THINKING ABOUT THE PLAYWRIGHT

THINKING ABOUT THE PLAYWRIGHT

Comments from Four Decades

Eric Bentley

Northwestern University Press
Evanston, IL

Northwestern University Press, Evanston, IL 60201

Printed in the United States of America

"Natural and Artificial" and "Reciting" are reprinted by kind permission of Mel Zerman of Limelight Editions, publishers of *What Is Theatre?*

Library of Congress Cataloging-in-Publication Data

Bentley, Eric, 1916-
    Thinking about the playwright.

    Includes index.
    1. Drama. 2. Theater. 3. Dramatists—Biography.
I. Title.
PN1623.B46   1987   792   86-31204
ISBN 0-8101-0732-5
ISBN 0-8101-0733-3 (pbk.)

For Irving Wardle
(another Bolton wanderer)
affectionately

ACKNOWLEDGMENTS

Perhaps the greatest psychic need is to feel needed. Since it is impossible in such short space to acknowledge all the friends and colleagues who have helped me in the past half century, I will limit the list to editors and publishers who made me feel they needed my services:

Ben Raeburn of Horizon Press
Harry Ford of Atheneum Publishers
Ann Hancock of Viking Press
Gilbert Harrison, editor of the *New Republic*
Robert Richman, literary editor of the *New Republic*
Robert W. Corrigan and Richard Schechner, editors at different times
    of what has usually been called the *Drama Review*
Gordon Rogoff, editor of *Theatre Arts*
Ross Wetzsteon and Erika Munk of *The Village Voice*
Jim O'Quinn, editor of *American Theater*
Joel Schechter, editor of *Theater*
Wendy Lesser, editor of *Threepenny Review*
Michael Zelenak and Brian Johnston of *Theater Three*
and last, not least,
the late Seymour Peck of the *New York Times*.

I omit the names of procrustean editors who "needed" me only when I'd been trimmed or stretched by them: they needed only my name.

E.B.
November, 1986

CONTENTS

PREFACE

The playwright is not the only subject of this book, but I am using the title *Thinking about the Playwright* not so much because I wrote a book called *The Playwright as Thinker* long ago as because the theatre has remained for me a playwright-centered universe.

The motion picture is director-centered, and since we live in the age of the motion picture (on big screen or small), directors have attempted to take over the legitimate theatre. A great director, Vsevolod Meyerhold, by his very greatness seemed to give the attempt validity, and every Tom, Dick, and Harry in his profession became the little Meyerhold of the local dunghill. Today you buy a ticket to *Hamlet* or any other classic at your peril, because what you will witness is the author's purpose subverted by the latest pipsqueak to graduate from drama school. There may even be a discussion afterwards in which the graduated director will call the atrocity he has committed a Metaphor or perhaps a Concept. When *Agamemnon* was produced by the New York Shakespeare Festival in the seventies, the program, as I recall, acknowledged, lower down the page, that Aeschylus had written it but announced, at the top, that it had been *conceived* by Mr. ——, the director. Gone is the modesty of Sam Taylor in the film of *Taming of the Shrew*—by William Shakespeare with additional dialogue by Sam Taylor. Aeschylus may in some sense be allowed to have *delivered* the baby but it had been *conceived*, nine months earlier, on the seacoast of Rumania.

Still, for all the talk of "theatre pieces," "nonverbal theatre" and so on, the dramatic theatre is still at its most distinguished when centered on playwriting, and even in 1986 its culture heroes are not Directors X, Y, and Z but Samuel Beckett and Harold Pinter, Sam Shepard and David Mamet, Peter Handke and Franz Xaver Kroetz . . . The reader who wishes to propose other names for this list is only reinforcing my point.

A word about the thinking playwright. The title of my earlier book had always been in trouble because many people read a title who don't read the book itself. These many—all too many—jumped to the conclusion that my book portrayed the playwright as mainly if not exclusively a thinker. I was reminded of the episode when later I called a short piece "A Play Is an Intellectual Thing" and a critic remarked that this, unfortunately, was what I'd always been saying: the playwright a giant brain, et cetera. The critic failed to notice I was misquoting Emily Dickinson's "A tear is an intellectual thing," of which remark the obverse is that the intellect weeps. The phrase "the playwright as thinker" was suggested to me in 1945 by my friend Jacques Barzun as a possible replacement to my own title for the book (used by my British publisher), *The Modern Theatre*. Jacques Barzun saw that I was trying to raise the intellectual status of dramatic art at a time when drama critics said it deserved no intellectual status at all, being an entirely un-intellectual thing with anti-intellectuals as its audience.

Amidst the polemics that ensued it was overlooked that when I interpreted the two playwrights who more than any others have been called cerebral—Shaw and Pirandello—my thesis was that they were no less impassioned than Ibsen or Strindberg. My anti-O'Neill thesis, also somewhat notorious in its day, was that while always implicitly claiming to be the most impassioned of playwrights, he was often bombastic and arid. I was not, of course, referring to O'Neill plays that weren't out yet such as *Iceman* and *Long Day's Journey*. I was referring to *Strange Interlude, Mourning Becomes Electra, Dynamo, Days without End . . .*

Such matters are further discussed in these "comments from four decades" without duplication of material from those of my books that have stayed in print. (Two minor exceptions: the short pieces on acting are in print with my collected theatre reviews, but they are not theatre reviews and make more sense here.) Without duplication of material and, I hope, without *mere* duplication of idea. The intention was, and is, to take any discussion a step further, probably modifying the previous conclusion, sometimes reversing it. If there are contradictions, it is to be hoped that they are unconcealed and visible: when contradictions are noticed, an argument can advance.

Such unity as this book possesses must derive from a certain singleness of purpose with which the question, What is theatre? was asked and answered during four decades.

PLAYWRITING

IBSEN IN 1956

1956 was the fiftieth anniversary of Ibsen's death, and, in celebration of the date, I delivered the following remarks in the Aula of the University of Oslo, ringed, as it is, with murals by Edvard Munch. What was running through my head at the time was that despite my reputation I was more an Ibsenite than a Brechtian. I did not know that 1956 was to be the date of Bertolt Brecht's death.

Ibsen's instrument was the Norwegian language. That is your instrument too, but not mine; so I come before you this morning, an amateur addressing professionals. And the position of the amateur has some advantages, albeit chiefly those of the fool rushing in where angels fear to tread.

In self-defense, I am going to invite you to remember that Ibsen was a *European* writer, by which I mean a writer known to the whole Western world—known, therefore, in all the languages of the Western world. Very few playwrights, even among the greatest, are European in this sense. Calderón, Racine, and Schiller, for example, are totally absent from the English-speaking theatre and almost totally unknown to readers of English. It was the special achievement of Ibsen and Strindberg—and Ibsen more than Strindberg—to conquer the foreigner. And so, if your critics blame us foreigners for our blindness to the Norwegian character of Ibsen's work, you should blame Ibsen himself for being so cosmopolitan that he appealed to us in the first place. To you, the action of A *Doll's House* takes place, crucially and unmistakably, in Norway. Bernard Shaw, however, said it took place in every suburb in Europe; and that, despite the notorious imperfections of Ibsen translations, is how it seems to all of us non-Scandinavians. Just as the

Germans came to speak of *Unser Shakespeare*, there is no non-Scandinavian country that did not come to think of *its* Ibsen.

All this by way of excusing the announced title of this address: What Ibsen Has Meant to Me, which has an egoistic ring. I hope the curse of egoism can be lifted from my observations this morning by the typicality of the experiences reported. It isn't what Ibsen has meant to me alone that I have in mind, but what he has meant to non-Scandinavians in general. Yet Ibsen taught us not to fear speaking for ourselves, for that way lies the danger of speaking, not for everyone, but for no one. I choose a personal approach in order, not to be more exquisite or eccentric, but to be more truthful.

When I was about fifteen, one of our teachers came to class and told us about a play that he'd just seen in London. He couldn't remember the names of the characters but he would call the leading one Sybil Thorndike because this actress played it. The plot was absolutely terrific—I think that was the way he put it—and the play ended with Sybil Thorndike's son going mad on stage, with poor Sybil Thorndike unable to make up her mind whether or not to keep her promise—which was to give him poison.

At a slightly later date, I came upon a copy of the play *Ghosts*, by Henrik Ibsen, in a small branch library of the Lancashire town where I grew up. Looking at the last page, I recognized my teacher's play. (A preface said something about an Italian actress who had evidently played Sybil Thorndike: the name was spelled DUSE, and I wondered how you pronounced it.) Reading the play through, I found the schoolmaster had exaggerated neither the circumstances of the story nor their effectiveness. I, too, found the play "absolutely terrific." The colloquial hyperbole seems, indeed, appropriate to the youthful enthusiasm I felt for an author who could stir me so deeply. I don't recall being so surprised by a book—caught off guard, as it were, completely "bowled over"—until, in college days, I read *Crime and Punishment*. Or until, also during my college years, I first saw Ibsen staged.

It was *The Master Builder* in London with D. A. Clarke-Smith as Solness and Lydia Lopokova as Hilda Wangel. I had not read the play, and, again, I was surprised. And, after all, at every moment, what a surprising play this is! Where are we? Who *are* these people? And what on earth is going on? This is distinctly old-fashioned theatre, is it not, in which, when a character says the younger generation is knocking at the door, a knock is actually heard at the door, and in walks the ingenue? Yet why is that knock so strangely startling? One jumped in one's seat. The story is not very clear, is it, or at least not very comprehensible? What is all this that happened so long before the curtain went up? Are we meant to believe it all? That Solness shook his fist at God from the top of a tower? And did he really make this girl the promise she speaks of? And is it credible that she would come to him after all these years and expect him to keep such a promise? No, obviously not. And yet—and yet—if the fable is so unclear and incredible, how does it happen that we find ourselves caught in it? And caught we are—at any rate, caught I was. And I could not believe that the web I was caught in was merely the web of adroit dramaturgy as, say, with Scribe. There was something altogether more Sophoclean about it. It seemed the web of fate. Not that I found the *idea* of fate in it—rather, the *sense* of it, the sense of inevitability and grand significance. Somewhere, behind the middle-class prose of the dialogue, a great bronze gong was sounding. I have in mind, not subtlety of meaning, but the power of the effect. The *impact* and *enthrallment* that publishers like to claim for any new work they print are actually rarities. But even those who rate Ibsen lowest should grant that, in the theatre, enthrallment is something he can establish in the first seconds of the action and sustain unbroken throughout an evening, while the impact of the work as a whole is seldom short of shocking.

And so it happens that the Ibsen evenings stand out so strongly in my recollection of nearly a quarter century of theatregoing. Though much is forgotten, the special quality of each production remains, even when it is only one of Ibsen's special qualities shining through bad acting and inept direction. Among the best productions I have seen is that of *Ghosts* as presented by the Old Vic just before the Second World War with Marie Ney as Mrs. Alving and Emlyn Williams as Oswald. Though long stretches of the performance have faded from memory, certain moments have stayed quite luminously with me. And this is not as unsatisfactory a state of affairs as it sounds, for, while the atmosphere is charged from the beginning to the end of an Ibsen play, it is at a limited number of moments that the charge explodes, sometimes in thunder and lightning, sometimes in the characteristically Ibsenian lightning without thunder. It was a thunderous moment, in that production, when the sanatorium caught fire, and the thunder had a mocking sound when Manders cried out in pain because the place wasn't insured. Lightning flashed without thunder in the quietness of Emlyn Williams's first entrance (when Oswald confronts Manders with his antitype), and in the hush of horror as Mrs. Alving hears the ambiguous noises from Oswald and Regina in the next room and realizes what they mean. (Miss Ney dropped a crumpled piece of paper, and one could hear it hit the floor.)

It would be easy to list the merits of other outstanding Ibsen performances I have seen—such as Michael Benthall's production of *The Wild Duck,* in which Anton Walbrook shuttled between the pathetic and the ridiculous with dazzling virtuosity—yet the point about Ibsen can perhaps be even better clinched by reference to a couple of performances that were not outstanding. A production of *Rosmersholm* at the Yale Drama School in 1940 demonstrated to my satisfaction—and perhaps to my surprise—that even moderately good amateur performance, if conscientious and sensibly directed, can enthrall an audience and have a shocking impact—in short, create in the theatre the Ibsen magic, the Ibsen world.

My last exhibit is that of the worst Ibsen production I have seen: *The Master Builder* as produced a couple of years ago at the Phoenix Theatre in New York with Oscar Homolka as Solness and Joan Tetzel as Hilda Wangel. A resolute attempt was made to eliminate the poetry, the mythic quality, the suggestion of great gongs sounding, and reduce the play to the cliché romance of a tired businessman and the spirited young lady he prefers to his weary and wearisome wife. That the attempt failed shows Ibsen's play to be actor-proof. The great effects were indeed weakened, but they were not eliminated. For all the pretense of putting Ibsen on firm naturalistic ground, the tremor of the Ibsenian earthquake was still occasionally felt.

2

I have been trying to say what it is in Ibsen that first takes hold of us, and I shall now try to say what it is in him that *keeps* hold of us. What would explain, in my own case, my starting with Ibsen in a first book on modern drama and my ending with him years later in a book on modern theatre? Or, to give the question a more academic form, what is his abiding relevance now that, in the mid-twentieth century, all the initial shock of Ibsenism has long been absorbed?

The world's attitude to Ibsen has gone through two phases and is now, as I see it, entering upon a third. The first phase was that of the late nineteenth century, at which time one either expressed one's detestation of the dramatist's iconoclasm or one's enthusiastic acceptance of it. Either way, the Ibsen under consideration was the revolutionary; and one accepted or rejected him according to whether one was oneself a revolutionary or not.

The second phase of opinion came with the acceptance of Ibsen in the early twentieth century by society at large. A gain of this sort is always, at the same time, a loss. For general acceptance implies only a cessation of hostilities, not an active interest in an author. To be accepted is the first step toward being ignored. When the rear guard accepts an author, moreover, the advance guard drops him. Necessarily so, as the advance guard's function had been to scold the rear guard for underestimating him. Not so necessary, but quite natural, is the advance guard's tendency to turn against those it used to champion, perhaps even reviving arguments against them that had first been formulated by the rear guard. In the nineteenth century, playwrights were warned against Ibsen by the die-hard, older critics; in the twentieth century they began to be warned against him by the advanced young spirits. Bertolt Brecht's Epic Theatre, beginning in the 1920s, was, on the technical side, mainly a revolt against Ibsen, whose forms Brecht has described as rigid and narrow.

More important than the technical side, perhaps, was the ideological. As the only fully worked-out Marxist theory of drama, Brecht's Epic Theatre is the purest example of collectivism in twentieth-century dramatic writing, and the extreme statement of his thought is to be found in the play *Die Massnahme (The Measures Taken)*, which celebrates the sacrifice of the individual to the group. Ruth Fischer credibly states that it is based on the experiences of her brother Gerhard Eisler as a Communist agent in China, and, by anticipation, it dramatizes the deaths of Radek and Bukharin, Rajk and Slansky, though not the subsequent admission, in 1956, that the confessions these men made were a pack of lies.

During the phase of history that produced Epic Theatre, collectivistic thought spread far beyond the confines of the Communist movement, and when I was in college in the thirties, the standard opinion was that Henrik Ibsen was *borné* and *petit bourgeois*—that he represented the end of individualism and not the beginning of the great new order. Only later did I learn that this view had first been expressed by Friedrich Engels himself and thereafter had been echoed by all Marxist critics from Franz Mehring on.

And Marx and Engels were right if their philosophy as a whole was right; it is a matter of that; while, equally, Ibsen will cease to seem *borné* and *petit bourgeois,* will become important again, to those who wish to stand *for* the individual and *against* what seems to them the hideous monolith of Soviet collectivism. To these—and you will realize that I am one of them—the great individualists of the nineteenth century are still great, Ibsen among them. Great and exemplary—for they possess what we have lost but must at all costs rediscover.

They possessed, first and foremost, what Lionel Trilling and others have been calling the mystique of the self: for their self-respect, and their belief in self-respect, went beyond opinion to sentiment, and beyond sentiment to faith. For them, there existed no Radeks and Bukharins—no people, that is, who could be asked to lie their lives away for an alleged collective good. In some much-quoted lines of verse, Henrik Ibsen once said that to live was to fight with the devils that infest the head and heart and to hold a Last Judgment over the self. The mystique of the self never found more pithy expression, nor the subject matter of Ibsen's plays more precise definition. Even where Ibsen criticizes an individualist—as in *Brand* and *The Wild Duck*—he does so not from any standpoint acceptable to Marxism, but from that of another individualism. Brand's flaw, after all, is a defect in self-knowledge. Instead of living in harmony with his own nature, he attempts to live according to an abstract law which he must constantly foist on himself and others by arbitrary violence. This individualist becomes less of an individual all the time. By a supposed attachment to the *super*human, he becomes *in*human.

Consider Mrs. Alving, the individualist as woman. We know she reads the right books, though Ibsen leaves them unnamed so that each spectator can supply the titles of his own favorites. She belongs to the nineteenth-century Enlightenment. But we find out that she achieves enlightenment in general while keeping herself ignorant in particular of precisely those two or three things which it would do her most good to know: above all, of her complicity in the tragedy of Captain Alving. When she tells Oswald—at the end—that she shared the blame, because, in her prudishness, her fear of sexuality, she had not welcomed Alving's joy of life, she is also telling herself. Catastrophe in this story plays, as it were, the role of psychoanalysis, bringing to consciousness the guilty facts which the protagonist has so zealously kept under. Mrs. Alving, reader of books, has come to know many things; but she has not come to know herself. She is not too much an individual, as Manders thinks, but too little.

My generation of undergraduates—that of the 1930s—reserved its greatest contempt for the person who was "only interested in saving his soul" and was therefore neglecting the real task, that of changing the world. We didn't realize to what an appalling extent the motive force of our reforming zeal was the fear of the self, the failure to face the self. We scoffed at the escapism of certain individualistic poets, and did not see that social collectivism could be the supreme escape, and conversely that there can be no healthy altruism which is not founded in self-respect. Yet, if we hadn't been tipped off that Ibsen was *petit bourgeois*, we might have learned our lesson from him. For he saw that the enlightenment in a Mrs. Alving was but the skin over the sore. He saw that the altruism of a Gregers Werle was the outgrowth of a sick conscience; Gregers persecutes Hedwig because he is running away from himself.

With the disrespect for the self that has been so prevalent in our time goes, naturally, a disrespect for the whole inner life of man, as witness the overtone that the word "subjective" now carries. The "objective" is real, the "subjective" is unreal—in other words, you get at the truth by getting away from yourself. If anyone remarked of Neville Chamberlain in 1938 that at least his motives were good, there was always a young Marxist on hand to remark that we must not judge by motives but by objective facts. Here again, Ibsen belongs to the earlier tradition. He believes the motive itself to be an objective fact and, in a strict sense, the primary fact—the one to start from. He would never have written a play about the rightness or wrongness of Chamberlain's policy, but he might well have written one about whether the man did indeed have good motives, whether his conscience was healthy. His plays are studies in *unhealthy* conscience, in lack of integrity. Naturally, then, he seems not only old-fashioned but even wrongheaded to those who assume that life begins after integrity has been surrendered to a party, a class, or a state.

But I do not wish to focus my whole argument upon Communism, because, in the present connection, Communism is only the extreme instance of a universal phenomenon—conformism parading as virtue. And in the West we encounter the danger less in the form of Communism than as a new attitude to life which the American sociologist David Riesman calls other-directedness—that is, being oriented toward other people, not just in external matters, not just, as it were, when other people are looking, but even in one's most intimate mental activity. Modern civilization lives under the sign of Mrs. Grundy.

The spiky, individualistic Victorians were, of course, inner-directed. Trained under strong fathers in the discipline of self-reliance, they hearkened to the inner voice, and went their independent way. Whether we can ever get back to anything of the sort is a question going far beyond the scope of the present statement. But even Mr. Riesman (who seems to be a fatalist) permits himself some unmistakably nostalgic admiration. And, certainly, the stock of all the Victorian individualists has been rising as men have come to realize what a frightful mess the anti-individualists have been making of the world. Ibsen is a great exemplar of the inner-directed culture. *Peer Gynt*, though not quite a prophecy of other-directedness, is about the danger of self-disrespect, of having no sense of identity, of being a human onion, all layers and no center.

By this time, I may have given the impression that What Ibsen Means to Me is Conservatism, the Nineteenth Century, Darby and Joan, or even Songs My Mother Taught Me. Certainly we have come to the point where Victorianism no longer suggests a narrow and enervating stuffiness but manliness, free intellect, abundant individuality—men like Henrik Ibsen rather than Parson Manders. Of course, the great Victorians were *not* conservatives but rebels against Victorianism, nonconformists one and all. In political theory, Henrik Ibsen leaned toward anarchism—of all *isms* the most remote from totalitarianism. His first audiences regarded him as primarily a rebel, and in the future, I think, he will be regarded as a rebel again.

Ibsen's plays are *about* rebels—from Catiline to Brand and Julian, and from Lona Hessel and Nora Helmer to Hedda Gabler and John Gabriel Borkman. And we should not need to be told by Ibsen himself (as we were) that he wrote only of what he had lived through, for rebelliousness is very evidently not only the subject of the plays but the motive force. Anticlericalism (as in the portrait of Manders and the Dean in *Brand*) and political satire (as in *The League of Youth* or the characterization of the Mayor in *Brand*) are merely the most obtrusive signs of a mentality that was critical through and through. As we retreat in horror, disgust, or mere boredom from the idea of the writer as Commissar or Official Mouthpiece, we come back to the old liberal conception, most adequately represented in this century by André Gide: the writer as questioner, dissenter, challenger, troublemaker, at war with his age, yet, by that token, standing for the best in his age and helping the age to understand itself. In Ibsen, as in Gide, we who live in a time of fake radicalism are confronted by a real radical.

In speaking of fake radicalism, I again have more than Communism in mind—more even than politics. I am thinking, for example, of all playwrights who are considered daring, and whose courage is rather lightheartedly connected by critics with that of Ibsen and Strindberg. As people these playwrights are often much more Bohemian than Ibsen. In fact, he seems distinctly prim by comparison. And, similarly, something much more quickly identifiable as daring is smeared over the whole surface of their plays, which deal with assorted neuroses not even mentionable in the theatre of Ibsen's day. But Ibsen is supposed to have given daring its start in *Ghosts* . . .

The mistake here is to imagine that the subject of *Ghosts* is syphilis. Lucky for Ibsen that it isn't, as the medical science of the play is now quite obsolete! His daring was not a matter of bringing up repellent subjects, though it included that. It consisted simply in his genuinely radical attitude to life in general, and it is therefore at the heart of his writing and not merely on its surface.

What is true in the sexual sphere applies also to the political. In our political plays today, we are given what is conventionally regarded as daring but what actually takes no courage at all to say—it is at best what used to be daring and is now calculated to produce cheers from a clique, class, or party rather than bad reviews in the press and rotten eggs from the gallery. An instance, oddly enough, is *An Enemy of the People* as freely adapted to the American stage in the mid-twentieth century by Arthur Miller. Ibsen's original, by contrast, though no profound piece of thought, and in my view one of his least vital plays, is genuinely daring, especially in its blunt challenge to the idea of majority rule. The reason the Miller version is dull is that Mr. Miller was himself offended by Ibsen's daring, made excuses for him in a preface, and proceeded to censor offensive passages. The dangerous thoughts of the latter-day quasi-radical are all completely safe; Ibsen's plays were so subversive they frightened, at times, even their author.

Another difference between the old radical and the new is that the former explored life while the latter lays down the law about it. *Die Massnahme* perfectly represents the latter procedure. Such a play is not even drama of discussion or ideas, for the author isn't talking it over with you, he is telling you. Still less is it drama of exploration, for the "play" is but a device to clinch the point the author started out with. *

Gerhart Hauptmann once remarked that the playwright must never reword thoughts which he or his character has already thought: dramatic dialogue must only present thoughts in the process of being thought. Which is another way of saying that the playwright must not be directly didactic, for it is the didactic writer—out, not to learn, but to teach—who concentrates on finding effective form for thinking that was finished long ago. Didacticism seems not to have been a besetting temptation for Ibsen as it is for Brecht. It is an irony that the man who is always considered the father of the drama of ideas makes so few explicit references to ideas in his plays.

Incidentally, I consider *An Enemy of the People* inferior Ibsen just because it is one of the few plays in which this author seems simply to be "telling us"—with upraised finger and an inclination to be very angry if we aren't good and do as we're "told." Generally, with Ibsen, we feel we are his companions in a search and therefore, in line with Hauptmann's principle, are not given summaries of what has been thought already but are present at the thinking. Mere summaries of experience (intellectual experience or otherwise) are without dramatic life. The pulse of the drama begins to beat at the moment the playwright begins to struggle with his experience. There is indeed no better evidence for this truth than the lifework of Henrik Ibsen.

Hauptmann's principle enables us to understand the radical difference not only between Ibsen and Brecht but between Ibsen and the Ibsenites. The more the latter agreed with the Master, the worse the result was bound to be: for they were starting where he ended—namely, with his findings. It is of course open to writers who do this to improve on their master in all the external qualities of literature—elegance, concision, clarity, and so on. For they are only paraphrasing. And it makes one realize that one values literature, ultimately, for other qualities than these. One will indeed suffer inelegance, inconcision, unclarity and the rest with a good grace if only there is a degree of inner movement, action, energy, conflict . . .

There is a lesson in Ibsen for our so-called profession of playwrights today. The profession—by definition, perhaps—acquires a certain craft

---

*This breezy summary of Brecht's play passes over the not-so-secret sympathy shown for the Young Comrade. Brecht was not a monolith and neither, it was soon to turn out, was the world Communist movement.

and then . . . uses it. In other words, the professional writer works within the resources he has found himself to possess. Such-and-such worked very well last time; the presumption that it may work well again is enough to prompt a second use, and a third and so on. Hence his youth is the professional writer's only creative period; there can indeed, on the terms just stated, be no development, but only a possibly increasing facility. Ibsen chose the path of constant development, accepting the risks, paying the price, and reaping the reward. The price is the forgoing of easy success and small perfection. Professional dramatic critics, out of something more than fellow feeling, will always tend to prefer the professional craftsman to the real artist: the merits of what the former has to offer are more easily recognized and measured, while the latter undoubtedly makes far more mistakes, and is not always improving. The payoff comes at the end, when the "mistake"—about which the critics have "rightly" been merciless—reveals itself as a needed part of a pattern. It has been said that all Shakespeare's plays taken together form one long play. Something of the kind can be said of the collected work of any real artist. Not the smallest fascination of Ibsen is the togetherness of his work, the profound meaning in the relation of play to play. To write both *Brand* and *Peer Gynt* is not just twice the job of writing one of the two; it is to force the reader to read the plays as thesis and antithesis in an artist's effort at synthesis. To follow up *Ghosts* with *An Enemy of the People* was more than an act of moral reprisal, and to follow up *An Enemy* with *The Wild Duck* was more than an act of self-correction: one thing leads to another in a drama which has *Catiline* for prologue and *When We Dead Awaken* for epilogue, the drama of Ibsen's whole *oeuvre*.

Henrik Ibsen meant a lot to me when I first encountered theatre, literature, and adult life, and I return to him a couple of decades later when trying, as we do, to come to terms with the theatre, the literature, and the life around us, trying to locate the essential problems, discard impeding prejudices, correct obstructive errors, see through the facts to the meaning of the facts—and, in all this, to accept the self that does the locating, discarding, correcting and seeing. For, while the Bible tells us to love our neighbor as ourselves, Henrik Ibsen seems to remind us how foolish that injunction would be for people who do *not* love themselves.

(1956)

STRINDBERG IN 1985

I stopped regular book reviewing long ago not because I was above it but because I was below it: I was not equal to its demands. The only review I'd written that gave me much satisfaction took me about two years to write; only because at *Kenyon Review* I had a very unworldly editor did it get printed, late as it was. But in 1984 Seymour Peck, my old editor from Arts and Leisure at the *New York Times*, found himself on the staff of the Book Review and was urging me to write for them. Sy was killed by a drunken driver on January 1, 1985, but the *Times* kept after me. I did not take on the Michael Meyer biography sight unseen. When I read it, what struck me was the analogy with Richard Wagner. It may interest Strindbergians that, after my review appeared in the *Times*, I received the expected indignant protests from the Wagnerites—but none from Strindbergians. That is as it should be, in the sense that Wagner spent his whole life acquiring hangers-on, while Strindberg spent his time losing any support he might have accumulated.

"Real superiority," Eugène Delacroix wrote, "admits no eccentricity. . . . The great genius is simply a being of a more highly reasonable order." He remarked, however, that the opposite view seemed to prevail at the time—1855. If only he had seen *Amadeus*, or read Allen Ginsberg, or had known that Sartre would describe Jean Genet, with only partial irony, as a saint! Since Delacroix's day, we have lived under the sign of one of his immediate successors, Arthur Rimbaud, who wrote that the Poet, albeit a Sage, was the great Sick Man, the great Criminal, the great Accursed. This conception, for a while nothing if not startling, is by now a received idea. By the standards of the modern man on the street, a Dylan Thomas is obviously a poet while a William Carlos Williams is not. To justify his men (or women), the biographer has to go back to the detail of their lives and discover the sinister, or at least

the scandalous, element. Ruskin, who had seemed one's primmest uncle, can be brought back—vindicated—as a child molester.

August Strindberg (1849–1912) came at a certain juncture in the
evolution of such expectations. Goethe had provided a clue in describing a whole lifework (his own) as fragments of a single confession.
Baudelaire had written under the rubric *mon coeur mis à nu* without
actually telling his life story in detail. Strindberg would fulfill the promise of these writers both by making a grand confession of his total *oeuvre*
and by penning a series of autobiographies.

The Strindberg autobiographies are world literature. They have also
proved a source of confusion. At first taken to be an author "coming
clean" and "telling all," they were later shown to be an author, if not
simply lying, at least creating an alter ego, Strindberg II, another drama
by one who was nothing if not a dramatist. Otherwise it might not
have been necessary for others to write his life: he would himself have
written the definitive biography. As things were, biographers were
needed, if only to measure the gap between the autobiographies and
mere fact.

Getting at the facts on Strindberg has not been easy for those who
read him only in English: most of what he wrote has not been translated.
Even Swedes are still discovering facts. The uncut text of *Miss Julie*
didn't come out in Swedish till 1984. The complete *Occult Diary* "has
appeared only in a limited facsimile edition," says Mr. Meyer. The
Strindberg letters, he adds, that came out in fifteen volumes between
1948 and 1976 are still some 3000 short of complete . . . No wonder,
then, that a biographer who has gone through all this material can still,
even in 1985, come up with surprises.

"Woman, being small and foolish and therefore evil . . . should be
suppressed, like barbarians and thieves. She is useful only as ovary and
womb, best of all as a cunt." "She can be replaced, dispensed with.
One needs only a constant temperature of 37° and a suitable nourishment fluid. Then man will be emancipated."

That is Strindberg on woman, coming to us through Mr. Meyer.
Here, from the same source, is the Swedish master on race: "Hjalmar
has negro blood in him . . . even [his] hair . . . was nigger." ("Strindberg
uses the English word," says Mr. Meyer.) "To squander, to pinch, to
pilfer, to be disloyal and show one's eyeteeth . . . that is nigger! Black
man is bad man. . . . If I rate the black race below the white, it is
grounded on experiences which have shown that the black are inferior
to the white."

Strindberg read what has proved to be one of the most influential
anti-Semitic books of the past hundred years, *Jewish France* by Édouard
Drumont, and proceeded to comment thus on his own Jewish publisher,
Albert Bonnier: "[His] tactic is to suck blood (i.e., money) slowly . . .

a Jew never forgives! He will not kill you, but he will take your job. . . . Jews do not believe in friendship or gratitude. . . . Read my play *The Father!* For Laura read Albert Bonnier and you will understand what a devilish fight I have on my hands."

I have the impression that the link which Strindberg himself here establishes between what we would call his sexism and his racism was of crucial importance to Mr. Meyer as he weighed his man in the balance. Each topic became more important in itself than it had ever been in the past, and both bore witness to the same hair-raising capacity to exclude from the legitimate human race untold millions—women, Jews, "pederasts"—of human beings. Not that Mr. Meyer's book is a disquisition on sexism and racism. It tells the story of Strindberg's life in more detail than it has ever been told in English before. But, as a biography should, it finally amounts to a portrait—the most shocking portrait of a major artist, probably, since Robert W. Gutman's magistral *Richard Wagner* in 1968. And the shock has much the same basis. It is the shock of discovering (or seeming to discover) that a very great artist aligned himself with evil, indeed with some of the worst moral abuses that were to plague the following century. (A previous biographer, Olof Lagercrantz, underlines the fact that Strindberg also idealized certain Jews. Which, I'd say, only modifies things slightly: if Jews are either submen or supermen, they are not men.)

Racism occupied an ever-larger part of Wagner's mind and was most virulent in his last years. Mr. Gutman, showing how much of it underlies the pious pseudo-Christian surface of *Parsifal*, perhaps goes too far when he would have us hear racism in the music itself, yet there is little doubt that Wagner's essays of the period laid the foundation of what would later be National Socialist theory, not to mention prose style. Strindberg's anti-Semitism has no comparable prominence or importance, nor does Mr. Meyer argue that it has. Rather, if Strindberg happens to be in conflict with, say, a Jewish publisher, he simply latches on to that anti-Semitism which the Christian tradition provided him with. Wagner's anti-Semitism is ideological and gigantic, Strindberg's opportunistic and petty. There is a reverse contrast in their misogyny. Wagner's is seen only in spite of himself and, initially, only through its apparent opposite: the glorification, the over-spiritualization of women. Later, in Kundry, it is naked enough, though hardly the central "matter" of *Parsifal*. It is Strindberg who was possessed by misogyny, as all the world knows: it is *all* that the world does know about Strindberg. For he does not condescend to woman in the traditional male way, or dread her secretly and pretend to adore her in the Wagnerian way, he confesses openly to both fear and hate of the other sex. Which, in the nineteenth century, meant that the cat was out of the bag. People don't say such things! Even Ibsen did not say such things. The husband of *A Doll's*

House neither hates his wife nor fears her. And that was what was bound to make the play quite unreal from where Strindberg sat, the actual dynamics of sexual relations being absent.

Mr. Meyer sits elsewhere. He is also—not only "also," but primarily—the biographer of Ibsen, who turns out to be the real hero of this biography of Strindberg. Long live Ibsen! His stature is not in question and if he, too, was sometimes on the "wrong" side, as in *An Enemy of the People,* where he sided with the elite against the masses, that wouldn't be noticed: instead, he would receive the homage of such ardent democrats as Arthur Miller. Returning to what was called The Woman Question: Strindberg's contention was that, beneath the advertised issues like rights, beneath even the question of who's boss (Lenin's "who whom"), as raised in *A Doll's House,* lurked massive resentments and, if the old "order" was upset, the result would be a war, a chaos. We who live in that war, that chaos, know who was well advised on this one.

"For men, the right to abuse women is elemental, the first principle. . . . Pornography reveals that male pleasure is inextricably tied to victimizing, hurting, exploiting. . . ." Thus Andrea Dworkin in her book *Pornography.* That women are writing this sort of thing in the 1980s would have stunned Ibsen but would not have caused Strindberg to raise an eyebrow. And the point is not that Ibsen was mistaken where Strindberg was correct but that, where Ibsen was a moralist, Strindberg—though doing some moralizing of his own from a wrong standpoint—was a prophet, and not in having second sight, but by having first sight, that is, by total immersion in actuality. The sexism was morally wrong but the power of observation was something that the morally right people—even the geniuses among them—did not have. *Could* they have had it? We are in deep water here and, instead of attempting to plumb the depths, Mr. Meyer is content to side with Ibsen and stress Strindberg's moral wrongness and psychic abnormality, not to mention his lesser faults, limitations, and eccentricities.

Whatever one makes of all that, one must challenge Mr. Meyer's appraisal of Strindberg's art. The weak element in his book is the literary and dramatic criticism in it. Is this pertinent in a biography? There is a widespread assumption to the contrary. There is a huge public out there that is interested in the artist and not in the art: literary biography thrives on their support and consequent oversupport by the book review supplements. And some artists' lives do hold a kind of interest—can sometimes be fascinating—without reference to their art. The artist who wrote *The Seven Pillars of Wisdom* is more interesting in books about him written by other people. But Strindberg? I cannot imagine that a lengthy life of this man could interest anyone except a student of his writings. A biographer must ask: what did Strindberg do? and the only comprehensive, significant answer is: he wrote. Mr. Meyer certainly records *what* he wrote, and provides background information that enriches our understanding of it. It is only that when he comes to the point—to what is written—he has very little to say. And that little derives more from the marginal documents (such as letters) than from the masterworks.

Strindberg was a *great* writer, yet, when he writes greatly, as in *The Father*, this is all that Mr. Meyer can make of it: "Brief, . . . savage, as unbalanced as *The Marauders* in its treatment of the sex war, as melodramatic in the climaxes of its last two acts as though Ibsen had never written, masochistic and self-pitying. . . . The play's faults were obvious; less so its scenic power and deep understanding of that twilight area where sanity and insanity merge." On *Miss Julie* Mr. Meyer has a real insight: "Miss Julie's tragedy is that she does not want to make love with Jean; she does not want to sleep with him; she wants . . . to be fucked by him, like an animal." But this is not as clear as it sounds. What is the difference, here, between making love to and sleeping with? How do we know what (other) animals want? "Strindberg," Mr. Meyer says, "unlike any dramatist before him, showed that men and women can hate each other yet be sexually welded." Certainly Strindberg was in the forefront, but the modernist approach to sexuality was happening all around him; the secrets of a masterpiece like *Miss Julie* are not susceptible of purely, or even mainly, clinical analysis, nor should critics of an art become just spotters of pioneers. It has been said of Mozart that he pioneered nothing, he was just better at all the old things. At one of the old things—melodrama—Strindberg was better, and the word should not be used to cut *The Father* down to size. Sometimes Mr. Meyer does not know what to say about even a major Strindberg work except that it's splendid but could use some cuts—to be made, presumably, by such as Mr. Meyer himself, whose published text of even Ibsen's *Brand* is abridged. If he appreciates the magnitude and subtlety of Strindberg's genius, one would never know it from his book. Which also means that he did not learn much from predecessors who did show such an appreciation. These include not only biographers (Martin Lamm, Lagercrantz) but also critics who couldn't avoid making a biography out of their criticism, notably Evert Sprinchorn.

On Mr. Meyer's final page, there is an interesting summation. It is not by Mr. Meyer, who seems to have quailed at the thought, but by the playwright John Mortimer, who says: "The exhilaration [Strindberg's] best work brings is not that it is intelligent (like much of life it is totally absurd) but that it is absolutely true." This has a modernist ring to it, definitely post-Delacroix, yet the famously misogynistic plays are acknowledged and *felt* to be among the greatest works of Strindberg, the truth in that misogyny, as I have already allowed, being precisely not absolute—but relative.

How can one characterize such a figure as unintelligent, let alone totally absurd? Could one even be interested in the artist described in this summation? Yet I, among many, have long been interested in August Strindberg: as an artist he wears extremely well. Can Mr. Meyer begin to tell us why? Or again have Mr. Mortimer do his work for him?

(1985)

UNCLE JACK MEETS HELEN OF TROY

My first book on drama, *The Playwright as Thinker* (1946), received its least favorable review from someone who later became a dear friend, Barbara Deming. A pupil of Francis Fergusson, who would also be dear to me later, she found my approach too biographical: I was too much interested in the playwright, too little in dramatic structure as set forth by Aristotle (and Francis). Hence, she argued, there was little or nothing in my book about Chekhov. Her argument drove me wild, as Chekhov was one of my favorite writers; indeed he still is four decades later. I resolved to write about him forthwith but learned, in doing so, that he is the hardest of the great modernist playwrights to write about and impossible to sum up. Thus it is that, in all the years, I have found it possible only to comment on this Chekhovian occasion and that, not to "do a book on him," not expound him *in extenso*, least of all explain him. Dropping in on Chekhov in this way turned out to be a delightful privilege. Some of the actors (and maybe the director too) would have little idea, or the wrong idea, of what they were up to, but always there were performers who would touch the heart of Chekhov and mediate between that rare spirit and mine. Theatre would suddenly be as solemnly important as religion, as accurately emotional as music.

It's nearer forty than thirty years ago now that, on a visit to London, I bought a ticket for the top of the balcony at a play I hadn't heard of with John Gielgud in it. The curtain went up on a man and a woman and the man said: "Why do you always wear black?" The woman answered: "I'm in mourning for my life. I'm unhappy." I'd never heard anyone talk like that, in or out of a theatre. I was enthralled. This was more real than all my realities. And I understood it too: what adolescent wouldn't? But how could anyone go straight to this, well, real reality and have his people talk so simply from the very center of their beings—from the very center of being?

The enthrallment lasted beyond the first two lines of *The Seagull,* beyond the reading of Anton Chekhov's other plays, beyond the discovery of the stories and the letters, beyond the professional reviewing I did in the forties and fifties of various Chekhov productions in New York, beyond the experience of making my own adaptations of several Chekhov farces and seeing them through production. At one time I studied Russian quite hard with the sole aim of reading the untranslated works of Chekhov.

I venture to strike this personal note because Chekhov is a writer who becomes precious in a very personal way. There has also been a personal development which may have general significance and interest: in the course of several decades of companionship with the spirit of Chekhov, I have come to respect him as much as Tolstoy or Dostoevsky. It is very possible that I *need* him more than them, and that at some point I shall definitely realize this. Four decades may not be enough time to digest the work of this writer who himself was given little more than four decades on earth. But the converse of this somewhat intimidating thought is that, even after four decades, further discovery, further illumination is still awaited.

Now what is there in this author that takes so long to understand? He himself would probably have roared with laughter at the very idea. He was like that. But then I wouldn't consider that his laughter really put me down, let alone proved me wrong. His laughter might also take time to understand. And yet this author got through to me in the very first moment in my seat at the top of the balcony? That too. This is perhaps the central paradox of a genius who can be interpreted only by way of paradoxes: he is the simplest of writers, but and at the same time he is the most complex of writers. Any reader, spectator, or critic who grasps but one of these two propositions has not grasped Chekhov. And indeed if Chekhov criticism may be faulted, it is not, usually, that critics saw what was not there but that they failed to see that the quality they noticed was offset by a not only different but opposite quality. When such critics fall to quarreling among themselves, the results are peculiarly unfruitful, for both can so easily be right—yes, Chekhov is conservative; yes, Chekhov is radical; yes, Chekhov is pessimistic and sad; yes, Chekhov is optimistic and joyful—yet both are very wrong, not only in limiting Chekhov to one side of his genius but, even more crucially, in failing to see that his greatness reveals itself to us precisely in the interaction of the two sides.

If Chekhov is assimilated slowly by an individual such as myself, it might be unfair to ask the world in general to be any faster. All the world felt when it first encountered Chekhov's stage masterpieces was that they were sad. This hit Desmond MacCarthy so hard he put Chekhov down as "the poet and apologist of ineffectualness." The Russian-born English critic David Magarshack wrote a whole book to prove MacCarthy wrong. Magarshack found a "gay affirmation of life in the final chorus of the three sisters," and elsewhere. What both critics claimed to find was indeed there, yet both falsify Chekhov not only in being one-sided but in missing the interactions. If MacCarthy was deeply moved, moved to deep sadness, by the ending of *Three Sisters*, he cannot be told he shouldn't have been. But Magarshack has a strong point too. The cheerful elements at the end are not there only to reinforce the sadness, as in many a romantic drama where the heroine's heart breaks to the strains of a Viennese waltz. They both reinforce the sadness and exist in their own right. "The music is so cheerful and gay and I want to live. . . . The music is so gay, so joyful, and it almost seems that in a little time we shall know why we live. . . ." Yes, it *is* a joyous, hopeful ending, though—by some strange magic—that has not stopped it from flooding us with sadness as no dramatist had done since Shakespeare.

Well, the magic is not so strange, it is just that the talent, the genius, of Chekhov is greater than even we, his admirers, have assumed. This is not just a writer of very good plays, though such are rare enough. He can "get away with" all sorts of things that the others, even the brilliant and successful others, cannot. And so what is true of the "art of the drama" as we have learned it from the others is not true for him. It is terribly true for his imitators. There the "lack of action" really does prove disastrous, the pessimism all-enveloping, the jocularity affected. Or they have to redeem themselves by qualities not at all Chekhovian. So the magic is but a synonym for supreme artistic greatness, the greatness not just of a Webster or a Corneille or a Schiller, those splendid dramatists, but of Euripides—and Aristophanes, Racine, and Molière. Nor should one shrink from the name of Shakespeare, even though this our Russian colossus died at forty-four with only four full-length stage masterpieces completed.

Colossus? Chekhov's laughter can again be heard from the grave. He tended to use words like "modest," as have his critics. Although I do not retract the Shakespearean comparison, I will concede that Mozart is a more persuasive analogue. Mozart, who, for a century, was thought pretty-pretty and who, as a man, had usually worn the mask of modesty. It took the world a century, not just to sound his depths, but to realize they were there to be sounded. So deceptive is "simplicity." If an artist is unsimple, there is a presumption from the outset that he is deep. It may not take the world a century to learn that he is not; but meanwhile a great career has been had. Of course there are also the unsimple who *are* deep, like Tolstoy and Dostoevsky. One falls headlong into their depths at the first encounter, and perhaps demands such a trial by drowning from every great artist thereafter. But that isn't fair—to the artist or to oneself. That way one never takes the full measure of a

Mozart or of a Chekhov. One is enthralled, but one has not received the full illumination. It is as if the gods challenged us to get the point and we didn't get it.

The "point" about Chekhov lies on the other side of the enthrall-ment I felt in my love-at-first-sight. It lies on the other side of Tolstoy's remark about one of Chekhov's stories: "It is like lace made by a chaste young girl"—though this is apt and beautiful. It lies on the other side of Maxim Gorky's comment on *Uncle Vanya:* "It is a hammer with which you strike at the empty skulls of the public." It lies even further on the other side of the praise of Stalin's lackeys, such as Vladimir Yermilov, who, as translated by Ivy Litvinov, wrote: "The purifying storm burst out and our native land began to be turned into a beautiful garden, the laws of its life became those of truth and beauty. 'What a pleasure to respect people,' wrote Chekhov in his notebook. We know this pleasure now," et cetera, et cetera.

There would be no need to take issue with the Stalinists in an American newspaper had not the errors of an excessively—to use the current word—"politicized" Chekhov crept also into American dis-course, and not merely on the Left. Anyone who has talked to more than one generation of American students knows that the Pessimistic Stereotype has in recent years been replaced by an Optimistic Stereo-type, and "all Russia is our garden" has become a prophecy of 1917, if hardly of 1936–38. Now it is true that the messianic hope of socialism hovers over Chekhov's work, as it hovered over the Russia of his time. It is true, too, that Chekhov is not against it. He is not an apolitical, anti-political, "pure" artist spewing contempt for political aspirations and interpretations. He can present messianic talkers with considerable sympathy.

And their opponents with equal sympathy? Here we come to a thorny problem. Is it neutrality, finally, that Chekhov affirms, as is often implied by critics who come to us fresh from the realization that he was not a naive partisan? No, Chekhov did affirm the will to radical change, even while presenting an attitude to the means employed, and to the role of the artist, which is contrary not only to Stalinism but to Leninism. A recent critic, Simon Karlinsky, has pointed to two radical elements in *Uncle Vanya:* an advocacy of "conservationism" or ecolog-ical sanity, and an attitude to women so revolutionary that it puts Chekhov's play outside all the conventions of nineteenth-century art from *Camille* to *Tristan.*

One reads that Soviet Russia is in as much need of ecological salvation as the United States, and has done as little about it. Certainly Anton Chekhov saw crisis coming, and we find evidence of his insight in more than one play. The issue is dramatized in *Uncle Vanya* by a character-contrast between a good reformer and a bad one. The bad one uses a smoke screen of idealistic gab to conceal greed and meanness of spirit. The good one drinks too much and is no hero yet lives out a real poetry in action, a poetry patriotic in the best sense: concrete love of the country, the country*side*.

More important in the play, of course, are the human, the sexual, relationships. In the age of the Fallen Woman, the very decade of Mrs. Tanqueray and Lady Windermere, Chekhov completely bypasses that mythology of marriage by which our grandparents hoped to evade the whole challenge of real sexual love. Here again our first realization must not be our last: if we begin by noting that Chekhov is a very candid observer, a great naturalist, we must not fail to note that here again he refuses to rest in an attitude of scientific neutrality. He passes judgment, a different judgment from any he could have learned at mother's knee. The will-she-or-won't-she? questions in his works aren't questions as to whether an accepted commandment will be broken. Instead, they are "realistic" questions, the queries of a critical humanist. Will she have the desire? The strength to see it through? No one's objection to sexual intercourse is at stake; it is all a matter of who wants what and how much and why. Nothing is forbidden. There could be an instant erotic utopia if the individuals concerned could so arrange their desires and mutual interests.

What an *if* that is! That they haven't the slightest chance is the fact of a human condition in which Chekhov the artist, the supremely great artist, finds his opportunity. No wonder his audiences, particularly those of fifty years ago, found the erotic scenes oblique! Audiences have their minds fixed on goals in quite another direction. Since all is relative, Chekhov would have the good right to call the love scenes *they* expected oblique. One of the principal measures he took had nothing to do with any notion of dramatic form but strictly with subject matter: his women are people in exactly the same sense as his men. For him a woman is not part of a man, much less a projection of male fantasy. He could identify himself with a woman as fully as many of those more recent playwrights who are famous for it, but who cannot, like him, also identify themselves with a man.

Chekhov was a free spirit. But here again, if we are going to use another of the big simple words, in this case the word *free*, we shall find that Chekhov refuses to be trapped in the big simple definitions. Free. He did not *float free* like some disembodied sprite. He did not even consider that he was born free. His grandfather had been a serf. Even as Goethe, the man of privilege, saw life as one long educational process, Chekhov, son of slavery, saw life as a process of liberation. At no point did he differ more from most of the revolutionaries of his day than in his conviction that the inner liberation of a single individual is possible as well as desirable. He had had to squeeze the slave out of himself drop by drop: the phrase is his own, and has been quoted by his countrymen right down to one of the underground songwriters who was expelled from the Writers' Union last year. Freedom. From what? "Freedom," Chekhov answers in a famous letter, "from violence and lies." In the glass house of Richard Nixon's USA we shall not throw stones at the USSR. And, in its quiet way, *Uncle Vanya* is about just that: the effort to be free from violence and lies, for violence is not just B-52 bombers, and lies are not a White House monopoly.

This is the age of the common man, when interest in man is typically an interest in what we call ordinary life. Chekhov has rightly received many compliments for his ability to illuminate this ordinariness. Although his ordinary people are singularly unproletarian, they have rightly been accepted, by the Left as well as everyone else, as one of the finest renditions of just plain folks in all literature. And now, as ever with Chekhov, we need the words *but also*. These ordinary folks embody the aspirations of kings and queens—which is to say your aspirations, reader, and mine, for democracy is our demand to *be* kings and queens and get those aspirations satisfied.

Democracy is a failure. Those aspirations are not satisfied. We are oppressed. *Uncle Vanya* is an archetypal image of our oppression. We are represented on its stage by a family that is dominated by a tyrannical father-figure, Professor Serebryakov. Anyone who has been taught that Chekhov has no villains in his plays should take a look at him (as well as at Natasha in *Three Sisters*). Chekhov in fact had a very strong sense of destructiveness—of evil, if you will—and knew how to embody it in really cruel—therefore not wholly weak—characters, such as this maybe "brilliant," but certainly dead, professor of art.

No one, of course, can oppress except as the oppressed let him, and this play bears the name, not of Serebryakov, but of Vanya, the most wronged, deluded, and abject of his victims. In an earlier draft, Uncle Vanya had committed suicide when he learned just how oppressed he had been, when, to be specific, he finds out that the professor proposes to cheat his own daughter Sonia out of that "estate" which is at once what the family lives off and a symbol of family and continued living, a stake in Russia. Such suicides are traditional in the theatre. Chekhov was untraditional in making Vanya live on. Bernard Shaw's generation got the initial message: instead of catastrophe, monotony; instead of death, dreariness. But, resting content with this analysis, that generation was soon complaining that Chekhov was too negative, if not also too feeble. And possibly it is fair to say that Chekhov's plays end not with a bang but a whimper, if we add that they also demonstrate that a whimper can signal more pain than a bang, that monotony can be the ultimate catastrophe, that dreariness can be death. Then again, this is not exactly how *Uncle Vanya* does end. As David Magarshack correctly states: a "young girl's faith and courage will rebuild the ruins." And this being a Chekhov play, the young girl—Sonia—is no fixed symbol of faith and courage. She has learned these virtues, in considerable part, before our eyes in the course of a dramatic action.

According to the dramaturgy Chekhov inherited, Sonia too would be a candidate for last-act suicide. Shaw said Chekhov's discovery was that in real life even the Hedda Gablers really don't "do such things." They live on. And just as one can get at the structure of traditional tragedy by working backwards from the end and seeing how the author arrived at his big death scene, so one can get at the structure of a Chekhov play by working backwards from the end and asking how this living-on, this sense of ongoing, flowing, unstoppable life, was arrived at. Even in this short piece, I have been able to cite one nodal point of action: the proposal to sell the estate. The other (if, as I feel, there is only one other) is erotic, for all drama in the comic and tragicomic modes hinges on money and love. If the professor's arrival, brief sojourn, and departure give the action its outline, that outline is filled in by the beautiful young wife he brings along. This Helen of the Chekhovian Troy arouses in Vanya and his friend Dr. Astrov not so much lust as love's "impossible dream," the dream of everything-solved-by-love, life transfigured by love into pure beauty. She couldn't, of course, realize that dream for them, even if she tried hard; and she is not a hard tryer. But, if, up to then, Sonia had hoped she herself could win Astrov, the dramatic action has stripped her of that hope.

Now if the money theme gives this drama a hard center, disproving any contention that Chekhov is a soft writer, the erotic theme, as it is handled, gives this drama a vast circumference—I might again cite *Tristan* and deny Wagner any claim to a greater range of intense feeling. "Eros shakes my soul," wrote Sappho, and the god of love, the only deity in Chekhov's pantheon, shakes his people. Shakes them down, indeed, till their belongings, if not their guts, strew the stage. And moves on soon after like a tropical storm. Astrov goes back into his solitude, the forests his only mistress. Into work, too, of course; which also must fill the solitude of Sonia and her uncle, everyone's uncle, Vanya.

Jack. Those for whom the word Vanya is exotic should call him Uncle Jack, for Vanya is but the familiar form of Ivan, which is our John. Why is the whole play named after him when the story, even as it appears here in broken outline, is about equally of Sonia and Helen and Astrov and Serebryakov? The professor is the mainspring of the action. Astrov, under the nickname Wood Demon, had been picked for the title of the earlier draft. In the final version, though, the move made by Serebryakov is countered by Vanya. The story builds to a climax at the end of the third of its four acts when the stage is set for

Vanya to kill the professor. In one of the trickiest and deftest scenes in all drama, he fails to bring it off. He is not a tragic hero. But he has a good claim to be considered protagonist of this tragicomic drama. He is weak. But then weakness, and not just his, is the subject. More than the professor's strength, such as it is; for he too is also weak.

Do the words *faith* and *courage* say everything about the ending? No words ever say everything about Anton Chekhov, or anything close to it. As I intimated at the outset: he's been dead nearly seventy years, and we still don't know him. My own ignorance was dramatized only the other day when I received a copy of a new edition of Chekhov's letters. I'd had an old edition on my shelves for decades. On one page of it, a person by name Toro is mentioned, and a footnote explains that Chekhov probably meant Tur and that Tur was a woman novelist. The new edition provides what I trust is the definitive correction. A word had been transliterated from our alphabet to the Cyrillic and back. This word was Thoreau. Our own Henry David.

We keep having to revise our impressions.

(1973)

THE LIFE AND HATES OF EUGENE O'NEILL

For Perry Miller

When I criticized the Broadway intelligentsia in some *Harper's* articles in the mid-forties, a friend described the event as the slaughter of the innocents. I wasn't so sure about the innocence. What was wrong, I thought, was that that intelligentsia had its list of sacrosanct and therefore untouchable figures. Eugene O'Neill stood at the head of the list, thus making himself the icon to be broken by any right-minded iconoclast. It was resented that I called him "promising." But that was in 1944–46 when he had not yet brought out *The Iceman Cometh* and *Long Day's Journey into Night*, plays in which his promise, if anywhere, was fulfilled. I was co-director of *The Iceman Cometh* in its German-language premiere at the Zurich Schauspielhaus in 1950, and I reconsidered O'Neill's whole lifework in the following essay, written for my friend Perry Miller and his anthology *Major Writers of America*, 1962.

[James] O'Neill assumed the role of the Christus in an adaptation of the Oberammergau Passion Play. In later years he always seemed most proud of having played this part, claiming to have been the "only actor on the English-speaking stage who has impersonated our Saviour." As late as 1918, James O'Neill still felt very strongly about the desirability of putting on this play. He declared that "it would be a relief after all the filth we get. . . . People have seen so much lewdness on the stage that they have become nauseated by it."

   —From *The Curse of the Misbegotten* by Croswell Bowen

Jamie jeered. "The curtain of eternity has been there a long time and I don't think that you're the one to tear it down. . . ." "The answer is that there is nothing behind the curtain when you do tear it down," Gene said. . . . "Life is a farce played by a baboon who feels in his invertebrate bones a vision that, being an ape, he cannot understand. He scratches his fleas absently, with melancholy eyes, and then hangs upside down on the nearest branch and plays with his testicles." "My trouble is that there is nobody who wants to play with mine!" Jamie said. . . .
—James O'Neill, Jr., and Eugene O'Neill, as reported in *Part of a Long Story* by Agnes Boulton

ACT II. SCENE 3. Platform of the Château d'If. Steps cut in the rock. Door of secret dungeons. Enter two gaolers carrying a sack enveloping a form.

FIRST GAOLER. *Are you ready?*
SECOND GAOLER. *Ready!* (They swing the sack into the sea.)
FIRST GAOLER. *An ugly night on the sea.*
SECOND GAOLER. *Aye, under, too.* (Exeunt. The moon breaks out, lighting up a projecting rock. Edmond Dantès rises from the sea. He is dripping, a knife in his hand, some shreds of sack adhering to it.)
EDMOND (on rock). *Saved! Mine, the treasures of Monte Cristo! The world is mine!*
—James O'Neill's version of *Monte Cristo*

I'm going on the theory that the United States, instead of being the most successful country in the world, is the greatest failure. . . . We are the greatest example of, For what shall it profit a man if he shall gain the whole world and lose his own soul?
—Eugene O'Neill, speaking to the press, 1946

1

The son of a famous romantic actor, his infancy and youth were spent in the atmosphere of the theatre while his father, James O'Neill, toured the country in *Monte Cristo* and Shakespearean repertoire. After a year at Princeton and a brief career as a reporter in New London, Connecticut, O'Neill went to sea on a Norwegian barque and at the end of two years earned his Able Seaman's certificate. In 1914, following a year in Professor [George Pierce] Baker's famous English 47 class at Harvard, he devoted himself exclusively to playwriting. Since then no fewer than thirty plays have come from his pen, and the whole world has sought to do him honor. Awarded the gold medal for drama by the National Institute of Arts and Letters and the degree of Litt.D. by Yale University, three times winner of the Pulitzer Prize for drama, he achieved his highest accolade when he was given the Nobel Prize for Literature in 1936. Eugene O'Neill's plays have been translated into almost all languages and have been performed in every civilized country of the world. His plays, next to Shakespeare's, are read by more people than are the works of any other dramatist, living or dead.

The foregoing is from an anonymous Note on the Author in *Nine Plays by Eugene O'Neill* (Modern Library). The tone is a little euphoric and one wonders where the statistics come from that would prove O'Neill is read by more people than Bernard Shaw. My reasons for quoting the excerpt are, first, that it does give an outline of the facts up to 1941 (when it was written) and, second, that it gives them in a distinctly typical way—typical of the O'Neill literature, typical of that American middlebrow culture which has been O'Neill's principal audience, typical of the world we live in and its Hollywoodian way of thinking about writers. The long and short of it is that O'Neill was a worldly success—in contrast, say, to E. E. Cummings, of whom Mr. Gilbert Highet has written: ". . . he has never made a really solid impact on his world. Up to this time, for instance, he has not been awarded the Pulitzer Prize. . . ."

The tone of a Note on the Author might be unimportant, only in this case the writer's assumptions are symptomatic enough to be significant. Not only, in his account, is the Harvard class a famous one. Harvard is famous too. Likewise the playwright's father. And the university at which he spent an undergraduate year. And when the playwright wrote plays, up rose "the whole world" and cried Hooray! "in almost all languages. . . ."

All of which provides an excellent cue for the question: *What really happened?* By way of answer I shall rehearse a few well-established facts.

The author's father, James O'Neill, was indeed famous: he was a star actor. Eugene O'Neill was born into the theatre and, as it happened, literally on Broadway, New York City. But Broadway is not much of a home to anyone and was not at all a home to Eugene O'Neill. "My first seven years," he has written, "were spent mainly in the larger towns all over the U.S. . . . I knew only actors and the stage. My mother nursed me in the wings and in dressing rooms."

It hardly even makes sense to say he was "sent away to boarding school"—away from where? (He went to school in Riverdale and Stamford.) The only approximation to a home that his parents ever acquired was a summer place in New London, Connecticut, which, therefore, was to play a role in their son's life.

The year at Princeton (1906–7) was a flop—otherwise it would have been four years at Princeton. O'Neill liked to make it out even more of a flop than it was, for he sometimes lent his authority to the myth that he had been expelled for throwing a bottle through President Woodrow Wilson's window. It turned out that the only person he had abused was the stationmaster. To top things off, he didn't take his exams.

At this point, the anonymous Note is seriously misleading. "After a year at Princeton and a brief career as a reporter in New London, Connecticut, O'Neill went to sea on a Norwegian barque. . . ." The word "barque" is very choice; the rest is fudge. The period under review is 1909–12. There were three voyages (to Honduras, South America, and England, respectively), not one, and each time O'Neill returned to his father—either to the New London summer place or a theatre somewhere. He also got married, stayed with his wife long enough to get her pregnant, attempted suicide, and was divorced.

Nineteen twelve was the most important adult year in O'Neill's whole formation. This was the year in which he not only worked as a reporter but also began to have his own work published. It was the year of his first divorce. It was the year of his romance with the girl whom he calls Muriel in *Ah, Wilderness!* And it was the year when he went to the hospital with tuberculosis.

I have no intention of putting down the facts of a whole lifetime— that has been done by others—but am setting the intellectual stage for interpretation. It is the early years, for anyone, that are formative. No need, at this date, to stress the importance of childhood, but there is a critical age of which much less has been said: the first years of adult-hood. This is a particularly trying time for the children of the famous— enviable as Fame seems to anonymous annotators and the anonymous millions. Or, rather, just because Fame is so enviable, it is embarrassing, to say the least, if your own father has got it. The problem of rivaling and replacing the father—or at least establishing one's own place on his level—is compounded. The only complete solution is for the son to be a Goethe or a Mozart, and then it's Father who has problems.

That solution was not open to Eugene O'Neill. He did say that his father would someday be known only as the father of Eugene O'Neill, and the prophecy has proved correct, but it was a disingenuous prophecy. For acting—or acting before the days of movies—is automatically for-gotten, while even a second-rate writer can "live" for a generation or two, and actually O'Neill's rank among dramatists has turned out to be about what his father's was among actors: high but not quite among the highest.

O'Neill was unable to defeat his father and then love him. He remained forever in the original state of ambivalence with which he first rebelled.

And the mother? As a girl she had been taken to see James O'Neill play Sidney Carton in Cleveland and had fallen in love with him, though she was by no means of the theatre herself, and had indeed thought of becoming a nun. Life proved less romantic than *A Tale of*

Two Cities, and, as the world has learned from *Long Day's Journey into Night*, Ella O'Neill took to drugs.

As the world knows from the same source, there was an elder brother, James, Jr. He was an alcoholic. He also kept company with prostitutes and made sure that his younger brother went along with him from time to time.

In the work of Eugene O'Neill the ideas of "nun" and of "mother" often go together. He was very much an Irishman, and the Virgin Mother composed an image he could not do without. He liked to use the phrase, "God the Mother." Otherwise, in the works of O'Neill, femininity is found largely in whores. The vices of James, Jr.—drink and whoring—are the standard recourse of any O'Neill character who has received a setback.

O'Neill married three times. From what has been published on the subject, it would seem clear that he looked less for a wife than for a mother—looked, indeed, for the image of the young Ella Quinlan, whom he had never known—and that he thought sometimes, in his second and third marriages, that he had found her. It would seem, too, that he was greatly loved by his wives but experienced the utmost difficulty in accepting love. It may well be that he portrayed this aspect of himself in Hickey, the salesman who kills his wife because she keeps forgiving him.

And his playwriting? The art of an artist is often outrageously left out of account by his biographers, as if it were not as much a part of his life as his relations with people. Thoroughly wise to this error, a psychoanalyst has shown that the writing of drama came as the solution, or partial solution, to O'Neill's main problem in living. Dr. Philip Weissman[*] points out that O'Neill's mode of living in the critical years 1909–12 constituted the "acting out" of the cruel ambivalence in his relation to his father. He would flee, and then return, time and again. But in 1912 that stopped: he had started writing. He wrote the story of his ambivalence again and again and again; devoted his life to doing so; was able to live only by doing so.

That isn't all Dr. Weissman says, but even this much helps us to understand the peculiarity of O'Neill's endeavor. He is no Broadway playwright writing to entertain, to make money, or to be one of the boys. Nor is he a man of letters with an interest in the whole give-and-take of literary, political, or scientific discussion. He lives, as it were, in a trance, writing and rewriting the story of the two Jameses, Ella, and Eugene. Or parts of the story. Or the story at a remove.

[*]"Conscious and Unconscious Autobiographical Dramas of Eugene O'Neill," *Journal of the American Psychoanalytic Association* (July 1957).

Whatever the isolation of writers from the average middle-class citizen, they at least belong to families, and as children were not so isolated after all. Yet in having the kind of family background most Americans think they want—namely a Famous one—O'Neill had a hideous and painful upbringing. Some think talent thrives on that sort of thing. More probably, he was born strong and made his way through innate strength. The handicaps were enormous, and his writing is marked by them. What important American writer has known so little of America—any part of the country or any class of its people? It is so taken for granted these days that the artist is isolated, is "alienated," that it is hard to realize that some artists are much more isolated than others. O'Neill was the outsider of outsiders. He did not "belong" in the beginning, and he did not try to belong later on. As a youth, he hankered after the *Lumpenproletariat* in waterfront dives or in Greenwich Village. When he made money, he used it to take himself away not only from the dives but from everyone. He chose the life of the luxury villa. Children embarrassed him, especially his own children, to whom, as to at least two of his three wives, he was extremely cruel. One son committed suicide, the other became a drug addict. Only his daughter made a go of things—on her own. Ever since he was in the sanatorium in 1913 he characterized himself as an invalid, and while occupied with his largest work—during World War II—he fell victim to Parkinson's disease. During the thirties he had separated himself even from his audience by not releasing plays for publication or production. His last years were a living death: he was separated even from his work. His hands shook too much to allow him to write; and he could not compose orally.

If there is much success worship in America, there is also a widespread belief that successful people are unhappy. Like unsuccessful people, they are. What distinguishes them from other folk is that they must suffer the effects of success. In other words, Eugene O'Neill had to try to cope, eventually, not only with his father's success but with his own.

For he did have success, and not merely in the newspaper sense of the word. He had success in solving the particular problem to which he had addressed himself: rivaling and replacing his father. How better, in any case, can a man outdo an actor than by becoming a playwright? The actor is the playwright's mouthpiece and victim. At least he can be; and O'Neill, Jr., made sure that he would be. His father's theatre—the Victorian theatre of Edwin Booth and Henry Irving—was an actor's theatre. The modern theatre would be a playwright's theatre, and Eugene O'Neill was one of the principal playwrights who made it so.

The texts of the plays bear a relation to James O'Neill, Sr., not merely in frequently portraying men who are like him but in doing so in a style he could never have accepted. O'Neill, Sr., was, as the *New York Times*'s obituary put it in 1920, "the last of the old school . . . a lover of all that is true and good in dramatic art, always holding up with authority the best traditions of the American stage." Early that year he had sat in a box at the premiere of his son's first Pulitzer Prize-winning play, *Beyond the Horizon*. Afterward he said to his son, "People come to the theatre to forget their troubles, not to be reminded of them. What are you trying to do—send them home to commit suicide?" Which certainly was to hit a bull's-eye; for to send one particular person home to commit suicide was, in a symbolic sense, precisely the intention.

The public discussion of O'Neill has by this time gone beyond the above-mentioned anonymous Note and embraced the fact—announced so openly in *Long Day's Journey*—that he was his father's enemy. The anonymous annotator's success story has been undermined, and another school of interpretation has taken over the public mind: the school that finds fame interesting *as an ordeal*. At this point, books and articles on O'Neill come to resemble books and articles on, say, famous actresses who tell it to Gerold Frank. In journalism, one stereotype follows hard on the heels of the next.

The newer school of thought will be willing enough to concede that the young O'Neill reacted against the elder O'Neill's type of theatre. "James O'Neill," we read in Croswell Bowen's *The Curse of the Misbegotten* (1959),

> was seeing the passing of his kind of American theatre with its old-fashioned, flamboyant acting. Melodrama, pathos, blood and thunder, hearts and flowers were already a little passé. They were yielding to the neo-realism—to the interpretation of contemporary experience—that constitutes the serious aspect of Broadway today, and which his son was inaugurating.

And again: "Before O'Neill, the American theatre had been cheap, sentimental, and tawdry. It was 'afraid of its own emotions,' as Eugene said. . . . It would not be too great an exaggeration to say that the emergence of an important American theatre is due . . ." et cetera.

Now it is true enough that Eugene O'Neill expressed contempt for *Monte Cristo*. As far as that goes, he even described his father, on one occasion, as the worst actor in America. The two statements may be equally personal and uncritical. Even if they are not, what does the younger O'Neill claim to be rejecting in the older theatre? Only, it would seem, what was feeble about it—hearts and flowers, no doubt, but not "melodrama, pathos, blood and thunder" by any means. What does the same commentator say of one of O'Neill's early plays? "*The Web* is remarkable in that it includes many of O'Neill's characteristic elements: violent death, cruelty, and a good deal of theatrical action." Exactly—these are the characteristics of melodrama.

Ambivalence is ambivalence. If Eugene O'Neill hated his father and his father's great role of Edmond Dantès, he also loved them. The proposition that he rejected Victorian melodrama will be useless to criticism unless it is accompanied by its opposite: O'Neill undertook to free melodrama from what was cheap and tawdry and ineffective, and to write a melodrama that would be truly melodramatic—a *Monte Cristo* raised to the nth power. If the rebellious son wishes to destroy the father, in his ambivalence he wishes nothing so much as to validate him and, if necessary, to rehabilitate him.

Eugene O'Neill is generally at his best when he sticks to melodrama, but Mr. Bowen's words about a "serious" and "important" aspect call our attention to a problem. Even good melodrama does not have the reputation it might have. That much is clear even from Mr. Bowen's own tone. And what the son does to, with, and for the father must win recognition—must have a good reputation, must gain prestige. Hence the paradox that though the younger O'Neill succeeded in melodrama he was not thereby satisfied. He had to be serious too. And he had to be acknowledged as such by pundits, professors, and institutions who award prizes even more august than Pulitzers—such as the Swedish Academy.

We have seen that he succeeded in his adventure into seriousness. The Swedish Academy and "the whole world" seriously approved. It remains a question, though, whether the seriousness was *artistically* successful, whether it even had any spontaneity, or any underlying purpose other than its author's private and neurotic one.

2

The writing career of Eugene O'Neill falls into three parts:

I. 1912–1924

The notable premieres were:
  1920: *Beyond the Horizon*
       The Emperor Jones
  1921: *Anna Christie*
  1922: *The Hairy Ape*
  1924: *Desire under the Elms*

II. 1925–1934

The notable premieres were:
  1926: *The Great God Brown*
  1928: *Strange Interlude*
       Lazarus Laughed (Pasadena, California)
  1931: *Mourning Becomes Electra*

III. 1934–1953

There were no O'Neill premieres between 1934 and 1946. The last three named below were posthumous.

1946: *The Iceman Cometh*
1956: *Long Day's Journey into Night*
1957: *A Moon for the Misbegotten* (Columbus, Ohio)
1958: *A Touch of the Poet*

Eugene O'Neill's earliest efforts are somewhat ludicrous, not least because the form of the one-act simply would not carry the kind of weight he tried to put on it. Soon he was wise enough to reduce the load, and the result was a kind of one-act not quite like anything else that had yet been produced in the genre. The little plays of the sea, later gathered together under the title *The Moon of the Caribbees* (1919), are sketches of maritime life organized largely by a certain sense of romance, of "poetry." Brevity was an admirable discipline, preventing O'Neill from launching upon the *longueurs* that ruined many of his later works. Though people nowadays think of O'Neill as the author of very long plays, he was in fact one of the many modern playwrights who have difficulty filling up more than one act. A lot of his best work is in the one-act form, and some of his seemingly full-length works are but one-acts slightly extended—I don't necessarily mean padded. *The Emperor Jones* is one of O'Neill's more satisfactory creations. Essentially, it is a long one-act, and the culmination of all his work in the one-act form between 1912 and 1920.[*]

Anna Christie is a play which proceeded splendidly for one full act but then went to pieces in the effort to become a full-length play. The tragedy of "old davil, sea" and its victory over Chris Christopherson was spoiled by the comedy of Anna and her Irish boyfriend. Two one-acts do not make an integrated full-length play, and O'Neill confessed his own dissatisfaction with the result. Nonetheless, *Anna Christie* remains a landmark. Such richly colloquial dialogue had not been heard in the American theatre before. Here the genteel tradition—of Clyde Fitch and the rest—ended, and the rhythm of modern life—in a sense Whitman himself would have recognized—was heard on the New York stage.

O'Neill's dialogue has often been adversely criticized, and not without reason: it is often prosy and ponderous; his ear was not a fastidious one; nor was his knowledge of real dialects—as against stage dialects—particularly sure. Even so he was responsible, more than any other one man, for a change in the tone of stage dialogue in general, and people "talk O'Neill" on the American stage to this day. Such an author as

---

[*]My topic is dramaturgy. On O'Neill's attitude to blacks, in this play and *All God's Chillun Got Wings*, there would be more to say. Paul Robeson did star in both.

Tennessee Williams may introduce local variations from New Orleans or St. Louis, but the basic pattern is still, I think, the O'Neillian blend of vernacular with a kind of artifice that wavers between rhetoric and lyricism.

The best commentator on O'Neill's work as a whole, Edwin A. Engel, has shown that evolution is the idea behind both *The Emperor Jones* and *The Hairy Ape* and that, while in the latter we see a man vainly trying to evolve, in the former we see him looking back at the stage he has evolved from. I would add that the Darwinian philosophy is less important than the psychological implication, which is the same in both cases: namely, regression. To be sure, Yank does not regress. It is O'Neill who regresses; and we with him. People who talk lightly of O'Neill the Able Seaman forget that his visits to stokeholes and waterfront dives were the slumming of an ex-Princeton undergraduate and son of a Broadway celebrity. That *this* man chooses to identify himself with Yank and Brutus Jones is what is significant—a maladjusted young Bohemian who, in real life, goes slumming.

To go to sea can be itself that ultimate regression—to go to sea as O'Neill went to sea, not for any practical reason but in evident quest of certain purely psychic satisfactions, and particularly, one would think, in quest of the mother he had never (sufficiently) had.

That it is not always desirable for an artist to become too conscious of what he is doing can be amply illustrated from the career of O'Neill's son-in-law, Charles Chaplin. When people explained to Charlie what was going on in his early films, he unloaded their explanations into his later films, which, consequently, are weighed down with explanations. Though the artist, qua artist, does not explain himself, in our day, explanatoriness has become the besetting sin of the cultural climber: Charlie Chaplin thought by explanations—symbolism, message, philosophy—to come up in the world.

Up to a point, O'Neill's background was similar and his ambition identical. The parents in both cases belonged to the popular theatre. The sons in both cases wanted all this and culture too. Here "culture" means recognition from people who write about such things. Here "people who write about such things" means the critics of those newspapers and magazines who lay down the law. Even if these men were giants of disinterested thought it would not be wise for a Chaplin or an O'Neill to have them constantly in mind. Since by and large what they have is not brains but vested interests, to pay much heed to them can only be a mistake.

The Hairy Ape has many of the merits of *The Emperor Jones* and the first act of *Anna Christie* but also marks the appearance on the scene of Eugene O'Neill the Intellectual. You only need to read it once through to gather that an explanation is expected of you. You only need to read it a second time to discover that the explanation has been supplied by the author in his dialogue. You only need to read it a third time to realize that this is precisely what is wrong with the dialogue. Perhaps for a brilliant reader three readings would not be needed, but for most, surely, the phonetic spelling will conceal for a while the far less uncouth mentality of the author. One cannot help thinking that the uncouth accents are only a device to cover intellectuality. Yank would not have talked about "belonging." The conception comes from the intelligentsia who have talked of nothing else for the past hundred years.

Desire under the Elms is a better play because it springs more directly from O'Neill's needs and preoccupations. So central is this play that Dr. Weissman has been able to take it as a sort of first draft of *Long Day's Journey into Night*. In other words, it deals with O'Neill's relations with father and mother.

Directly incestuous relationships are avoided, in fiction as in other fantasy, by making the mother-figure only a stepmother. The device is at least as old as Euripides, and is familiar to many of us from Schiller's *Don Carlos*. A modern touch is added by O'Neill, who brings the story nearer to overt incest by stressing that Eben Cabot has a "fixation" on his dead mother—as well as an affair with his live stepmother. That Eben loves both his mothers and hates his father is perhaps not so remarkable in modern writing as that the stepmother murders their child to prove she loves Eben. In the context, there is some logic in this act, because Eben has been told she bore the child only in order to get an inheritance. The murder does disprove the allegation. The question that arises is whether, even so, it is credible. Infanticide is a crime that has often been committed. Nonetheless, few women will kill their child just to prove a point. What is beyond debate is that O'Neill's fantasy gave birth to a woman who commits an atrocity that is not only inhuman but also quite rare because it is quite unfeminine. O'Neill's plays are full of items like this, which are of interest chiefly in relation to their author's life and makeup. Psychoanalysts to the contrary notwithstanding, this is a limitation.

Though it has a flaw near its center, *Desire under the Elms* remains a superior play because most of the time O'Neill stays well within his emotional range, within the kind of world that is truly *his* world. The landscape is neither pretty nor varied. The father is an Old Testament tyrant re-created with something of the appropriate majesty. If in many later plays O'Neill tends toward the overabstract, here the father is not derived from a bare idea. He seems to grow from the soil. The soil is given a reality, not, to be sure, through true local color, or sensitivity to the life around him, but by a curiously vivid sense of the bovine which O'Neill found, surely, in some marshy tract, not of New England, but of his soul. It is a nauseating play, but nausea is at least a thing of the senses, and one must grant that O'Neill at his best could communicate strong emotions, particularly negative ones. I am not even convinced that the negative emotions he most readily commanded are those he has been praised for commanding, such as terror. Are they not, rather, the mean and masochistic feelings? One may admire *Desire under the Elms,* but one can hardly relish it.

3

O'Neill's more ardent admirers have been admirers above all of his second phase (1925–34). The rest of us feel compelled to regret that this phase ever happened, vain as it always is to scold artists or tell them, even beforehand, that they mustn't do what their hearts are set on doing.

I have stressed that playwriting was for O'Neill something much different from what it is for your Broadway entertainer. It may be well to elaborate at this stage a point of Dr. Weissman's. O'Neill was so disturbed in the period 1909–12 that he kept alternately fleeing from and returning to his father. That activity constitutes neurotic "acting out" and nearly went as far as suicide. Then it subsided considerably. Why? Presumably because O'Neill, in 1912, took up writing. At first he wrote precisely about the voyages and the returns, a theme which, for that matter, he would revert to later. The career of O'Neill should interest those who see a connection between art and neurosis, and it would indicate that art is not so much a symptom as an attempt at cure. O'Neill was never cured—which of us is?—and he deserted wives— one in 1909, it is true, but one also in the middle twenties—as he had deserted parents. Yet it is quite tenable that only his writing kept O'Neill going at all. And why did it? Not, obviously, because it was art, but because it seemed a weapon in a personal battle. Everything we know about O'Neill suggests that he never emerged from the Oedipus conflict but remained in the immature and adolescent relation to both father and mother.

What O'Neill did was to take Victorian melodrama and add. When what he added was chiefly his own personal vehemence—as attached to his own complexes—the result could be impressive and even unpretentious. When he added more than this, the result was to many even more impressive—and very pretentious indeed. The *New York Times* was impressed. Which is to say that middlebrow culture was impressed, as well it might be, for what had O'Neill added to melodrama but the stock of ideas and attitudes which constitute middlebrow culture? O'Neill may have flunked out of Princeton but, down the years, he had been reading, reading, reading, and was now a rather formidable autodidact.

He had a theory of theatre which I for one am so far from taking issue with that, on the contrary, I would applaud nearly all of it.

What was this theory? We have seen that O'Neill wanted to reintroduce the powerful emotions fearlessly. That perhaps was the main wish, and one that could not harm him unless he had it too much in his *head*. He also saw through the cult of character—the schoolteacher's idea that playwrights must portray "individuals, not types"—and realized that even better than "individuals" are archetypes. He also realized that no kind of character—even an archetypal one—is enough, that the playwright should try to get at "the Force Beyond," at the part of the world that is *not* contained in the characters themselves, and at the problem which Goethe himself thought transcended all problems, that of belief.

In short, Eugene O'Neill saw through not only the tawdry everyday commercial theatre of his father's time but also through the drab or homey naturalistic theatre of his own time and ours. Like most autodidacts, he had a nose, too, for the kind of reading that would mean most to him, and this nose led him unerringly to the philosopher who, of all philosophers, has entered most deeply into the spirit of tragedy, and who also happens to be the philosopher who laid the foundations of modern psychological understanding: Friedrich Nietzsche. One result of all this thinking of O'Neill's, and all this reading, was that he was able to reinvent Expressionism on his own. For I believe we can take him at his word when he tells us he knew very little of the German Expressionists. There is ironic justice in the fact that one of the German Expressionists considered *Lazarus Laughed* the best of all Expressionist plays.

Unfortunately, all this proves no more than that Eugene O'Neill came to some good conclusions. No number of good conclusions will make a good play. And he also came to some bad conclusions. More precisely, he came to adopt an outlook which could affect actual playwriting—for the worse. There is no word for this outlook that I know of. I will call it psychologism. It proceeds by substituting notions about people's minds for actual observation of people's minds and contact with them.

Now an artist can often get by with few formulations, provided he enjoys lively contact with people. He need not *know* what people are like but he certainly need *sense* what they are like, and he certainly must be able to communicate that sense. O'Neill came to maturity in the era of psychologism. Freud was then—as now, I suppose—chiefly a fad. One had to know his name. One had to bandy Freudian phraseology, actual or supposed. O'Neill had some canniness, it is true, and tried to avoid being a faddist. He denied having read much Freud. But in that atmosphere nonreading was insufficient protection. Freud was "in the air." Worse: Jung was in the air. Then too, O'Neill said he *had* read Jung.

More important than the leading psychologists were the hundreds of nonleaders whose books and articles flooded the market. One of O'Neill's closest associates, Kenneth MacGowan, was coauthor, with Dr. G. V. Hamilton, of a psychiatric treatise, *What Is Wrong with Marriage?* The heading for a chapter entitled "Oedipus Rex" reads: "Evidence that supports Freud's dictum of the part the mother-image plays in a man's choice of his wife. . . . The happiest group of men have wives on the mother-pattern. Yet the fear of inbreeding makes men marry away from the mother." The next chapter is headed by the words: ". . . fear of incest, added to the fear of inbreeding, makes the women even less fortunate than the men in their marriage choices." This chapter is entitled "The Tragedy of Electra."

When Malcolm Cowley visited O'Neill in 1923, the latter

> picked up a green textbook-type volume from the table and explained that it was William Stekel's treatise on sexual aberrations, *The Disguises of Love*, recently translated from the German. He said there were enough case histories in the book to furnish plots to all the playwrights who ever lived. He turned to a case history of a mother who seduced her only son and drove him insane.

The poet Meredith wrote, "Passions spin the plot." It was left to O'Neill to imagine that case histories spin the plot. There could be no more clear-cut example of the kind of half-baked thinking that mars his work. *Strange Interlude* stands condemned right there: it is a gigantic appendix to Dr. Hamilton's *A Research in Marriage*. "My husband is unable to give me a healthy child. What shall I do?" In the spirit of the lady columnist running her readers' private lives, O'Neill writes out not, to be sure, what we *should* do but what Dr. Hamilton or Dr. Stekel says we *have* done.

I do not find *Strange Interlude* boring. Though not lowbrow, it is soap opera, and soap opera doesn't have to be boring, it only has to be foolish. Soap opera larded—or should one say lathered?—with would-be serious and up-to-date ideas is doubly foolish. The solemn farce got its deserved comeuppance when Groucho Marx—in *Animal Crackers*—did an imitation of its manner.

Groucho used the comedian's privilege of attacking the weakest spot, which was the device of asides placed at the service of psychologism. The things that people think and don't say were written into the dialogue as long and numerous asides, delivered while everyone on stage stood petrified. The petrifaction would have been bearable had the monologues been bearable, but the principle behind the latter was simple-minded. It was that when a man is saying to a woman, "I love you!" he is murmuring to himself, "No I don't, I hate you, you bitch!" Of which the reverse form, even commoner in O'Neill, is: "I hate you, you bitch!" followed by: "Oh, what a cad I am, I don't hate her at all, I love her!" If, as one might certainly maintain, ambivalence is the main theme of O'Neill's writing, as of his life, this is no adequate way to present it.

What about the mask? It is the very prototype of theatrical artifices, and it was O'Neill's idea that it could be used to express ambivalence. For example, a mask may express innocence, while the face is haunted with guilt; a mask may exude confidence, while the face exudes timidity. This is one of a very few ideas by which *The Great God Brown* stands or falls. It proved more interesting in discussion than effective in the theatre. So did the idea of having two actors play opposing sides of the same man in *Days without End* (premiere 1934).

More of course was involved than technical devices. The plays of O'Neill's middle period were a very bold attempt to realize on the stage the vision of theatre of O'Neill's generation. This was particularly the vision of three of his close associates, George Cram Cook, Robert Edmond Jones, and Kenneth MacGowan. Jones was the most gifted American stage designer of his day. He and MacGowan had toured the European theatres shortly after World War I and had returned to write and rhapsodize about "the theatre of tomorrow." Like all such dreams, this one had a good deal to do with yesterday. It had specifically to do with Wagner and Nietzsche, Adolphe Appia and Gordon Craig. The vision was of a release from realism, a release upward, as it were, toward the sublime and downward toward the instinctual. Cook's particular enthusiasm was Greece. It is Cook whom O'Neill is echoing when he speaks, in a letter, of the Greek dream being the noblest of them all. The word "dream" recurs a good deal, and the reference is less to Freud than to Apollo, whom Nietzsche regarded as a symbol of the dream world in contrast to Dionysus, who stood for drunkenness.

The word "Dionysus" recurs even oftener. Bred a Catholic, and educated in popular Hellenism by Cook and others, O'Neill liked to see life as a conflict between the ascetic and the pagan spirit. Hence the name of the hero of *The Great God Brown*, Dion Anthony—Dionysus the drunken God and Anthony the ascetic saint. Closely related to Dionysus is "the great god Pan," with whom O'Neill contrasts the American businessman of the Babbitt era—the great god Brown.

One can only say of these antitheses what I have already said about O'Neill's whole theory of drama. In themselves they are splendid and full of possibilities. Very similar antitheses underlie tragic art of the greatest epochs. It was a contemporary of Shakespeare's who wrote:

> O wearisome condition of humanity!
> Born under one law, to another bound,
> Vainly begot and yet forbidden vanity,
> Created sick, commanded to be sound.
> What meaneth nature by these diverse laws,
> Passion and reason, self-division's cause?

And it was certainly permissible for O'Neill to champion passion against reason—instead of reason against passion as the Elizabethans had done. This he was inclined to do in the middle twenties when he took a Nietzschean position. Once, in the early thirties, he seemed, rather, to champion Anthony against Dionysus in a play that ends in reconciliation with the Catholic church, *Days without End*. But this was a momentary point of rest, not a final conclusion.

The question was never of the permissibility of the ideas themselves but of O'Neill's ability to handle them—or, more exactly, of their suitability to the kind of work which he could do in art. In *Hamlet* the conflict between passion and reason is deeply sunk in an Action as well as in characters inwardly felt. Neither passion nor reason have to be mentioned by name, and, when they are, we do not have an embarrassing feeling of "There goes the main theme again." This embarrassing feeling is just what we do have in *Strange Interlude* when we hear:

> a lot to account for, Herr Freud! . . . punishment to fit his crimes, be forced to listen eternally during breakfast while innumerable plain ones tell him dreams about snakes . . . pah, what an easy cure-all! . . . sex the philosopher's stone . . . "O Oedipus, O my king! The world is adopting you!" . . .

and:

> she has strange devious intuitions that tap the hidden currents of life . . . dark intermingling currents that become the one stream of desire . . .

and:

> Perhaps he realizes subconsciously that I am his father, his rival in your love; but I'm not his father ostensibly, there are no taboos, so he can come right out and hate me . . .

and:

> Yes, perhaps unconsciously Preston is a compensating substitute.

and:

> I was only a body to you. . . . I was never more to you than a substitute for your dead lover!

and:

> I can remember that day seeing her kiss him . . . it did something to
> me I never got over.

These passages prompt the question: In what way should literature
be psychological? It is good that great writers should be psychologically
deep, and that Freud should say so, but is it good that an artist should
read Freud and reproduce him? Is it good that characters should sum
themselves up, should spend their time diagnosing themselves—and
everyone else? That, by consequence, human character should come
to the audience in the form of summation and diagnosis? On the contrary, it is a disaster. The drama should provide an image of experience
and character such as might be analyzed later. To begin with analysis
is to put the cart before the horse—with the same result: immobility.

What is true of psychological ideas is true of all ideas in drama.
The playwright Friedrich Hebbel put it with witty overstatement: "In
drama, no character should ever utter a thought: from the thought in
a play come the speeches of *all* the characters." Now, if this principle
applies to the relatively modest ideas of *Strange Interlude*, how much
more is it called for when we confront *The Great God Brown* and *Lazarus
Laughed!* So little are the ideas of these plays sunk in the action and
the characters that neither action nor characters have any effective
existence except to illustrate the ideas. And if there are obscurities, as
in *The Great God Brown* there certainly are, they are cleared up not
by more work on action or character but by a letter to the newspapers
explaining the philosophy and the symbolism.

Lazarus Laughed is probably the most ambitious American play ever
written by a gifted playwright. It cries out to be compared with the
work which presumably prompted its writing, Nietzsche's *Thus Spake
Zarathustra*. ("This book," writes O'Neill's second wife, Agnes Boulton,
"had more influence on Gene than any other single book he ever read.
It was a sort of Bible to him, and he kept it by his bedside. . . .") Both
works would ring out an old era, and ring in a new. Both authors would
denounce the old era with the terrifying finality of a Jeremiah and, in
hailing the new, reach the highest peaks of ecstasy. Nietzsche, however,
was a master of ideas, and was not attempting drama. In *Lazarus* the
ideas are too few and too grandiose ever to become active and interesting, while not enough is done by way of dialogue, action, and character to give us a real play. And if O'Neill had not had much success
in depicting self-division, it was a false way out that he found in *Lazarus*
when he picked a hero who was not divided.

O'Neill's Lazarus has little to do with the biblical character and
a great deal to do with the Greek god whom Nietzsche had already

opposed to Christ: Dionysus. Following Nietzsche, O'Neill takes Christianity to be life-denial, the religion of Dionysus to be life-worship. One worships life and denies death. In that perhaps rather peculiar sense, one believes in immortality. "The fear of death," O'Neill wrote,

> is the root of all evil, the cause of all man's blundering unhappiness. Lazarus knows there is no death, there is only change. He is reborn without that fear. Therefore he is the first and only man who is able to laugh affirmatively. His laughter is a triumphant Yes to life. . . . And life itself is the self-affirmative joyous laughter of God.

Whatever we make of this as philosophy, we can hardly make much of it as theatre or psychology. Theatrically, O'Neill asks laughter to do more than laughter *can* do. For an actor to be laughing so often and so loudly when he isn't even amused is to court confusion, even assuming he can keep it up. Laughter is not a pretty noise or a majestic one, a fact that is related to the psychic side. Laughter is not a suitable symbol of, or outlet for, affirmation because there is so much about it that is inherently and unmistakably negative. Laughter sounds aggressive for the good reason that it *is* aggressive. It is impossible to hear roars of laughter in which one is not personally involved without wishing to shut them up.

O'Neill was not always kind to his audience. *The Iceman Cometh* opens with a lot of men asleep on stage. In the theatre, sleep is contagious, and some audiences have at once dozed off. Did O'Neill hate not only his family but his public? Lazarus's laughter would prove very annoying. Was that O'Neill's unconscious intention? If so, it is a pity that no conscious intention interfered. It is hard to resist the conclusion that O'Neill sometimes liked to flout his own theatre sense because he identified it with his father. If the laughter of Lazarus stems from thought, it is an instance of the way in which a playwright should *not* be a thinker.

Though not more ambitious, *Mourning Becomes Electra* is a much longer play than *Lazarus Laughed* and is ambitious enough to invite the comparison with Aeschylus. Some of the most respected critics of the time, such as George Jean Nathan and Joseph Wood Krutch, thought it could sustain the comparison. For a time it was possible for many intelligent people to think of this play as at least one of the supreme American masterpieces like, say, *Moby-Dick* or *The Scarlet Letter*. Today there is no need to take issue with an opinion which is gone with the wind: it can serve only to educate us in the ways of the world. And there is an interesting human and historical problem: what was it about *Mourning Becomes Electra* that at first made a big impression and later did not?

The idea behind the play is that of an equivalent in terms of Freudian, or perhaps Jungian, psychology to the *Oresteia* of Aeschylus: an equivalent and, following the reasoning of the man in the street, an improvement. As Croswell Bowen puts it, "*Electra* is based on sound modern concepts of psychological and biological cause and effect, not upon the inspiration of the Furies." It is certainly based on concepts. That may be the main trouble. Whether these concepts are so much sounder than Aeschylus is also open to debate. They are certainly more depressing. The *Oresteia* celebrates the establishment of community: it shows the rule of law take the place of the vendetta. *Mourning Becomes Electra* shows the vendetta going on and on and on. In place of the liberating, creative, and inspiring ideas of Aeschylus come ideas that at best are sobering.

The key terms reverse their meanings. Where Aeschylus describes a curse that can be lifted in the name of a justice that is real and that can be assured by a human nature not wholly lacking in wisdom, for O'Neill living is itself a curse, death is a release, and justice is not the opposite of revenge but the same thing.

The psychology of *Mourning Becomes Electra* runs as thin as the philosophy. One thing leads to another in all too naive and mechanical a way. It is as if a couple of psychoanalytic concepts, taken in ridiculously simple form, were held sufficient to demonstrate what tragic life is like. Daughters, for example, hate their mothers and love their fathers. This must have seemed a thrillingly novel idea in 1931, or how could anyone have thought O'Neill's presentation of it anything but monotonous? To do without the Furies is nothing but a loss if all you put in their place is the rhetoric of psychologism.

Orin grows to resemble his father, and Lavinia her mother. Such a development comes under the heading, in psychiatry, of "psychotic identification," and it seems that O'Neill has been "confirmed" by recent medical writers. Dr. Weissman congratulates him on his insight, but is it so remarkable? Isn't this particular "insight" in the logic of the whole argument? Isn't it also very much in the spirit of melodrama? And finally, do such "insights," however correct, constitute dramatic art?

Insofar as any big play can be summed up in a sentence, cannot *Mourning Becomes Electra* be summed up in this one: Eugene O'Neill feels that people wish to kill each other? O'Neill seems to have been imbued with hatred as Saint Francis, say, or Gandhi was imbued with love, but how creative is mere hatred, even in art? Certainly, it is permissible for O'Neill to keep inventing people who kill each other or want to, but isn't it equally permissible for us to wonder that they don't have any other interests?

The question sounds like a jibe, and those who leap to O'Neill's defense might ask if one could not wonder the same about the frantic characters of Strindberg and Dostoevsky. I doubt it. The world of Dostoevsky's people, and even of Strindberg's, is a far larger one than that of O'Neill's. The Captain in Strindberg's *The Father* is a scientist and his intellectuality is made quite real to us. The Captain's fury attains to full dramatic force just because we have been made to feel his love of knowledge. Does not every author who presents the negative side have to make us feel the positive side even if he never shows it? Is an artist ever really a monomaniac? Must he not always be able to *imagine* an alternative even if he does not propose one? Dostoevsky often did propose one. Not all his characters are possessed, unless one were to say that some are possessed by Christian love. O'Neill sometimes presents an alternative—but inadequately. The few characters not propelled downward by the death wish are mere dummies. Peter and Hazel, in *Mourning Becomes Electra*, are examples.

For all his reading, O'Neill remained horrifyingly barbaric. Culture existed for him, it would seem, only as those books he lifted ideas from and in no degree as culture—the cultivation of the spirit and the tradition among men of such cultivation. In this respect, *Mourning Becomes Electra* stands at the opposite pole not only from the Greeks but from such characteristic attempts to revive Greek tragedy in modern times as Goethe's *Iphigenia in Tauris*. There, the poet's search was expressly for whatever in the myth might tend to the schooling of man and the taming of the beast in him—whatever might tend to the enhancement of life in possible sweetness and grace. Reading or seeing Goethe's play, we enter his mind and find it a spacious and truly edifying dwelling place. The paradox of *Mourning Becomes Electra* is that O'Neill took up a great testament of humane culture in order to spit in the face of humanity.

How is it no one said so? People bring such charges against authors much less guilty of them. Obviously, if O'Neill's points got across at all they did not carry a sting—which is to say they did not carry conviction. For when all is said against O'Neill's ideas, it must yet be admitted that such ideas might have gone to the making of very powerful drama. They did so when Wagner used them. (For is not the "tragic philosophy" of *Mourning Becomes Electra* much less that of Nietzsche than of Nietzsche's archenemy, the author of *Tristan and Isolde* and *The Ring of the Nibelung?*) If initially one tends to reject this *Electra* because of the view of life it presents, one rejects it even more emphatically because it does not get this view across the footlights.

We are now perhaps in a position to answer the question as to what people were impressed by back in 1931: not by the nihilistic view of life, which did not come home to men's business and bosoms, but merely by the rhetoric of psychologism. One might not know exactly what the main intent was, but certainly much of the talk in scene after scene was close enough to the talk at the cocktail party before the show. Now even dead ideas can seem to come alive in a play when they happen to be alive in the current conversation of the public, and surely such ideas—though they may not be the main themes of the plays—come up in all the plays of O'Neill's middle period. They return to their graves as soon as they are no longer part of the current chatter, "the new small talk."

4

By 1930, the success story was written: Eugene O'Neill was far more prominent in the American theatre than his father had ever been and a Nobel Prize winner, Sinclair Lewis, was telling the Swedish Academy that

> had you chosen Mr. O'Neill, who has done nothing much in American drama save to transform it utterly in ten or twelve years from a false world of neat and competent trickery to a world of splendor and fear and greatness, you would have been reminded that he has done something far worse than scoffing—he has seen life as not to be neatly arranged in the study of a scholar but as a terrifying, magnificent, and often quite horrible thing akin to the tornado, the earthquake, and the devastating fire.

How to survive such praise? After the success of *Mourning Becomes Electra*, what O'Neill attempted was to re-enter his past. In *Ah, Wilderness!* (premiere 1933) he based a play upon that same New London summer of 1912 which later would yield *Long Day's Journey into Night*. After reading both plays, one comes to doubt that O'Neill meant even the latter to be pure autobiography. In any case, it is almost incredible that both plays present the same O'Neill in the same year. In neither play does he see himself as the actual twenty-three-year-old who was already a father and was in the process of being divorced. In *Ah, Wilderness!* he sees himself as an adolescent and a virgin, dreams of belonging to a regular American home in a regular American town, and so relives the kind of childhood he had never lived in the first place. In *Days without End* he dreams himself back into the Church of his fathers. Incidentally, the priest he consulted on theological matters got no impression that O'Neill wanted more than to dream. The two plays belong to a moment of wistful pause, and perhaps of hesitation, before O'Neill embarked upon the most grandiose of his grandiose schemes: a cycle of plays in which he would write the spiritual history of his country. Six of these plays were undoubtedly completed, and five others planned. But in 1953 O'Neill sat down with his wife in the Hotel Shelton in Boston and tore up all the finished plays. "We tore them up bit by bit, together," says Mrs. O'Neill; "I helped him because his hands—he had this terrific tremor, he could tear just a few pages at a time. It was awful. It was like tearing up children."

Why Mrs. O'Neill cooperated in the tearing up of O'Neill's children shall remain, for the present at least, her business. A writer's life, on the other hand, belongs to the world, and the world has already speculated on Eugene O'Neill's reasons. All he said was, "I don't want anyone else finishing up a play of mine." But the plays, says Mrs. O'Neill, *were* finished—except for cutting. It is impossible not to connect this terrible act—which any fellow writer feels in the pit of his stomach—with O'Neill's many other destructive acts. He had killed himself as son, as father, and several times as husband—why not also as writer?

Everything that happened since the plays of the early thirties remains somewhat mysterious despite the labors of the biographers. O'Neill had lived the life of a wealthy man ever since he *became* a wealthy man in the early twenties. If he changed now, it was mainly to let it be known that he was going off—presumably forever—to work on the giant project. He seems to have worked on it regularly until 1939, and to have resumed it with less assiduity several years later. Shortly before the end of World War II O'Neill had a stroke. Afterward a tremor of the hands which he had had for some time was much more marked, and he could not write. Echoing Mrs. O'Neill, I have already said that since he could not compose orally his writing days were over. This is an incomplete statement. Many men would have gradually learned to compose orally. Mrs. O'Neill says, "He died when he could no longer work—spiritually died and was dragging the poor diseased body along for a few more years until it too died." This does not explain why his will to work was insufficient to overcome his aversion to dictation. One must assume that this will was already dead or dying. Following such a clue, one might then move backward into the mysterious years when the Cycle was being written. Did the plays of the Cycle, when finished, disappoint O'Neill? One, A *Touch of the Poet,* has survived and is certainly not among, say, his dozen best plays. Did the Cycle, in O'Neill's opinion, deserve to be destroyed? He seems never to have expressed the opinion that it was, as it was meant to be, the crown of his writing career. Could it be that most of the writing he did in California did not represent his further development as a playwright but a progressive withdrawal from the theatre, a long day's journey into night? This is not a conclusion drawn by Dr. Weissman but he provides evidence for it.

If O'Neill's "love affair with the world" was over, he sometimes longed for his old mistress, and we find him dropping the Cycle in 1939 and writing two of his best plays: *The Iceman Cometh* and *Long Day's Journey into Night*—as well as *A Moon for the Misbegotten,* which is by no means one of his worst. To think of O'Neill's "final period" will always be to think of *The Iceman* and *Journey.*

Both are explorations of the year 1912. Neither is merely a memoir. *Long Day's Journey* does seem wholly a memoir the first time one reads it; at least it did when the facts of O'Neill's background were not yet public knowledge. One read the play with amazement at what the O'Neills went through. Dr. Weissman soon pointed out that O'Neill had omitted facts of the utmost relevance, such as that Edmund is not represented as a father and divorcé. Dr. Weissman conjectures that these facts had been "repressed," and thinks that Barrett Clark also did a little "repressing" in his biography. This conjecture I find uncalled for. Clark said what he was allowed to say, and tried to give the impression he was supposed to give. O'Neill never stated that *Long Day's Journey* was pure history, and he was a good enough playwright to know that history and drama must ever be distinct. O'Neill "played" with the facts of 1912 in no less than four dramas—*Hughie* is the only one not already mentioned here—and always in a different style, always with a different angle on the facts. In *Long Day's Journey* the camera is still at an angle to the subject, though admittedly a less oblique one.

If O'Neill was nihilistic in his views, and Bohemian in some of his conduct, he was not disorderly in his work. Indeed his work spelled order for him, just as it spelled somewhat better mental health. *The Iceman Cometh* and *Long Day's Journey*, prompted to some extent by the outbreak of World War II, were islands of order in the sea of a personal and more than personal chaos.

Long Day's Journey is a kind of classical quartet. Here O'Neill eschews the luxury of numerous minor characters, crowds, and a bustle of stage activity. He has a few people and they talk. This has given the public an impression of shapelessness. Bowen says, "The play is essentially plotless . . . the deliberate formlessness of it all is enervating. Still, it is a dramatic achievement of the first order. . . ." A biographer—in this case at least—is not a critic, or one might ask him how a piece of enervating formlessness can be a dramatic achievement of the first order. *Long Day's Journey* is a dramatic achievement which at first glance *seems* formless. Later, one discovers the form. The play has the outward calm and formality—not formlessness!—of French classical tragedies. Like them, and like *The Iceman*, it observes the unities. The form reveals itself in the interrelationship of people. The principal relationship here (dramaturgically speaking at least) is that between Edmund and his mother. The classical dramatist has to pull together on one day events which in actuality happened over a longer period. O'Neill found his action and his drama in the—presumably fictitious—coincidence of Mary's final relapse into drug addiction with the discovery of Edmund's tuberculosis. But a situation is only a premise of drama, not its realization. Before we have drama, the situation must move, and the dramatist must have discovered what makes it move. In *Long Day's Journey* Edmund has come to the point where he needs his mother very much.

He is moving toward her. And only a short while ago he would have had a chance. But she has now relapsed, with an obvious finality, into drug addiction. She too is moving. She is moving away from Edmund, away from everyone. She is moving to the point—reached during the play as its culmination—where no one can reach her any more. That Mary moves away just when Edmund moves toward her is—in terms of dynamics—what makes possible the play and enables O'Neill to rescue it from "formlessness."

Admittedly, this is to speak only of two of the four main characters. Before the play is over we have got inside each of the four. As people, James, Sr., and James, Jr., may be just as salient: in the dramatic structure, as I see it, they are subordinated to Mary and Edmund because the action turns on the question, What is happening to the latter pair?

Sincerity has done far more for O'Neill in this drama than ambition could ever do for him in the "big" plays of the second period. In the handling of ambivalence, for example. Had it ever really been necessary to invent devices to show the phenomenon? The method O'Neill used in the later play was to work through to his feelings, and then let them speak. It is the hard kind of sincerity, and he must surely have been gratified to see how—under this dispensation—a character can turn from expressing his hate to expressing love without any kind of device at all. It "just happens."

The process called "working through" implies deliberately living through an experience a second time, to the end of understanding and liberation. If Aristotle's word catharsis implies a sort of thorough cleaning out of the emotional system, then it exaggerates what normally happens to us at the theatre, even when there's a tragedy on. Perhaps it is not spectators but authors who experience catharsis. Mrs. O'Neill has given the following account of the composition of Long Day's Journey:

> He came in and talked to me all night. . . . He explained to me then that he had to write this play. He had to write it because it was a thing that haunted him. . . . I think he felt freer when he got it out of his system. It was his way of making peace with his family and himself.

Catharsis, if I understand what Aristotle meant, is a matter of physical and mental health, but I cannot hold wholly mistaken the now discredited view that he may also have had moral considerations in mind. Whether or not Aristotle had them in mind, moral considerations do at once come up. Catharsis means purgation, and purgation is purgatorial. After it, if one is lucky, one is ready for heaven. It is the road on which a man learns to forgive.

The deeply human thing about this often inhuman artist, Eugene O'Neill, is his concern to be forgiven—and to be capable of forgiving. The absence of catharsis is a notable, and ugly, feature of the "big" plays. As Engel has put it, instead of catharsis, O'Neill proposes narcosis or necrosis. Not that even *Long Day's Journey* ends with anyone on stage actually forgiving anyone. Their journey is truly into night, not into love, but the dignity of the ending lies in what is *not* said. There throbs in the final speech that sense of an alternative, that sense of having lived and of having deserved to live, which I deplored the absence of in the "big" plays:

> I had a talk with Mother Elizabeth [says Mary Tyrone]. . . . I told her I wanted to be a nun. I explained how sure I was of my vocation, that I had prayed to the Blessed Virgin to make me sure and to find me worthy. I told Mother I had had a true vision when I was praying in the shrine of Our Lady of Lourdes on the little island in the lake. I said I knew as surely as I knew I was kneeling there that the Blessed Virgin had smiled and blessed me with her consent. But Mother Elizabeth told me I must be more sure than that, that I must prove it wasn't my imagination. She said, if I was so sure, then I wouldn't mind putting myself to a test by going home after I graduated and living as other girls lived, going out to parties and dances and enjoying myself, and then if after a year or two I still felt sure, I could come back to see her and we would talk it over again. I never dreamed Holy Mother would give me such advice! I was really shocked. I said of course I would do anything she suggested but I knew it was simply a waste of time. After I left her, I felt all mixed up, so I went to the shrine and prayed to the Blessed Virgin and found peace again because I knew she heard my prayer and would always love me and see no harm ever came to me as I never lost my faith in her. That was in the winter of senior year. Then in the spring something happened to me. Yes, I remember. I fell in love with James Tyrone and was so happy for a time.

5

The Iceman Cometh was almost as much of a new departure for O'Neill as *Long Day's Journey*, and it is equally the end of a long day's journey for the author. It marks the end of his voyagings after new forms and a "theatre of tomorrow." Here, finally, O'Neill settles for the theatre of yesterday. The form of *The Iceman* is conservative and contains nothing that would have surprised his father. The Jones-MacGowan rejection of realism is itself rejected. We are back with the kind of theatre of low life which Gorky envisaged for his *Lower Depths*. Gorky's naturalism was not, however, the dramaturgic model. There is nothing episodic about *The Iceman*. The structure is unified and, though large, almost symmetrical. It is possible that O'Neill was compulsive in this, and allowed himself too little freedom. Note the stage manager's pedantry with which he lays down in a lengthy stage direction just where everyone is to sit!

This is how I summarized the main action of the play in my book *In Search of Theater:*

> There is Hickey, and there is Parritt. Both are pouring out their false confessions and professions, and holding back their essential secret. Yet, inexorably, though against their conscious will, both are seeking punishment. Their two stories are brought together through Larry Slade, whose destiny, in contrast to his intention, is to extract the secret of both protagonists. Hickey's secret explodes, and Larry at last gives Parritt what he wants: a death sentence. The upshot of the whole action is that Larry is brought from a posturing and oratorical pessimism to a real despair. . . . Larry is . . . the center of the play, and the audience can watch the two stories being played out before him.

The summary is accurate enough, but what strikes me after a ten-year interval is that it betokens more interest in the intellectual than in the emotional dynamics of the play. I continued:

> The main ideas are two: . . . that people may as well keep their illusions; second, that one should not hate and punish, but love and forgive. . . . In a way the truth-illusion theme is a red herring, and . . . the author's real interest is in the love-hate theme. . . . O'Neill is unclear. . . . It is his play, and not life, that is unintelligible.

I now think that the play becomes more intelligible if we follow up this hint: "the author's real interest is in the love-hate theme." Hickey really hated his wife, as Parritt really hated his mother. These are the repressed truths which it is the function of the action to bring to the light of day. In Hickey's case,

> I remember I heard myself speaking to her, as if it was something I'd always wanted to say: "Well, you know what you can do with your pipe dream now, you damned bitch!"

The implication could hardly be clearer, yet what follows can be confusing. "Good God," Hickey cries, "I couldn't have said that! If I did, I'd gone insane! Why, I loved Evelyn. . . ." The idea appeals to Harry Hope. It gives him an "out." It gives all the men an "out." It enables them to discount all that has happened and return to their pipe dreams. Hickey is taken aback at this turn of events. After all, had he not embarked on his long, long narrative with exactly the opposite purpose in mind: finally to persuade them to abandon their dreams? He starts to object: "I see what you're driving at, but I can't let you get away with—" Then he thinks twice about it and, after a pause, gives in: "I *was* insane." He has decided to let them keep their dreams after all. Why? It is not a simple question. Ten years ago I would probably have answered: because he now sees the need which weak people have of illusions, for I thought of the play as a footnote to Ibsen's *The Wild Duck.* Today, I would find the clue in O'Neill's own stage direction:

"Harry Hope's expression turns to resentful callousness again." It is to check this "resentful callousness" that Hickey agrees to be considered insane. Ten years ago, I wrote: Hickey "is a maniac," and there is a case for applying such a word to men who murder their wives under the illusion that they love them. Nonetheless, the dramatic point is different. Hickey regards himself as sane, but is willing to be regarded as insane by the others, so that Harry Hope will stop being "resentfully callous" to him. We are back with the love-hate theme.

And there is a whole dimension of *The Iceman Cometh* about which I find nothing in my earlier account of the play: the drama of love and hate, merely recounted in the speeches of Hickey and Parritt, is re-enacted in the drama of this very recounting. One recounts *to* someone. This play presents what Theodore Reik calls the "compulsion to confess." The intent of Hickey's confession—whose weight and position make it the climax—as of his previous shorter declarations, is to bring "peace." The source of this peace is his supposed love for Evelyn. But where previously, before the men tried unsuccessfully to drop their dreams, Hickey's speech-making did elicit love—made this well-liked salesman even better liked—now they are all angry at him. They hate him. And Hickey, like many O'Neill characters, if not all, is a man completely at the mercy of other people's love and hate. As Evelyn's love drove him to hate and kill her, so the men's hate drives him to declare himself insane—and rush toward the electric chair.

Aristotle said that the chorus should be regarded as a character in the play. The men in Jimmy the Priest's are the chorus of this play, and a way of looking at the action perhaps just as valid as the one I have quoted from myself would be to take it as arising from the reciprocal relationship of Hickey and the chorus. Nowhere more than in the scene where the men rise up and try to make a new life do we feel the power of O'Neill's playwriting. We see, as various critics have noticed with approval, a pipe dream take shape before us. But is that just an incidental bit of virtuosity? Is not the chorus equally important—and dramatic—in the final scene?

An analogy can be drawn between *The Iceman Cometh* and *Lazarus Laughed*. If they are very different, it may well be because the pattern has been exactly, and perhaps deliberately, reversed. *Lazarus* was O'Neill's attempt to affirm life and love, and put down death and hate. Most of his life, as in *The Iceman Cometh*, death and hate dominated his thoughts and seemed to him to dominate the world: it is no bridegroom that cometh with love,* it is an iceman—bringing death. As for love, it is

---

*"Behold, the bridegroom cometh" (Matt. 25:6). In the biblical context, the bridegroom himself symbolizes death, and the moral drawn is *memento mori*: "Watch therefore, for ye know neither the day nor the hour wherein the Son of man cometh." Not that O'Neill loses contact with literal bridegrooms, whose "coming" is the consummation of mundane marriage.

only lust—as is implied by popular sayings concerning housewives and their affairs with icemen. Now if we have in mind these two contrasting attitudes to life and death, we can take Lazarus and Hickey as corresponding figures. Both are salesmen to a clientele. Lazarus is selling love and everlasting life; Hickey is selling hate and everlasting death; but where Lazarus is candid, Hickey claims to be selling—precisely what Lazarus is selling! The earlier play is direct; the later, ironical. This is one factor, I believe, that makes *The Iceman* the superior play, and it would seem that O'Neill's natural bent was toward what is called "realism," for what seems awkward and "arty" about the chorus in *Lazarus* falls into place in the everyday setting of *The Iceman*.

That the average spectator at *The Iceman* is not forced to think of a "chorus" at all but can just think of men shows something good about the play. At the same time, those who wish to explore O'Neill's mind cannot but be interested in the Nietzschean intention behind the "realistic" disguise. The Dionysian element is still large—even if it appears under the form of alcoholism or a birthday party or the euphoria of a drummer's "pitch" with its background of midwestern revivalism. The chorus remains an integral part of the drama and has its own curve of action. As in *Lazarus Laughed*, the crowd is excited and inflamed by a savior, only later to be disenchanted. They end in *Lazarus* shouting, "Hail to Death!" They end in *The Iceman*, first in complaints, and then in the noisy relief of a return to pipe dreams.

In this way, *The Iceman Cometh* is seen to have its own peculiar emotional dynamics, and the ending effects a negative catharsis: the expenditure of emotion leads not to a new beginning but to the admission of exhaustion. There is something audacious and almost quixotic about the application of so much histrionic ingenuity to such negative ends. "Life's a tragedy, hurrah!" the young O'Neill used to say in humorous acknowledgment of a contradiction that vitiated all his thought. It is futile enough to profess pessimism in any art—but above all in the drama. For a play cannot but be playful.

If in *Long Day's Journey* O'Neill transcends his usual vision, *The Iceman Cometh* is the quintessence of O'Neillism. I have already tried to show how the word "justice" loses its meaning in O'Neill's world. Of necessity, the word "punishment" must also lose. If by justice O'Neill means only revenge, by punishment he means only inflicted suffering—as when a boxer "takes a lot of punishment." Hence, in *The Iceman*, though there is a Dostoevskyan sound to the word when we hear that Parritt seeks punishment, he actually is seeking only suffering and a conclusion. He is a masochist. He wants Larry to hurt him, and he has lost the wish to live, or will have as soon as he is hurt. He wishes his own death—the only alternative in O'Neill's bleak world to wishing other people's death. Life equals murder and suicide.

This conception deprives O'Neill of what would normally be the dramatic content of his material. Our story would normally be dramatic so long as we think of our men—Hickey and Parritt—as seeking punishment as we understand punishment, and, after all, one of them is heading for what we take as the very embodiment of punishment under its usual definition: the electric chair. But if life is not a blessing, death is not a punishment: in which case *The Iceman* has a happy ending!

We suffer some confusion of the feelings as to the direction, happy or unhappy, in which the main characters are traveling, but, in a very clever play, O'Neill does something very clever about this: Hickey's punishment is over before the cops arrive; Parritt's punishment is over before he kills himself. By that token, their punishment takes place before our eyes during our whole evening at the theatre. Parritt is punished by Larry Slade, not at the end—which is a release—but all through. Hickey is punished by all the men—again, not at the end but all through, except for one moment of vertigo when it seems they may be transformed.

This is where the pipe dreams of the three main characters come in. The illusions are what stand between them and the punishment they seek. In what he thinks about illusions, O'Neill is systematic. Best is not to lose one's illusions and die as soon as possible. Second best is not to lose one's illusions and die later—like most of the men in *The Iceman*. Third best is to lose one's illusions and die as soon as one does so—like Hickey and Parritt. The worst fate of all is to lose your illusions and live on. This fate is reserved for Larry Slade—whom, in this interpretation as in others, we find to be the central figure in the composition. Now the spectator figure in literature is nearly always a portrait of the author. I imagine that Larry Slade represents a piece of self-criticism on O'Neill's part, that O'Neill puts into Larry his own tendency toward an empty and oratorical pessimism (an inversion of the official optimism of American society), and, since it is not in the cards that either Larry or O'Neill should turn optimist, the most that can be achieved is that the pessimism should turn from spurious to genuine. Larry learns sincerity, which was what O'Neill was learning in the final phase of his career.

Larry learns sincerity, which is something; not love, which would be everything. However, O'Neill does try to cope with love in *The Iceman Cometh*, and the topic is a suitable one with which to close this consideration of the play and of O'Neill's whole "life in art." Taking my cue from O'Neill's own words and those of his biographers, I have spoken of ambivalence as a central fact, perhaps *the* central fact, both of the life and the work. If the word "ambivalence" implies an exact balancing of opposing attitudes, the formulation, finally, seems inexact. The relevant attitudes, in O'Neill's case, are love and hate, but we do not find them balanced: we find the former swamped by the latter.

This is not surprising in itself. The negative emotions are more prominent than the positive ones throughout the whole of literature. What is important, and disappointing, about O'Neill is that, while he does deal with love, it is always a very inadequate kind of love that he deals with, while the hate he feels would be adequate for blowing up the universe. I do not speak just quantitatively. It is the quality of the love that is insufficient—I mean of course for the purposes which O'Neill himself proposes. If we consider, for example, the relationship of Hickey and his wife Evelyn, we learn that she loves him, and we are given to understand that her love is simply wonderful because she keeps forgiving him. But to reread Hickey's long account is to realize that O'Neill, as his habit was, has equated true love with maternal warmth while leaving sex to prostitutes. Yet he does not use this fact to characterize Hickey with, because it is not a fact he can *see* as an artist. It is a fact that he is involved in as a man. The perfect marriage which Evelyn offered was the union of mother and child. What the play "ought" to have been about is Hickey's unresolved Oedipus complex, but it could not be about this because O'Neill's Oedipus complex was unresolved.

Which helps to explain, I think, why Freudian critics, upon reading O'Neill, prick up their ears and reach for their pencils. He needs them to finish a job that he could not finish himself. Ibsen said, "to be a poet is chiefly to see," and I am assuming here that in literature the writer's complexes are not wallowed in, they are seen. And one can see only from a distance. The fantasies which derive from a writer's troubles must not merely exist; they must be transcended. They resemble the ordeal by fire and water: you have to pass through, yes; but you also have to emerge on the other side. Perhaps this is a matter of character, perhaps of talent, perhaps of both; or perhaps our terminology is inadequate and neither "talent" nor "character" tells the whole story. But anyone who uses psychoanalytic ideas at all must start out with at least a tentative answer to this question: Why cannot any literate person with an Oedipus complex write an *Oedipus Rex*?

The Iceman Cometh is a typical O'Neill work in that, while it has high merit, it does not achieve the transcendence I am speaking of, but substitutes the standard O'Neill pessimism—or rather a more sincere brand of it, as I have also tried to show. It is arguable, as I have indicated, that O'Neill did achieve transcendence in *Long Day's Journey into Night* and perhaps in some of the plays of his youth. An author's talent is often most abundantly at work in his least "serious" efforts, and it may well be that such an item as *The Emperor Jones* will withstand time better than the big plays, just as *Charley's Aunt* withstands time better than *The Second Mrs. Tanqueray*. The reed withstands the hurricane better than the oak.

(1960)

AMERICAN DRAMA AT MID-CENTURY

From 1952 to 1956 I was drama critic of the *New Republic*. Most of my reviews are in print in the eighties in a volume called *What Is Theatre?* (Limelight Editions). What follows here is a kind of interim report on the reviewing experience, first presented as a lecture at the Library of Congress in 1954. It is not important that the reader share my verdicts on particular plays: I myself have changed my mind about some plays and have come to have much greater respect for one of the authors discussed here — Tennessee Williams. (He wrote a lot after this report was written. Many of the reviews he got for the later works were far too negative. That was because the reviews of the earlier works had been far too positive. Such is the American way: our "critics" erect pedestals far too high and then enjoy themselves dragging their victims down from them.)

THE ECONOMICS OF IT

It costs anything from forty to a hundred and fifty thousand dollars to put a play on Broadway. It cost $23,000 to put on *Life with Father* in 1939, and $85,000 to put on *Life with Mother* in 1948. *Mother* cost three and a half times as much. One could cite wider differences. A famous William Saroyan play was put on before the war for about $5,000. A famous Tennessee Williams play was put on in 1953 for $115,000.* That is twenty-three times as much. It would take a more expert statistician than I to say what is the average increase since 1939.

*Extreme cases. *My Heart's in the Highlands* was done only at special matinees. Few straight plays in 1953 cost as much as *Camino Real*. Musicals, on the other hand, cost much more: *Kismet* cost $400,000. There are further particulars, highly relevant to this chapter, in two important *Harper's* articles by John Houseman: "No Business Like Show Business," September 1949, and "The Critics in the Aisle Seats," October 1951.

Place it anywhere you wish between three and a half and twenty-three, and you have an increase such as any business might find it hard to meet.

These figures help to explain the state of dramatic art better than any conceivable remarks about dramaturgy. However, instead of discussing union regulations, the "real estate situation," competition from movies and television, I shall simply note the principal condition they impose on theatre—namely, that no play shall be performed unless a small group of wealthy men will bet on its having a long run. For it takes months of playing to capacity houses for investors to so much as get their money back.

What kind of play is the safest bet? No one quite knows, and that is perhaps the one happy aspect of the situation: think how dreadful it would be if we knew for certain that good plays always flop! Nevertheless, though no one lays claim to certitude, and an extraordinary number of hits are surprise hits, there *is* a general prejudice on Broadway against certain types of drama and in favor of others. Other things being equal, a play that can in any sense be defined as highbrow is considered a bad bet. It is not equally true that a play considered lowbrow is always considered a good bet. At this point, other criteria enter in. For example: all those who have opinions about plays seem to agree that one recent Broadway show, *The Fifth Season*, is an execrable play. Yet it was a hit; and its success was predicted by people with opinions, not about plays, but about garment workers, pretty girls, and Menasha Skulnik. A producer's job is not to judge plays but to "know the angles"—in more academic language, to know what criteria are relevant to success. That is, this *would* be his job, if it were possible. Since it has seemed to be impossible, what we witness is prejudice against so-called highbrow works and sheer guesswork among lowbrow works. "If only it were easier to tell good shit from bad shit," a producer said to me. We need not pity such a producer too much—we have our own troubles—but many of us do have some feeling about the prejudice against the so-called highbrow: we resent it. We have a prejudice against that prejudice.

I have simplified the producer-speculator's problem if I've suggested that he bets directly on the public's response. Actually, he doesn't ask about Tom, Dick, and Harry but about Brooks Atkinson and Walter Kerr. "What will the critics think?" When the first performance is over, the producer presides over a dismal supper party till the small hours of the morning when the eight reviews are relayed to him by phone. If he has produced a serious play, and the reviewers don't like it, he is done for. If some of them like it, he is done for. Only if all of them write of it in a vein of corny exultation is he sure of a hit.

Many people still blame this state of affairs on the critics, but, as the latter are always pointing out, that is unfair: it isn't their fault if people take so much notice of them. And it is not true that they are unusually dogmatic men. On the contrary, one might more justly complain of some of them that they play the role of the crumply little man who apologizes for having an opinion at all. They make such admissions of ignorance that one might say their motto is: "I thank thee, God, for my humility."

Why does the New York public pay so much more attention to the newspaper critics than it used to? Is it the higher price of a ticket that makes the customer more cautious? Is caution the best description of credulous dependence on eight reporters? Or is such behavior a straw in some more horrible wind? A token of an abject reliance on pundits that brings us nearer to George Orwell's 1984?

The Fifth Season is a play that succeeded without the critics, as musicals and other light entertainments not seldom do. The paradox of the critics' position is that they completely control the serious drama which they hardly even claim to understand, while no one very much cares what they say of light entertainment which they are quite at home with. Where they have competence, they have no power, and vice versa.

I should not like to leave the subject of economics without admitting there are exceptions to the rule that no play shall be performed unless a small group of wealthy men will bet on its having a long run. There *is* a noncommercial theatre which has three great sources of income outside the box office: private philanthropy, the local community (or group philanthropy), and the state legislatures. That is, there *are* producers who will put on certain shows—with little or no hope of profit—because they like them; there are community theatres, such as those of Cleveland, Pasadena, and Dallas; and there are the theatres of the great state universities supported by the taxpayer. Such are the American approaches to a subsidized theatre. (Even the Federal Theatre of 1936–39 was not a state theatre in the European sense but a freewheeling, hyper-American interpretation of a public relief program.)

Noncommercial theatres deserve all the encouragement we can give them except that of flattery. The fact that we want to get more and more money for them is no reason for overlooking their present limitations. Let us admit that they are more often a provincial substitute for Broadway than an alternative to it. To call them collectively the Tributary Theatre is misleading. They do not pour their own waters into the larger stream. They are rather the Parasitic Theatre, drawing what little life they have from New York.

An extreme—if, therefore, special—case is the Summer Theatre, which manages to be considerably more hidebound than Broadway. In New York, an actor's name is seldom enough to draw an audience; on Cape Cod, nothing else matters. In New York, a "name" actor usually—

not always—has also to be a good performer; in a summer theatre, any nincompoop from Hollywood will do. The formula is a movie star, even one who hasn't acted in twenty years, any old company, any old director, and any old hit play.

So if you come along with a new play which is not too easy or too stupid, which is not identical in pattern with a dozen accepted hits, it may be hard to get it produced on Broadway but it may well be even harder to get it produced anywhere else. A corollary of this fact is that many plays that are worth seeing are done in New York and never sent out on the road afterward. The most recent works of Arthur Miller and Tennessee Williams are examples.

There is also the matter of how the plays are done. But before I tell what I have seen, I should like to describe my angle of vision.

THE CRITICIZING OF IT

There is daily reviewing, and there is weekly reviewing. Most of the daily reviewers are weekly reviewers too, inasmuch as they add a Sunday article to their daily notices. But in principle daily and weekly reviewing differ. The daily reviewer is a reporter setting down right after the performance the responses of an "ordinary" playgoer. It is a very hard job—as reporting on anything, a football match or a street accident, is hard: it calls for a more observant eye and a more fluent pen than most of us possess. The weekly reviewer has the privilege of more time both to write and do his homework. And his aim is different. On most magazines the task he is called on to perform is dual: he has to judge the show as an expert on shows (not an average playgoer) and he has to entertain his readers with his thinking on and around the subject. Since the fate of a play in New York has been settled before the weekly magazine reaches the stands, weekly criticism has no immediate effect. To the weekly critic this seems both good and bad: it is a relief to know that you aren't doing anyone out of a living when you pan a performance, and on the other hand it is depressing to feel that what you say has no practical importance. I sometimes feel my reviews have been dropped into a bottomless well, that they are contributions to a discussion that never takes place.

Even if I feel sure I am writing for a reader, it is hard for me to know his identity. The weekly reviewer has to satisfy New Yorkers who have seen the play or will see it; he is also read by many outside New York who will not see it. Ninety percent of *New Republic* sales are outside Manhattan. But then the Broadway audience is to a large extent composed of out-of-towners. So I have no idea what proportion of my hypothetical readers sees the shows. I find the thought of two distinct types of readers rather disturbing. I intend each article for both "inside" theatre people and for nontheatre people on the outside; yet there is some evidence that the former find my pieces too full of known information while the latter find them overallusive and obscure. I should perhaps give the job up as hopeless but for the example of Stark Young, who performed it so well for over twenty years. His procedure was simple: he set down what was of interest to him and left readers to fend for themselves.

The *New Republic* has a tradition in dramatic criticism. My two[*] predecessors on the magazine—Stark Young and Harold Clurman— stand apart from most of their colleagues in being less concerned with journalism than with theatre. Both have worked on the other side of the footlights. The personal relations with actors which such an interest entails set the critic problems of tact that are susceptible of no perfect solution. It is impossible for him to be both as frank as he should be and as discreet as he should be, as ruthless as he should be and as charitable as he should be. He is always either bowing and scraping or bending over backward. He knows too much. On the other hand, very few people have ever learned much about acting and production from seats out front after the rehearsal period is over. These are arts you learn as playwright, actor, director, designer, not as theatregoer, nor yet as critic.

Whatever a man's estimate of the total intelligence of drama critics, high or low, he cannot fail to notice that—except for a Young or a Clurman—they know far less about acting and directing than about literature. Which is another funny thing about this remarkable class of men. They know something of literature though they are antiliterary; they are pro-theatrical but know little of acting. And so, as was noted above, a mediocre performance of a mediocre play is often greeted as a magnificent performance of a bad play. A brash actor who ruins a play will not be found out. He may very well be praised. The ruin is blamed on the playwright.

This scolding of the reviewers leads to my next topic:

THE STAGING OF IT

Nowhere more than in stage design is the matter of expense the decisive one. America spends a lot on stage design and doesn't get very much for its money. Costs are so high that many of the best ideas have to be dropped as too expensive. This is the main fact to consider in making any comparison with the German or Russian stage. Producers breathe a sigh of relief if they are assured that a play can be done with one set. So we get stereotypes. The chief old-fashioned one is the stage drawing room with its familiar rows of bookshelves full of unread books,

---

[*]Strictly speaking, three; and the third, Irwin Shaw, has also had a lot of theatre experience; but he stayed with the *New Republic* only a few months.

the couch here, the armchair there, the staircase, the door, the piano, and of course the phone. The chief new-fashioned one is the interior-and-exterior-combined (*Death of a Salesman, Rose Tattoo, Streetcar*), of which the porch-and-surroundings is a variant (*All My Sons, Picnic*). Some sets of these two types have been very fine pieces of composition, but the possibilities of variation are limited; and the alternatives to the standard modern patterns seem also to run to type. Thus there is the gorgeous-gaudy show, lowbrow in musical comedies, highbrow in opera; brains and ingenuity and a certain lush taste go into these things; but no style is achieved. Then there is Shakespeare with platforms and drapes. Though the scheme has its points, they are not as many as at one time was expected. The same could be said of that more recent scheme: central staging.

If we look at the designs of Christian Bérard of Paris, Teo Otto of Zurich, or Caspar Neher of Salzburg, we find more of a style—more of a realized modernity—than even the most brilliant men are giving us here. We don't give our men enough practice, and we don't give them wide enough powers; so they find themselves caught between musical comedy with its miles of gaudy, old-fashioned scenery and the one-set play with its inevitable porch or its inevitable bookcase. We have fine craftsmen, but they work under restrictions both artistic and technical that prevent their giving any adequate account of themselves. Ask why, and we are back again with economics. *

In this brief survey I shall not attempt to speak of directing: acting is more important. And, at that, directing today is less the mounting of giant spectacles, the marshaling of crowds, the unfurling of scenery, than it is the training of actors. Because we have no national theatre and no network of repertory theatres, we offer our young actors far too little either of variety or continuity. Still, certain remedial measures have been taken. The creation of the Group Theatre was one such measure—back in the thirties. It was followed by the creation of the Actors Studio in the forties. In these organizations, a new generation of American actors has been trained, and a new type of American actor has evolved. The easiest way of telling the layman about the new acting is to inform him that he has seen it in *Death of a Salesman* or *A Streetcar Named Desire*. It is a deliberate American alternative to the elocutionary "style acting" that we import from England. It seizes on the nervous excitement of American life—healthy or unhealthy—and communicates it. It makes older-fashioned acting seem stilted, slow, and emptily declamatory. I never felt this so sharply as when seeing *Tea and Sympathy*

---

*There are other resources we don't use beside the human ones. I am not equipped to expound the theory and practice of George C. Izenour of Yale. But it is pretty clear that his researches have rendered the switchboard—and therefore much of the stage-craft—of all our theatres quite obsolete . . .

as directed by the head of the Studio, Elia Kazan, the night after a Margaret Webster production (*The Strong Are Lonely*). It was like finding myself on an express train after sitting yawning in the waiting room. On the other hand, reviewing plays which are acted by members of the Studio, I have had frequent occasion to note the narrow scope of the newer acting. It almost seems limited to the portrayal of violent and neurasthenic types.

Two other kinds of acting are expertly practiced in America. The first is musical comedy acting, which includes singing and perhaps dancing. The second is light comedy acting. The lay public scarcely distinguishes the two; yet the distinction is in fact a fairly broad one. Musical comedy technique starts—I think—with song: not so much with the music as such, not with singing, but with the art of performing a song, handing it to the public by means of singing, half-singing, interpolated speaking, and pantomime. Then the postures and gestures—the whole art of putting a song over—extend themselves even into the parts of musical comedy which are not sung; so that, if you see a musical comedy actor in a straight play, you say: it seems as if he's always just going to sing. His bouncy manner, the little springs he takes from one foot to the other, the way he keeps lifting his arms in salutation or extending his fist in a punch—all these things come from the pantomime of a singer. It is quite a jump from this to light comedy— from, say, Alfred Drake in *Kismet* to Elliott Nugent in *The Male Animal*. Light comedy has an inner connection with broader forms (like the musical) but conceals it; and that is the joke. There is a portentous pretense of grave reality. The vitality of a performance in light comedy depends on the degree of tension between the seeming reality and the concealed madness. The comic climaxes are reached when gay and furious imps of folly come surging up into a hitherto decorous situation. Any drunk scene is likely to be a simple instance of the pattern; and, in a sense, all light comedy is drunken comedy.

Domestic drama, musical comedy, light comedy—these are what American actors are trained to perform. They aren't all of theatre. If we want to do Shakespeare or Wilde or Shaw or Eliot we are in trouble. British actors are called upon, and—to the extent that Actors' Equity lets them in—a provisional solution is arrived at. In the long run American actors have got to be trained to do these other kinds of work themselves. Shakespeare in particular is an author each country has to study and interpret for itself. The American Shakespeare might even be better than the British; at any rate, it would be different.

THE WRITING OF IT

Many of the most serviceable scripts of the past ten years have been in the less serious categories—musical and light comedy. The book of a musical is seldom impressive of itself; you go to musical comedy for everything except the words; yet, behind the music and dancing, the book may be efficiently doing its job.

Light comedy tends to have witty words wittily spaced out and arranged. If one were asked, what is the best American play? one might not have the temerity to say *The Male Animal* or *Born Yesterday*, yet they are better plays than most of those that have a higher reputation; and certainly, if you want a good evening, a light comedy is nowadays more likely to supply it than the so-called serious drama. During the 1953–54 season, for instance, one of the dullest evenings was an earnest treatise on the United Nations called *The Prescott Proposals*. One of the brightest was a joke about a comic-strip artist called *King of Hearts*.

Even inferior plays in the lighter vein often have something rather striking about them. It was agreed that a play called *Men of Distinction* was one of the very bad plays of the 1952–53 season; yet there was something very good about it. In fact, it had one virtue of such a provoking sort that not only the deficiency of the play but also its merit militated against success. This virtue was a cocky satirical humor totally unsoftened by sentimentality. There being no nice character in the play "to root for," you were unable to detach yourself from the non-nice characters. What made matters worse, they seemed nice. One of them was a Harvard man as personable and charming as Harvard's represen-tatives on Broadway, Brooks Atkinson and John Mason Brown. But he was a pimp. (I said at the beginning that the fate of a play at the hands of the reviewers was unpredictable; *Men of Distinction* is an exception.)

Turning to plays of more serious intent, I do not know which are the best of the past ten years. *The Iceman Cometh* would be a candidate, *The Autumn Garden* another, *The Country Girl* a third, yet all three are in the nature of postscripts to a communication written in an earlier decade. I prefer to pick out for discussion plays which belong more exclusively to the period under review. Of course they have traditions behind them—two traditions in particular: that of the social drama and that of the psychological "mood play."

It is agreed that the most interesting social dramas of the period are *Death of a Salesman* and *The Crucible*. Sidney Kingsley's version of *Darkness at Noon* is just as skillful a piece of craftsmanship, is in subject matter much closer to the center of social conflict and makes a much clearer statement, but, for all the exciting bits that are its component parts, it is not quite a satisfying play. One reason for this is that the statement it makes is not only clear but obvious, not challengingly a little ahead of public opinion but boringly a little behind it. Why pay five dollars to be told that Communism* is unpleasant and immoral?

---

*The reader is again reminded of the date of this piece—1953–54—at which time Communism was monolithic and Stalinist.

Maybe some people wish to. In that case, I shift my ground and say they shouldn't. We shouldn't go to the theatre to have our already inflated self-righteousness further blown up by ritual denunciation of an acknowledged villain's villainy. The theatre should be less serious than that—or more so. It should be a place either of innocent frivolity—or of moral responsibility. There is an unending war to fight in our theatre against those who are frivolous without being innocent and moralistic without being moral.

But not many people did wish to see *Darkness at Noon*.

They saw Arthur Miller's plays. Why? How could Mr. Miller's plays be more interesting if, as I have said, they are no better in craftsmanship, are less clear in meaning and further from the center of social struggle?

At the center of things nowadays is the matter of Communism. Mr. Kingsley put his play together to say so, and the play falls a little flat because we hold the truth of the proposition to be self-evident. What does Mr. Miller say about Communism? He doesn't mention it; yet the word—spoken or not—is likely to be at the center of a discussion of Mr. Miller. Now which fact is more important—that Mr. Miller doesn't mention Communism—or that you don't discuss him without mentioning it?

Suppose we ask in any group of liberal intellectuals, do *All My Sons* and *Death of a Salesman* present a Marxian analysis of American society? Or, does *The Crucible* say that American Communists should not be investigated? Some will answer yes, others will answer no; a certain heat and anxiety will get into the discussion; and a very vocal group will resent the fact that the questions have been asked in the first place. Mr. Miller may hold such and such a position, but, we shall be told, it is not—definitely not—playing fair to say so. In short, we encounter certain ambiguities and we find that these ambiguities have a strong emotional resonance among our fellows.

What is the nature of this resonance? What would explain so large an investment of emotion in Mr. Miller's plays on the part of those who don't wish us to ask questions? Take *The Crucible*. It is a play in which Mr. Miller complains that the accuser is always considered holy, the accused guilty. We think of McCarthyism; and we think of it again when we find that Mr. Miller's story is about a witch hunt. What is unusual about Mr. Miller's treatment of McCarthyism? One thing above all others: that he sets up as the offense which the seventeenth-century McCarthys accused people of an offense which it is impossible to commit: the practice of magic. If to the Mc-Carthyites (of both periods) an accused man is almost automatically guilty, to Mr. Miller he is almost automatically innocent. If one were to ask, what fantasy would give most perfect expression to a Communist's feeling of innocence in the face of McCarthyism? one couldn't do better than reply, Mr. Miller's story. Mr. Miller has missed the essence of our political situation. He has thereby missed a more interesting dramatic situation. But he has hit upon a wish-fulfilling fantasy that, conceivably, has a stronger appeal than either; and with it he has soothed the bad conscience of a generation.

Just as the good liberal is not supposed to mention Communism when discussing Mr. Miller in general, so he is not supposed to mention Communism—or McCarthyism—when discussing *The Crucible* in particular. The production of the play was preceded by a quarrel between Mr. Miller and Elia Kazan. Mr. Kazan went on record as a former Communist and named some of his former comrades; in the last scene of *The Crucible*, Mr. Miller presented a man whose dignity consists in refusing to talk under pressure of the investigators. But that one is not supposed to find any connection between that scene and the Kazan incident I discovered when I tried to get some remarks on the subject into a liberal journal. The play, I was told, was about the seventeenth century. I gathered that, though I could have criticized Mr. Kazan's attitude, I mustn't criticize Mr. Miller's.

It is no business of mine—in this context—that Mr. Miller may be wrong. I am contending that he is ambiguous, and this in a way that would amount to trickery were it deliberate. I assume that, like the rest of us, he doesn't deliberately deceive others but involuntarily deceives himself. What gives this fact public importance is that so many of our fellow citizens want to share these particular self-deceptions with him. Let me illustrate. Indignation is Mr. Miller's stock in trade: his writing has Attack.* But what is he attacking? And is he really attacking it? "He's attacking the American way of life," says someone. "Why, nothing of the sort," says someone else. "He shows great sympathy for it." The punch is threatened; and then pulled. We are made to feel the boldness of the threat; then we are spared the violence of the blow. Now isn't this particular ambiguity strikingly characteristic of that large wing of the liberal movement which has been overawed by Communism? They admire the audacity of Communism all the more because they don't share it. They admire fearless outspokenness above all things; yet if outspokenness is actually to be feared, they fear it,** and choose fearless silence. *The Crucible* is a play for people who think that pleading the Fifth Amendment is not only a white badge of purity but also a red badge of courage.

---

*"Daring is of the essence. Its very nature is incompatible with an undue affection for moderation, respectability, even fairness, and responsibleness."—Arthur Miller in "Many Writers: Few Plays," *New York Times*, August 10, 1952.
**"But we have an atmosphere of dread just the same, an unconsciously—or consciously—accepted party line, a sanctified complex of moods and attitudes, proper and improper. If nothing else comes of it one thing surely has—it has made it dangerous to dare, and worse still, impractical."—Arthur Miller, *ibid.*

Another habit of the quasi-liberal mind has been to say that of course so-and-so is not a Communist and yet, when it turns out that so and so is or was a Communist, to register no dismay, not even surprise. Of course he wasn't a Communist; but, if he was, so what? This ambiguity has been given rather powerful expression by Lillian Hellman in *The Children's Hour*, which was revived in the 1952–53 season with changes expressly calculated to suggest the play's relevance to McCarthyism. The play can be translated into political terms as follows. Someone is accused of Communism and says, "How absurd, I never heard of Communism, this is a witch hunt, my accuser is psychotic," and you believe him and your heart bleeds. Then this someone says: "Well, maybe I do carry a party card, either it's all this red-baiting that's driven me into the arms of Communism or, well, being a Communist isn't as bad as you assume. The social system *is* pretty terrible. You admit *that*, I suppose? I'm going to kill myself in a minute. My death will make you feel awful. Please be indignant about it."

The Crucible and *The Children's Hour* represent a type of liberalism that has been dangerous and is now obsolescent. *Darkness at Noon* is more defensible on political or even moral grounds; yet it fails to stir us for reasons I have tried to state. If these are our best social plays, one wonders what the future holds for the genre. Shall we ever have a social drama with the purity and force of *The Power of Darkness* or *The Lower Depths?* *

Perhaps the creative forces in America are no longer running into political art. More prominent, certainly, in our theatre than social drama is the "mood play." I am referring to the school of playwrights— the only American school of playwrights—which is headed by Tennessee Williams and includes Carson McCullers, William Inge, and Jane Bowles. In a recent book, *Playwright at Work*, John van Druten has hailed this school as a fine new drama gloriously superseding the old in much the same way as William Archer hailed the school of Ibsen half a century ago. One has one's doubts.

The moral weakness of the social drama is that it scorns or neglects the self. Liberal idealism of the sort I have described springs from fear— even hatred—of the self. The new psychological drama, school of Williams, is equal and opposite. It springs from fear of the Other, of society, of the world, and from preoccupation with the self. Now art that doesn't spring from the whole man but from one side of him tends, I think, not to become art at all but to remain neurotic or quasi-neurotic fantasy. The archetype of political fantasy is, perhaps, an imagined oration to

*A couple of shows from the 1953–54 season—*End as a Man* and *The Caine Mutiny Court Martial*—suggest that the New Conservatism may have a vogue in the theatre under the slogan: Respect Authority. Both shows have force; but it is scarcely the force of their message; and both are as impure and equivocal as any liberal effort.

a Congress of the Party of your dreams. The archetype of nonpolitical fantasy is an imagined confession to a psychoanalyst. Are the attitudes we find embodied in dramatic fantasies of either kind any more adequate for good drama than they are for the good life?

However this may be, one can certainly take exception to the view of form and structure implied in the new works and openly championed by their admirers. Mr. van Druten puts this view in a nutshell when he says he'd like a play to be all atmosphere and no plot. He says he finds inspiration and guidance in *Member of the Wedding, The Glass Menagerie,* and *The Cherry Orchard.*

These are not plays I should wish to attack: one is a masterpiece; all are good evenings of theatre. However, none of them seems to me as mysteriously structureless as Mr. van Druten implies. Perhaps Plot is the name he gives to a structure he finds bad or at least obtrusive? Or is it just that he enjoys economy of means and the audacity with which a playwright can push big, tempting events into the background: Chekhov could push a duel-to-the-death off into the wings while the center of the stage is occupied by someone reading a newspaper and whistling a tune. Mrs. McCullers kills off the little cousin between scenes of *Member of the Wedding.* This is not to say that either Chekhov or Mrs. McCullers has no plot, though Mr. van Druten admits that *Member of the Wedding* is open to criticism on the grounds that its action is too slender; which is to say it has a plot but not a very big—or perhaps a very good?—plot. Only by the beauty of the lines, the addition of music, romantic lighting, and the personality of two fine actresses could the play command a whole evening. It is a little story prolonged by theatrical legerdemain.

Picnic I do not know in the state the author left it but only in its final state as directed by Joshua Logan. Mr. Inge clearly contributed admirable character sketches, group portraits, local color, anecdotes . . . Can one venture to say that it took the showmanship of a musical-comedy director to give *Picnic* the size of a complete show?

Jane Bowles's *In the Summer House* posed a similar problem but met with a different solution. This play had rather a *succès d'estime* in New York, largely, it is said, because of a performance by Judith Anderson which the critics called magnificent. Magnificent or not, this performance had little relation to the character Mrs. Bowles conceived. Yet—and this is my point—I don't know that the play would have stood up by itself. It needed a buttress made of harder material; and *that* Miss Anderson certainly is.

I am not interested in establishing that any of the plays I mention is weak but only that it might have been stronger had the author not followed current fashion and assumed he could get along without the traditional kinds of support. I do not mean that a bad playwright could ever become a good one by dropping one attitude and taking up another—only that mistaken notions can hamper a good writer. (I assume that writers we take an interest in are to some extent good.) Nor am I saying that Mr. van Druten's book is having a bad influence. Rather, it sums up—and is influenced by—the view of drama which the more sophisticated people in the theatre had already come to hold.

This view is largely false. Chekhov's plays (for example) have a cast-iron structure, only it is concealed, like the girders of a modern building. Tennessee Williams (for another example) is no model of plotlessness. The fashionable components of plot may have shifted since Archer's day but A *Streetcar Named Desire* has a strong, straightforward story, organized on principles that would be familiar to any earlier generation. What is the play in fact but the American version of *Miss Julie*? Even *The Glass Menagerie* has what I would call a plot. In short, I cannot see that the plays Mr. van Druten admires were constructed according to the theory he expounds; on the contrary, they seem to me to have merit insofar as they contravene this theory.

CRITICIZING THE CRITICIZING OF IT

Having stated where I think our playwrights are going wrong, I should like to end by saying where criticism, including of course my own, may go wrong. I shall go wrong if I imagine that the playwright needs me to tell him what to do. Drama criticism is not a disguised and prolonged course in playwriting. If a man can write plays, he doesn't need a critic to push his pen. If he can't, he doesn't need a critic to dig his grave.

A critic is only a judge. A judge doesn't help you to commit your crime or even to abstain from committing it. His verdict—too late to influence the actions under consideration—has value, if at all, not for the prisoner, but for society at large. I implied earlier that the drama critic mustn't be modest and pretend he's the man in the street. (Between aisle seat and desk chair he knows only the inside of a taxi.) I am insisting now that he also lay no claim to direct influence on writers. If by chance he does exert such an influence, and it is salutary, so much the better; this is service over and above the call of duty. All he regularly and imperatively does is help to create the climate of opinion in which the playwrights live.

That is no small matter. The cultural air has often become oppressive. And it has done so, not when criticism was keen and demanding, but when it was nonexistent. One writer who resented the power of critics got himself made propaganda minister and legislated criticism out of existence, substituting *Kunstbetrachtung*—that is, reportage and eulogy. This was Goebbels. In Russia, critical analysis is dismissed as formalistic. A writer is praised as a yes-man or silenced as a saboteur.

Though the direct influence of dramatic criticism is small, its indirect effect could be considerable. Bernard Shaw stated the converse of this proposition when he spoke of the "ruinous privilege of exemption from vigilant and implacable criticism." There is, of course, a converse of this converse: that the right to criticize enjoins the duties of vigilance and implacability.

(1953–54)

MOTHER COURAGE IN 1962

In the fifties, the world discovered Bertolt Brecht. And that included the academic world, East and West. If an author has theories, academia will see his works as exemplifications of those theories. There is Epic Theatre, ergo *Mother Courage* must be an example of Epic Theatre. And of course it *can* be an example of Epic Theatre, depending on what Epic Theatre is defined as. But there are other perspectives, and *Mother Courage* will survive scrutiny from these: such is its many-sidedness and its power. In preparing a preface to a Methuen edition of the play in 1962, I proposed a stoical Mother Courage. If I borrowed spectacles, it was not from Brecht himself, or from Marx, his master, but from C. V. Wedgwood, Herbert Read, and Rainer Maria Rilke.

As we look back today upon the career of Bertolt Brecht (1898–1956), two periods of maximum creativity define themselves. The first came with the onset of manhood. Brecht had written some of his finest poetry, dramatic and otherwise, before he was twenty-five; *The Threepenny Opera* was written at thirty. The second period came when he had perforce to withdraw from the hectic political activity of the Depression years and lead the life of an exile during the later thirties and earlier forties. This is the period of *The Good Woman of Setzuan*, *The Life of Galileo Galilei*, *The Causasian Chalk Circle*, and of what many regard as his very greatest play, *Mother Courage and Her Children*.

In this play, and *Galileo*, Brecht withdrew, not only from Nazi Germany but from the twentieth century, and it is not without interest that the century he took in exchange was, in both instances, the seventeenth. It is the century of greatness, a century that opens with William Shakespeare and closes with Isaac Newton. Brecht finds in that century the roots of his own philosophy of life, scientific humanism.

"Of all the days," he writes of the day when Galileo had to decide whether to abjure Copernicus, "that was the one / An age of reason could have begun." This at any rate is the "thesis" in the dialectical process: the "antithesis" is represented by the Thirty Years' War (1618–48).

For Germans, this is not "just another war." In the way it bore down upon whole cities and populations, it remained unique in German history until 1944–45. Since Brecht's play was finished before World War II began, this "cross-reference" has a sadly prophetic character.

One wonders if some friend mailed Brecht a copy of an English book that came out the year before he wrote *Mother Courage*, *The Thirty Years War* by C. V. Wedgwood. Here is Wedgwood's summing up:

> After the expenditure of so much human life to so little purpose, men might have grasped the essential futility of putting the beliefs of the mind to the judgment of the sword. Instead, they rejected religion as an object to fight for and found others.
>
> As there was no compulsion towards a conflict which, in despite of the apparent bitterness of the parties, took so long to engage and needed so much assiduous blowing to fan the flame, so no right was vindicated by its ragged end. The war solved no problem. Its effects, both immediate and indirect, were either negative or disastrous. Morally subversive, economically destructive, socially degrading, confused in its causes, devious in its course, futile in its result, it is the outstanding example in European history of meaningless conflict. The overwhelming majority in Europe, the overwhelming majority in Germany, wanted no war; powerless and voiceless, there was no need even to persuade them that they did. The decision was made without thought of them. Yet of those who, one by one, let themselves be drawn into the conflict, few were irresponsible and nearly all were genuinely anxious for an ultimate and better peace. Almost all—one excepts the King of Sweden—were actuated rather by fear than by lust of conquest or passion of faith. They wanted peace and they fought for thirty years to be sure of it. They did not learn then, and have not since, that war breeds only war.

Whether or not Brecht read C. V. Wedgwood, there is an author we can be sure he did read: Hans Jacob Christoffel von Grimmelshausen (?1610–76), author of *The Life of the Arch-Imposter and Adventuress Courage*. Yet this work does not stand to *Mother Courage* as *The Beggar's Opera* stands to *The Threepenny Opera*. What Brecht took from Grimmelshausen was not a structure, nor yet a story, nor yet a protagonist. He took a name, and he took atmosphere. He entered Grimmelshausen's world—the world not only of his *Courage* but of his *Simplicissimus**— and carried some of it away with him. He carried away, especially, Grimmelshausen's sense of death—death on a tremendous scale and all a result of man's inhumanity to man.

*I have written introductions to both, as published by the University of Nebraska Press.

Mother Courage and Her Children is coming to be accepted universally as one of the important plays of the past half century. Critics in
the East wish it had an optimistic ending, and critics in the West wish
it was a traditional tragedy; which is to say that it is a play that both
parties worry over, and which neither can get around.

"Pessimistic" or "untragic" as he may be, Brecht has put his finger
on what Sir Herbert Read has shrewdly called "the problem of our age":

> The problem of our age is not a problem of conscience or commit-
> ment—of why people choose to die in wars for or against communism
> or fascism. The problem is rather why people who have no personal
> convictions of any kind allow themselves to suffer for indefinite or un-
> defined causes, drifting like shoals of fish into invisible nets. The problem
> is mass-suffering, mute and absurd. . . .

Oddly enough, this quotation is taken from a passage in which Read
is complaining of the absence of tragic poetry in our day:

> We live in a tragic age, but we are unable to express ourselves in
> tragic poetry. We are inarticulate and our only art is mockery or self-
> pity. Our fatalism gives us a stoical appearance, but it is not a genuine
> stoicism. It is a dull animal endurance of misfortune, unfocussed and
> unexpressed. . . . There seems to be a direct connection between our
> inarticulateness, which implies a lack of emotional purgation, and our
> readiness to respond to mass appeals. Modern war in all its destructiveness
> is a dumb acceptance of this anonymous fate. Our armies, as Matthew
> Arnold said, are ignorant and clash by night.

But supposing this dull animal endurance, this inarticulateness, this
dumb acceptance of anonymous fate is precisely the subject? Suppose
the writer is not lost in it but sees it? Suppose he himself is not "ignorant," but can show the "clash by night" in a flood of light? We
might still conclude that Brecht has not achieved tragedy (that is a
matter of semantics), but we shall begin to see the point of his whole
approach. It is because he is not identified with Mother Courage as
academicians, East or West, want him to be, that he does not fall into
the trap of self-pity. "Our only art is mockery or self-pity." There is
plenty of mockery in *Mother Courage*, but surely it is not such persiflage,
or defensive irony, as Read presumably had in mind? This mockery
helps to *dispel* self-pity.

It also includes a robust humor through which the protagonist ceases
to be "average" in the usual modern sense—a sort of lowest common
factor, the human animal seen abstractly, as in public opinion surveys—
and becomes someone who, however lacking in the attributes of saint
or heroine, is every inch a person.

When *Death of a Salesman* came out, there were discussions as to
whether the story of such a "little man" as Willie Loman (low man)
could be regarded as tragic. If not, it was implied, then the poor chap

would be left all alone with his littleness in outer darkness. About Mother Courage, one need have no such worries. Brecht need not rise up, like Arthur Miller, to broaden the theory of tragedy lest his protagonist be left out of things. Not being the abstract "little man," Mother Courage can stand the outer darkness. She may even light it up. She represents, one might say, an alternative to tragedy.

But she does not represent Marxist optimism except when a director—as in Moscow, 1960, it was reported—changes the ending and has her become a pacifist. Of traditional tragedy, *Mother Courage and Her Children* retains the sense of overriding fate, the sheer inevitability. Is this pessimism? That, too, is a matter of semantics. I think it makes good sense to say, No, and again to claim that Brecht's work comes as an answer to a problem formulated by Sir Herbert Read: "Our fatalism gives us a stoical appearance but it is not a genuine stoicism." Mother Courage doesn't present a stoical appearance but she does embody a genuine stoicism. Though her name is an irony, and she is, in the first instance, a coward, she also, in the last analysis, needs courage—needs it merely to continue, merely to exist, and this courage is there—inside her—when she looks for it. A human being, she has human resources.

To clinch the point one need only ask oneself what a naturalistic playwright would do with Mother Courage at the end of his play. Would he not kill her off, probably by her own hand? Yet how grotesque this "solution" seems to anyone who has inhabited the world of Brecht's drama! With the same good right as the aristocratic Rilke, Mother Courage can say: *Wer spricht von Siegen? Überstehn ist alles:* "Who talks of victories? To see it through is everything."

(1962)

TWO HUNDRED YEARS OF MACHEATH

If I was complaining above about academic criticism of Brecht, I must complain here that some of it was not academic enough. I refer to that part of it that concerns the main source of *Threepenny Opera*: John Gay's *Beggar's Opera*. A volume entitled *Brechts Dreigroschenbuch* claims to bring together, in German, all pertinent material, but since what is offered as a translation of *Beggar's Opera* is itself a free adaptation, the German reader is not permitted to compare Brecht with Gay, not to mention that the editor of the volume thinks Jonathan Wild was the model for Macheath (he was the model for Peachum). To clear up in my own mind what Two Hundred Years of Macheath have meant, I had recourse not only to such Brecht scholarship as James K. Lyon's book on Brecht and Kipling, but to Ronald Paulson's splendid Hogarth and above all to: *Polly Peachum and "The Beggar's Opera"* by Charles E. Pearce and *Gay's "Beggar's Opera"* by W. E. Schultz. My "quotes" below from Johnson, Gibbon, Dickens, and Taine are taken from Schultz.

The Threepenny Opera is a work of high originality. At the same time, to report that it is based on *The Beggar's Opera* is not to imply that the earlier work was base metal to be transmuted into gold by Bertolt Brecht and Kurt Weill. Though much is new in the later work, much that is true of *The Threepenny Opera* (1928) was already true of John Gay's *Beggar's Opera* (1728).

Both works have delighted two classes of people and outraged a third, and, making allowances for changes in social structure during the passage of two hundred years, we may add that the two delighted classes and the one outraged class were the same in 1928 as they had been in 1728. The delighted classes were, first, the upper- and middle-class theatregoing public and, second, the intellectual elite, "intelligentsia" if you will, the cognoscenti as the eighteenth century preferred to say, the Bohemians, the radicals, the professional critics, and fellow artists. Outraged in both periods was another section of the middle and upper classes, the one that sees itself as the guardian of traditional values, the enemy of anarchy and all threatening innovations, the friend of conservative censorship: the Moral Majority.

It is true that, in the eighteenth century, most writers themselves wished to be upholders of traditional morality, and thus we find Dr. Samuel Johnson telling Boswell and Sir Joshua Reynolds that "there is in [The Beggar's Opera] such a labefaction of all principles as may be injurious to morality." In more relenting mood, Johnson conceded, however, that Gay wrote less to encourage highwaymen than to entertain the rest of us. For that matter, Johnson slyly added, "highwaymen and housebreakers seldom frequent the playhouse." It is obvious at any rate that The Beggar's Opera was a phenomenon that could not be ignored, and even the author of The Decline and Fall of the Roman Empire gave his opinion on the controversial question of encouragement to highwaymen. It was that the play "may perhaps sometimes have increased the number of highwaymen, but that it has had a beneficent effect in refining that class of men, making them less ferocious, more polite, in short, more like gentlemen." Edward Gibbon had almost arrived at Oscar Wilde's "manners before morals."

Few moralists were as humorous or as sophisticated as Edward Gibbon, however, and more than forty years after The Beggar's Opera opened, a London magistrate was still trying to get the play banned. The issue was always the attractiveness of Gay's highwayman, and Gay's failure to hang him at the end: to have done so would also have been proper literary practice in that Augustan Age, as carrying out the law of poetic justice. Gay could have retorted that his ending was irony, comedy, satire, parody, or whatever, but his less literary opponents could have counter-retorted that the "crowd" (mob, the less literate audience) is less interested in such niceties than in cheering an attractive rascal. Incidentally, it was not just the magistrates who thought this way, nor did such thinking end with the eighteenth century and its aristocratic paternalism. In a preface to Oliver Twist, we come upon Charles Dickens himself finding in Macheath a dangerous idealization of crime, showing a "very flowery and pleasant road . . . to Tyburn tree." And the language in which Dickens's contemporary, the great French materialist Hippolyte-Adolphe Taine, speaks of Gay's work sounds to our ears like that of reactionary critics of The Threepenny Opera, circa 1930: "fiercest and dirtiest of caricatures," "a cruel keenness sharpened by a stinging irony," "[The Beggar's Opera] proclaims the dishonor of . . . society."

Taine's language calls attention also to a shift in emphasis in the nineteenth century: The Beggar's Opera has now become a "dirty" play. As such, it need not be banned by a magistrate: the Good and the Just who run things can simply make sure either that it is not performed or that, if it is, it is bowdlerized. The Theatre history indicates that *The Beggar's Opera* was never completely abandoned by the English theatre, though by the late Victorians and Edwardians it was very neglected. I have not been able to verify that either Wilde or Shaw ever saw a performance, though the latter was friendly with Nigel Playfair, who successfully revived the play in the 1920s. (Shaw saw *The Threepenny Opera* in Moscow in 1931, and himself thought of making a topical, updated version of *The Beggar's Opera* long before Brecht did.)* The extent of the tampering that took place with Gay's text is impossible to measure, as most of the prompt scripts, if they existed at all, have not survived. But even the claim that the full text was restored in the London revival of 1920 is belied—by, for instance, a published lyric in which the word "whore" is replaced by "trull."

Still, it was the permissiveness—the "naughtiness"—of the twenties that did revive Gay and—perhaps not immediately—for the first time rendered *The Beggar's Opera* fully acceptable. Obviously this was, in one way, a cultural gain, and one can sense the dimensions of the gain in, for example, performances of Benjamin Britten's arrangement of the work. There is a relaxed quality here that was never (I think) present before, a sheer joyousness. Such is *The Beggar's Opera* unbanned and unbound.

If you are more relaxed, you are less tense, and the age of permissiveness meant a loss of tension for *The Beggar's Opera*. Certain values that had been hidden before could emerge, but others were lost, and a new danger presented itself: that of blandness, innocuousness. If one can believe in providence, one must see the advent of *The Threepenny Opera* as providential. At least it filled a gap, and answered a challenge. Macheath thereby became controversial once again, and this story won back all its tension, was recharged with electricity. If it again had enemies, it again had ardent champions and cheering (not merely smiling) audiences. This was what happened in Berlin in 1928.

The Threepenny Opera was banned from 1933 to 1945, and had been a storm center in the years when it had played all over Germany (1928–33). I have said that the enemy was the same element in the population that had opposed *The Beggar's Opera* two hundred years earlier. It remains to modify this statement and to be more specific. Conservatism had now gone fascist, so it wasn't only straightlaced old magistrates who were up in arms, it was just as often loud young punks. But of course the Nazis linked up antisocial violence with prim-and-proper narrow-mindedness. In an article in *Die Weltbühne* in 1930 the

*Letter to Cecil Sharp, dated February 17, 1914: "I have had the Beggar's Opera idea for a long time."

great satirist Kurt Tucholsky identified the enemies of *The Threepenny Opera* as the middle-aged who long for the good old days and who loathe "socialism, Jews, Russia, pacifism, abortion, threats to their morale and their businesses." He added, "The Nazis are in there strong, whose view of art takes in, not the body of a work, but only its foreskin." Kurt Weill being Jewish, it followed that *The Threepenny Opera* had no foreskin.

To Nazi nostrils what emanated from *The Threepenny Opera* was a bad smell. Of what? *Judentum?* A fairly factitious issue—a nonissue—Brecht not being Jewish, the subject not being Jewish, and the music? Well, you had to be *told* the composer was Jewish. But the Nazis were against all *Modernismus*, and this work was surely modern in a big way, as well as bringing with it another aroma: that of late-nineteenth-century *Dekadenz*. Then there was the content. Like its source, *Threepenny* would be considered "dirty." "Permissive" is perhaps the word, especially since Brecht permitted himself a reference to abortion—at least in a verse of the tango that was always omitted in performance. And *Zynismus?* Whether or not you would characterize *Threepenny* as a whole as cynical, you cannot blink the fact that it does bristle with cynical remarks and attitudes—a very threatening thing for people demanding a savior, a führer.

It would be hard to find works that have given more offense in their time than *The Beggar's Opera* and its successor. John Gay was known as a gentle soul, but in his *Opera* he attacked the prime minister of England (who would attend the opening) as well as the most prestigious form of entertainment of the day, Italian opera. Some of the literature on the subject takes these as his real, his ultimate targets. The magistrates knew better. One need not share their belief in censorship to concede that their analysis of *The Beggar's Opera* went deep. There *is* something subversive of established social order in the Macheath theme, something deeply rebellious, potentially anarchic. And to show such a figure sympathetically is indeed an act of provocation: at best a bit of harmless rabble-rousing, at worst a demagogic attempt actually to arouse and mobilize the "rabble." Here is a villain-hero who gets away with murder to thunderous applause from the mob.

What is the story? What is its pattern, its archetype? Surely it is the man with the charmed life, the cat with nine lives. He keeps getting caught but always gets away again. He is the "gray goose" of folklore who is shot at and shot at but always survives. He is beyond good and evil, so that the people (crowd, mob) don't ask for a judgment: they identify themselves with him and hope he'll escape. When he does so, they experience a catharsis and cheer.

If these thoughts seem confined to mythology and fantasy and art, I would point out that, to the contrary, *The Beggar's Opera* is realistic and far closer to contemporary actuality than is *The Threepenny Opera*. It is built on a firm foundation of various real-life Macheaths and Peachums and Lockits. Now if Gay had had only one real-life Macheath in mind, that would undoubtedly have been Jack Sheppard (on whom Daniel Defoe and many others wrote). Unlike Macheath, Jack was finally hanged. But his trip to Tyburn tree proved a triumphal procession. He was a popular hero. The mob loved him, and not because now he was going to his death, but because he had eluded the Grim Reaper—and the authorities—so deftly and so often. A contemporary work about him was called *The Prison Breaker: The Life and Adventures of John Sheppard*. In his notes to *Threepenny*, Brecht was to give a rather strained, formal explanation why Macheath has to be captured twice. No explanation is called for: Macheath is "the prison breaker," the man who always escapes. John Gay's decision to reprieve, instead of hanging, him was a stroke of genius: it expresses, in the concrete way of dramatic poetry (as against explanations), who Macheath is: the man who *always* gets away with it, thus going one better than Jack Sheppard. Sheppard is the actuality, Macheath the Platonic idea of such a one. Yet without Sheppard—and others such—there would have been no Macheath.

> During the year 1725 Jack Sheppard, his exploits and his execution, formed the one topic London people were never tired of discussing. Throughout the autumn of 1725 Sheppard provided sensation after sensation by his daring escapes from prison. The sympathy of the mob was with him, not so much on account of his hardihood, as because of their hatred of Wild [this is Jonathan Wild, prototype of Peachum and his gang of informers—to "peach" was to "inform"], and of their delight in Sheppard's defiance of the brutal criminal laws in force in those days— the days of beheadings, of hangings, whippings, disembowellings, and the tortures of the press-yard and hulks.

No wonder that Harrison Ainsworth, when he wrote a popular Victorian novel about Sheppard, had him visited in Newgate Prison by Hogarth and Gay: Gay tells Sheppard he should write his life story, but Sheppard says it will have to be written by Gay.

Bertolt Brecht changed the characters of *The Beggar's Opera* rather more than the story,* eliminating Lockit altogether in order to make of Lucy's father an entirely new character, Tiger Brown, sheriff of London. As for Macheath, he is updated and he is diminished. "Mac-

---

*Indeed, the story should probably have been altered more to fit the new characters the better. Irving Wardle writes: "Basic plot points are unaccountably missing. The Peachums' horror at their Polly's marriage is barely established. The idea of Peachum and Macheath representing an underworld counterpart to legal capitalism is pushed off course by the sexual events. Polly, elected leader of the gang when Macheath first goes into hiding, fails to go on to her expected criminal career."—*Times* (London), March 15, 1986.

heath" means "son of the heath," and Hampstead Heath survives to remind us that Old London was surrounded by such heaths. Coaches were held up there by highwaymen like Gay's Macheath. Brecht's Macheath, however, is only a burglar or organizer of such. No horse for him, only a "stick with an ivory handle." Though a "gentleman" in the special sense which Brecht gave to that English word—very pseudo, very seedy—he would have been no gentleman in the eyes of Edward Gibbon. He is a "hero" of sorts—a mock hero—but the mock-heroic here reaches an extreme at which he himself mocks heroes (notably in "The Secret of Gracious Living"). Brecht's notes show that Brecht tried to persuade himself that John Gay—or at least Hogarth—was already that unheroic. But the Macheath figure in the scene which Hogarth painted some half a dozen times is classically mock-heroic, and an art historian has pointed out that his stance is that of the Farnese Hercules. When we find Jonathan Swift suggesting that Gay should have likened Macheath at one point to Alexander the Great we are in that same world. Or should we say, more simply, that there is a touch of the Douglas Fairbanks daredevil in Gay's hero? Brecht's antihero, though not, in my view, without passion, is without romance—a burglar's prose to the poetry of Gay's highwayman.

It is a complex matter, not least because Brecht applied so many fine peripheral touches of humor and fancy. Central is that his Macheath is a very bad man. Gay's Macheath did deteriorate, and at the end began to show a treacherous streak not seen at the outset (thus giving the character a significant development), but Brecht's Macheath—if we step outside all the joking for a moment and sternly ask ourselves what is what—is so bad from the start he could hardly get any worse:

POLLY: . . . you've killed two shopkeepers and committed more than thirty burglaries, twenty-three street robberies, arsons, attempted murders, forgeries, perjuries, and all in eighteen months. You're a terrible person, Mac, and in Winchester you seduced two sisters, both under the age of consent.
MAC: They told me they were twenty-one.

In John Gay's text the arch-criminal had been Peachum, to whom was assigned the notorious and ultimate crime of the historical Jonathan Wild: that he did not respect even "honor among thieves" but turned in his own men to the authorities. That was "peaching." In the Brecht, Macheath "peaches" and so is deprived of any moral superiority to his competitors and colleagues: the point would seem to be that the whole world of *Threepenny* is without ethics. Polly, who had been an innocent in the Gay, is here at best ignorant, losing not innocence but ignorance as the action proceeds.

Even so, to deny Macheath moral superiority should not be to deny him all superiority, all positive qualities, as has been attempted in stage productions claiming to be ultra-Brechtian and paying special attention to notes which Brecht wrote at a date later than the play itself and when he was more of a Marxist. For a totally negative Macheath one should go, if anywhere, to the screenplay Brecht sketched (but which was not filmed) or to *The Threepenny Novel* derived and developed from this. In *The Threepenny Opera* there survives in Macheath a Brechtian stud or fertility god from earlier Brecht works, notably *Baal*, and this character *is* superior to Peachum, not morally, but simply in having feelings, in having sexuality, and thus in having human weakness: he can and does succumb to passion. Being immune, being sexless, Peachum is better fitted to win battles. But one cannot like him. One cannot approve of Macheath, but one cannot *dis*like him—even with the help of the author's notes. One actor I saw in the role more or less succeeded in making Macheath consistently repellent, but the result was that one was then repelled by the play itself. That surely cannot be desirable? No, it is not accident, much less error, that Macheath generally charms everyone, even the "true Brechtians" who don't want to be charmed. That is of his essence. It is even of the essence of Bertolt Brecht, as his other plays illustrate. (Mother Courage is not supposed to be charming but she is . . . and so on.)

Now, if I am right in all this, Brecht was not merely reiterating one of his own themes but making use of one of the archetypes embedded in his source, *The Beggar's Opera*. For, as we have seen, one thing that made that work popular, explosive, and highly controversial was that Macheath—whatever might be said against him—continued to win all hearts, a circumstance which virtuous critics always read as the seductive appeal of evil to sinful man. I have intimated that the real appeal of Macheath is the appeal of success to the unsuccessful, of resourcefulness to the helpless—ultimately the appeal of survival, and a gift for survival, to the dying and to those under sentence of death.

In the Brecht, there is also an appeal to the down-and-out that is not to be found in the Gay. Gay offers to those who want it the spirit of romance: the oppressed will not be among the takers. Brecht offers to the down-and-out the notion that if they keep out of sight (out of the headlines and the advertised power struggles), and are prepared to be bad in a small way, they can—if the goddess Fortune happens to favor them—have quite a good time for a while: sing, dance, make love. Brecht's Peachum argues that Fortune will *not* favor them:

> We all are running after luck
> But luck is running last.

Important, crucial, is that the "hero" is not Peachum but Macheath and that he not only has to be arrested a second time because of his jailbreak but is then reprieved. True, someone then says this is only because it's an opera and unlifelike. But who is the someone? Not

Brecht but—Peachum, spokesman for a bankrupt capitalism, spokesman for nihilism and nothingness. *The Threepenny Opera* affords us few consolations and no comprehensive philosophy, but when it ends there is a twinkle in Macheath's eye—and in Bertolt Brecht's.

Where does *The Threepenny Opera* diverge most widely from its predecessor? In two features: its characterization of Peachum and its songs. The "shock value" in Gay's Peachum lay in the circumstance that one whom we expected to be only a receiver of stolen goods in fact goes on from there to "peach 'um"—that is, to betray his own associates and protégés to the authorities. He is perhaps the only person in *The Beggar's Opera* who has gone all the way with evil (and, to provide a perfect polarity, his daughter Polly is perhaps the only wholly innocent person). Since in *Threepenny* everyone is bad in a bad world, if Peachum stands out, it has to be for something other than pure wickedness. Here Brecht's notes are not misleading:

> [Peachum] is undoubtedly a villain, and indeed a villain in the convention of the oldfashioned theatre. His crime consists in his conception of the world. . . . He regards misery as a commodity.

He belongs, body (and soul, if any), to capitalism, to the acquisitive society, but, much to the surprise of anyone who expects a *Daily Worker* cartoon of a capitalist:

> Money means nothing to him. To him, who mistrusts everything which might arouse hope, even money appears to be a wholly inadequate defense.

"He regards misery as a commodity": his brainstorm is that poverty can be wealth. Such is Brecht's complete transmogrification of the very idea of a "beggar's opera." For John Gay, there is a single beggar, he has written our opera, and has already produced it many times for an audience of fellow beggars. We shall never see the latter, however, as our Beggar-Poet is now offering his script and score to a Player in the public theatre. No one in the 1728 audience would need telling that this Beggar was little more than a representation of Gay himself, who was wont to beg, often unsuccessfully, for patronage. His Beggar refers to St. Giles-in-the-Fields, near Holborn, where the beggars lived, and in *Threepenny* it is as if Brecht had moved the action out there. His single Beggar is no longer the author, nor is he a suitor to a playhouse. He is a narrator. (*Moritat*-singers made ballads out of the latest news for their illiterate public.) And he is out in the streets—as also is Brecht's action at its climax in the final act. Structurally, Brecht's Beggar is the thin end of a wedge, the thick end being a whole army of beggars on coronation day. To switch metaphors, Peachum's army of beggars gathers momentum like an avalanche that would indeed descend but for the famously phony happy ending. Such is the big drama that Brecht constructed. Nothing experimental about it, formally speaking: the climax is as traditional as it is splendid. If it carries the old story right out of John Gay's world, it has grown not from the theory of Epic Theatre, but from Brecht's conception of Peachum.

As for the songs, a large part of the credit must obviously go to Kurt Weill. Even a critic of music such as T. W. Adorno, who would have preferred outright *Modernismus*, school of Schoenberg, Berg, and Webern, congratulated Kurt Weill on the way in which, instead of using the new resources, he had revived and transformed the old ones. Adorno saw also that Weill was not merely exploiting American pop music but—and I would add, perhaps more importantly—was proving adept at the already old-fashioned show tune and/or popular ballad. It has been remarked that the time of the *Threepenny* plot is "vague." The coronation would have to be that of Queen Victoria, though nothing in the writing suggests the 1830s. The jazz element in the music suggests the 1920s, but the rounded and nostalgic popular tunes of the songs suggest nothing so much as songs of the 1890s. Vagueness is too vague a concept. One has a sense, not of no period at all, but of two distinct decades: the nineties and the twenties. (Add a third if you produce the show in the eighties.) It is Kurt Weill's achievement that he can fly us to these different worlds on wings of song.

But even if there were as yet no score for *Threepenny*, the lyrics would alone dramatize the dual time scheme. And, if John Gay's is the name that cannot be avoided in discussion of this work as a whole, the name that cannot be avoided in discussing the lyrics is that of Rudyard Kipling, poet of the nineties. (As early as 1891 William James described Kipling as "distinctly the biggest literary phenomenon of our lifetime. He has such human entrails, and he takes less time to get under the heartstrings of his personages than anyone I know.")

Kipling's name is omitted from present-day programs and title pages, though this was not always so, and, during preparation of the first production, Brecht included German translations of two complete Kipling poems: Macheath was to sing "The Ladies" while preparing to visit the whorehouse, and Lucy was to sing "Mary, Pity Women" in the scene that contains "The Jealousy Duet." Both these items were canceled before opening night, but this bit of the second poem was given to Polly:

> Nice while it lasted an' now it is over
> Tear out your 'eart and goodbye to your lover!
> What's the use o' grievin' when the mother that bore you
> (Mary, pity women!) knew it all before you?

But the importance of Kipling for *Threepenny* does not lie in direct quotation from him. A Brecht song, even when "original," is quintessentially a Kipling ballad, a "Barrack Room Ballad" if you will, and this is Brecht's link with the nineties. Which is rather obvious in a case like "Song of the Heavy Cannon" that brings to mind Kipling's *Soldiers Three*, but it is equally true when there is no allusion to Kipling at all, as in "Pirate Jenny" and "The Barbara Song." If the refrains are something of a giveaway, the tone is equally indicative: no one but Kipling ever spoke in that voice. The subject matter, and the author's attitude thereto, also fit the pattern.

Kipling being the poet of imperialism, Brecht the poet of Marxism, the influence of the one on the other has too often been taken to be superficial and incidental: Brecht stole a little ammunition from the enemy, and so on. Actually, they are kindred spirits, who happen to disagree on politics. And even in politics the disagreement is not total. Fundamental to Kipling's politics is hostility to "anarchy" and anarchism, a commitment to authority, to centralized power when this is governed by correct ideology. What Kipling hoped for from London is not all that different from what Brecht hoped for from Moscow. Kipling readily conceded that London did not "deliver," and in his last years, especially, Brecht was aware that Moscow had not "delivered."

In *The Threepenny Opera* Bertolt Brecht—and it is the miracle of this text—beautifully blended no less than three kindred spirits: John Gay, Rudyard Kipling—and François Villon. The last-named was already an old friend in 1928, for Brecht had already written a poem about him, and had based the title role of his play *Baal* partly on him. In *Threepenny*, the borrowings from a modern German translation of Villon were so blatant that Brecht was accused of plagiarism, found guilty, and forced to pay the translator. Yet the Brecht-Villon relationship is less direct than the Brecht-Kipling relationship. Villon's vocabulary may be drawn on more, but the sense is changed and very often inverted.

A single instance will suffice here. The song "The Secret of Gracious Living" (act 2, scene 3) is based on Villon's "Ballade: Franc Gontier Refuted." Franc Gontier was a peasant hero who stood for toughness under hard conditions. Villon would rather have a life of pleasure, especially sexual pleasure. That's his "refutation," and his verses carry the refrain: "Il n'est tresor que de vivre a son aise." "There is no treasure like living at one's ease." Now Macheath's song is also a "refutation" (read: "repudiation" both for Villon and Brecht) but what he is repudiating is idealism. I have hinted above that this is the idealism which makes romantic heroes of highwaymen. But the point is broader than that. The idealist is one who "thinks of books and does not think of dinner," who puts morality before mere material considerations: "Erst kommt die Moral, dann kommt das Fressen." To which Macheath's answer in another song with the most famous line Brecht ever wrote:

"Erst kommt das Fressen, dann kommt die Moral." My English version reads, "Till we've had dinner, right and wrong can wait," but literally the line means: "First comes feeding [eating as animals eat], then comes morality." And here in "The Secret of Gracious Living" Macheath is saying, "put money in thy purse." A Villon poem which simply pits the grim life of the hardworking peasantry against the easy life of the frivolous is replaced by a Brecht poem that says, "Never mind about high ideals, just make sure you have a high income."

Thus, in the very act of quoting—plagiarizing—Villon, Brecht turns him inside out. Where the spirit of Villon comes through directly—where he is displayed as a truly kindred spirit—is not in the quotations but in the characterization of Macheath, to which any discussion of either *The Beggar's* or *The Threepenny Opera* must inevitably return again and again: on this all the enemies of both plays* agree with all the friends. The "bottom line" of the role, I have suggested, is the archetype of the "prison breaker." Then there were models aplenty in real life, and especially Jack Sheppard. So far, however, we only have the action, the plot, of the role. What kind of person is he, and what were Brecht's models there? John Gay's Macheath, obviously. But here he is changed. To what? To whom? Watching this Macheath singing, one might well see in him the young Brecht in some nightspot in Schwabing (the Greenwich Village of Munich). Kurt Tucholsky said that all of *Threepenny* is "Bavaria stylized," and it could be that Brecht had said to himself: "John Gay put himself into the play as the Beggar: I aim higher, I'll be Macheath." If the poet-philosopher has portrayed himself as a burglar, he has also portrayed a burglar who seems to be a poet-philosopher. (We never see him burgle. We incessantly hear him philosophize.) Yet is this really Bertolt Brecht? Only in the sense that "the poor B.B." of his famous poem is himself: a self-dramatization, an imaginary self. In the image of whom? Perhaps more than one man but, if only one, then François Villon.

(1981)

---

*Yes, plays. The word "opera" in both titles is simple irony. It is also a metaphor like such expressions as "song and dance." And what the metaphor means is made quite clear in the lines about happy endings in both works. Each is "a comedy with songs."

SHAW IN 1978

What follows was originally a talk at the Shaw Festival in Ontario. One member of my audience said he had twenty volumes of Shaw in his library, and he'd swear my "quotes" from the master were not to be found in any of them . . . My impression was that the Shaw Festival had never discovered Shaw, but was offering his plays in the style of *Charley's Aunt*. One should not be hard on the Canadians. There has yet to be a Shaw on any stage that one could call post-Brecht (or perhaps I mean post-Stalin). I was flattered to find my audience familiar with my own defense of Shaw, published in 1946, but weren't there other things to say now?

Bernard Shaw's play *Major Barbara* holds interest for an audience eighty years after it was written. How could it fail to? Its subject (all its subjects) are interesting. The wit often scintillates, and at certain climaxes there is really deep emotion. Finally there is something definitely challenging about this play. But it is here that we run into problems.

Who is challenged is clear enough: ourselves. And who we are taken to be is clear too: educated, middle-class persons, with a prejudice against what is now called the Establishment—a sympathy for the underdog, a lack of sympathy for the overdog, persons who favor David over Goliath, Jack over the Giant. Oddly enough, this class of persons includes people who, outside the theatre, are closer to Goliath than David. For many of us lead double lives. In the part we call reality we are of the government's party. But in fantasy we are liberals, if not revolutionaries. And fantasy is of itself liberal and revolutionary and never champions the Giant against Jack, Goliath against David.

Or seldom. One of the exceptions is Christopher Marlowe's *Tamburlaine*, in which the sympathy for mankind is slight and the envy of the conquering mass-murderer considerable. It can only be popular on occasions when the customary fantasy is reversed and the common man chooses instead to imagine what fun it would be to be Attila the Hun or Hitler. This is different from wishing that six million Jews would be gassed, for that was justified on grounds of idealism—a service to the Aryan race. Tamburlaine despised all races. The justification is the fun of conquering, enslaving, and slaughtering. History proves that such notions do not lack appeal in real life but not that people are willing to admit it very often in the theatre. We would rather sneak a little sadistic pleasure from, say, Richard III's wickedness, and then return to the normal fantasy of poetic justice. Shakespeare, a much more popular artist than Marlowe, obliges us, the populace, by punishing Richard in the end, whereby the thought that, in truth, we are aligned with his victims reclaims us from the service of Satan.

Now what of *Major Barbara*? Its author would like to have broken down these divisions between theatre and life, fantasy and reality, and first on the agenda would be an attempt to dramatize the incongruity between the two. Comedy has always done that, and Shaw is in the classic tradition of comedy.

Take this proposition: "In theory my sympathies are messianic and salvationist. Major Barbara is my hero. In practice, however, well, give me a strong, cynical businessman. I know which of those two I'd trust my money to. I'll give him not just my cash but—just to be really honest—my endorsement as a human being."

That is tolerably close to what the play *Major Barbara* does say, and the first-person singular in the proposition is Bernard Shaw. Our first conclusion is that in this play Shaw has rejected the various socialisms in favor of an improved capitalism. Yet we know that he was a socialist. What are our options now? Just to say he was inconsistent? To make him a renegade who has repudiated what he had believed? To say he is not serious and will say anything for a joke? Over the years, the play *Major Barbara* has elicited all these varied responses. None of them should be disallowed. Shaw himself admitted to being too much of a paradoxer, and was sometimes willing to drop his argument for a laugh. Consistency was not his forte any more than it had been Nietzsche's, and beliefs he acquired he would at times rebel against or simply give up on. A critic of *Major Barbara* has indeed to ask himself if in this case a socialist author has not written a paean in praise of capitalism. I addressed myself to this critical question years ago and answered it in the negative. I said that, while Major Barbara's idealism was inadequate, so was Undershaft's realism, and that Adolphus Cusins was brought forward in the final act to suggest a synthesis that would go beyond either and combine both. I reluctantly conceded that this synthesis might not be fully convincing dramatically.

Those who respect the play as a whole have generally entered this proviso: the solution at the end—the final act as a whole—is unconvincing. And one might cite, for confirmation, that Shaw himself seemed to sense that something was wrong. The third act of *Major Barbara* seems to have been one of the few passages in his plays that didn't come readily into focus. Contrary to his usual custom, he did much rewriting on it.

He also consulted his friend Gilbert Murray, the classical scholar upon whom the character of Cusins is based. When Murray asked why Undershaft must always be in the right, Shaw answered: because he *was* right. It's an interesting reply, particularly for dramatic critics, as it suggests that Shaw might have been prepared to sacrifice his play, as work of art, to a conviction about one of his characters. Propagandist playwrights often *are* so prepared, and certainly Shaw regarded himself as a propagandist. Is *Major Barbara* propaganda for capitalism?

Shaw's more thoughtful critics have answered this question in the negative. The play, they explain, is not a balancing-off of capitalism and socialism at all. That is not the issue. That is not what Undershaft is right *about*. What he is right about is realism, yes, but "realism" is too broad a term. He is right about something far more specific and, as would always be the case with Shaw, something that is fully verbalized in the play: "Nothing is ever done in this world until men are prepared to kill one another if it is not done."

Had Shaw been planning to make the capitalist system as palatable as possible he would hardly have taken as the typical capitalist a merchant of death. This could only disrecommend capitalism the way Mrs. Warren's whoring and procuring had done, and indeed *Andrew Undershaft's Profession* had been an earlier title of our play. One has to remember that, for Shaw, capitalism versus socialism, though a prime question, was never the ultimate one, nor did he think the situation so simple that damage done to capitalism was necessarily a service to socialism. Twenty years after *Major Barbara*, when Shaw had taken a position much more decisively "leftist" and revolutionary, he was still writing:

> We must build up Capitalism before we can turn it into Socialism, but meanwhile we must learn how to control it instead of letting it demoralize us, slaughter us, and half ruin us. . . .

In the second half of the twentieth century, which Shaw did not live to see, we are aware that a socialist country like Poland can call in an Andrew Undershaft from the Krupp factories in West Germany to help build up and control its own factory system. Capitalism and socialism are not hell and heaven. There are principles of action and organization more universal than capitalism and socialism and valid under either social system. Shaw is proposing *readiness to kill* as a touchstone of effectiveness under these systems or any others and conversely *unwillingness to kill* as a guarantee of passivity, capitulation, default, and failure. If we don't kill, we will be killed, and we'll have asked for it.

Such is the gospel of Andrew Undershaft and, according to his author, he is right. All the other characters are placed in the wrong except insofar as they come around to this point of view. It is therefore not just the gospel of one character but is intended to be the message of the play. Two questions: *Is* it the message of the play? And second: Is it true? Is it even sufficiently plausible to be accepted as possibly true, as the truth for some reasonable men?

The first question can be answered summarily, and the answer enables us to describe more closely what is wrong with the play *Major Barbara*. The meaning of a play emerges, less from any particular statement therein, than from the sense of life that the whole drama gives off. Although one character in the play affirms that the law of life is "kill or be killed," the play as a whole does not affirm this. It is hard for a drawing-room play to give off a sense that life essentially takes place outside drawing rooms. Not that all of *Major Barbara* takes place inside drawing rooms. But the first act anchors it quite firmly in that style of living, talking, and believing, and none of the other acts, not even the last scene of the last one which takes place in a munitions factory, ever lifts that anchor. The Undershafts and Cusinses take their drawing rooms with them both to the slums and to the factory. In, say, the movie of *All Quiet on the Western Front* we see "kill or be killed" in action, but in *Major Barbara* we see forms of life in which "kill or be killed" is not only not the working principle but is not really conceivable. We have got a play that, if valid, refutes the gospel of Andrew Undershaft. If this is really a world of "kill or be killed," there is no room in it for the plays of Bernard Shaw. Well, that, you will say, could be the point, and to be sure, this author was wont to feel out of things on this planet. Still *my* point remains that what is intended as the message of this play does not, and cannot, come through as such. What does come through is no clear message at all but a contradiction between tenor and vehicle, a conflict between the author's will and the author's art: a blur.

My second question was whether the gospel of Andrew Undershaft was valid anyway. Is this really a world of "kill or be killed"?

There is a piece of truth to that proposition that no one would dispute: that, in human affairs, at their most crucial, especially in politics, demands are made *on pain of death*. But generally one can save one's life by making a lesser sacrifice. Your money or your life! At knife point, one gladly surrenders one's purse instead of one's blood. Shaw is postulating that far more outrageous circumstance in which one can only survive on acceptable conditions by taking the other fellow's life. Such a circumstance would commonly be called war, and what Shaw is saying is, in effect: Politics is the continuation of war by other means.

He is able to have a field day in one part of the polemical territory. The propaganda of war has seldom dared to make much of killing. It has made much of dying: "dulce et decorum est pro patria mori," "greater love hath no man than this, that a man lay down his life for his friends. . . . " Willingness to lay low one's enemies, on the other hand, has been left to drill sergeants. On this subject, our culture, the whole human race, cannot but carry a mighty load of guilt. Shaw is mocking that guilt, and calling for unwonted candor. We are all frontiersmen at heart, he seems to be saying; it's my scalp or the Indian's, why not admit it? Where there was capitulation—refusal to kill, in order to be spared—there was defeat, as in France 1940.

Bertolt Brecht wrote a play which embodied a sense of all this: *Days of the Commune*. The men of the Paris Commune of 1870 are represented as having been killed because of their reluctance to kill. Humanitarianism is defeated by humanitarianism.

Opponents of what has been called Appeasement, in the 1930s and later, taking the lead from Churchill, a statesman Shaw nearly always disagreed with, are people saying "do let's be prepared to kill him when the enemy moves to kill us." In Bernard Shaw's last press interview, published on August 6, 1950, he said:

> As long as war exists as an institution, every nation must to the utmost of its resources keep its armed and drilled forces up to the level of its most formidable rivals.

He adds that this is clear both to Stalin and Truman, and we might add that we have heard nothing different in recent years. It is the conventional wisdom of power politics, an assumption made by all the rulers of the world we live in.

The play *Major Barbara* is saying (a) that we can't avoid this assumption and, (b) on the contrary, we could actually rejoice, as Undershaft does, in our readiness to kill at the appointed times. Why? First because one is happy to be open and candid, rather than furtive and hypocritical. Shaw is inclined to overdo this out of his delight in himself as iconoclast, but he has another argument up his sleeve, and it has vaster import.

In the years just before he wrote *Major Barbara*, Shaw protested the inadequacy of reforms or rather the inadequacy of the people whose lives were being reformed. The average man was not worth much and he was not active but passive. He was not revolutionary but conservative. He must therefore be abolished. *The poor must be abolished*. The preface to *Major Barbara* is full of things of the sort. There is a joke involved. Shaw said that the poor agreed with him and *wished* to be abolished, which presumably meant they preferred to be rich. *

Our wars and famines did help to kill off populations in the early twentieth century, but not enough to satisfy Bernard Shaw, who in the thirties championed extermination—his word—as it was practiced by Stalin. He compared the first head of the Russian security police to Ibsen's Button Moulder, who treated the average mediocre human being as a badly made button to be thrown back in a vat and remade. Though the Russians offered him the euphemism liquidation, Shaw himself, while sometimes willing to talk euphemistically of "weeding the garden," fastened on the word extermination, and explained that it goes on all the time, and that his study of capitalism had taught him how industrial change exterminated whole classes.

The innocent liberal may want to interject that these other exterminations were not deliberate. So much the worse for them, Shaw will answer; they were unscientific. They often exterminated the wrong people. Surely the *planned* economy is what we want? The "plan" will be to exterminate the useless and the dangerous . . . The idea is implicit in *Major Barbara*, written more than a decade before the October Revolution, and I'm ready to answer the question: is Undershaft's gospel true?

It is not true, nor partly true, nor even "all right" for some people to believe. "Nothing is ever done in this world until men are prepared to kill one another if it is not done." Nothing? Are no human affairs of importance that do not produce such threats? We can make allowance for hyperbole in Shaw's rhetoric, but is not this a rhetoric which radically falsifies life by placing too much value on things that are killed for? What are the things that "are done" when men *are* prepared to kill? Most often, there is much killing, and little positive result. Shaw would be the first to concede such a point. What then are these rare occasions when the "something done" could truly be said to be worth the sacrifice, not of one's own dead only, but of the enemy's dead too?

A kind of positive answer could be offered to this question. Successful wars of national liberation, for example; though I don't know if Shaw would consider Ireland's perennial war of national liberation to have been worth all that readiness to kill and all that readiness to go on killing. And if so many things that were done because men were prepared-to-kill-if-they-were-not-done, if so many of even these special things are of dubious value, can one really go on to say: "but then

---

*When he despaired of politics, Shaw tried to believe that the answers would come from eugenics. Positive eugenics would mean that his beloved superior few could mate with each other. Negative eugenics would mean . . . extermination of the undesirable.

nothing is *ever* done in this world except under these conditions"? Does reluctance to commit political homicide *never* have any value?

That question *is* rhetorical but, in the context of the Shavian-Stalinist argument, it had to be put. Isn't it appalling that it had to be put? Can we understand how someone like Bernard Shaw came to provoke us into such a question? Does reluctance to commit homicide never have any value? The question could only arise among people who are reluctant to commit homicide. It assumes such a reluctance to be widespread, and willingness to commit homicide the exception.

Is that our problem, or don't we have to deal with a too great eagerness to kill? A much too small price set on each human life? Shaw may counter by saying, "If *they* put so small a price on each human life, *we* can't afford to do differently," but it is rather clear that he makes an exception of his own life, in which case it is others he sacrifices, particularly the poor and "worthless," the non-geniuses. Would it not be better to follow the example of the great religions and set a high value on the life of even the lowliest human being?

We all know how important it was to Shaw to feel he was a genius and tell everyone so. But why? If it was so, wouldn't that come across anyway? He made a joke of his egotism, but, since Freud, we know about jokes. This was a man too preoccupied with the notion of his own superiority. And this sense of the self as genius, what is it, socially speaking, but pharisaism—"I thank thee, God, that I am not as other men are"? It is a factor that deprives Shaw, in his political writings, of feeling he is *discussing* any topic—tossing out ideas that others may toss back again in changed form. He is sure in advance they will have difficulty understanding. Let them just listen and try to take it in, never answer back. This paternalism vitiates, to a great extent, the otherwise great merit of *The Intelligent Woman's Guide to Socialism and Capitalism.* The title and procedure are, on the surface, a compliment to the female, as more likely to grasp the truth, *but* the truth is being released from on high by a male god. Like the men, the women must listen, and not answer back.

"I was . . . at my ease," Shaw wrote, "only with the mighty dead." It is not enough people to be at one's ease with. The non-mighty dead have their merits, not to mention the living mighty and less mighty. I am not taking a cheap shot. The famous self-promotion of Bernard Shaw was not a slight fact which, given a little Shavian humor, one can lightly dismiss. It was real. Shaw seems to have thought all he was doing was overcoming a natural shyness by an affectation of confidence, but the shyness was rooted not only in superiority but in—well, what?

Late in life Shaw brought out a book called *Sixteen Self Sketches.* The title of one of the sketches informs us that he is going to release "a secret kept for eighty years." The Freudian in us pricks up his ears.

Shaw was not apt to speak of secrets of childhood. What could the secret be? The other half of his title is "Shame and Wounded Snobbery," and what we learn is that for eighty years Shaw could not tell anyone that when he was thirteen he encountered lower-class children.

Where others might remember rape or incest, what Shaw remembers is: *his discovery of the poor.* "My artist nature," he goes on, by way of describing a childhood trip to the slums, " . . . would not accept poor people as fellow creatures." And indeed his artist nature was never going to accept poor people as fellow creatures. They were just the misshapen buttons to be scrapped by the Button Moulder. They were the misbegotten to be eliminated by the science of genetics. They were the backward and reactionary elements to be liquidated—exterminated— by Stalin. On some things the inconsistent Shaw was consistent.

Obviously, Shaw advanced some good arguments and was able to adopt the stance of a man who will not stand for any nonsense but will penetrate all illusion and expose all fantasy and wishful thinking. The very tone of Shaw's writings—especially in such instances as Undershaft's speeches—shames the reader or listener into feeling he is the deluded ignoramus who needs to have his consciousness raised by this engine of enlightenment. It is odd that Shaw is held to be fond of discussion, since what his rhetoric tends to do is: *put topics beyond discussion.* Brilliance after all doesn't make one see. It dazzles. Clever rhetoric bewilders. Torrential eloquence snows one under. Arguing to win intimidates. As he said to Murray, Undershaft is right. We don't discuss *if* Undershaft is right: his most devastating scene is the dialogue with his son Stephen, who, theatrically speaking, is just the straight man for a comedian-with-all-the-answers.

The radicalisms and socialisms of the eighteenth and nineteenth centuries had mostly, by Shaw's time, been set down as impractical idealisms, but one form of socialism, Marxism, had offered itself as the positive answer to what was now the key question: is there any way of combining the chief aims of the revolutionary outlook with a realistic practice? Now the goal of nineteenth-century revolutionism was *anarchy*: individual freedom through freedom from state control, through, finally, abolition of state power. On that, Marx was at one with Bakunin and Kropotkin. The stance that Marx took which was comparable to Bernard Shaw's was the realistic one. State power, being real, must be accepted, even if only provisionally, with all that goes with it: oppression and class war. And class war has always been seen by Marxists as hot war, not cold. Which in turn means that behavior hitherto only allowable in wartime became allowable *all* the time because the class war is incessant. "Kill or be killed" is the law of war and peace alike. Liberals are shocked when the Communists in Brecht's *Measures Taken* kill their young comrade as soon as he endangers their mission. But it is a military mission, and all armies assert the right in wartime to shoot the insubordinate. (Liberals do not recognize class war as war.) Shaw was not in all respects a Marxist, but without Marxism there would have been no Undershaft, who might well have said with Friedrich Engels, "Violence is the midwife of social change," the point being, not that violence is to be reluctantly accepted, as it is by everyone not a pacifist, but that violence is welcomed as offering positive opportunities. You will achieve *nothing*, Undershaft has it, unless you are prepared not just to die but to kill.

Still, in the nineteenth century, the assumptions of the Marxist movement remained majoritarian, democratic. The faith was in the people, no longer envisaged as the middle-class average man, but definitely as the bottom class, the base of the social pyramid, the worker. That is still what Marxism was like in Germany during World War I under such leaders as Karl Liebknecht and Rosa Luxemburg. It was Lenin who, even more in practice than in theory, modified the idea in what we might call a Shavian direction. Whereas to Rosa Luxemburg proletarian revolution must mean that the masses themselves revolt, for Lenin it was sufficient that a minority party revolt in their name, maintaining, without taking a vote on it, that the masses were at least acquiescing and at most lending sympathy and support. In Russia it was certainly the Party that revolted; and that ruled; and that was endorsed by Bernard Shaw.

And quite early on. Already in an essay of 1921, "The Dictatorship of the Proletariat," his support for that element in the Russian revolution which most radicals found hardest to swallow is apparent:

> To them [the Russian Communists] dictatorship [of the proletariat] means overriding democracy. For example, though there are elected Soviets everywhere in Russia, and it sometimes happens that on some vital question the voting is 20 for the Government and 22 against it (the opposition consisting of Social Revolutionaries, Mensheviks, Syndicalists . . .), the Government does not thereupon say "Your will be done: the voice of the majority is the voice of God." It very promptly dissolves that Soviet, and intimates to its constituents that until they elect a preponderantly Bolshevik Soviet they shall have no Soviet at all. It may even treat the majority as rebels. The British democrat is scandalized by this. . . . The Russian statesmen reply that they are fighting a class war, and that during a war an Opposition is the enemy. . . . They add that any party . . . which refuses in a highminded manner to take any action until it is supported by a constitutional majority is clearly led by *fainéants* (not to say cowards and incapables). . . .

By 1931 Shaw, on his visit to Russia, was ready to give a wholehearted endorsement of Stalin, and explicitly to embrace Leninism as the one hope of the world. None of the subsequent events of the thirties and forties changed his mind. It is his prefaces of those decades that contain his defense of the theory and practice of exterminating whole sections of the population.

All this was recognition of harsh facts with a vengeance, but, alas, it was accompanied by its own romanticism, as for instance the romanticizing of Stalin's personality. Shaw saw Stalin as not only immensely capable but all-wise, and even full of humor and charm, a superman in fact, like his own Julius Caesar, though less vulnerable and therefore even more admirable. In his youth, Shaw had objected to the Marxist melodrama of a virtuous people versus a wicked bourgeoisie, but when Stalin invoked exactly that melodrama in a 1934 interview with H. G. Wells, who objected, Shaw took Stalin's side.

What was it in Shaw's eyes that gave the Bolsheviks the right to "treat the majority as rebels"? The idea seems to be that whoever has seized power in the name of socialism must hold on to it even at the expense of democracy. Any of the other groups would have been equally acceptable. The thing is to get there first. Any authority is better than none:

> There is only one alternative to government by police, and that is government by massacre. . . . The Turks, in the Balkans and in Armenia, and we, in the Indian hills and in Africa and Australia, have found that, where our police stops, its place must be taken by raids of soldiers, killing, burning, and destroying indiscriminately until enough is judged to have been done to keep the district in awe for some years to come. The fact that we call such expeditions massacres when the Turks resort to them and punitive expeditions . . . when we resort to them does not change their essential character. . . . Though the reign of terror is necessarily cruel, anarchy is apt to be crueler still, and the reign of terror is thus forced on us. . . . In the territories of the United States . . . the revolver and the bowie knife reigned . . . the sixteen-inch gun and the submarine torpedo reign in Europe at present. . . .

A paradox unfolds. Although anarchy was the original aim of nineteenth-century revolutionism, including Marxism, for such as Bernard Shaw it became what they chiefly feared. He had long been a state socialist, and with his excessive respect for power and authority, came more and more to stress the value of strong government. Thus the diametric opposite of Shavian politics is not capitalism but anarchism. In this, too, Shaw resembles Stalin. To maintain the appearance of being still a Marxist, Stalin had to believe that anarchy remained the goal, but it was no longer part of any predictable future, it played no part in practical politics. The reality was the State, gigantic and omnipotent.

What for Kropotkin or Emma Goldman would have been the longed-for freedom was for Shaw a dreaded chaos. In his book *From Radicalism to Socialism*, Willard Wolfe has convincingly argued that Bernard Shaw began as an anarchist. This means that he originally was able to feel the lure of freedom from authority, of individual autonomy. Later Shaw decided that any such attraction was a snare and a delusion: a dream that for him was pure nightmare. His reverence for power was rooted in panic and indeed in neurotic fear, the fear he had felt for lower-class children, and had rationalized as pride in class superiority. It is not uncommon. Snobberies rule the world. Without the German middle class's panic at the thought of proletarian revolt and supremacy there would have been few Nazis.

It is true that very much of British radicalism in Shaw's time was still under the sign of Thomas Carlyle and his hero worship. H. G. Wells was no less an elitist than Shaw. In the Victorian age, even John Stuart Mill believed the educated should have two votes to everyone else's one. If we are after precedent we could run all the way to Plato, who, for European mankind, *created* the idea of government *for* the people but *by* an elite. Plato's convictions, like Shaw's, were rooted in dread of mob thinking and mob rule.

That was over two thousand years ago, when any democracy on the grand scale would certainly have been an empty dream. Plato's dreams were not empty. He was free of that modern curse, intimidation by high authority, was not fascinated with power, did not want it for himself, did not want to grovel before any who might have it. Shaw, on the other hand, was overimpressed by power and the powerful. It is the obverse of being underimpressed by the powerless, by common people. If it was the special characteristic of Jesus that he loved the common folk, then Shaw's opposition to Christianity is founded on something more than a theological difference, it is founded on a difference in personality and inclination, in which the founder of Christianity has the advantage. "When men are animated by the charity of Christ, they feel united, and the needs, sufferings, and joys of others are felt as their own." This is how Pope John XXIII put it, and another Christian, Thomas Merton, has made a further application of the principle. "It is both dangerous and easy to hate man as he is because he is not 'what he ought to be.' If we do not respect what he *is* we will never suffer him to become what he ought to be: in our impatience we will do away with him altogether."

Liberty, equality, fraternity: this is democracy, is it not? Shaw dispenses not only with liberty but, even more disastrously, with fraternity. He lacked the common touch, and for a democratic politics it is a fatal lack, not so much because it leads to anti-democratic, elitist doctrines and schemes, as because it means that the spirit of brotherhood is not there as a bond and an inspiration. Here Walt Whitman, little as he knew of politics, let alone of socialism, is not only more democratic than Shaw but more radical. That warm-blooded love of comrades which he practiced and preached is the proper foundation of the whole democratic adventure, a *sine qua non*. To have nationalized industries without such brotherhood is to have . . . well, the present-day Soviet Union. A figure like Emma Goldman, not comparable to Shaw in intellectual expertise, was a far greater servant of liberty, equality, and fraternity. She loved the common people and they loved her: she was one of them, a common woman while at the same time being a woman of uncommon intelligence and courage.

Given his aspirations, the snobbery Shaw noted in himself was a fatal flaw. Its nemesis was that the man who thought he was at home only with the mighty dead like Shakespeare and Mozart was also at home with the mighty living like Mussolini and Stalin. The man who was incapable of warm-blooded fraternal love for the oppressed was capable of cold-blooded approval of their extermination at the hands of "supermen" who were really submen.

The Depression years inspired Shaw to give a lecture under Fabian auspices "in praise of Guy Fawkes," whose comment on his attempt to blow up the Houses of Parliament was: "Desperate diseases require desperate remedies." But blowing up a house of Parliament will do no more good than setting fire to a Reichstag. The hypocrites and fools who talk, talk, talk represent a lesser danger to the world than the self-appointed great leaders who remove and replace them. Even if readiness to kill is sometimes necessary (as a nonpacifist I am not entitled to say it is not), such readiness will settle few problems of itself, and is not the one thing necessary nor yet the thing most necessary. I would suggest that the *readiness to disobey* deserves as high a mark, and has wider application. It is the prerequisite of self-rule. It suggests the way to nip future Stalins in the bud.

As an anarchist epilogue to *Major Barbara*, I propose the removal of both Undershaft and Cusins from their position of leadership by a unionized work force that will itself take over the ownership and administration of the whole concern. To make it stick, that might require a general strike throughout all England. Which would be revolution. The only people it should be necessary to kill would be the occasional recalcitrant Undershaft or the occasional worker who wants to be the great leader, the new Lenin. Power must be diffused. The state is dispensable. The Houses of Parliament, kept intact, might be put to some useful purpose, as schools, libraries, and auditoriums.

(1978)

NIETZSCHE AND WAGNER

In 1983 the hundredth anniversary of Wagner's death was being celebrated, mainly, of course, by musicians and music historians. I accepted an invitation to speak at the New School for Social Research in New York, not to match myself against the musicians, though I yield to none in my love of music, but to return to old hunting grounds. My writing career had begun with Nietzsche, whom I "discovered" in the stacks of the Yale library when studying for my doctorate in 1940. His ghost haunted my first book, *A Century of Hero Worship*, 1944. Nearly half a century later, he—with William James and I might add Schopenhauer—is the only philosopher I read habitually. My experience of Wagner is a little different. I returned to his music in my sixties after ignoring him for several decades. There is no recovering the madness of one's youthful Wagnerism, though I catch an echo of it when I hear Melchior and Leider singing the Love Duet on an old record.

Nietzsche had an outwardly uneventful life. It could be said that the only thing that ever happened to him was that he met Richard Wagner.

There is certainly only one thing that Nietzsche is known to the world for: he is the inventor of the Superman. But the Superman was not invented, he was discovered, and his name was Richard Wagner, the man who could do everything, and do it bigger and better than anyone else, the master, not of a single art, but of all the arts, combining them, as he did, in a gigantic *Gesamtkunstwerk*, outdoing Beethoven by combining him with Shakespeare, thereby outdoing Shakespeare too, reviving Greek tragedy but adding to it all the glory of modern German music . . .

Nietzsche wanted someone to look up to, a father surrogate for one who had been fatherless since the age of four. Wagner became that father surrogate with a vengeance, Nietzsche's vengeance. He fitted the role. Nietzsche was a failed composer and a minor poet. Wagner was no major poet but he had a theory to get around this point and the claim he implicitly made for his music dramas* was to be second to no one in either music or drama. An older Nietzsche used the phrase *non plus ultra* to characterize *Tristan*. If Wagner hadn't existed, the young Nietzsche would have had to invent him.

And then later, kill him, of course; Wagner had it coming. It is the way of sons with powerful fathers. No one in any case could possibly have lived up to Nietzschean expectations. We are all human, all-too-human, and Wagner's human weaknesses were very marked indeed, not to mention his prejudices, his errors, his stupidities, and his effronteries. If Nietzsche had cast himself as Siegfried, Wagner would be Wotan, the god in twilight or, as Nietzsche would put it, the idol in twilight.

And so, while Nietzsche spoke of Wagner as a "case," one can even more plausibly speak of Nietzsche as a case, and in his disarming way— if he has said something, he will invariably be found to have said the opposite—he has fully admitted as much. The admission is perhaps his primary statement to the world: I am a case, study me as such, I am a sick man and my sickness is that of the age, nay, that of *Homo sapiens* as such. Behold the man—the crucified! *Behold man crucified.* He defined Richard Wagner as one of his diseases.

Six years after his break with Wagner, Nietzsche writes his friend "Peter Gast":

> On Sunday I was in Naumburg to prepare my sister a little for *Parsifal.* It felt strange. . . . I said . . . "I wrote this kind of music as a boy" and took out the old ms and played it—the identity of mood and expression was fabulous, wholly Parsifalesque. . . . It gave me a fright to realize how closely I am akin to Wagner. . . . You will understand, dear friend, this does not mean I am praising *Parsifal.* What decadence, what fake magic!

He did live to praise the prelude to *Parsifal,* and we learn, too, from these words of praise that when he had *dispraised Parsifal* earlier he was speaking only of the libretto and had not yet heard the music:

> I recently heard the prelude to *Parsifal* for the first time. . . . Did Wagner ever compose anything better? The finest psychological intelligence and definition of what must here be said, expressed, communicated in the briefest and most direct form for it, every nuance of feeling pared down to an epigram; a clarity in the music as descriptive art, bringing to mind a shield with a design on it in relief; and finally a sublime and extraordinary feeling, experience, happening of the soul at the basis of the

Gesamtkunstwerk. Music Drama. The German compound was little used by Wagner himself and, as to the term *Musikdrama,* he disapproved of it. Yet both expressions now belong to the vocabulary of Wagner criticism—usefully, it seems to me.

music, which does Wagner the highest credit, a synthesis of states which will seem incompatible to many . . . with a severity that judges, an altitude in the terrifying sense of that word, an intimate cognizance and perspicuity that cut through the soul like a knife—a compassion for what is being watched and judged. Something of that sort occurs in Dante, nowhere else. Has any painter ever painted such a melancholy gaze of love as Wagner in the last accents of this prelude?

Fairness was never Nietzsche's forte. He preferred a fight, and at the basis of his attack on Wagner was an error, namely, that the older Wagner was different from the younger, the difference constituting a capitulation and a betrayal.

Toward the end it was a Wagner grown old whom I had to fight; as for the true Wagner, I still expect to become in good measure his heir.

It is curious how both those perfect Wagnerites, Nietzsche and Shaw, had to invent a change of heart in Wagner to account for the part of him they didn't approve of. He was supposed to have changed from Siegfried to Parsifal, from rebellious, fearless champion to *reiner Tor, durch Mitleid wissend.* Thus Shaw thinks of the pessimistic *Götterdämmerung* as something added many years later to *The Ring* when in fact the libretto, the drama, had been there more or less from the beginning. And Nietzsche thinks of Wagner's religiosity as a later phase when in fact Wagner had planned to write a music drama about Jesus early on. The years of Nietzsche's Wagnerism, 1868–76, were simply years when he chose to ignore the other half of Wagner's nature. Again, it is Nietzsche who is the "case," though, to be fair to the unfair one, we should recall that he had reservations about Wagner from early days, and was always an *imperfect* Wagnerite.

And an ignorant one. Today, many thousands of music students— and even nonprofessional listeners—are more familiar with Wagner's music, are familiar with more of Wagner's music—than Nietzsche ever was. Of course, he did not have the opportunity to play anything over and over on a phonograph, but he also lived most of his life out of touch with opera houses. He seems to have seen even *Tristan* only twice, and a number of Wagner operas not at all. Being a composer himself, albeit self-taught, and perhaps not very talented, he was able to work through piano-vocal scores at the piano. Yet, when we look closely at his most telling remarks against Wagner, we find they are remarks about the libretto:

Who if not Wagner would teach us that innocence prefers to redeem interesting sinners—the case in *Tannhäuser?* Or that even the Wandering Jew is redeemed and settles down when he marries—*The Flying Dutchman?* Or that old corrupted females prefer to be redeemed by chaste youths—Kundry? Or that beautiful maidens like best to be redeemed by a knight who is a Wagnerite—*Meistersinger?* Or that married women too enjoy being redeemed by a knight—Isolde? Or that the old god, having compromised himself morally in every respect, is finally redeemed by a free spirit and immoralist—*The Ring*? . . . Other lessons may be learned. . . . That it may have the direst consequences if one doesn't go to bed at the right time—*Lohengrin*. . . . That one should never know too precisely whom one has married—*Lohengrin*. *Tristan* glorifies the perfect spouse who . . . has only the single question, Why didn't you tell me that before? Answer: I cannot tell you: what you ask you can never know. . . .

Nietzsche is having a good time, but what he is having a good time with is not the music.

Even his attempts to sum up the whole Wagnerian *oeuvre* seem prompted less by the music than by the words. For example, this phrase: "the most seductive blend of everything the world today wants—the three great stimulants of the effete—the brutal, the artificial, and the innocent-idiotic." Or this on the roles played by the Wagnerian *Heldentenor:* "sovereign beasts of prey with spasms of thoughtfulness, generosity and boredom." Or this on Wagner himself: "chewing the cud of moral and religious absurdities till he chokes."

He has most to say about the music when he likes it, as in the passage about the *Parsifal* prelude already quoted, or this about the *Meistersinger* overture:

> It strikes us now as archaic, now as strange, tart and too young, it is just as capricious as it is pompous and traditional, it is not infrequently saucy, still more often coarse and rude, it has fire and courage and at the same time the loose dun skin of fruit that ripens too late. It flows broad and full—and suddenly a moment of inexplicable hesitation, like a gap opening up between cause and effect, a pressure triggering dreams, almost nightmares—but already the old breadth is restored by the current of well-being, old and new happiness, including the artist's happiness with himself. . . .

His hostile characterizations of the music are full of memorable phrases and brilliantly chosen epithets. In the string of adjectives "cloudy, sticky, histrionic, and pretentious," *sticky* is as exact as it is malicious. But the philosopher's love of generalization does not make for good criticism, and Wagner becomes a victim of Nietzsche's wish to define decadence. Nietzsche tells us that Wagner makes a thunderous, intoxicating assault, tries to sweep us off our feet, in order to state his preference for an art that seeps gradually into us. Even when Nietzsche tries to come down to cases, he doesn't do so, but deals with *Tristan* in this sweeping sentence:

> The part becomes lord over the whole, the phrase over the melody, the moment over time and tempo, pathos over ethos (character, style), esprit over sense.

Nothing is added to persuade the reader that this is so. But such persuasion would be needed to convert mere declaration into criticism.

The show is given away in Nietzsche's handling of the Wagner/Bizet contrast. Wagner being at this point all that is bad, Bizet is the answer, and all that is good. This message is repeated a number of times with the usual Nietzschean stridency, but the last reference to Bizet in Nietzsche's letters is this:

> What I say about Bizet you should not take seriously. The way I am, Bizet does not matter to me at all. But as an ironic antithesis to Wagner, it has a strong effect; it would have been in inordinately bad taste had I used an encomium on Beethoven as my starting point.

In short, Bizet has also fallen victim to Nietzsche's desire to set up dramatic antitheses, driven, as he was, by his desire to transcend the concrete in the general. It is not Bizet he is really talking about, and in a sense it was not Wagner he had been talking about, ever. In Nietzsche's so-called Wagnerite phase, Wagner had been the symbol of the Nietzschean artist-hero, re-creating tragedy out of the spirit of music; later, Wagner was the Devil of Nietzschean theology, the Decadence that would be overcome by the spirit of Zarathustra.

Nietzsche's most ardent champion in recent decades and in this country was my late friend and colleague Walter Kaufmann. He elevated Nietzsche to the rank of hero of anti-anti-Semitism. If this is justified, then in Nietzsche and Wagner we have to see hero and villain. Wagner said, "The Jewish race is the born enemy of pure humanity and everything that is noble in it." He found it amusing that forty-seven Jews were burnt to death in a fire. And so on and so forth. Nietzsche's later works, to the contrary, are full of jibes against anti-Semites. He called his own sister an anti-Semitic goose, registered a strong dissent from her own and her husband's proto-Nazi politics, and after his breakdown wired Bismarck, "All anti-Semites will be shot." So far, so good. But it is also true that, like other categories, the Jewish category fell victim to Nietzsche's boundless polemicism. He was giving hell to his own— the Germans. Wagner thought Germans were all that's good, the French all that's bad; Nietzsche inverted this proposition. Anything non-German was better than anything German. He invented a Polish ancestry for himself, discovered modern Russian literature, praised Gallic wit . . . Such a polemic would have been incomplete if the Jews had not been included among the heroes.

Now Nietzsche's early letters show marked traces of the conventional anti-Semitism of his place and time and class. Nor, in his youth, do we find him protesting the anti-Semitism of either Wagner's writings or his behavior. We read that Nietzsche would keep his Jewish friend Paul Rée out of Wagner's way in deference to the latter's anti-Semitism.

I am speaking now of Nietzsche's Wagner period, but Wagner's anti-Semitism is not the bone of contention even in Nietzsche's anti-Wagner writings later on. Nietzsche is interested now in Wagner as decadent, not as proto-Nazi. More important, though he distanced himself from the anti-Semitic movement, he was always anti-Jewish in philosophy—anti-Jewish exactly as he was anti-Christian—because he saw both Judaism and Christianity negatively. Both stood for herd morality.

Nietzsche wanted Wagner to be against both Judaism and Christianity, but Wagner was only against Judaism: *that* was his crime. And here it is not just the paranoid Nietzsche who suspects Wagner of cheating. The Christianity of *Parsifal* is not cogent. As one of the Wagnerians (not Nietzscheans) has said, to write *Tristan*, Wagner had to fall in love with Mathilde Wesendonk, to write *Parsifal* he had to fall in love with Christianity. An opportunist, then, for art's sake.

We learn from Hermann Rauschning's *Hitler Speaks* that the disingenuousness of *Parsifal* was apparent to that most perfect of all the Wagnerites, Adolf Hitler. According to Rauschning, Hitler said, "Beside the absurd externals of the story with its Christian embroidery and Good Friday mystification, it is not the Christian Schopenhauerist religion of compassion that is acclaimed but pure and noble blood."

Yet one need not share Nietzsche's revulsion from the play-actor in Wagner. It seems to be not just revulsion from moral hypocrisy but revulsion from the histrionic, from theatre, as such. This is where the two men are furthest apart. It was true enough, as Nietzsche insisted, that Wagner was an utterly histrionic personality, a Proteus, and with Nietzsche it was a point of honor to be—or try to be, since this may not be possible for anyone less "evolved" than Superman—just the opposite, a single self to which one is always true. Nietzsche's method is exposure, with emphasis on self-exposure, while Wagner, the actor, is forever changing mask and costume. Still, the attraction of Nietzsche to Wagner must have been precisely the *attraction* of an opposite, which later, by all means, he could come to see as a fatal attraction—that of the homme fatale of the epoch. This opposition is obvious enough at the social level: it is the contrast between the prim, professorial, Lutheran, middle-class, probably virginal bachelor and the Bohemian womanizer whose mistress at the time Nietzsche met them was pregnant with the Siegfried-to-be, not to mention costume, stage design, and perfume:

> Violet and red dominated . . . heavy carpets, deep cushion, plush chairs, and poufs, the whole accented with garlands, passementeries . . . and lace. . . . Through these settings [Wagner] flitted in satin pants with matching slippers and jackets, almost everything padded and lined with fur. . . . In Prague . . . he had appeared in a yellow damask dressing gown, pink tie, and voluminous black velvet cape lined with rose satin.

. . . He asked Judith [an *amie*] to ship limitless amounts of amber, milk of iris . . . Rose de Bengale. . . . His study in Wahnfried was directly over the bath which he would inundate with rare odors. . . .

As Robert W. Gutman, from whom I take these passages, relates, it was in such a perfumed setting that Wagner embarked on *Parsifal* . . . The contrast with Nietzsche is not merely social, it is archetypal like some of the antitheses dear to Nietzsche's heart, Apollo and Dionysus, Dionysus and Christ. How define this particular antithesis? In his later writings, Nietzsche is thinking of it as the contrast between the Sick and the Healthy, the Decadent and the Supermanic, and this is a contrast between Wagner's music and his own late prose which in his final megalomaniac phase he overpraises but does not misrepresent. (He ventures that it is the next step after Luther and Goethe . . .)

Great as is the contrast between Wagner and Nietzsche in this respect, we must finally see the two men—Nietzsche himself was capable of doing so—as remarkably akin. Take again the hostility of both to Judaism. Like Christianity, Judaism—as they both see it—stands for herd morality. In his youth, Wagner had been touched by the democratic ardors of 1848. They didn't last long, and an early, "democratic" plan for Bayreuth was abandoned: Wagner progressed from a populist conception to a royalist one. His faith moved first to the Wittelsbachs, then to the Hohenzollerns and the new Reich and the stand he hoped the Reich would take for *Deutschtum* against Jews and other undesirable aliens. Nietzsche accepted none of this, but was even more ferociously opposed to democracy, a factor which must not be seen in narrowly political terms. This philosophy is at bottom misanthropic. Most of mankind is written off as worthless. Only great men are worthwhile.

Now it is entirely traditional to see democracy as mob rule, not preferable to autocracy or oligarchy. However, the traditional view is that, though not *by* the people, government is *for* the people. Not so for Nietzsche. The aim is to have a few great men. In order to have them, the exploitation of the many is both inevitable and justified.

In our culture today, nearly everyone disagrees, and yet there is very little discussion of what seem to me the two underlying problems. The first is in the nature of the whole discourse. To whom are Nietzsche's writings addressed? Not to the herd. Thus, if *we* are reading him, we have already declared ourselves above the herd, we are the free spirits, we are the Nietzschean elite. But think for a moment. We are not really an elite. There are too many of us. (The question, who are the masses? has been wisely answered by Raymond Williams: *we* are the masses.) We are only members of the herd, flattered by Nietzsche into an illusion of superiority. Is that not a trap one should get oneself out of?

Second, in the matter of misanthropy, what is reported by misanthropes about their fellow men may be accurate, yet it raises the question whether misanthropy is good for the misanthrope. We need to ask, how does misanthropy affect the misanthrope, what does it do to him?

Nietzsche was one of the most intelligent men who ever lived. His insights never fail to amaze. But he failed to see that the supreme political problem of the democratic era—which he knew we are in— is that of the rapport or lack of it between leaders and peoples. That Stalin did not love his people has great political, as well as moral, importance, as, conversely, has the fact that Gandhi did love his people, or that Martin Luther King, Jr., loved his.

Nietzsche can, of course, be explained by opposites. He himself favored such explanations, and was eager to state that for him the greatest danger lay in pity:

> "Pity" has always been the *main* cause of trouble in my life. . . . For this is not only a softness which any magnanimous Hellene would have laughed at, it is also a grave practical danger. . . . One has to keep a nice tight rein on one's sympathy, and treat anything that goes against our ideal (for instance, such low characters as Lou [Salomé] and Rée) as enemies. You will see this is how I read a moral lesson to myself but to attain this wisdom has almost cost me my life.

But what a Gandhi feels for Indians is not pity, nor is what a Martin Luther King feels for American blacks. The short word for it is love, the long word is solidarity. That pity is a problematic sentiment and often a bad one is a well-established idea—William Blake was aware of it. That is because it operates *de haut en bas*. The paradox of superiority is, however, this, that Gandhi would have been a less great man had he distanced himself from non-great men. You may have a higher IQ than your neighbor, but if you punish him on this account, that is not a demonstration of higher IQ . . . Much of Nietzsche's thinking is vitiated by his low opinion of his fellows. His creation of Superman is the obverse of this. An absolutely fruitless notion. Or if fruitful, the fruits are Adolf Hitler and the Superman comic strip.

Nietzsche is extremely vulnerable. Wagner, on the other hand, was extremely successful—*the* success, perhaps, of the successful century— the century that believed both in success and in itself *as* a success. To top it off, he was a success in a field—music—in which Nietzsche, though trained, hardly excelled the accomplished amateur. When the young Nietzsche met the old Wagner, the latter was what the former wanted to become but never would, or could, become, in achievement or in recognition.

Obviously then, once Nietzsche turned against Wagner, his vehement anger would carry with it all the suspect force of "sour grapes," and it is hard for the reader to realize that the speaker of those harsh words is not some social peer of Wagner's, enthroned in some other Bayreuth, but an impecunious invalid living from hand to mouth in one rented room after another, racked by bodily illnesses which would have put anyone but him out of action altogether.

"The whirligig of time brings in his revenges." Today Wagner is extremely vulnerable—as anti-Semite and proto-Nazi. Easy, then, especially after the holocaust of the 1940s, to see him as the Nazi Goliath and Nietzsche as the David of anti-anti-Semitism. This is how Walter Kaufmann did see the matter. But in this way too easy—too utter—an antithesis is created. Nietzsche, after all, came to Wagner in the first place because he found him *sympathisch*. This may initially have been a matter of musical style, since he knew the music before he knew the man, but the style is the man, and particularly the Wagnerian style declares at once all those characteristics which anti-Wagnerians find obnoxious, and especially a rush to overpower, to inundate and overrun. Imperialism—the wish to overrun the world, if not the universe—here finds an objective correlative in music.

> In dem wogenden Schwall
> in dem tönenden Schall
> in des Welt-Athems
> wehendem All

It may be said I am wrenching these lines from the proper context, since in *Tristan* they are promptly followed by:

> ertrinken
> versinken
> unbewusst
> höchste Lust.

But I am not offering analysis of *Tristan* here, merely alluding to one of the great dreams of the nineteenth century, which was that the world could be taken over and transformed by individual genius. Neither Shelley nor Marx, neither Wagner nor Nietzsche offered anything less than a world overpowered and then transfigured by their rhetoric. It is a long journey, not in years, but in experience, from there to Eliot's *Waste Land* and Kafka's *Trial*. It is a long journey from the *Ring* to Berg's *Wozzeck* or even to Debussy's *Pelléas*.

I have mentioned that Nietzsche called Wagner one of his diseases. Since Nietzsche had so many diseases, we must now ask, which one? I would propose megalomania, the megalomania of the nineteenth-century "romantic" artist. I am not thinking of vanity and arrogance themselves but of a distortion of vision and values consequent upon vanity and arrogance. One's superiority in talent may be enormous—

as Wagner's was, as Nietzsche's was—but in solving some problems it compounds others and brings its own illusions, delusions too, and notably those of grandeur. Psychology has stressed that we all harbor fantasies of omnipotence. These are blatant and pathetic in conspicuously weak and inept persons. But strong and capable persons have them too. Winston Churchill is said to have believed that World War II could not be won without him, and each nineteenth-century sage who believed the world could be utterly transformed, probably in a very short time, seems also to have assumed the world needed him to transform it. Thus the crazy Nietzsche who sent messages declaring himself Jesus or Dionysus was in essence no different from the non-crazy Nietzsche offering a transvaluation of all values. Or Marx offering to initiate the history of human freedom. Or Wagner setting up Bayreuth, and helping to set up that Second German Reich which would be followed, in how Wagnerian a style, by the Third, Hitler the ultimate Master Singer of Nuremberg.

It is hard for us to recapture the perspectives of the nineteenth century. Not a few then hoped to see the world transformed and transfigured, whereas we (to adapt Albert Camus) would be relieved to find the world won't be blown to bits. Not a few, then, had large, strong egos. Their strength was the strength of ten because their hearts were pure. (That's Galahad—Lord Tennyson's Parsifal.) In the wake of Napoléon, only a bit more modestly, followed Bismarck and Disraeli and Cecil Rhodes and Theodore Roosevelt.

Likewise the intellectuals. Not just the court jesters. Also what has been called the adversary culture. All those who dared to say No, from the real giants to the dwarves that imagined themselves gigantic and capable, with a little help from their constituency, of turning history around and transforming this globe at lightning speed. The sages of the nineteenth century are not only reformers but transformers. They are prophets who undertake to provide the advice that will lead, if not to Utopia, at least to some highly improved condition humaine: Bentham and the Mills, Fourier and Comte, Marx and Engels, Carlyle and Ruskin and the Russians. Above all, perhaps, the Russians. After one has exhausted the names that come to mind, Tolstoy and Dostoevsky,* Kropotkin and Bakunin, one is aware that there were many names one has forgotten, also offering that shining future . . . if only one assented to their opinions . . . This, we can say in the complacency of hindsight, was dreadfully overdone. There must have been many readers who, even in the nineteenth century, after enjoying a few pages of confidently

---

*Dostoevsky, to be sure, was anti-utopian. Still, the radical Right, down through Solzhenitsyn, just like the millennial Left, is imbued with a vision of Russia transfigured, the modern being transfigured into the medieval. The artist is nothing if not a prophet.

bright prophecy, smiled sadly and closed the book. But it is now almost the twenty-first century and we have forgotten that our great-great-grandparents did write things like this:

> My philosophy will play a part in the world such as no other philosophy in ancient or modern times.
> Within the limits of human knowledge, my philosophy is the real solution of the riddle of the world.

Both these quotations are from Arthur Schopenhauer, role model, for a while, of Friedrich Nietzsche and, for a longer while, indeed for the duration, of Richard Wagner.

Am I changing the subject from history to geography, from the nineteenth century to Germany? Yes, because it was in Germany that the nineteenth-century tendency I am talking about reached its logical conclusion—or should I say was reduced to the absurd? You will appreciate the difference between Germany and some other places if you agree with me that Giuseppe Verdi was just as great a composer as Richard Wagner, and just as great a man of the theatre, but that, while Verdi merely composed his operas and enjoyed such success as they brought, Wagner had to begin with grandiose theorizing and end with grandiose practice. Bayreuth was the only opera house in the history of the world where only one composer's operas would be performed, this opera house no ivory tower but rather an extra mailed fist for Kaiser Wilhelm in his fight for German supremacy in Europe.

German visionaries and would-be visionaries of the nineteenth century revived an age-old dream, which was that of a Third Empire succeeding whatever one conceived of as Europe's first two stabs at imperial perfection. What they got, what we all got, was the Third Reich, whose supreme culture hero was Richard Wagner. Pierre Boulez, for one, shakes his head at that, and ruminates on the unfairness, the grossness, of politics. He does not wish to know that Wagner, his music hero, is the culture hero of the anticulture that reviles humanistic values, Gallic wit, and the Jews, and offers as its role model—SIEGFRIED, the blond and blue-eyed Teuton of much brawn and little brain, who will stop at nothing in the way of aggression, because he is inhuman and fears no one and nothing, even God.

The first World War, or so I have read in very respectable literature, was caused by Nietzsche, the second by Wagner. From this one might deduce that, if intellectuals cannot produce a New Jerusalem, they can produce Armageddon: if not Utopia, then Hiroshima. But the respectable sources I am citing are also hysterical sources: these accusations against Nietzsche and Wagner are taken from Allied war propaganda.

They are grotesquely false. But Wagner and Nietzsche both asked for it when they dramatized themselves, and they constantly did, as not only world-historical but world-shaking figures. When the world shook, they inevitably got the credit.

(1983)

WAGNER AND IBSEN

Long ago I had let myself be guided by Shaw to the twin sources of modernism in the theatre: Wagner and Ibsen. So when an institution called the American Ibsen Theatre asked for a talk, I resolved to return to the original meeting place of these three seminal minds: Wagner, Ibsen, Shaw. The point I am returning from—the late twentieth century—suggests a non-Shavian view of the Ibsenite quintessence.

Two little books of the 1890s did much to advance the cause—and cause it was—of Wagner and Ibsen. I'm referring to *The Perfect Wagnerite* and *The Quintessence of Ibsenism* by Bernard Shaw. Like many others I have been deeply affected by both, but when I re-read them today I find Wagner and Ibsen wrongly conceived, or at least as they cannot be conceived in the late twentieth century or perhaps ever again in the future.

The first edition of *The Quintessence* ended with a quotation from Wagner. Wagner is saying that "man" up to now has been a slave of Religion, Nationality, and the State, but that in the future he should and can liberate himself from all these and become real man, free man. Bernard Shaw is using this passage to define Ibsenism, the emerging point being that, while Wagner and Ibsen created different types of drama, they were at bottom in sympathy philosophically. In another place, Shaw says: "Every one of Ibsen's plays is a deliberate act of war on society as at present constituted. . . . Ibsen undertook a task of no less magnitude than changing the mind of Europe with a view to changing its morals." He is talking, of course, of a fundamental change, just as Wagner had, and Brecht would later: "Change the world, it needs it." Up to now we have had slavery, after Wagner and Ibsen we can have emancipation.

The topic is the idea of progress, and the artist's relation to it. An older Shaw would both question and redefine the idea of progress, but the young Shaw is still committed to it in what had become the established way, and if you ask, established by whom? I should have to take the story back at least as far as "the heavenly city of the eighteenth-century philosophers." Carl Becker was criticized by his fellow historians for applying this phrase to a whole century. It was just one school of thought, the Utopian school, the school that believed the Heavenly City could be built on earth and if not today then next week. Though this was not the creed of Voltaire or Rousseau or Diderot, it still proved, in a sense, to be the Master Idea of an epoch, and for some people lives still. More people, probably, would agree that, though the world has indeed changed, it has not changed according to the Master Idea. To misquote Camus again: the nineteenth century expected to transform the world into Utopia, the twentieth century would consider itself lucky to keep the world in existence. Detention camps invented by British imperialism to hold Boers in 1900 had been developed by 1942 into extermination camps that in three years brought death to six million people. In the third of those years, the first atomic bombs were dropped and destroyed two cities.

Shaw claimed to find that he, Wagner, and Ibsen shared a very heady optimism, and this optimism, this belief in progress, this belief in an attainable Heavenly City of the eighteenth-century philosophers, had become a kind of orthodoxy among those who considered themselves enlightened. Today, only politicians profess optimism, and even they prove their case only by smiling before television cameras. People who consider themselves enlightened are now pessimists—Samuel Beckett is their counterprophet and antihero—for it is no longer reasonable to think that humanity will solve its most pressing problems. Even if we don't go to war, we are changing the world, *but for the worse*, by overpopulating it and destroying the environment. H. G. Wells, whose name most people still associate with progress in science, ended up after World War II with a little book called *Mind at the End of Its Tether*. Karl Kraus wrote *Die letzten Tage des Menschheit* during World War I.

Shaw was of course entitled to speak for himself, and in the twentieth century he tried desperately to hold on to his nineteenth-century perspective. I say desperately because, in 1931, we find him saying that the world has only one hope left, the Soviet Union. One wonders what he would say to the Soviet Union of 1986.

Leninism might be defined as the desperate form of Marxism, an attempt to save Marxism by Machiavellizing it, but Marx's own work is in my view also marked by desperation. From the start, Marxists maintained that on the road to the Heavenly City we would encounter Armageddon or what the Internationale of 1871 called *la lutte finale*, the final conflict.

C'est la lutte finale!
Groupons-nous et demain
L'internationale sera la genre humain.

The idea is at least as old as the last book of the New Testament, but it has always been a desperate idea: peace reached only through war, heaven only through hell (not through purgatory). Yet it is now a dead idea because since 1945 any *lutte finale* would destroy both sides and perhaps the planet itself. . .

Was Shaw right about Wagner and Ibsen? He quoted Wagner's own words, and there are words of Ibsen's that could be introduced to affirm that he wished to ennoble the human race and/or to smash the State. In *Emperor and Galilean*, Ibsen tried to make a contribution to the Heavenly City of the philosophers, but Shaw is wrong about both artists. He is wrong (in a rather interesting way) about *Der Ring des Nibelungen*. He asks us to believe that the last part of the cycle, the *Götterdämmerung*, spoiled a masterpiece. Because he finds it to be opera rather than music drama, he declares it inferior, and does not take its pessimism seriously but insists that Wagner's original scenario, in which Brünnhilde would carry Siegfried to a Heavenly City, Valhalla, which would never burn down, is what we should respect. Wagner allegedly let too much time go by, and lost touch with his own creation.

Now it is true that the music of the *Götterdämmerung* was unfinished until many years later, but it is not true that the unhappy ending waited that long. On the contrary, it had been worked out in the years immediately following the abortive 1848 revolutions, in one of which Wagner had played a part, and Shaw's quotation from Wagner in *The Quintessence* belongs to Wagner's very short revolutionary period (as short as Wordsworth's in another revolution, or many a poet's in the 1930s in yet another). If there is such a thing as representative Wagner, this is not it. As for *Götterdämmerung*, it has long been recognized as the finest of the four parts of the cycle musically, and dramatically has proved the most astonishing and prophetic. If Wagner had originally intended something in the tradition of Shelley's *Prometheus Unbound*, which of course is the tradition of the Heavenly City of the eighteenth-century philosophers, he changed course rapidly after the failures of 1848 and composed what is among other things a classic of political disenchantment—one of the great themes of the later period, our period, *the* archetypal images of our time being, alas, The End of the World, Der Untergang des Abendlandes, Apocalypse Now, The Waste Land, Journey to the End of the Night, Endgame, Die letzten Tage des Menschheit, Mind at the End of Its Tether. *

---

*Maurice Valency brings our attention at book length (469 pages) to the fact that Proust's *Sodome et Gomorrhe* has this sentence in it: "C'est beau, n'est-ce pas, la fin du monde?" Over 100 of the 469 pages are about Giraudoux, whose *Sodome et Gomorrhe* directly dramatizes the end of the world. —*The End of the World* (New York, 1980).

One of several reasons why the Patrice Chéreau production of *The Ring* (Bayreuth, 1976), reaching us on American television in 1983, carried no conviction except in the first of the four operas was that it was based on Shaw's misunderstandings of Wagner written down nearly a century ago. (Avant-garde and rearguard are the same thing.) Except for a very brief period in which he composed no music, Richard Wagner was not an old-fashioned optimist but a new-fashioned pessimist, and he himself was the first to realize that his model philosopher was not Bakunin but Schopenhauer.

Christianity, to be sure, is the most optimistic of religions, conquering for us our two archenemies, Time and Death, by a Grace all too amazing, but when Wagner writes his "Christian" superopera *Parsifal*, the Christian spirit is far to seek, and Hans-Jürgen Syberberg's avant-gardism in his *Parsifal* film is not open to the kind of criticism I've made of Chéreau's. Here there was truly a case for the director as critic and iconoclast. Syberberg's "statement" was that the music is great, should be sung straight and left intact, but that the drama is in many ways unacceptable and deserves to be given a rough time . . .

The Ibsen experience was so liberating for Shaw's generation that they took it for granted Ibsen was a liberationist. In his speeches and letters, they could cite chapter and verse, not to mention again that massive tribute to eighteenth-century cosmic optimism, *Emperor and Galilean*. But where is the optimism in *Brand*, *Peer Gynt*, or the whole roster of modern prose plays that followed? *A Doll's House* may have made some feminists cry "Hurrah for Nora!" at the end, but it has made more people ask how Nora now proposes to get along. Then there is Ibsen's highly somber, and wholly negative, account of the workings of modern liberationist ideas in the lives of the folk who accept them, such as Mrs. Alving and Mr. Rosmer.

How curious, by the way, that a twentieth-century feminist should choose to call herself Rebecca West when, though no doubt Rebecca was ideologically modern as of the 1880s, she was more conspicuously a woman who, from sexual jealousy, drove another woman to suicide. Some have tried to resolve our dilemma by maintaining that Ibsen was optimistic in his social plays, though not in plays that are more psychological or metaphysical. This theory falls down the moment we look at the most exclusively social of the major plays, *An Enemy of the People*, and note how far from confident the conclusion is.

Shaw proposed a nineteenth-century revolutionary Ibsen, just as he proposed a nineteenth-century revolutionary Wagner. We should turn down both proposals. The work of both men has a prophetic character that brings them to a twentieth-century position that Shaw perhaps himself never reached—though, again, *Heartbreak House* may prove that, on and off, he did. Wagner had not read Schopenhauer when he created works that he later came to regard as Schopenhauerian, but like Schopenhauer he had a prophet's insight into the present and its potential for the future.

Politically Shaw and Ibsen were not very close. When Ibsen heard of the Shaw lecture that became *The Quintessence*, his pleasure at hearing he was approved of by the socialists was marked by surprise. The one kind of socialism that Ibsen was ever attracted to was anarchism. Now anarchism was the first kind of socialism to appeal to Shaw. However, he rejected it fast with all too much thoroughness, and set out on the road that led to Leninism and to Sidney and Beatrice Webb's book *Soviet Communism: A New Civilization?* Compared to Shaw, Ibsen is unpolitical. If his subject is society, he is an extreme individualist where Shaw was collectivist, individualistic only when the individual was a Great Man: he had good words for Mussolini, Hitler, and Stalin as individuals, but the most shocking item in his later prefaces is his assent to the idea that a good government is entitled to liquidate whole sections of its population for the benefit of those who remain. This view leads straight to Auschwitz, and is the quintessence of non-Ibsenism.

Having said that Wagner and Ibsen are twentieth-century figures *avant la lettre* in their sense of a *Götterdämmerung*, an *Untergang des Abendlandes*, I am now championing Ibsen for his individualism, a typically nineteenth-century phenomenon, as against the eventually brutal collectivism of those "great individuals" Hitler and Stalin. There is an organic connection between the two sides of my argument: for a decline in respect for the individual itself constitutes the decline of the West, or at least is both a cause and a symptom thereof.

The respect for great individuals *only* which we find in late Shaw— even more so, his respect for individuals who weren't really great—is the obverse of his disrespect for people in general. Under the Christian dispensation, the individual was (in theory) sacred; each soul unique, and loved by God. And now that God was dead? Was everything permitted, including the misanthropy of Schopenhauer, Nietzsche, and Shaw? Like them—like anyone perhaps—Ibsen could occasionally be swept away by the winds of misanthropy, and wish he could have torpedoed the Ark, as he once put it. But the absence of God from the world of his "modern" plays only serves to stress the centrality of man— once sacred as related to God, now uniquely sacred, sacred and alone. A priest has been quoted to the effect that Auschwitz didn't matter all that much because those people would have died a few years later anyhow; what are a few decades of earthly life compared to an eternity in other worlds? But Ibsen is a modernist. This earthly life is all we can count on. The individual life is precious indeed. And the individual life might be, can be, noble. Still, the prospects are not good. That middle-class culture which pretends sympathy for the individual is actually inimical to his well-being. Which is one way of stating—if it can be reduced to a single sentence—Ibsen's chief preoccupation. Around the bright light of the individual soul, the dark sky of a dying—a killing—culture.

Some of the texts have, it is true, been given optimistic readings. G. Wilson Knight, one of the most interesting commentators any playwright could have, finds sublime transcendence in the ending of *When We Dead Awaken*. Knight was not a Jungian, but at points like this his criticism resembles, say, the Jungian view of the end of Wagner's *Ring*: what to the unenlightened would seem one of the great images of death and collapse—the decline of the West, the death of God, and so on, as I've been saying—can be reinterpreted, à la Jung, as the exact opposite: death into life, resurrection, that very Christianity which Wagner was to pretend to espouse, later, in *Parsifal*. In myth, we are told, death equals life, which one is sure can be quite true, only whether it becomes true in a work of art depends whether the artist creates that truth anew. Thus psychoanalytic categories do not automatically apply. It is the same with symbolism generally. Freud can say an umbrella symbolizes a penis. But a poet can make it symbolize something else, or even use it without making it symbolize anything. Nothing in poetry symbolizes anything except as made to do so by its context . . .

I am giving reasons not to impose general mythic patterns on *When We Dead Awaken*. Ibsen has therein created a specific pattern which, in my judgment, reflects disenchantment if not despair. If there is a philosophy that is close to *When We Dead Awaken*, it would seem to be Schopenhauer's: the final thought is of release from life's bondage, resignation to dying and departure.

On the surface, *Little Eyolf* has an optimistic ending but, since Hermann Weigand in the twenties, most critics, including myself, have taken this ending to be ironical, which is to say unhappy or happy only illusorily.

Wagner was smart to spot Schopenhauer as, from where he sat, *the* modern philosopher. Modern drama has stayed with Schopenhauer—not with his metaphysical argument but with his *Weltanschauung*, his outlook and general attitude. *Long Day's Journey into Night*, its title almost a manifesto, is Schopenhauerian in spirit, whereas Brecht, who attempted drama that was optimistic and Marxist in spirit, never quite had the (aesthetic) courage of those (philosophic) convictions, and what comes through in his would-be optimistic theatre is despair. His two plays directly about revolution are both about classic defeats, 1870 in Paris, 1905 in Moscow.

In the twentieth century the writer has not been able to sustain the nineteenth-century self-confidence. One might almost say that twentieth-century writers don't have ideas, at least not ideas of their own. Not seeing themselves as a source of thought or action, they join an organization. A church or party tells them what to think. Things were different in the early days of industrialism when Shelley and Carlyle attributed to themselves, and presumably some others, the gift of prophecy, a gift that sometimes seemed to approach omniscience and infallibility.

> My philosophy will play a part in the world such as no other philosophy in ancient or modern times.
> Within the limits of human knowledge, my philosophy is the real solution of the riddle of the world.

These sentences, already cited above,* illustrate what Santayana called the egoism of German philosophy, even a sort of elephantiasis of that celebrated German *Geist*. They belong to the same phase of history in which a Richard Wagner was not content to be the composer of splendid music but had to pretend his operas were Aeschylus, Shakespeare, and Beethoven combined and transmuted in a synthesis grander and greater than any of them. And if Nietzsche was the first to diagnose this illness, one reason was that he, too, suffered from it.

The idea that "small is beautiful" has indeed been a radical one in our day because in the previous century big was beautiful. With big egos and big claims came big (long) works with big intentions. Indeed many of the masterworks of the nineteenth-century drama—from *Faust* through *Peer Gynt* to *Man and Superman,* and one is tempted to add *The Dynasts*—are monster dramas, just as *War and Peace* and *The Brothers Karamazov* are monster novels, while some masters who wrote shorter novels (Scott, Balzac, Zola) strung them together to make a Monster Series that covered Everything. Is the trend wholly redeemed by the genius of masters who contributed to it? This is an unanswerable question, but one can certainly present evidence that the Idea of the Gigantic misled as talented a poet as Thomas Hardy into that mistake of genius, *The Dynasts,* and so talented a composer as Gustav Mahler into his *Symphony of a Thousand* (the Eighth), not to harp on the ponderosity and pretension that flawed the great works of Richard Wagner, nor to overstress that the Idea lived on to inspire Eugene O'Neill's mammoth tragedies and that play of Robert Wilson's, in the seventies, that dragged on all night.

And Henrik Ibsen? The first part of his career was lived under the sign of *Faust* I and II. *Peer Gynt* is a masterpiece, but there must be serious doubt about *Brand* and *Emperor and Galilean*. There are marked

---

*P. 108. And what to Schopenhauer was the riddle of the world was to Karl Marx the riddle of history, which he solved: "[Communism] is the true solution of the conflict between existence and essence. . . . It is the solution of the riddle of history. . . . " The proletariat needed a bourgeois philosopher, nineteenth-century style, to come to its rescue.

signs of strain in Ibsen's effort to be gigantic. And then what happened? He wrote the "modern" plays. Why? In order to *be* modern. That is the argument of Ibsen himself when he speaks of the influence of Georg Brandes's lectures, and "modern" in those days meant in prose not verse and with a structure modeled on the well-made play, not on *Faust*. And that is all? I would suggest that the main point here is being missed, and that it lies in Ibsen's choice of the smaller instead of the larger Idea. Small *is* beautiful, or as Goethe more subtly put it: "In der Beschränkung zeigt sich erst der Meister," "the master's touch is found, first of all, in self-limitation." More Ibsenites than fully admit it really think Ibsen descended from the heights of *Brand* and *Peer Gynt* to wallow in the bourgeois swamp of plays like *A Doll's House*. I believe that, to the contrary, Ibsen sensed the dangers inherent in Gigantism and committed himself to the opposite principle: less is more. If this is true, then the change to "modern" playwriting was an achievement, even a breakthrough.

I would not say he achieved the perfection of a Racine, who had the advantage (among others) of having a model for his work which was itself characterized by a kind of perfection: the work of Euripides. The model for Ibsen's "modernizing" of himself in the domestic, prose plays was a highly *im*perfect one. This was the *pièce bien faite* of Eugène Scribe, charlatan of genius, genius of charlatanism. Or perhaps, since to Scribe is attributed the perfecting of this Well-Made Play, we should speak of an empty perfection. Shakespeare's plots certainly seem imperfect by comparison, less tidy, less neat. The tidiness and the neatness have their handicaps. For one thing, they call attention to themselves just when that kind of attention is most damaging. By the same token, they victimize the characters, who cannot, as it were, develop in a forward direction to what may turn out to be their fate, but are controlled by the outcome, the whole play having been written backwards. And if it be said that Euripides and Racine must also in a sense have written backwards, in that they certainly knew how their stories would come out, the just retort is that, even so, they did not so enmesh and entangle their people in a clever and complex imbroglio as to eliminate all freedoms along the way. Not that plot can be natural. Plotlessness is natural. But the *pièce bien faite* constantly calls attention to its own unnaturalness, as a conjurer calls attention to the cleverness of his legerdemain.

The final effect of the tidiness, neatness, and cleverness is, paradoxically, ponderous and clumsy. One concedes that the puppeteer moves his marionettes deftly, but one would have preferred not to see the wires. As far as perfection is concerned, not all great artists come as close as Euripides and Racine. "The more there are great excellencies in a work, the less am I surprised at finding great demerits." This is

Edgar Allan Poe speaking. The case of Ibsen would not have surprised him.

If Ibsen did not offset the Victorian cult of bigness with perfection, or even perfectionism, he did offset it with something more modern and modernist: the pursuit of authenticity. In his early work such as *Brand* and *Peer Gynt,* this is a theme, *the* theme. Later, it becomes the work itself. I have quoted Goethe on the value of accepting narrower boundaries. Let me quote now his great phrase (which also I have quoted before this) about the gift a literary artist most needs: "eine Fantasie für die Wahrheit des Realen," "the power of imagining the truth of the real." Ibsen's early plays have their champions, but I cannot see that, when he wrote *Emperor and Galilean,* he was consistently able to imagine the truth of what was real about Julian the Apostate, even though he had much to say on the subject that may be true and is certainly of interest. To *become* able to imagine and project this truth would be a breakthrough, the breakthrough into the modernist plays.

Goethe's phrase helps us to understand, also, what Richard Wagner did *not* achieve. He had an imagination of great and mythopoeic power. But it was not an imagination that would ever break through into anything that could be called the truth of the real. *Parsifal* is indeed the test case. In intention, it bursts the bounds of theatre and exhibits Truth, revealed and supernatural. Nietzsche smelled incense, and thought of Rome. This is not accurate. *Parsifal* is not even Christian. But given that Nietzsche identified Christianity with mystification, his reaction was inevitable. Important here is that *Parsifal* was not a spiritual breakthrough. It served the purpose of allowing Wagner to develop musically, which justifies its existence certainly, but dramatically it is just another *Tannhäuser* fantasy. If Nietzsche overdid his case against Wagner, it was because, at a time of much Wagner worship, to which he himself had contributed, he sensed something profoundly wrong, something absolutely *inauthentic.*

Yet, as Nietzsche admitted, he and Wagner do not make a dramatic antithesis: there was too much Wagnerism in Nietzsche. Wagner might, for example, be too histrionic, but nobody could be more histrionic than Nietzsche, who even in his madness was still role playing and indeed leaping from one role to another which would be its opposite. A better antithesis to Wagner is he whom Shaw proposed as the leader of the "other" school of modernist theatre, Henrik Ibsen. Shaw intended thereby only to indicate alternate but equally valid modes: drama of feeling and drama of thought, respectively. For us today, Ibsen represents a more admirable alternative in his will to truth and his ability to imagine truth—the truth of the real.

(1984)

ACTING

I was a teacher of drama before I was a play reviewer. I undertook play reviewing to learn what the library could not teach. The library offered me writings on acting in Shakespeare's day by scholars who, if they had seen much acting, had given it little thought. So I ventured, in the two *New Republic* pieces that follow, to question some of the received notions about what acting is.

NATURAL AND ARTIFICIAL

Trying, some time ago, to discover how Shakespeare was acted in his own time, I found that scholars classify acting as either *natural* or *artificial* and put Shakespeare into whichever category they prefer: Shakespeare's own principal utterance on the subject—Hamlet's advice to the players—lends itself equally well to either interpretation. Though my first impulse was to reject these categories altogether, I soon caught myself reintroducing them in disguise: *natural* reappeared as *realistic*, *artificial* reappeared as *stylized* when I disliked it and as *the grand manner* when I approved. And looking back over the history of theatre, I realized that critics have fallen into two classes: those who say acting has become so natural it lacks beauty and those who say it has become so fancy it lacks naturalness. The critic's plea is either for a return to the grand manner or for a return to reality. But this is not to say that we all stand either for one style or the other, simple or grand, natural or artificial. On the contrary, so soon as we think about it, we recognize that dramatic, like all other, art necessarily involves both imitation and selection, nature and artifice, truth and beauty. We want the right balance, so we put our own weight on the side which contemporary theatre is neglecting. To interpret Hamlet's advice correctly we would need to know whether Shakespeare's contemporaries were leaning too far toward the natural or toward the artificial: Hamlet was against the unbalance, whichever it was. *Natural* and *artificial* are not names of rival styles in acting; they are names for lack of style in acting. Acting is both natural and artificial, yet to the extent that it comes off, to the extent that it is *good* acting, it is not notably either. At this point, we seek more laudatory words. We replace *naturalness* with *reality*, *artifice* with *style*, nor would we grant that a performance had *reality* till we felt it had *style*, or *style* till we felt it had *reality*. Hence, though we can divide bad actors into two widely different schools—natural and artificial— we shall find that good actors have a great deal in common with each other. We must not be misled at finding a great actor of the past assigned by critics to the natural or to the artificial category. This, if it means anything, and if the actor was really great, means that he corrected the balance, was *natural* in counteracting excessive artifice, or *artificial* in counteracting excessive naturalness. The terms are relative. Forbes Robertson is often cited in pleas for the grand manner; he has also been called the most natural of actors. Much the same is true of Eleonora Duse. Henry Irving has become a byword for rant and artifice, yet he shocked his Victorian public with his harsh, abrupt "realism." Thomas Betterton and David Garrick were congratulated on their naturalness, but just compare their portraits with performances by actors of our current nose-picking school! To say that their naturalness had its limits is only to reiterate that they were actors.

Have good actors so much in common that we should not readily notice stylistic differences between them? Differences that can partly be described by words like *natural* and *artificial?* These are rhetorical questions, and I agree with the implied answer but think it less important than the fact that even the minimum requirements of good acting are so considerable that Burbage, Betterton, Garrick, Kean, and Forbes Robertson *must* have had more in common with each other than any one of them had with a defective, one-sided actor, natural or artificial. When a critic contrasts one actor's style with another's he is almost invariably saying that one is right, the other wrong, one a good actor, the other a bad. Thus, Leigh Hunt does not present Fanny Kemble and Edmund Kean as great actors who have little in common; he is telling us that Kemble is not great. So with Shaw on Sarah Bernhardt and Duse; he finds Bernhardt's acting faulty; those who think him prejudiced in favor of Duse's greater naturalness should read his good-natured demolition of one of the better natural actors of the time, John Hart. If you grant that good acting is neither "natural" nor "artificial," you will not find it very profitable to describe one good actor as "more natural" or "more artificial" than another: this will only be to say that good actors are not *wholly* good. Again, if you compare the relative "naturalness" of eighteenth- and twentieth-century acting, you will have to discuss what the two periods consider natural. Which in turn involves what *is* natural in the two periods. And naturalness is relative to place as well as time: a gesture that is natural to an Italian is unnatural to an Englishman . . . In short, though the word *natural* may lead us into interesting speculations, it leads away from the subject of acting; it is not a convenience but a distraction. It follows that the same is true of *artificial,* its antithesis. In a given period, the tendency of bad acting (thus of the acting profession as a whole) is "natural" or "artificial"; and the critic will be busy deploring the tendency. As for good acting, its being both or neither forces the critic, if he is to come to grips with it at all, to more specific description. For, though in transcending the natural and artificial, good actors have a technique in common, what interests us is what they do with their technique. Having come out into the clear, where do they go? Classifications a good deal more helpful than natural and artificial are no doubt possible. But more interesting for the student of theatre than the generalities are the particulars. For, once an actor has his technique (i.e., *is* an actor), his individuality shows itself. He has shed everything that passed for his personality in the days when personality meant the part of him that was accessible to his conscious mind and to the minds of fans and publicity men. He now has his personality as an artist. The one *persona* is an obstacle, the other an instrument. The critic, for his part, if he has put bad acting in its place, and knows a false *persona* when he sees it, is free to forget about styles and talk of actors' personalities. The best recorded writing about acting is sheer description of performance, and amounts in each case—I am thinking of certain pages in Colley Cibber and G. C. Lichtenberg, William Hazlitt and C. E. Montague— to a portrait of the actor.

(1952)

RECITING

Praising the Drama Quartet,[*] people are saying how nice it is to do without scenery. I do not share their implied disdain for stage design, but I am not surprised at it. What surprises me is the assumption that, when a play is read to us, nothing is missing but decor. Or does the fact that readers use gesture make them actors?

You can say yes to this, and cite the sages. Dr. Johnson wrote that we go to the theatre to "hear a certain number of lines recited with just gesture and elegant modulation." John Dryden seems not to have demanded much more: "All passions may be lively represented on the stage if to the well-writing of them the actor supplies a good commanded voice and limbs that move easily and without stiffness." And when Johnson says, "A dramatic exhibition is a book recited with concomitants that increase or diminish its effect," we know where we are. This is the notorious "literary" view of theatre, bluntly restated by a Shakespearean scholar only the other day: "In the theatre, as in the study, the poet's words are all that count." Of more interest than the untruth of this statement (whatever can be so flatly asserted can, I presume, be as flatly denied) is its motivation and background: it has its origin in the study of a theatre where the words did in fact play a much larger role. Of this theatre Bernard Shaw once wrote: "In Shakespeare's time the acting of plays was imperfectly differentiated from the declamation of verses; and description or narrative recitation did what is now done by scenery, furniture, and stage business." Anxious to restore the long speech and the "rhetorical" way of delivering it, Shaw preferred what he thought of as the older method to the newer. And his special perspective gave him special insights: his insistence that Shakespeare's lines not be broken by "business" is still called for today. But as usual—one

[*]Charles Boyer, Cedric Hardwicke, Charles Laughton, Agnes Moorehead.

should rather say, on principle—Shaw overstates the case. A fair amount of "business" is to be inferred from Elizabethan scripts, and the scantiness of stage directions cannot be taken to mean that the Elizabethans did not insert "business" even where the scripts do not infer it. Nor was the Elizabethan stage as bare of furniture and scenery as scholars in Shaw's early days thought. As for acting, we know nothing, really, of the style which Edward Alleyn or Richard Burbage practiced, though the praise accorded these men in the roles we know they played certainly suggests that they did more (for example, with *character*) than a mere reader would. And this is to speak of tragic acting only. The comedians, we know, were acrobats and dancers; speaking was but one of their several accomplishments. (For that matter, the wary Dr. Johnson admits that the "literary" view of the stage is inapplicable to comedy: "Familiar comedy is often more powerful on the theatre, than in the page; imperial tragedy is always less. The humour of Petruchio may be heightened by grimace; but what voice or what gesture can hope to add dignity or force to the soliloquy of Cato?") To these empirical remarks I would even venture to add a syllogism: all good acting has more to it than recitation, Alleyn and Burbage were good actors, therefore Alleyn and Burbage did more than recite.

The man who best helps us to see this is Constantin Stanislavsky. Many think of him primarily as the bringer of the new style—the style that works with scenery, furniture, and stage business, rather than with language; for a time, undeniably, a particular form of this style—naturalism—*was* what he stood for. What he stands for in the long run, however, will not be this style or any other. It will be his approach to acting—in any style. It will be what he has to teach *anyone* who wishes to act. He understood the minimum requirements of good acting, one of which is to put words in their place. This is not necessarily to make words less important; it is, rather, to make them more effective. The "place" of words is in the mouth of the speaker—and, beyond the mouth, in his body and mind. A stage director has to "sink" his author's words into the actors, and then help the actors, as it were, to hoist them out again. In short, words are, for actors, not statements but responses to stimuli, like gestures. We, the spectators, should not have the words simply handed to us—we should see them springing from a situation, from a character, from a query, a blow, or a snort. A minimum requirement for an actor is that he enable us to see them in this way. William Gillette called it giving "the illusion of the first time." I am not happy with this phrase, for it seems to me that much more is involved and that an actor should on occasion give the impression that a thing *has* been said before. But that the "gesture" of real speech is always necessary is certainly true. And with it goes gesture in the literal sense. Describing gesture as a "concomitant" of "recitation" may be accurate enough from an outsider's viewpoint, but anyone who has learned to act would, I think, have to approach it differently. Stanislavsky said this when it much needed saying. But actors, and teachers who trained actors, must surely have known it at all times. For the actor, it is more practical to consider the "book" as the "concomitant" and the "gesture" as the main thing, if we can a little stretch the meaning of the word "gesture" to include "posture," and the word "posture" to include the posture of the mind as well as the body. That we have to stretch the meaning of words is of course no accident. The art of theatre is poor in precise terminology; that must be one reason for confusion. But it surely makes sense to differentiate between the working actor's attitude to words and the spectator's. For the latter, the words will be predominant—if the play is of the type where words predominate. But, even with such a play, the words must become secondary for the actor as he works. He must subordinate them to the context from which they spring, or they will never gain the importance which their author wishes them to have.

Another element of confusion comes in because reciting is not the opposite of acting, it is halfway to acting. The Drama Quartet half-acted their play. Radio actors half-act their plays, as anyone knows who has watched them in the studio. Now half-acting is only successful when practiced by whole actors: what enables Charles Laughton to portray Shaw's Devil is not his practice in reciting but his practice in acting. A generation trained in reciting would not recite well. It is therefore a mistake to regard the method of the Drama Quartet as a solution to our problems. We can settle for nothing less than acting, as it was, is, and ever shall be.

(1952)

How many man-hours have been given by American actors to talk about Stanislavsky—
since his visit to New York in 1923? More than have been given to acting, we can be
sure. One cannot sum it all up nor even—though it has been tried—reduce it to a
formula. One also cannot ignore it, so what I did was write a couple of "notes in the
margin," calculated to remove a couple of common misunderstandings.

DID STANISLAVSKY KNOW ANY PSYCHOLOGY?

In his essay "Emotional Memory" in *Tulane Drama Review*, Summer 1962, and subsequently published as a pamphlet by Samuel French, Inc., Mr. Robert Lewis traces the phrase "emotional memory" back as far as 1925 and adds: "During the Group Theatre days, in the Thirties, we called it 'Affective Memory' (a term borrowed from an earlier French psychologist). But, by whatever name, it is accomplished, roughly as follows."

The name is actually given in David Magarshack's *Stanislavsky: A Life* in these words:

> Stanislavsky was struck by the fact that in his most successful part of Dr. Stockmann he had unconsciously endowed it with a number of external traits which he had observed in life and kept buried in his memory till the moment came for them to be combined in the delineation of a character with whom he felt a strong affinity. He at once realized the importance of these hidden memories, which he embodied in his system first under the name of "affective memories" (he had presumably been reading Th. Ribot's work *Problèmes de psychologie affective*) and later under the name of "emotional memories."

If Mr. Magarshack means to suggest that Stanislavsky necessarily took the phrase Affective Memory from one particular book of Ribot's, that would be a mistake, but one which the English-speaking reader might have difficulty in tracking down, for this is how the only published translation of the key passage reads. It is to be found on pages 156–67 of *An Actor Prepares* (Theatre Arts Books, 1958):

> "As for *emotion memory*: there was no sign of it today." When he was asked to explain that term he said: "I can best illustrate it as did Ribot, who was the first person to define this type of memories, by telling you a story. . . ."

However, some of us who may not be up to reading all of Stanislavsky in Russian have read quite a lot of him in the admirably complete

German translations. I will translate literally this same passage from the German edition (*Das Geheimnis des schauspielerischen Erfolges*, Zurich: Scientia, n.d.):

> "As for the memory of feelings, there was no sign of it today." "The memory of feelings?" I tried to make this clear to myself. "Yes, or, as we wish to call it, the 'emotional memory.' Earlier—following Ribot—we called it the 'affective memory.' This term is now rejected without having been replaced. But we have *some* word for it and so, provisionally, we're agreeing to call it the memory of feelings: Emotional Memory." The pupils asked him to explain more clearly what was understood by this word. "You will best understand it from the example which Ribot gave. . . ."

In short, there is no mystery at all as to where the author Stanislavsky took the term. Mystery is created only when a translator decides to leave out so much that is of interest, or when a teacher decides to relegate a distinguished scientist to the status of an unnamed "earlier French psychologist." Even Mr. Magarshack, himself a scrupulous translator of Stanislavsky, is not, evidently, so close a student of psychology or he would know that it need not have been the *Problèmes* that Stanislavsky was reading, as Ribot mentions Affective Memory in other places, some of them better known. Nor must the American reader study French to become acquainted with Ribot, several of whose books were published in English.

All this, however, does not mean that we can trace Stanislavsky's teaching on Emotional Memory back to the scientific psychologists. Even on the terminology Stanislavsky seems misinformed. It is not true that Ribot spoke exclusively of Affective Memory, and that only later writers spoke of Emotional Memory; nor is it true that, for Ribot, Affective Memory was an earlier term, Emotional Memory a later one. We find him using the former expression in the late work (1910) which Mr. Magarshack cites, whereas the phrase Emotional Memory is found more than once in such an earlier work as *The Psychology of the Emotions*. I cite the latter title in English because it was published in that language (1897) in quite a popular series, "The Contemporary Science Series," as edited by Havelock Ellis. The fact is that both terms were common currency among psychologists of the time.

So much for terminology. The ideas are quite another matter. Whether there was really such a thing as Affective or Emotional Memory was NOT agreed upon by the psychologists. Ribot himself, though inclined to accept the notion, records the doubts of his colleagues, and surrounds his own assent with such stern provisos as: "The emotional memory is nil in the majority of people." Even this debate was not quite in Stanislavsky's field, for it concerned whether people spontaneously do have emotional (as against intellectual) memories, not whether emotional memories can be induced by exercises. Ribot's answer is that *some* people have them. And he cites a contemporary man of letters as saying that women have them and are therefore monogamous while men don't have them and are therefore polygamous.

Hence, when Mr. Lewis speaks of Emotional Memory as something that is "accomplished" he is not talking about what Ribot was talking about. And when he implies that, though the *name* may vary, the *process* which both the psychologists and the theatre people have been referring to is the same, he is exactly inverting the truth. For what has happened is that theatre people have been invoking scientific terminology *for the sake of its authoritative sound:* anything with a scientific name must have a scientific basis. Once we see through this fallacy, we realize that "exercises" given to actors may not actually do the work they are supposed to do. But this is not to say they have no value. By way of analogy, take prayer. There may not be a God sitting Up There listening to it, but that is not to say the person praying feels no better for it. Some of the older actors did pray before going out on stage: and prayer was probably a better preparation than dressing-room chatter, let alone alcohol or drugs. Likewise exercises in emotional memory. They are the prayers of the age of science. As such it is doubtful if they could be improved by the study of science itself. I do not recommend Ribot to actors. Rather, perhaps, Ignatius Loyola's *Spiritual Exercises*, a book which embodies the science of the age of prayer. Ribot, for that matter, does refer to St. Ignatius's great work, and years ago Francis Fergusson introduced the topic into the discussion of the Stanislavsky system. When the news reaches the Moscow Art Theatre, Russia will perhaps get reconverted to Christianity.

(1962)

ARE STANISLAVSKY AND BRECHT COMMENSURABLE?

"How does Brecht's system differ from Stanislavsky's?" I have often heard this question asked, sometimes in exactly these words, and probably we shall all live to see the question appear in much this form on college examination papers. I recall, too, that as a young admirer of Brecht's, nearly twenty years ago, I myself described an actor in one of his plays as having gone "beyond Stanislavsky." Will the acting profession soon be divided beween Method actors and Brechtians?

Possibly it will, so far as nomenclature is concerned, and so far as the actors' declared allegiances are concerned. It is obviously possible for some actors to love Stanislavsky, others, Brecht. What I would question is whether there are indeed two systems, two ways of life, presenting the actor with an either-or choice.

At least some of the differences between what the two men said stem from the fact that they addressed themselves to different subjects: that they differed about the *same* subject remains to be proven. Take Stanislavsky's alleged preoccupation with subjective elements and Brecht's alleged preoccupation with objective elements. Brecht speaks of what is done in a finished performance. As a director, he tells actors to do what is presumably to be done "on the night." Some Method actors will protest that it is wrong of him to tell them this: he is "working in terms of results" instead of stimulating their subconscious. Some Brechtian actors will retort that theatre *is* results, that drama is action, that the notion of a subconscious is bourgeois and decadent . . . And so the issue is joined.

But it is an imaginary issue. We can sidestep it by remembering that Brecht was a playwright, Stanislavsky an actor. For Brecht, actors were the means toward the full realization of his plays. Because he had the good luck to work in a highly professional environment and with actors of very great talent, he could with reason take it that the actor's craft was simply *there* to be used. At worst, it only needed adjusting to a new kind of playwriting. At best, it could give the new playwright ideas *on* playwriting. (Some of Brecht's "theories" are deductions from the work of particular actors.) Brecht, who regarded his scripts as forever unfinished, forever transformable, and his dramaturgy as young and developing, tended to regard the actor's craft as given and as already there in finished form. He assumed that the actor in one of his shows *was* an actor, and had his training behind him, while he made a different assumption about playwriting: namely, that he was constantly giving himself an education in it. Brecht's rehearsals, while they trained the playwright, did not, in any such direct way, train the actor. This is but another way of saying that, in a playwright's theatre, the actor is there to do what the playwright says, and he better know how to do it pronto and not hold the playwright up: that's what he's paid for. For Stanislavsky, on the other hand, it was the play which was a *fait accompli.* We do not read of his reworking his scripts either in the manner of Brecht or of the Broadway directors. He was too busy reworking the actors. I suppose every director looks for clay to mold. For Stanislavsky, the clay consisted of actors; for Brecht, of his own collected writings.

I know that the antitheses I am using oversimplify. What antitheses don't? In his last years, Brecht was beginning to mold actors, beginning, in fact, to *learn* to mold actors, and beginning to talk of acting schools and the younger generation. And conversely, perhaps, examples could be given of Stanislavsky's editing and adapting plays. Such factors, however, imply only slight modifications of the point I have made. And by consequence what Brecht, in his theoretical pronouncements, is talking about is what actors, finally, can and should do, while what Stanislavsky is talking about is the question of how they may be brought to the point where they can do this or anything else. Brecht is talking about the end result; Stanislavsky about education, about the actor's training. To say this does not provide us with all the answers. Rather, it opens up new questions.

For example, did Brecht assume that the present-day actor can give him just the result he wants? Stanislavsky, it is well known, presupposes just the opposite. In his view, it is because the actors cannot produce the right results that the Method is needed and that the emphasis on education and training is justified. Hence, when the Brechtians protest that a director must not degenerate into an acting coach, the Stanislavskyites can retort: "Yes, he must—at a time when the actors are not perfected professionals but still need coaching." And indeed that our "professional" actors attend acting schools and the like until middle age testifies less to their modesty than to the fact that we do not have a profession any more. Was this not true in Brecht's Germany? Another hard and ambiguous question. I would say it was on the whole not true of the Germany of Brecht's youth and therefore that his reliance upon a realized professionality was justified. That he began to get interested in training young people after World War II represents not a change of heart on his part but a change of situation in his country. It was not to a land of well-trained Helene Weigels, Oscar Homolkas, and Alexander Granachs that he returned, and so in his latter days Brecht acquired an interest in what had been Stanislavsky's lifelong concern: the development of young people into actors.

If the generalization still stands—that by and large Brecht is concerned with getting the play produced, Stanislavsky with training the actor to be in it—would it necessarily follow that an actor trained by Stanislavsky would be a bad actor for Brecht's plays? Were Stanislavsky alive today, one can be reasonably sure he would answer this question in the negative, for it was his aim to create an instrument which could be used for *any* honorable theatrical purpose. And it is clear that he regarded this aim as attainable.

The Brechtians have their doubts—or should, if they wish to tread in the Marxian steps of the *Meister*. Stanislavsky's notion of a universally valid training and a possible omnicompetent kind of acting they will (or should) describe as bourgeois. And they will call for a more historical view of things, according to which Stanislavsky belongs to one class and one epoch, the Brechtian theatre to another class and another epoch.

Nonetheless the record indicates that while Brecht's efforts show a single direction, Stanislavsky, like Max Reinhardt, produced all kinds of plays, and could train actors to excel in each of them. In my view, this is only to repeat that he was a director (a director has to work with the whole repertoire) while Brecht was a writer concerned with writing (chiefly his own). It has been the tendency of the Berlin Ensemble to impose Brechtianism upon plays by other authors; but the results are unfortunate except when the other authors are quite Brechtian. Stanislavsky on the other hand was by no means the servant, let alone the prisoner, of one style or school. It is true that he created stage naturalism in Russia. But equally he might be said to have created stage symbolism there, by his productions of Maeterlinck and Leonid Andreyev. Given a few more years of life, would he have created a Brechtian theatre? The dangers of historical "If's" are notorious. And who would wish to overlook the obvious: that Stanislavsky and Brecht were such utterly different men—different personally, as well as in nationality? And though they both came of the upper bourgeois class—which is amusing—their relation to that class is different in quite an ironic way. Stanislavsky— prize exhibit of Stalin's Russia as he lived to be—remained genteel to the end. Acquiescent in the New Society, all that he was he brought from the old. He did not like the new Communist plays, and his theatre became a museum for the best in "bourgeois" drama. While Stanislavsky was not even a rebel against his own family background, Brecht was nothing if not just that; and his love of "the people" is pale indeed beside his rage against his own class. Hence, while it is ironic enough that Stanislavsky should be the darling of a terrorist regime, it is doubly ironic that supporters of that regime should champion him against an artist who had gone out of his way to praise Stalinist terrorism.

That part of the story would be irrelevant to my present argument except that the Communists, for their own reasons, have so handsomely contributed to the confusion that reigns concerning this Stanislavsky-Brecht relationship. In 1953, a spokesman for the German Communist Party declared Brecht's theories to be "undeniably in opposition to everything the name Stanislavsky stands for. The two leaders of the Ensemble must surely be the last people to hide their heads in the sand when faced with these facts." At that time the "two leaders" of the Berlin Ensemble were Brecht himself and his wife, Helene Weigel. Frau Weigel attended a Stanislavsky Conference (East Berlin, 1953) with the laudable aim of showing that Brecht and Stanislavsky were not as incompatible as all that. But if, as I gather, all she had to offer was a rehash of the Nine Points her husband had printed the year before in the book *Theaterarbeit,* she could only have made the confusion worse. For, like the Party leaders, the Brechts identified the word "Stanislavsky" with the word "Soviet." And one notes that the New Society is as given as any American orator on Commencement Day to orotund platitude. Stanislavsky believed in Man, Brecht believed in Man; Stanislavsky regarded Truthfulness as a duty, Brecht regarded Truthfulness as a duty; Stanislavsky had a sense of responsibility to society, Brecht . . .

When Brecht was not busy blotting himself out (like his Young Comrade) in order to be Stalin's organization man, he was apt to express hostility to Stanislavsky, as in two passages which John Willett rightly cites in *Brecht on Theatre* along with the Nine Points. In the first of these passages, the target is naturalism:

> What he [Stanislavsky] cared about was naturalness, and as a result everything in his theatre seemed far too natural for anyone to pause and go into it thoroughly. You don't normally examine your own home or your own feeding habits, do you?

In the second, the target is not only the strictly naturalistic theatre but any theatre that depends too heavily on empathy. Brecht finds in the hypnotic kind of theatre a soporific intention based on fear of the audience's intelligence: "The audience's sharp eye frightens him [Stanislavsky]. He shuts it." Such passages remind us that *Brecht knew very little about Stanislavsky* and, like the rest of the world, thought of him as the lackey of one style of theatre. If the word "Soviet" does not define Stanislavsky's general outlook, neither do words like "naturalistic" and "empathic" define his theatre as a whole.

To revert to the question of whether Stanislavsky, had his health been better and had he lived on, would have proceeded to create a Brechtian theatre, or at least to have achieved some authentically Brechtian productions, one would probably be wise to answer: No, he belonged too unalterably to the pre-1914 world. He would not have been any more at home with Brecht than he had been with the Russian Communist playwrights—or with his own rebellious sons, such as Meyerhold. The difference between generations is a difference of spirit and temper. *But this is not to say that Stanislavsky's approach to acting will have to be discarded if Brecht's plays are to be well performed.* First a man can become an actor—with the help of the Method. Then he can learn to adapt himself to different kinds of plays—including Brecht's. Is the difference between Brecht and all other playwrights greater after all than other differences which actors have already learned to confront— say, between Shaw and Shakespeare, Wilde and Arthur Miller? Brecht's assault upon the idea of Empathy and his defense of Alienation sound more threatening in their abstract theoretic grandeur than in practice they turn out to be. The "alienation effect" is not alien to the tradition of comic acting as Stanislavsky and everyone else knew it—what Brecht is attacking is the tragic tradition in its attenuated form of domestic, psychological drama of pathos and suspense. But the Charlie Chaplins and Zero Mostels* practice Alienation as Monsieur Jourdain composed prose. Perhaps it takes a German intellectual to make such heavy weather of the thing.

Incidentally, Brecht never considered that "epic" acting had really been achieved either by the Berlin Ensemble or anyone else. So there is his own authority for saying there are no Brechtian actors. Evidently *what he had was a vision of what acting might become,* given not only changes on stage, but also in the auditorium. Should that vision ever be realized, it is conceivable that Stanislavsky may prove to have been one of the contributors to it.

(1964)

*While I was directing him in *The Good Woman of Setzuan* in 1956, Mostel dropped me a note in which he was content to say of Brecht: "I knew Brecht fairly well and perhaps in an unguarded moment he expressed admiration for my work. . . . Brecht liked my personality."

POLITICS

THE POLITICAL THEATRE OF JOHN WAYNE

Twice in my life I have had a working relationship with the *Nation*, and twice it was shattered in an altercation with my editor there. The first quarrel, in the forties, had to do with high matters of state, the second, over John Wayne, in the sixties, with low matters of state. The *Nation* didn't wish me to say John Wayne was the most important person in America because *Nation* readers, I was told, would not sense that I was being ironical. Well! And was I being ironical? Wasn't I just right? Now Wayne is gone, the position has gone to his colleague, Ronald Reagan. This piece in lighter vein is also a piece in heavier vein, alas.

Mr. [Charles] Chaplin, *who retained his British citizenship during 40 years residence in the United States, left this country in 1952. James P. McGranery, then Attorney General, announced that the comedian could not re-enter this country unless he could prove his "moral worth."*
—New York Times, October 14, 1971

Showing up in Dallas to accept the Veterans of Foreign Wars Americanism Gold Medal, John Wayne said: "I have found that a peaceloving man fights if he has something to fight for. The V.F.W. represents many who died to give this country a second chance to make it what it is supposed to be—God's guest house on earth."
—New York Times, August 17, 1971

"Your generation's frontier should have been Tanganyika," he [Wayne] contends, recalling the African country—independent Tanzania now—where he made Hatari. "It's a land with 8 million blacks and it could hold 60

*million people. We could feed India with the food we produced in
Tanganyika! It could have been a new frontier for any American or English
or French kid with a little gumption! Another Israel! But the do-gooders
had to give it back to the Indians! Meanwhile your son and my son are
given numbers back here and live in apartment buildings on top of each
other."*

—*Life*, January 28, 1972

Of recent years I have repeatedly heard two things said of the blacklist in the theatrical profession. One is that it is now a thing of the past. The other is that the good guys got reinstated, whereas the bad guys, like Joe McCarthy himself, curled up and died. Happy ending. Triumph of the democratic process. And if not without tears, at least working itself out automatically and predictably: God is good.

Well, there is no denying the disappearance of those particular bad guys. To the younger generation, Godfrey Schmidt and Vincent Hartnett would simply be Godfrey and Vincent who? yet the first was president of Aware Incorporated, and the second was one of its directors as well as coauthor of *Red Channels*. In 1954 Aware called for a "full-fledged official investigation of the entertainment industry in New York" and got together with the House Committee on Un-American Activities to put it through. Where are the snows of yesteryear?

There is no denying the reinstatements and rehabilitations. Dalton Trumbo lives, and his screenplays are attributed to no one but himself. Vincent Hartnett and his collaborator, Laurence Johnson, a Syracuse supermarket owner, were sued by the blacklisted actor John Henry Faulk, who won a three-and-a-half-million-dollar libel verdict (even if he didn't collect). Pete Seeger appears on television (even if the script is censored to save face for Lyndon Johnson, the face unsavable). Millard Lampell and Lionel Stander report former privations in the *New York Times* and contrast them with present glory.

Yet one can only relax in satisfaction, or even sigh with relief, if one sees the conflict as a self-contained one between two small and rather peculiar groups: the theatrical profession on the one hand (including the term "movie and television people") and the radical right in business. This has been how the nonradical right has seen it, not to mention the center and the public at large, including many who consider themselves liberal. The moral drawn is that our system, if not always fast enough, of itself rejects such madness and restores the country to sanity—a thesis which has lost its cogency of late in that Vietnam has hardly been sanity. And Vietnam is not an isolated phenomenon but the result of strict, if horrifying, logic, all things working together for bad.

In the perspective of the sixties, a perspective still deepening and darkening in the seventies, the fifties must be differently seen, not, alas, as some kind of social measles that we had and could not have again but as a spreading virus which we still have, and have much worse. Joe McCarthy was not really a failure, any more than other martyrs. Like these others, he only agreed to take the rap, and he complaisantly allowed himself to be a guinea pig in experiments not equally successful in all directions. But the battles he lost were stages in a war which his side still hopes, not without its reasons, to win. This was not a war against the theatrical profession, nor was it, really, a war against the tiny Communist Party of the U.S.A. It was a war against the Soviet Union, the People's Republic of China, and the Third World, against all socialists who still believe in socialism and against all liberals neither enthralled nor intimidated by anticommunism. To prosecute this war it would be necessary for the United States to attack as well as defend and so, implicitly, to pass from nationalism to imperialism. Imperialism in turn implies racism, in which the United States was in any case uniquely schooled by its handling of the red, the black, and the brown.

The radical right at times let the cat out of the bag by admitting much of this, even boasting of it. Overfrank rightists tend to share the fate of McCarthy, and no one denounces them more shrilly than the main body of anticommunists, but the latter really owe the former a debt of gratitude, though it would hardly be shrewd of them to admit it. Better to accept the services of such rightists and disown them. For the new imperialism must not call itself imperialistic, any more than a member of an all-white golf club calls himself racist. There are indeed differences between the new imperialism and the old. The old was less hypocritical. The problem of the new order is: how to be hypocritical successfully, a problem not economic or military but political and diplomatic, to be solved in the communications media. Which is how it becomes the problem of those of us who write or speak or act, particularly if we do any of these things for a powerful constituency.

The most important American of our time is John Wayne. Granted that all good things come from California, Richard Nixon and Ronald Reagan are only camp followers of Wayne, supporting players in the biggest Western of them all, wagons hitched to Wayne's star. In an age when the image is the principal thing, Wayne is the principal image, and if the soul of this image is *machismo* (a topic for another essay, a topic for a book, for *the* book of our time), its body is the body politic, and its name is anticommunism.

The 1947 Hollywood hearings of the Un-American Activities Committee have never been entirely forgotten. Forgotten, however, is that those hearings would probably not have happened but for California's own Fact-Finding Committee on Un-American Activities (1941–49) under Jack B. Tenney and the Motion Picture Alliance for the Preservation of American Ideals, an organization founded in 1944 for the greater glory of free enterprise and what is now called Middle America, or, in its own words, to combat "the growing impression that this industry is made up of, and dominated by, Communists, radicals, and crackpots." It was made up of what a HUAC member called "old-time American producers, actors, and writers," and its president was John Wayne. "Let no one say that a Communist can be tolerated in American society and particularly in our industry," said Wayne on March 22, 1951. "We do not want to associate with traitors. . . . We hope those who have changed their view will cooperate to the fullest extent. By that I mean names and places, so that they can come back to the fellowship of loyal Americans. The bankers and stockholders must recognize that their investments [in the movie industry] are imperiled as long as we have these elements in our midst."

If, as Kierkegaard thought, purity of heart is to will one thing, Wayne's strength was always as the strength of ten, and his career described one consistent curve from that time forth until the day when Richard Nixon saw him on screen at the California White House and rushed out to say to the whole world that this was good old America, whereas bad new America was represented by gunmen of a different stamp like Charlie Manson, whom it seemed the president might have mixed up with Abbie Hoffman. In an age when God's son became a superstar, why shouldn't a superstar become God Himself?

Patron saint anyway. England's patron saint had slain a dragon. America's—even if camouflaged as a paper tiger—would slay all dragons. All alike had red blood, and Wayne made some anti-red movies, culminating, if that is the word, in *The Green Berets*, which was advertised with a picture showing Americans happily blowing up little, no doubt yellow, villagers. But the movies labeled anticommunist were the least of it. Motion pictures, as Nixon intuitively recognized, are by nature anticommunist, if only they are good pictures, healthy-minded, and put together by old-time American producers, actors, and writers. That they are so is the meaning of John Wayne's whole career. It is amazing that students of art and politics have ignored this fact, and even more amazing that critics of a conservative turn of mind have remained skeptical of the power of propaganda, "conservative" propaganda at that. It is all too true that the concerted efforts of antiwar propagandists have failed to prevent, let alone stop, a single war. John Wayne on the other hand, an explicit champion of pugnacity and an implicit instigator of aggression, might claim to have got wars started. Along with the statesmen of the Pentagon Papers, he is one of "the people who brought you Vietnam."

Have I made it any clearer what the blacklist was all about? Out of the thirties came a sizable red, or at least pink, minority. This minority was generously represented in our profession. If even Helen Hayes could be considered pink (and she could), you can guess how flaming red, in HUAC's eyes, were Tom, Dick, and Harry. Sociologists will find reasons for the radical enthusiasm of theatre folk, some flattering, some not— some, that is, having to do with our generosity of soul and some with our rootlessness and vagabondage.

World War II created a special situation. Soviet Russia was for the first time a political friend of the United States. It seemed all right, also for the first time, for reds to be *openly* pro-Soviet, but when the war ended in 1945, the German menace had been removed, thus leaving (from the American viewpoint) the Russian menace all over again, in fact more so, or (from the Russian viewpoint) the American menace all over again, in fact more so. Which is how it has remained. And which is what put John Wayne ahead, and started the careers of his friends and colleagues, like Nixon and Reagan. Before 1945 life had several aims, which for the common man has advantages, since he can hope to get lost in the shuffle. After 1945 it had only one aim: to combat communism. I read in the *Times* just the other day a comment on the Pentagon Papers by a member of LBJ's cabinet who said that, in occasionally disagreeing with LBJ, he hadn't meant to rock the boat, he just meant that *Vietnam might not be ideal terrain.* Life still had only one aim. And if Wayne was the icon, Nixon has long been the iconographer. It has been said that Nixon played rough, or even dirty, in the kind of opposition he offered to Jerry Voorhis and Helen Gahagan Douglas, who obstructed his first steps to power. But why not? If liberalism in that era was tainted by communism, and even chained to it, then Voorhis and Douglas were, in effect, Communists, who, in turn, are Russian espionage agents. Only a few years later—and while Hiss was still in jail—J. Robert Oppenheimer was declared a Soviet spy in so many words by a United States official who never apologized and was never reprimanded. Indeed it is characteristic of this whole era in America that many were punished for words that did no provable harm to anyone whereas others were permitted to speak with maximum destructiveness and mendacity and were not punished at all.

Conceivably, Nixon bore no ill will to Voorhis or Mrs. Douglas, nor will it suffice to describe them as victims of his personal ambition alone. They were victims of something much more important, in which I would not doubt he believes with complete sincerity: anticommunism. I have never heard that Hartnett and Johnson hated Faulk. If they did, the case would be an exception. This was no war of individuals, and if it was a war of groups, it was not a war of these groups only: all were participating in the great religious war of our age, which differs from the religious wars of the past in that the religion is only superstition or, more accurately, melodrama. Hence, an actor who fell in this war was not the victim of personal venom, nor yet of a group feud between, say, sponsors and performers. No one bore him any grudge. It was just that as a Communist—well, a pink, a liberal, what have you—he was a Russian agent, and Russian agents are always sending atomic secrets to Moscow. The minute the Russians have stolen our atom bomb they will drop it on New York, you can be sure of that.

Why did certain actors have to be blacklisted? Because they were Russian agents, as I have just proved. And why is it bad to have Russian agents strutting our stages? Because, as I have suggested, they may be making a long-distance phone call in the intermission. There is another reason, just as important in the long run, if there is a long run. We gotta keep old-time America the way it always was, and those guys (red, pink, what have you) are in the way: they must go.

I would ask the actors not to get too discouraged at the thought. After all, we often hear the argument that actors are of no political importance anyway; probably they should stay out of politics altogether; when they go in, they don't do too good. Actors, says a friend of mine, are just *children*. To this I would answer, first, that we are all just children in many respects, and I don't see that actors can claim any kind of monopoly there. Second, it is not just "going into politics" that has political importance. More important is *what an actor seems to the public to stand for.* On this point we must hand it to John Wayne that he never keeps his public in the dark. Off screen, he does not, like many liberals, hesitate to join organizations or to sign declarations. He even seeks, which is fairly unusual in Hollywood, to put his art at the service of his beliefs, and, even in his less deliberately propagandist efforts, he succeeds. As his president has acknowledged, he is a definite part of the education—or should we say conditioning?—of most Americans. If John Wayne is the artist a president like Nixon deserves, Nixon is the president a nation of John Waynes would deserve.

While some people say it doesn't matter what actors think and stand for, the Establishment knows it does matter what actors think and stand for, because actors are in the public eye, are the royalty and aristocracy of a society that still craves these things after getting rid of them, are idols in a society that has lost its gods. For "actors" read "theatre people" generally. It was always said that investigators and blacklisters were publicity hounds. They were, but not altogether wrongly. Publicity is a huge reality in our America, and our friends of the HUAC felt threatened by the publicity which attended radical activities in the theatre as elsewhere. I don't think they all believed their own mythology, which would have made Russian spies of all their opponents, yet their invention of such a mythology proves how lively their hallucinations were. Hallucinations are real. Rather than be crushed by the power of anticommunist propaganda, shouldn't we take these people at their word and retort, "You think we are important? O.K., we'll be important. To borrow a phrase from Khrushchev: We will bury you."

Around 1950 a section of the Establishment decided that the world situation was so grave America had better move anyone suspected of communism out of any responsible public position. Theatre and film artists of left-wing persuasion resisted the trend at first but, in considerable part, surrendered to it later. Before the director Robert Rossen could work again in Hollywood he had to undergo, or pretend to undergo, or hope he'd undergone, a conversion. "I don't think," he reported, "that any one individual can indulge himself in the luxury of individual morality or pit it against what I feel today very strongly is the security and safety of this nation."

It is true that none of these people ever seems to have felt these things spontaneously, but only when threatened with the loss of contracts. At the same time one has to allow for the communism of some having been as insincere as their subsequent anticommunism: people are only people. And people are various. All degrees of sincerity were exhibited. Then again the definition of sincerity is an open one, and the value of certain types of sincerity is unproven.

I am not digging up this "ancient history" to score points off anyone, but I do think the preparation for the disasters of the sixties goes further back than the Pentagon Papers, and I do think the exposures should cover material of the fifties, and perhaps earlier. The aim should be to understand our plight now, which all agree to be dire. I don't think we of the entertainment world have played a very large part either for good or evil, but some part we have played, and we owe it to ourselves to assess it. If we are not that important, we are—and this is my real point—not that unimportant either, and if a John Wayne can labor so manfully (that's the word) to prolong a certain social order, others in his profession can labor, instead, to replace it. They did so in the past, I know, but latterly I have seen them get very discouraged. One actress told me she could never again do any "signing or joining," though she agreed in her heart with many of the current causes: her back had been broken by her experience of the McCarthy era. In such an instance we see the lasting strength of McCarthyism: it works. As much as we let it. It fails to work insofar as we stop it. If some members of our profession passively suffered under the blacklist and HUAC, or even surrendered to them and the forces behind them, others did not. At least one man recanted his communism at the behest of HUAC and the FBI and then later recanted his anticommunism at the behest of his conscience. This was the actor Sterling Hayden, who wrote in his autobiography that he was "a stoolie for J. Edgar Hoover."

(1971)

The two pieces that follow were five or six years apart in my thinking, but they should appear together here, as I believe them to be entirely continuous if not entirely consistent. Together, the two pieces make up the hardest essay I ever had to write. In the first piece I was torn. I was myself both Pro and Con. The second piece is an attempt to strengthen the case Pro—in the light of what was going on at the time, namely, the Vietnam War. For further argument I might refer the reader both back to "More Than a Play?" in my *In Search of Theater*, where the Con in me was more prominent, and forward to the next piece in the present book, "Writing for a Political Theatre."

POLITICAL THEATRE, PRO AND CON

CON

One's thinking on this subject begins with the assumption that all the arts have a certain social importance. But do most members of most societies make this assumption? Probably not. So that, at the outset, the thinker finds himself in conflict with the world, and that is why what he says will be polemic rather than philosophy. But most thinking is polemical.

It is certain that one is forced into a defensive posture. One is the champion of art against the philistines. And so it comes about that, in a world that doesn't believe in art at all, art is nearly always represented, in print, as having far more importance than it really possesses. A few great artists—Plato, for instance, and Tolstoy—have refused to swell the chorus of art worshipers, but every sophomore learns to dismiss their opinions on the point without for one moment entertaining the possibility that they should have been given a hearing.

If Plato and Tolstoy were mistaken, they are mistaken in the same way as most of their critics: they overestimated the influence of art. If the artist is not as dangerous as they thought, it is because his work doesn't have that much effect one way or another. I am speaking of tangible and overt influence—social influence. Didn't "good" works like *Uncle Tom's Cabin* have much less effect on history than Tolstoy thought? Isn't the same true of works he deplored, such as his own masterpieces?

Not that these questions are dead simple. The violent emotions that many experienced when reading Harriet Beecher Stowe are certainly "effects." What I am questioning is whether such emotions played a decisive, or even a large, part in the freeing of the slaves. And if one followed up that discussion, one would have to ask to what extent these good emotions are truly good. The emancipation was itself highly ambiguous, and if Mrs. Stowe had influence at all, we should also reckon with the way in which she antagonized the enemy and helped to create the present-day Southern intransigence. If her book is useful today, it is useful chiefly, say, to a Governor Faubus, who might justly cite it as an instance of Northern incomprehension.

At that, I will stand by the position that literature is much less important, in the worldly sense, than it has usually been assumed to be. Governor Faubus can get along very nicely without Mrs. Stowe. Don't be misled by the fact that literature can *seem* to have a political importance much larger than it actually commands. Boris Pasternak, for instance, has truly become important politically, but that is not to say that his writings have political influence. For one thing, they are profoundly unpolitical writings, but what I have in mind is, rather, that the name Pasternak does not stand, in the eyes of the millions who know of him, as the author of words they have read, but as the author of words they have read *about*. America is full of people who wept when they read in the paper of Pasternak's fate but who snored when they got to page ten of Pasternak's book. So what has this incident to do with the influence of literature?

From literature and politics, let me turn to drama and politics. I have had the lucky opportunity to observe at close range the most political of all modern dramatists, Bertolt Brecht. According to him, the drama was to be nothing if not social, and in an era like our own it was to do nothing if not contribute to social and revolutionary change. Brecht was a far more gifted writer than Mrs. Stowe, yet can his contribution to history be considered any larger than hers? And, as with Pasternak, we must distinguish between the writer as a name to conjure with and the writer as mere writer. The name of Brecht was more valuable to the Communists than were the works of Brecht. Society's interest in art may be slight, yet society may at the same time accord prestige to the artist—just as one may revere a scientist like Einstein without having the least idea what he has done that deserves revering. The sociology of art should, I think, deal with such factors as these.

The theme of drama and propaganda is full of paradox. Brecht's intention had been to take art down a peg, and to model his work on science. Ultimately, his error was the usual one made by artists and critics of art: the overestimation of art. For he attributed great political importance to the theatre, an institution that has very little effect on politics. Just as one can justifiably ask of someone who prefers Russia, why doesn't he go to Russia? so one can ask of someone who prefers science or politics, why doesn't he go into science or politics? A playwright with a few notions about Galileo is never going to match the scientists on their own ground.

The sobering, and perhaps shocking, fact is that the artist has been and today remains a slave—or, if you prefer, a lackey. Communist critics have never tired of illustrating this fact with data from ancient, feudal, and capitalist society. There was always the patron, and there is still the patron today, even though his name be hidden behind that of a newspaper or a magazine or a publishing house. What we have become acutely aware of since 1930 is that Communist countries—except in the performing arts—have made matters worse rather than better. In Western society one can at least become the lackey of some rebel prince—let's say of a millonaire who supports a Communist magazine. The fates of Meyerhold and Eisenstein tell us what happens to rebels in Russia.

We should not lose sight of the fact that the rebel artist plays just as subservient a role in rebellion as his brother plays in conservation. God help any regime—and God help any rebellion—that depends heavily on its artists! They are on the whole, not a dangerous lot, as Plato thought, but a useless lot. A brutal government might logically ship them off to forced labor—as one hears that the present Chinese government is doing.

Our exploration of drama and society should begin with the realization that there has been prevalent a gigantic illusion on this subject: the illusion that the artist is characteristically the master rather than the slave. Perhaps, of course, this is the characteristic illusion of the artist—whom sheer powerlessness drives to dreams of power. The image many people have of the artist as sublime and Promethean only holds for very great artists. The average artist is not a Prometheus but a Walter Mitty.

In approaching the subject of drama and society, I address myself first to propaganda, because it is through propaganda that drama most simply can cope with society. Yet even this relatively crude subject has its ambiguities, as we have already been finding. The phrase "propagandist drama" suggests different things to different people. To most it suggests a drama that furthers social change and particularly total change or revolution. But, after all, the "other side" has its propaganda too, and plays can be written in the interests of the status quo: Shakespeare's histories are a case in point.

I am speaking of works which directly champion the preservation of the status quo, and implicitly recognize some threat to it. Works in which the status quo is merely accepted, and no alternative imagined, would not be propaganda unless we considerably extend the word's normal scope. Precisely this has been proposed by many people in the past fifty years—chiefly people influenced by Marxism. There is the slogan: Art is a weapon. And one used to hear people say—perhaps one still would everywhere except in this country—All Art is Propaganda. Such a phrase has its utility in reminding us that even classic writers of wide academic acceptance had some axe to grind. It is still a little puerile to lump together in this way Clifford Odets's *Waiting for Lefty* and Dante's *Divine Comedy*. So I will hold to the older understanding of the word as implying a direct effort at changing history, if, in some cases, only a little bit of history. For example, a work which seeks to convert you to a religion is propaganda. A work which merely presents that religion, or embodies its author's belief in it, is not. Admittedly, a person might be converted by the second type of work, and it has often been urged with some justice that propaganda is bad propaganda: the proselytizer makes fewest proselytes. But this is to comment on the limitations of propaganda, not to change the definition of it.

It is commonly assumed that propaganda is fundamentally offensive rather than defensive. That is because only its offensives are visible. If one can generalize at all in this matter, I would say that the stance of the propagandist is a defensive one, and that, if he hits, it is only when he believes he is hitting back. The starting point is a threat, real or imagined. Hitler's plot to take over the world is the dream of a man who felt persecuted. His persecutions are at once a revenge for and a forestalling of persecutions to himself, more imagined, of course, than real.

It is common, in this connection, to give the origin of the word: *congregatio de propaganda fide*, a committee of Cardinals who were given charge of propagating the faith. If we stop here, we might make shift with the positive conception of the process and the impulse that leads to it. The date when the congregation was set up tells us otherwise. It is 1622—at the height of the Counter-Reformation. What brought this, the original, propaganda into being was the threat of Protestantism. From the Counter-Reformation on, the word propaganda has kept the connotation of fanaticism, or at least zeal. It is the work of men in a tremendous hurry, which they believe is imposed on them by events. Propaganda is a weapon, and it is an emergency weapon, one to use when police methods have failed. When literature won't work, so to say, you may be forced to try propaganda. One sees writers reaching this conclusion whenever there's a war on. And always with us are people who say there's already a war on, and so the time for the use of this heavy artillery is now. "It's later than you think!" Act before it is too late! This assertion, which prompts propaganda in the first place, is nowadays its content, too. And again one would have to point to the illusion of believing that the propaganda makes very much difference. Brecht said, in effect, that you don't paint a still life when the ship is going down. He seems not to have realized that you don't paint at all when the ship is going down. A few artists *have* voluntarily given up their art in view of the urgency of a social situation, but if all artists were so consistent, propagandist art would be self-liquidating. At this point one sees that emergency art is based not only on an illusion but also on a bit of trickery. The ship is going down, and though one hasn't time to paint a still life, one has time to paint a picture of ships that are going down because the ship owners want to collect the insurance. This picture is justified by its future utility, but actually took as long to paint as a still life. If that utility is imaginary, the whole operation stands revealed as a double cheat. Meanwhile, the artist has brought painters of still lifes into disrepute, while securing automatic praise for his picture of a shipwreck on the grounds of its urgency, utility, right-mindedness and so forth.

I am giving in a parable the story of social art in our time. And don't let anyone say that it all passed away in the thirties. More to the point is that what we call here the spirit of the thirties is now strong in Western Europe, while something not unlike it is sweeping Asia and Africa. So much for what is wrong with the whole notion of propaganda in art.

I have been talking as if a work were either pure propaganda or not propaganda at all. Yet the propaganda in Shakespeare's histories has lost all its urgency and some of its plausibility, while the plays remain alive because they have the virtues of good plays of the non-propagandist sort. An author may intend a piece of propaganda, and inadvertently produce a work of art. Or he may have two separate intentions, in conflict or in harmony. It is a complex and mixed phenomenon.

One should distinguish, too, between preaching to the converted and preaching to the heathen. The original Congregation of Propaganda was dedicated to the conversion of the heathen. And a pattern of social drama that existed in the 1930s showed an irresolute person, characteristically a liberal, being forced into choosing between Communism and Fascism and choosing or failing to choose the former. Here the old reversal at the center of the plot is combined with a quasi-religious conversion. The real question—whether a person *is* forced into that particular dilemma—is begged. Propaganda was never strong on philosophy—the point is "not to interpret the world but to change it." Dramaturgically, one might say that the skill in manipulating situations which is usually applied frivolously is in propaganda plays applied unscrupulously, as by a Machiavellian or Jesuitical extremist. Certainly the type of drama that is addressed to the task of converting people seldom tries to do it by reason. If you proceeded by pure reason, you wouldn't invoke the aid of theatre in the first place: another point overlooked by Bertolt Brecht, who often thought of theatre as being as rational as a laboratory. But Brecht was consistent at least to the point of writing only one straight conversion play, *Señora Carrar's Rifles*. Since his own more characteristic type of drama was devised to deal with our modern emergency, it is curious that he gives this emergency as his pretext for reverting to conventional drama in the play I am speaking of.

Bernard Shaw has come closer than anyone else to writing plays calculated to persuade. At least we think of him as such a playwright. Coming down to cases, we perhaps have only one play to come down to, and it is only part of a play at that: the Don Juan scene from *Man and Superman.* That is a piece of persuasion if there is a piece of persuasion in all of world drama. But is it actually persuasive? By this, I don't mean, was Shaw right? I mean, even assuming he was right, are the tactics of this masterpiece calculated to win over someone who disagrees? One assumes that Shaw agrees with Don Juan. Yet he also gives the Devil his due. Don Gonzalo and Ana do not argue, but they embody parts of human life not embraced by the Don. A favorable response to the play is not likely to take the form of feeling won over. Rather, we feel we have shared a noble vision of life. And that is another way of saying we have taken the scene to be, not propaganda, but drama.

There exists a series of works which are persuasive but are not quite dramas: Plato's dialogues. I go by fairly orthodox definitions. Shift the normal definitions, as Georg Kaiser did, and Plato's dialogues can be the quintessence of drama. They certainly have many of the obvious characteristics of the dramatic form, and the death of Socrates can be presented on stage as a tragedy with very little changing of the text. Are Plato's dialogues propaganda? Again, it is, in the first instance, purely a semantic question. I have suggested that urgency—a plan for immediate, overt change—belongs to the definition. That is why I couldn't include Plato among the propagandists. That is also why practical persons call him a utopian.

Not very much writing actually tries to persuade, though quite a lot pretends it does. We are familiar with this kind of pretense from conversation and oratory. The motions of persuasion are gone through, but the audience actually envisaged is already persuaded. Before an audience of fellow Republicans, a Republican gives his answer to the Democrats—a different thing indeed from a Republican's persuading a Democrat to be a Republican. Much drama that makes controversial points relies, without ever admitting it, on the audience's prior agreement. No Broadway play about Negroes tries to persuade a conservative Southerner he is wrong. Every such play seeks to confirm the anti-Southern Northerner in what he already feels. Hence, what is called the "boldness" in the presentation calls for no boldness in the author. On the contrary it tempts him toward demagogic self-congratulation.

Is there a propagandist drama which is deliberately addressed to those who are already convinced? Under this head comes religious drama addressed to a particular denomination, or political drama addressed to a particular party. Here the issue is not the truth or untruth of the cause but only its celebration and its defense. Shakespeare put no case for nationalism in *Henry V.* He addressed his fellow nationals and fellow nationalists and called them to a feeling of solidarity—called them also to hatred of the French. The religious drama of the Middle Ages is not propagandist at all under the definition I am following, because it is not defensive. The religious drama of the Spaniards in the seventeenth century is often another matter: it is the literature of the Counter-Reformation.

In most of the liberal and left-wing drama of our days there are ambiguities. Some of it might be read as an attempt by Communists to make converts of liberals. But something like a trick, and a double trick at that, was often played. The author didn't admit to his Communism. At the same time he strongly implied that the progressive view, as currently accepted by the Party, is already acknowledged as truth by any right-minded person—so no good man really needs any converting in the first place.

The equivocation invades even the writing of professed Marxists and fellow travelers like Brecht. A certain amount of deliberate falsification was involved. For example, Brecht once wrote a scene to show that the Communists and Social Democrats continued to fight even when they were fellow prisoners in Nazi camps. On the advice of a better Communist than himself, he changed the scene to say just the opposite. The facts of the camps had not changed, but it was wartime, and the policy was a united front against Hitler. A useful lie was told; but what, actually, was its usefulness? Not, obviously, that very many people took Brecht's word for it and said: we can all sink our differences and fight Hitler. That is a supposed reason which few will accept as the real one. The actual effect was to give an impression that Marxist theory was softening in view of the fact that Bertolt Brecht no longer saw Social Democrats as the enemy.

If Brecht's plays are taken as argument, they must often be taken as arguing in a circle. What is proved at the end of *The Good Woman of Setzuan* is assumed at the beginning, and no fact is presented along the way except as exemplifying the initial assumptions.* Brecht says, "These are the facts—and look what follows from them." Anyone is free to reply, "If those were the facts, those would be the consequences. But those are not the facts." In short, Brecht really had in mind an audience of people who wouldn't question his version of the facts. There is no exploration in any of his plays of what the facts are. The truth is something established before the first line is written. The questions that arise are questions like: Will a person (his St. Joan) come to see this truth? Is a person (Galileo) strong enough to stand by this truth?

---

*But see page 177 below.

Brecht is said to have declared himself the last Catholic playwright, and certainly one remarks his tendency to write about martyrs of his faith. Doubts about the faith are seen, not as possibly reasonable differences in opinion, but as signs of personal inadequacy or outright cowardice. To make this point, Brecht attributes to Galileo views he could never possibly have held. The thesis is: Galileo held a modern progressive's view of history and even doubted the existence of God; if he didn't say so, it is because he was afraid of instruments of torture.

We have also seen in our time a revival of drama in the churches. Not much of it is propaganda in my definition, but I was surprised to hear T. S. Eliot say not long ago that *Murder in the Cathedral* was intended to be propaganda against the Nazis. His Becket was meant, apparently, as a sort of Pastor Niemöller in conflict with the state. Curious that such an intention should be revealed only years later, as in a note explaining an obscure line of *The Waste Land*. Anti-Nazi propaganda could scarcely be effective if kept such a closely guarded secret.

How effective is *any* propaganda in the theatre? I have already expressed my skepticism about propaganda generally. I can hardly waive it in this instance. What *Murder in the Cathedral* could have done against the Wehrmacht and the SS would in any event have been negligible. Persuasion, we have seen, is seldom attempted and, when attempted, seldom succeeds. With pretended persuasion, we come to propaganda drama that is really addressed to those already convinced. What can religion do for the converted—by theatrical means? and in the way of propaganda? The aim would be to fill with emotional content what may otherwise be a feebly "intellectual" tenet. You are made to feel strongly about a certain thing, and if the dose is repeated often enough, your feeling will perhaps harden into a habit. One believes this; yet one cannot measure any of the factors involved. For example, the theatre might help to inculcate patriotism, but if a theatregoer is a patriot, how can you tell how much of his patriotism actually comes from the theatre? I cannot imagine any attitude becoming socially important unless many more people than the dramatists are fostering it.

I speak, of course, from a twentieth-century background. The drama is now surrounded by radio, movies, and television. Things were different in the days when the theatre was the principal source of entertainment. Yet even then the home, the church, and the school were more important training grounds. Our Puritan forebears thought the theatre more likely to be a place where wisdom is unlearned. They had a good deal of evidence to go on.

We cast about for big claims to make. The arts seem to prompt people to grandiose pronouncements. Threatened, we make propaganda for theatre—as well as demand a theatre of propaganda. We even read in the papers that in asking some millionaire for money to build a theatre, a high-minded managing director has offered him in return all manner of high ideals. If a New York impresario wants to show us the Comédie-Française, he starts to burble about international peace, and we have visions of general disarmament resulting from transatlantic crossings.

The theme of drama and society suggests to me, in the first place, some of these big claims and, in the second place, their falsity. They can, of course, be understood. They belong to a phase of American evolution, and maybe of world evolution, in which masses of people are having their first inkling that the arts might be a good thing and might even enter their lives. I myself come of unlettered parents who, when they gave me an education, had to envisage the arts I studied on the analogy of religion. Their religion being evangelical, like most of the religion of England and America, they thought of the arts as being the way their son would do good to people, and perhaps abolish war, not to mention drunkenness. And I might confess also that, as I had been intended for a missionary of the church, I find it hard at times not to see myself as a missionary of culture.

Then there is the guilt we all feel, or have felt, at the fact that we are fiddling while Rome burns. The impulse to join Schweitzer in Africa, or Klaus Fuchs in East Germany, is felt by more people than actually do it. Many have tried to appease their guilt by saying, I will practice the kind of art that helps democracy, or that helps Stalin, or that helps God.

This making of excessive claims for art comes, oddly enough, from having too little faith in it. We search far afield for its purpose only because we cannot look it in the face. It is to gain the whole world for us, because it has lost its own soul. What worries us is the modesty, the intimacy of art as it really is: its real effects are small, internal, personal, and hard to describe or even to observe. Hence, though the purpose of the Ninth Symphony may be to introduce universal brotherhood, the chilling fact is that it has failed to do so. Shall we join the Salvation Army, which undoubtedly has more success in that direction? I would respect the man who drew such a conclusion more than the man who trumpets that our modern artists must strive to succeed where Beethoven failed.

There is a third possibility: to find what the Ninth Symphony can actually do for people—what it has done for some and will do for others. What actually happened to you when last you heard that work may seem rather a small incident compared with the invention of the atom bomb, but must you have an inferiority complex about this? The arts depend for their existence on our respect for such small incidents. The exploration of drama and society must properly start from respect, not for society, but for the individuals whom it comprises, and in the first instance, for their private experience. Second, artistic activity must be taken as a good in itself and therefore not needing justification on grounds of its utility in other fields, such as religion or politics. It satisfies a natural and not unhealthy craving. It is part of the good life. It is not suspect. It need not be on the defensive. If these two points—which are really one—are accepted, we must conclude that whatever, if anything, the arts may do for a society, they make a contribution to the life of individuals.

PRO

But aren't the arts social—and not just in the sense that society is made up of individuals? The question is unmanageably large, but it will be helpful, perhaps, to note that the various arts vary greatly in the degree of their "sociability." While lyric poetry is presumably the least social of the arts, drama is very likely the most social of them all. For a play in performance (how often we hear it!) is the fruit of a collaboration among many, and it is then presented to many more, who sit as a crowd before it and lose, in some measure, their individual identity. "Sociability" permeates theatrical life.

It is true that critics of theatre have grossly exaggerated its crowd psychology to the end of defending their anti-intellectual outlook, yet the theatre *is* sociable—even in ways they seldom mention. For example: when you wish to enjoy art alone, you read a book. You go to the theatre when you wish to enjoy it in company with someone else—not so much all those strangers in the other rows as the friends in your own party. Theatre is not necessarily a mass meeting: it *is* necessarily a gathering. There is no maximum size for an audience, but I would say the minimum is two. To relish theatre, you have to relish enjoying an art together with at least one other person. Even the critic who revels in his detachment from the audience as a whole is much influenced by his wife—not necessarily by her opinions (for he is a subtle fellow and on guard), but certainly by her smiles, her scowls, and her murmurs of, Really! Such influence is not any less when it works in reverse. The critic who hates his wife reverses the judgment that he judges her to have made.

If theatre, like other arts, feeds the inner life of individuals, more than other arts it depends for its existence on groupings, or societies, of individuals. The theatre is a society within society. And a theatre is created by persons who feel the need to create a society within society—a refuge, if you like, a haven, a little world. That is the smallest thing a theatre can be. At certain moments in history the theatre has been more. Though still physically small at these moments, it is a match for society as a whole. The people is its audience, and the life of the people is seen steadily and whole in its dramas.

Such was the miracle of fifth-century Athens or seventeenth-century Spain.

You cannot create those moments by wanting to. They were created by a confluence of many circumstances, most of them outside the drama itself. Much has been written about the changes that have come about since the seventeenth century, but it is well to recall that even before that there were few ages of great drama. Nor must we assume that the drama necessarily has an endless future. Artistic forms come and go more quickly than biological species. With these cautions in mind, let us turn to our situation today.

The world is in a troubling but fascinating period of transition between aristocratic culture and a culture that will be in some sense of the term democratic. It is surely not surprising if many features of this transition are bizarre or just plain deplorable, yet people who cite the bizarre and deplorable things nearly always assume that aristocratic culture was characterized throughout by truly aristocratic qualities. What about the aristocrats of czarist Russia? They are depicted by the aristocrat Leo Tolstoy in his novel *Resurrection*. The aristocrats of nineteenth-century England were characterized by Matthew Arnold as the Barbarians. Milton described those of the seventeenth century as drunk with insolence and wine. Mozart's life was one long indignity as a result of their callousness and stupidity.

True, those who hoped for a flowering of culture with the onset of democracy have been disappointed. They supposed that once the working man had leisure, he would take to arts and crafts; and actually he takes to automobiles and television. Some people will never recover from their surprise and disgust at this fact. That is why they either refuse to contemplate any more heartening phenomena, or hasten to "explain" them. The explaining is mere explaining away, as when one is invited to attribute the new mass interest in classical music to the personal glamour of Leonard Bernstein. And why must we cast a cold eye on personal glamour? Mr. Bernstein makes the wide public feel welcome in the halls of culture. Is that bad? On the contrary, it helps us to see that what stood between that public and the enjoyment of great music was partly a social apparatus that made them feel excluded. Opera and symphony were addressed to dowagers. The working man didn't have the right clothes for the occasion, or the right accent, or the right kind of chitchat. Invited to a concert, he could hardly be expected to feel like anything but a pariah.

Much the same is true of theatre. In America that institution is still amazingly upper class in its mores, and extraordinarily inconvenient in its prices and its schedule for anyone who earns a modest living. How true this is one only realizes fully when the prices and the schedule and the social atmosphere abruptly change, as they did on the creation of the Federal Theatre in the thirties. Millions of Americans who "never go to the theatre" suddenly went to the theatre.

It is easy to be overcome with gloom as we contemplate the recent history of what has come to be called mass culture. Indeed, stronger than all the evidence provided by writers on the subject is the sadness in the writers themselves—covered though it conventionally is by a devastating smartness of tone. But the prospects for anything good are always black. The good things were often flatly impossible until they happened—it is only afterward that they were found to have been inevitable. If we bow to what is inevitable beforehand, what we are going to get is George Orwell's 1984. Still lifes get painted by people who are determined to paint them even if they are on board ship and even if the ship is going down. Sometimes there are enough lifeboats. Sometimes land is in sight.

Alongside Broadway, alongside television, there exists a certain hunger for high art. That does not mean that art is always liked, let alone understood. But one would have to be a fanatic pessimist to assert that it is uniformly disliked and misunderstood. Those of us who have a professional interest in culture are inclined to let our irritation at modern vulgarities blind us to any concomitant achievement. We are acutely aware that many of the classical phonograph records that are bought are not really listened to but are used as a background to work or conversation. We are less inclined to concede that some listening does occur. We note the incongruous context of classical paintings when they are reproduced in *Life* magazine. We overlook the fact that a serious interest in painting might stem from a reading of *Life* magazine.

Or consider the notorious bad taste of the large public. One form it takes is that of a naive earnestness which leads it to consider the latest domestic drama on Broadway as just as profound as Ibsen or even Shakespeare. Lionel Trilling recently made a cutting remark about the dramatists who write these plays of modern life. It was to the effect that he studiously refrains from seeing their work. The remark was a deserved rebuke to the pretentiousness of certain playwrights and to the ignorance of such devotees of theirs as do not know that the same sort of thing has been done much better by others. A play like *Death of a Salesman* gets to be taken more seriously than it deserves to be.

Mr. Trilling, I gather, sees the public's undiscriminating earnestness as a wholly negative factor and has proposed as a sort of alternative a light comedy called *Two for the Seesaw.* Here I believe his sophistication has betrayed him. The fact that he will see or read so few Broadway plays has permitted him to believe that *Two for the Seesaw* has considerable distinction. It really hasn't. Such items abound on the Broadway program, and when you've seen three, you've seen the lot. More important, the earnestness which Mr. Trilling rejects out of hand is not all bad. At bottom it is a demand for high seriousness and as such not only a good thing but a supremely encouraging thing to anyone with the interests of high theatre at heart. It is because this demand is imperious—because the public will not take No for an answer—that something has to present itself as Highly Serious several times every season. Much is passed off as sublime that is in fact only earnest— something that no one has failed to notice who has given Broadway more than a cursory look. The public, as is well known, is likely to find *Death of a Salesman* just as noble and profound as *King Lear*. The invalidity of this proposition has prevented critical people from seeing the corollary: *King Lear* is just as noble and profound as *Death of a Salesman*—in other words, the mass public has nothing, finally, against *King Lear*, but is willing to be as moved and impressed by it as by a much more easily accessible modern work.

In the cultural revolution that is under way all over the world, the theatre could play a leading part. Most of music and painting is inaccessible except to people of a certain training. The same is true of poetry. Fiction is a little more approachable. I know people who left school at thirteen whose reading for pleasure embraces most of Tolstoy. But the drama—not in its printed form, but on the stage—is the most accessible of all high arts. That fact seems to me to give it a certain responsibility. And here I do not have in mind a drama that is in any intentional or overt way didactic. I am thinking, rather, of plays that speak to the heart. But then all good plays speak to the heart, not least those of the supposedly cerebral playwrights, such as Shaw. The masterpieces of dramatic art may have subtleties in them that it takes generations of scholars to decipher. They certainly have a characteristic that is far more important socially: they are emotionally powerful, and their principal emotions are such as make an immediate impact on a crowd. I think one might even say that the subtleties are at the periphery and that the center of each great drama is a certain simplicity. I do not, of course, mean superficiality, but rather that inessentials are so fully eliminated that we face an elemental and universal subject in its nudity. In this sense, the story of the Crucifixion is simple as told in the Gospels, even though men still disagree as to what it means.

One of the most sophisticated of modern plays is Pirandello's *Enrico IV*, and much has been written of its philosophy. At the core of the play, however, is something that all men feel keenly about: growing old. This is a play about a man of forty who clings to the image of himself at twenty. That is to say, this is a play about Everyman. Writing for a literary magazine, you assume that this fact is clear to all and you proceed to argue about the philosophy; and many writers for literary magazines come to identify the nonobvious with the essential. A theatre audience does the opposite, and is less wrong. It has a better starting

point for judgment: with the primary emotional experience. *King Lear*
may contain all manner of Elizabethan lore concerning kingship for
scholars to talk about. But if they have not started from actually feeling
what Shakespeare says here about fathers and children, they have not
started from the center. A public that picked up the points about parents
and children would have responded more properly to the play than one
that picked up points about Elizabethan culture. And that is under-
stating my thesis, for it is not really a matter of points to be picked up,
but of spontaneity versus sophistication.

As for great drama, I am saying something even simpler: that while
there are barriers between it and the great public, these barriers can
often be broken down by the fact of theatre, the act of performance.
And that without any jazzing up or deliberate popularization. Literary
people complain that in performance the subtle passages whiz past before
one can take them in. For nonliterary people that is an advantage. A
play whose value lies in the subtlety of separate passages is not a popular
play. Nor have any plays of that sort ever been considered great. When
a subtle play is popular it is because behind the subtlety lies a human
simplicity, a limited number of universal and powerful emotions. People
will tolerate any amount of subtlety provided they can ignore it, and
they can ignore it with pleasure if they are borne along by even one
unsubtle, strong emotion. In the theatre, who ever notices that the
first act of *Hamlet* contains much more information than we can retain?
We are preoccupied by the one, simple, central situation: the death of
the father, the remarriage of the mother, the desolation of the son, the
appearance of the father's ghost.

"Theatre," notoriously, is mostly mass entertainment of low artistic
quality. Some mass entertainment is of high artistic quality—one thinks
of some of the comedians who have been the darlings of the modern
masses—but, by and large, the artistic theatre is a thing apart for people
with not only an education but a special interest or hobby. This apartness
implies a division in modern society as a whole and has been widely
discussed in such terms as highbrow and lowbrow. The discussions are
unpleasant. Both high and lowbrows have ferocious champions, and
the middlebrows, as becomes them, have milder ones—or perhaps only
snider ones. No real discussion is possible because the statements of
the various teams imply accusations that are also insults. The champion
of the highbrows implies that his opponents have no taste. The champion of the lowbrows implies that his opponents are undemocratic—
the most violent epithet in the American vocabulary.

I have contributed on the highbrow side to this polemic. But the
returns are not all in. Much has yet to be learned about the nature of
popular taste, as also about the possibilities of so-called highbrow theatre
among those presumed to be lowbrows. When this kind of theatre was

suddenly made available in America at prices the mass audiences could pay, and in places where the mass audience lives, the mass audience attended the theatre and paid. I refer again to the Federal Theatre. Jean Vilar has been having "highbrow" successes with huge popular audiences in France, and has also been making discoveries about popular predilections. His audiences like best the plays which are not of the type known as popular. They like the plays they are supposed to dislike. A prime instance is Kleist's *Prince of Homburg*. Frenchmen don't like Germans, especially not Prussians, and especially not Prussian Junkers; but Kleist was a German and a Prussian and a Junker and suddenly this play of his, considered in German to be esoteric, appeals to a mass audience in France. I should add that it was produced with the greatest possible austerity—that is, quite without all the devices of deliberate "popularization." Another case in point is that of Paul Claudel. To the Communist press, he is a Catholic apologist, and the working-class audience in France is powerfully influenced by the Communist press. Claudel's style, furthermore, is what an English critic has called Mandarin—it bears all the marks of the highbrow caste. Yet the plays of Claudel have been captivating mass audiences in France.

Various conclusions could be drawn. What occurs to me is that, though the motive of going to the theatre is "to be entertained," a great deal more than entertainment may be painlessly added. The common man's demand not to be bored is a reasonable one. But once you have succeeded in not boring him, you have indeed "captivated" him: you can do what you want with him and he may even approve. For it is possible that, once relieved of boredom, even the least artistic person wants to be treated as a work of art will treat him. After all, it is not necessarily the substance of a great work that the public fears. People who cannot read Racine may just be scared of verbiage—look at the endless lines, lines, lines! The passions which are the real substance of Racine are not rejected—they are unperceived.

Despite the movies, radio, and television, there is still a lot of interest in the theatre. Indeed, it has never conclusively been shown that this interest has declined. Losses in one respect seem to have been recouped in another.

I want to make a suggestion which is almost practical. Leaving alone the kind of theatres we already have, I think it is desirable to add to them certain theatres in which great drama is produced for popular audiences. This has already been attempted more than once, but in most cases there has been what I have just called deliberate popularization. That is, the producers did not trust to the primary emotions of the classics—or their great universal themes—to put the material across. They relied on external devices, and particularly on the red pencil. The text was cut to ribbons, and what was left was arbitrarily modernized. If, before bringing a classic before the public, you convert it into just another modern entertainment, what point are you making? That the public doesn't like the classics? Quite often, for that matter, the public hasn't taken to the modern improvements.

You can set a Shakespeare story in present-day Texas or Edwardian England, but you cannot thereby hide the tameness of tame acting. Conversely, if the acting is not tame, it does not need such external aids to success.

Yet how often our failures are misinterpreted! "Shakespeare won't 'go' even when you give 'em Texas costumes"—et cetera. It has not occurred to people who say such things that the Texas costumes might be worse than a waste of money—that they might positively hamper the show. But I don't wish to make much of even that possibility. Even with Texas costumes Shakespeare could be well acted and so win its audience. I am saying we should place our faith in the power of the writing and the power of the acting. My almost practical proposal, then, is for the creation of troupes which will perform the classics for popular audiences but will address themselves wholly to the best possible performance, ignoring entirely what is called popularization. I think my point has already been granted in the realm of music. Any good conductor would give the same performance of the Ninth Symphony before a mass audience that he would give before fellow musicians. He would see no alternative to just doing his best.

What of dramatic literature? That propaganda falls far short of its objectives—we are speaking of the propaganda of artists, not of politicians and advertising men—is no reason why an artist should not be moral, or even didactic. It is not even a reason why he shouldn't write propaganda if that's what he wants to do—a comment I make uncynically, meaning thereby that, ultimately, artists do what they can't help doing, whether it works or not. In any event, an artist cannot give up regarding himself as the conscience of mankind, even if mankind pays no attention.

Will what we have all called the Social Drama have a future? First it should be established what we have—or should have—meant by the term. If, as is sometimes said, all drama is social, then the expression has indeed no value. Nor is there much more point in using the word "social" as an accolade and awarding it, as Arthur Miller does, to all the plays one approves of. It makes more sense to reserve it for its usual application—that is, to plays which are, in their main emphasis, political, sociological. The Germans have a term, *Zeitstück*, for a play that tries to cope with a problem of the day. A leading playwright, I believe, might be expected to cope with *the* leading problem of the day. It will, of course, be of the highest interest *what* he considers that problem to be.

There exists the possibility that the leading problem of the day cannot be coped with at all—at any rate by playwrights. One of our playwrights has, in fact, taken the position that it cannot. "The world of today," writes Friedrich Dürrenmatt, "cannot be envisioned because it is anonymous and bureaucratic. . . . Creon's secretaries close Antigone's case." And yet Dürrenmatt writes plays, and these plays do present what the author quite evidently intends as an image of the characteristic reality of our time. The essay I have just quoted from also contains this avowal: "Any small-time crook, petty government official or cop better represents our world than a senator or president. Today art can only embrace the victims, if it can reach men at all."

A rejoinder to Dürrenmatt's essay was written by Brecht himself. Brecht said the world of today could be mirrored on stage if it was presented as alterable. Such was the softened version he gave in 1955 of the belief he had held since 1928 that a playwright could present life in our time only with the help of Marxism.

Both playwrights need the formula: Today art can only . . . Both make, in effect, the statement: "On the face of it, the world of today simply cannot be got on to a stage. And yet it can: with the help of *my* philosophy." Since both of these dramatists have written social drama of some distinction, one could argue that both are right—and that perhaps a third playwright could turn the trick with a third philosophy. Which amounts to saying that both are wrong, and that it was not the rightness of the philosophy in question that wrought the miracle. *Mother Courage,* to take an example, is one of the best social dramas of the century. Marxism enabled Brecht to state in this play that war is the continuation of capitalism by other means. But is it this statement that interests any admirer of the play? Is it this statement, even, that makes us feel the play is burningly relevant? On the contrary, it is the fact, admitted by all philosophers and nonphilosophers, that war has become the supreme problem of our society. When the play urges that simple fact, it speaks to the whole audience. When it links that fact to a particular sociological theory, it speaks to theorists—in the gray language of theory. Both Brecht and Dürrenmatt seem to tell us that it is as doctrinaires that they will survive. Their plays tell us another story.

The problem of poverty is now eclipsed by the problem of atomic war; nor can most of us agree that the two problems are one. A new orientation is called for; one can even see it coming. In its 1959 Christmas issue, the socialist *New Statesman* featured a cartoon in which the stable of Bethlehem cowered beneath a super-store selling television sets and streamlined cars with fins. A board read: We Never Had It So Good. Now when a radical cartoonist protests, not against poverty, but against prosperity, a landmark has been reached in the history of radicalism. At this point much of the old social drama becomes obsolete.

Not just the drama of the virtuous poor versus the wicked rich. Although war remains an issue, has in fact become *the* issue, many of the old war plays are obsolete. There is a theme in Brecht's war plays, including *Mother Courage*, that is as dead as a doornail: the theme of jingoism, the idea that what endangers the peace is the gleam of swords and the glamour of uniforms. The illusion that war is fun has gone. The only sword that now has symbolic value is the sword of Damocles.

And yet *Mother Courage* has a validity, which stems, not from "Das Lied vom Weib und dem Soldaten," but from the direct portrayal of a devastation distinctly similar to that of Hiroshima. Which is to say that the valid part of this "social drama" is not optimistic; but there is no need to describe it as pessimistic either. We have to do here with a vision of horror which is a vision of truth and therefore necessary to any sane outlook, stormy or serene.

Atomic explosion: there will be plays about what it means to live under this particular mushroom. We must expect a literature of terror and defeat, which is to say, of nihilism. Insofar as the artist in our time simply sits and broods, he will write *Waiting for Godot* and *The Chairs*. Is sitting and brooding satisfactory? Is it even preferable to Stalinism? (The question, for Brecht, for instance, was not a rhetorical one.) And yet: what else is possible? A few years ago men hoped to remake the world. Nothing short of that seemed worth exerting oneself for. Now we would be happy to stop the world from destroying itself. Do we think we can? And do we really want to?

To ask such questions is to realize that while war is the immediate problem, the ultimate problem is: what would we do with peace? A generation ago the liberal movement answered: "Feed the poor. Whatever is done about freedom, let the poor be fed." Sometimes the poor were fed; and always freedom was sacrificed. The reorientation that is at hand today will entail placing the question of slavery and freedom again at the center of liberal (radical, revolutionary) activity, especially intellectual activity. For, as Camus said in Stockholm, "the nobility of our calling will always be rooted in two commitments . . . the service of truth and the service of freedom."

The literature of freedom—our generation's literature of freedom—began as a response to a situation not unlike that of today. As the whole world now lives trembling beneath the shadow of a bomb, so Frenchmen of the Resistance lived from 1941 to 1945 under what seemed the shadow of final Nazi victory. The literature of what may then have seemed a special situation has now become the literature of the universal situation. As certain Frenchmen in 1942 had to regard the future as black, yet fought, regardless, against enslavement, so the writer today, unable to see through that mushroom cloud to the light of the sun, can proclaim his faith in that light, can struggle toward that light.

(1960)

AFTERTHOUGHT, 1967

When the avowals of the first part of this essay gave offense—as they did both to pro- and anticommunist readers—I realized that this was because the second part does not meet the arguments of the first point for point, does not, perhaps, even balance the first in weight of logic and evidence. I knew I would have to give the whole subject further thought and proceed to conclusions which, in 1960, I had not reached. Such conclusions are to be found below in the essay "The Theatre of Commitment."

Oddly enough—if it really is odd—in that essay I take a position that is haughtily dismissed in the first part of the present essay without being vindicated in the second: namely, that "propagandist" literature can be not only healthy and inevitable (as is conceded), but also useful and even politically necessary. It is not that one's philosophy of literature changes of itself: my respect for the great body of art which is not propagandist is undiminished. It is a matter of events outside literature. "Urgency" is not to be swept aside as the Con part of me swept it aside in this essay. Also, I think even the unpolitical poetry of, say, Robert Lowell will be the more vital because of the commitment he made to the Vietnamese people in 1966.

"The illusion of believing that the propaganda makes very much difference": if my Con spokesman was to bandy phrases like this, my Pro spokesman should have reminded him that even to make a very little difference can be a very big achievement, necessary to a social cause as well as to one's personal honor.

THE THEATRE OF COMMITMENT

A recent literary conference announced its topic as Commitment or Alienation. I take this to mean that the public relations men believe, first, that these words are the great eye-catchers of the moment and, second, that they represent alternative ways of life for artists today. The Committed artist is one who is publicly protesting against American policy in Vietnam; the Alienated artist is one who is sitting the war out and waiting for Godot in sulky solitude. Artists who are following any other line of action or inaction simply aren't "with it."

I start with public relations because that and not the garden of Eden is where things nowadays do start. Also, public relations sheds its aura of unreality on the whole topic, and it is hard to get at the reality without first dispelling the aura. Further, public relations has its own dialectic. Beginning by flattering a subject, lending it importance by means of a glamorous terminology, it ends by throwing suspicion on it, and all persons connected with it. Take the observation I have just made that—once we have uttered the words Commitment and Alienation—artists following any other line of action or inaction would not be considered "with it." This means that, once these words are published, with capital initials, they impel artists to declare themselves Committed or Alienated lest they find themselves in outer darkness. To say this is to impugn the motives of all the committed and all the alienated: nothing is involved, it is suggested, but the desire to be in the swim.

Naturally, in any social movement, there is much mere fashion-following. "I will join if you will, and you will join if the neighbors are joining or if those you look up to think it chic to join." But this situation is not what I am calling attention to. I am calling attention to the way the situation is now exploited by the publicity racket. They need labels to attract attention. They intend a compliment by using them. But the final result is an insult to the thing labeled.

It makes no difference, by the way, that the public relations men are often employees of colleges and universities. And of course it is often the case that they don't regard themselves as public relations men. Their official titles may be president, dean, or plain professor.

Take symposia on television, especially so-called educational television. It all begins with the commendable desire to get the best men, and the modish topic is assumed to be what will attract them, not to mention the public. Commitment. Alienation. Theatre of the Absurd. Theatre of Cruelty. Half a dozen celebrities are brought before the cameras. An academic public relations man mediates between them and the attendant masses. Much smiling. Not much thinking. The millions have heard of Theatre of Cruelty, and it is concluded that there is a Cultural Explosion. (What an apt expression the phrase Cultural Explosion is—suggesting as it does some cultural equivalent of Hiroshima and Nagasaki.) The trick is this: the public is to think the half-dozen celebrities were brought before the cameras for some lofty, cultural reason; if no such reason is apparent, that is because culture is a mysterious business. Actually, the purpose of the whole thing was merely to bring half a dozen celebrities before the cameras. In educational television, that is a self-justifying act. And on commercial television it is justified, if not by itself, then by the increased audience for the commercials.

I have accepted the word Commitment for my title because I am not willing to have it relegated to television symposia and Sunday supplements; more than a mere fashion is involved. Behind the current discussion of Commitment is the perennial discussion as to whether art should teach or give pleasure. Of that discussion I would only observe here that it is full of paradoxes, and inevitably so, since to be taught can itself be a pleasure, while, conversely, to be given a pleasure may also be to be taught something. Over the course of Western history, the didactic view of art has predominated. Aristotle took the view that the purpose of poetry is pleasure but, on the other hand, he divided pleasures into higher and lower; and one man's higher pleasure is another man's edification. Also, Aristotle said that the most pleasurable thing of all was the learning process.

Perhaps the relevant question for us is why this subject has become urgent again in the past hundred years. For this period has produced not only the doctrine of Commitment but the theory which stands at the opposite pole—the name was not Alienation originally, but Aestheticism, Art for Art's Sake. The idea was to keep art pure from the world's vulgarity, and that vulgarity was seen as covering a great deal of territory. The pure artist is not a philistine, nor a politician, he is not even a man of ideas. Instead, he "walks down Piccadilly / With a poppy or a lily / In his medieval hand." The Pre-Raphaelite image of the artist became dated long ago, but just the other day a British poet protested against all the Commitment in modern England with the remark that he thought poets should be nightingales, and one of the great efforts at tragedy in twentieth-century drama—Hofmannsthal's *The Tower*—has as its subject the losing fight which in our time the artist puts up to preserve his human purity. Wallace Stevens said, "In the conflict between the poet and the politician the chief honor the poet can hope for is that of remaining himself." So strong was Mr. Stevens's commitment to non-Commitment.

Wallace Stevens's words could be taken another way. Everything depends on time and place. Suppose we heard that the two Soviet writers who recently went to jail had said, "In the conflict between the poet and the politician the chief honor the poet can hope for is that of remaining himself"? We would then find the pronouncement utterly political and conclude that the speakers were committed to liberalism. Similarly, what some consider the aestheticism of Pasternak was an active anti-Stalinism. We have grown used to conceding that silence is an act, and an act of cowardice, when speaking out in protest might do some good. We have to concede also that silence is an act, and an act of courage, when speaking out in conformity and flattery is expected of one. The "aesthetic" Pasternak withdrew into his "ivory tower"; was silent for a long time; then came out with highly "aesthetic" poetry and fiction. This sequence indicates a Commitment, a protest against politics that itself implies a politics.

It was not only with the generation of Stevens and Pasternak that aestheticism came to be a form of Commitment. We see something parallel in the life and creed of Oscar Wilde. Wilde said art was perfectly useless. He meant that he didn't want art reduced to the role of little moralistic mottoes on Auntie's mantelpiece. He was attacking the exploitation of art by a narrow and philistine utilitarianism. He actually considered art the most useful thing in existence, so far as the good life and the making of a good world are concerned. Only, since art itself provides an image of the good life, and the world an image of the bad life, he wanted the world to learn to be useful to art, not art to be useful to the world. He was the most committed of men. He not only preached anarchistic socialism; his parading of the aesthetic way of life was his form of direct action. As an anarchist he refused to leave the changing of the world to history and to movements and insisted on creating a small new world wherever he personally trod.

Am I arriving at the conclusion that all artists are committed? Well, all serious authors are; but that is not what is meant when we speak today of Commitment with a capital C. We mean a political Commitment. And we do not only mean that an artist has political views; we mean that his political views enter into his art.

Translators of Sartre have been explaining that the French word "engagement," which they render as Commitment, has two implications: first, that one is involved in politics willy-nilly; second, that one voluntarily accepts the consequences of a particular political stand. Uncommitted writers are those who don't concede the willy-nilly involvement or who don't concede that it makes any difference. They also are apt to reject a particular political stand on the grounds of its unpleasant attendant circumstances. By declaring allegiance—the Uncommitted are quick to complain—you make yourself an accomplice of the crimes and errors of your leaders and associates. Committed authors retort that the Uncommitted are accomplices of the crimes and errors of whatever leaders they have merely acquiesced in. Inaction is also a moral posture. Being in the world at all entails complicity. The Uncommitted consider themselves innocent because they have not done certain things. That their abstention from these actions may have had terrible consequences is something they *won't* consider. That their non-abstention may have been indispensable if the good was to result is something else they won't consider. The Committed say with Sartre in his letter to Camus,

> To deserve the right to influence men who struggle it is first of all necessary to take part in their struggle; it is first of all necessary to accept many things if one wishes to try to change several of them.

Sartre's play *Dirty Hands* is the classic presentation of this point. Its main message, surely, is that we have to be willing to get our hands dirty; that is, bloody.

Is the literature of Commitment by definition on one political side rather than another?

That is a historical question, and speaking historically one would have to answer it in the positive. Relative to the general social situation, the literature of Commitment is radical. It is a literature of protest, not approval, of outrage, not tribute. This proposition is only reinforced by the fate of attempts to disprove it in practice. There was a Jesuit play written to defend Pius XII against Hochhuth's *The Deputy*. That is a doomed kind of project, whatever the talent of the author, because the roots of the Hochhuth play are in a sense of outrage preexisting in the playwright and other people. Saying they shouldn't be outraged is beside the dramatic point. If the counterplaywright should succeed in presenting a Pius who is not outrageous, he will thereby be producing a play that is not dramatic.

You could have a viable play against J. Edgar Hoover, but not one in favor of him. The Commitment of literature could easily be to Robin Hood, less easily to the sheriff of Nottingham.

Again, you can be for Goliath against David. In politics, today, that is called being pro-American. But Goliath cannot find a literature of Commitment to back him; David always could—only in fact from that literature do we know his story. Poor Goliath!

In the 1930s the Commitment of many writers was to anti-Hitler literature. It is true that certain writers supported Hitler, and that some of them attempted to produce a literature of Commitment in support of the Führer, but they got nowhere, for essentially what Hitler wanted was sycophancy. Failing that, he would settle for . . . Art for Art's Sake.

Take the theatre. After 1933 the radical German authors couldn't be performed any more. But this did not mean that the theatres were flooded with Nazi plays. There weren't enough Nazi plays to make a trickle, let alone a flood. The German theatre chiefly stages classics, and continued to do so in the Nazi period. The classics had suddenly become all the more necessary. And so the Nazi regime cherished the classics, at any rate when the classics had no offense in them—that is, when they were pure; that is, when they were apolitical. So Art for Art's Sake had a second lease on life—with a second, somewhat revised significance.

It would seem that Art for Art's Sake is very often what the Attorney General's office calls a *front* for other activities. In Oscar Wilde's case, it was, if you insist, a front for anarchism. In the case of the Germans of a generation ago, it was a front for Nazism and made a special appeal to the German cultured philistine who likes his art noble, archaic, and reassuring. Such was the "reaction-formation" following upon a great era of uncomfortable modernism. It is remarkable, but, in that era, going to a Mozart concert could be a gesture directed against the "Jewish conspiracy in world music" (that is, Schoenberg or, if you prefer, Kurt Weill).

What about Alienation? It is not my subject, but if it can be journalistically touted as the opposite pole from Commitment, it may have some place in a discussion of the latter that would like to be dialectical or at any rate not one-sided. The term was taken by Marx from Hegel, and applied to the divorce of the laborer from the fruits, and from the significance, of his labor. From there it has declined—in recent years rather sharply—into signifying merely the younger generation's feeling that it has been left out of things by its parents and teachers. That the term Alienation popularly has this rather unsubtle meaning only makes it the more surprising that Commitment should be popularly regarded as its opposite. When there is a relationship between the two, it is surely not of opposition at all but directly temporal and causal: *after* being Alienated, and *because* one is Alienated, one the more readily Commits oneself. I am, of course, thinking now of the American youth who passes from merely negative revulsion against parents and teachers into espousal of a cause. But that is such a simple and old and well-known sequence that the big words, ponderously if lovingly translated from the revered German and French respectively, are not needed to describe it.

Do the terms Commitment and Alienation serve to describe the two current ways of writing drama? At any rate, if someone said they did, one would know what plays were being referred to. The Committed playwrights are Brecht, Sartre, the social playwrights of modern England, such as John Osborne, and the new generation of German playwrights, such as Rolf Hochhuth, Peter Weiss, and Martin Walser. The Alienated playwrights are those otherwise coming under the rubric Theatre of the Absurd: Beckett, Ionesco, Genet. Peter Weiss's *Marat/ Sade* might even be seen as a battleground on which the armies of Commitment and Alienation fight it out. In which case, was Peter Weiss himself Committed or Alienated when he wrote that play? There has been fierce debate on the point, and this again makes me wonder if the terms must be used antithetically. No doubt not all persons seen as Alienated must also be seen as Committed? If a Commitment, as I have suggested, properly implies a radical protest, then it is not likely to be made except by those who have already made a radical break. And what we call making a radical break could also be seen as a process of recognizing that a break has already occurred: one was alienated, one was repulsed and rejected, and, knowing it, one rose up, a rebel against the alienators, against the alienating society. I am now trying to give the words back a little legitimate dignity so that they might again refer to something more than adolescent tantrums and sulks.

The alienation Marx spoke of is reflected in the literature of the epoch he spoke of and the epochs that have followed. That is well known. Nonetheless, pure alienation would not produce art at all. The absolutely alienated worker is a desolate, a spiritually annihilated creature. He can only either languish and die or let rage give him back a portion of his humanity and rise in revolt. After the revolt, alienation will be ended in this world; and even before the revolt, it has been mitigated, rendered less complete, by revolt itself. Literature, for its part, may express and dramatize alienation in images unutterably blank and painful, yet it is exposed to the paradox that the act of doing this is not itself blank and painful. The writer takes pleasure in expressing alienation, and his audience takes pleasure in responding to the expression. Any "literature of alienation" is therefore a partial conquest of alienation, just like the fighting worker's efforts on the barricades.

In Samuel Beckett, the positive, or non-alienated, element is not limited to factors one could isolate as purely technical or purely aesthetic. His work also has features which show moral conviction and, second, revolt. Godot may not be coming, but that does not diminish our moral approval of the two tramps who kept their appointment. The philosophy is firmly stoical, and the humor of the whole proceeding suggests cool defiance.

Is this to say that Beckett is not Alienated but Committed? Not under the definition I am using, which insists on political Commitment. But could not *Waiting for Godot* be political theatre all the same? When Jan Kott was asked, What is the place of Bertolt Brecht in the Polish theatre? he answered: "We do Brecht when we want Fantasy. When we want sheer Realism, we do *Waiting for Godot.*" The most apolitical of writers—as we have already seen—can become political in given political circumstances. To be apolitical may indeed be to take a political stand, just as—notably in Poland—to be religious may be to take a political stand. And so it has been the paradoxical destiny of *Godot* to express the "waiting" of the prisoners of Auschwitz; as also the prisoners behind the walls and barbed wire of Walter Ulbricht; as also the prisoners behind the spiritual walls and barbed wire of totalitarian society generally; as also the prisoners behind the spiritual walls and barbed wire of societies nearer home. And there is no doubt a lesson in the fact that these things had not really ever been expressed in works that tried to express them more directly. As A. Alvarez has written in *Commentary:*

> The real destructive nihilism acted out in the extermination camps was expressed artistically only in works like Beckett's *Endgame* or *Waiting for Godot,* in which the naked, unaccommodated man is reduced to the role of helpless, hopeless, impotent comic, who talks and talks and talks in order to postpone for a while the silence of his own desolation.

But this is to put it too negatively. Estragon and Vladimir do not only wait. *In* waiting—the original title is "*En* attendant Godot"—they show human dignity. They have kept their appointment, even if Godot has not kept his. A lot of comment on Beckett has gone wrong in taking for granted that Godot will not come, but hope does spring eternal, and even Auschwitz prisoners hoped to get out. In this element of hope lies the politics of the play. Without it, *Godot* would be antipolitical, inviting its audience to lose itself in complete despair or to seek redemption from despair outside the world depicted (presumably in the other world of religion).

Many a play acquires urgency through special circumstances, and one should think of political drama less in terms of the script alone than in terms of when and where it is presented, not to mention how.

What I have said up to now is essentially about literature in general, or about drama as literature, but there exists a drama of Commitment which is not just another instance of literature of Commitment. It is *theatre,* and puts its message across in a special way, a way that is perhaps especially suitable to the purposes of a Committed author. It also differs from other forms of drama, and especially from the traditional patterns of tragedy and comedy. Let me again—and this time at some length—cite *The Deputy*.

A priest was quoted in the press as saying that it would all have mattered so little if only *The Deputy* had not been a play. This comment suggests, more than anything one is likely to read in dramatic criticism, that a play can somehow both focus and enlarge discontent. Books have been written on Catholicism and the Nazis, some of them with a viewpoint similar to Hochhuth's, and one more such book would make little difference. *The Deputy* made a big difference, so we are authoritatively informed, *because it is a play*. A play—this is the first meaning we derive from the statement—is by definition a "dramatization": it brings out what is memorable and striking in the material, possibly to the point of sensationalism. Dramaturgy implies a whole armory of devices for bringing order out of the chaos of facts and fictions. Greater intelligibility reinforces greater vividness. The unmanageable becomes manageable, even as the blurred becomes the clear. It is not hard to see what interested parties have to fear. If they have a bad conscience, they have to fear the *dies irae* when the truth will suddenly out and the malefactors will be punished. They have to fear the hard outline which a play can draw around the truth; they have to fear the power of conviction a play can carry. If they have a good conscience they have to fear what they will see as the specious plausibility of the drama. Pirandello has it that life, because it is fact, need not be plausible, but that art, because it is fiction, has plausibility as its *sine qua non*. How terrible, then, the plausibility of a fiction which poses as fact! Pirandello used to notice how much more cogent were his mad wife's fantasies than his own recollection of the truth. How ruefully those who consider *The Deputy* a mad fantasy of Hochhuth's must think of their own unavailing efforts to counter the play with *their* recollection of the truth! They cannot but consider Hochhuth's recourse to the dramatic form as in itself a trick.

Luckily for their peace of mind, such persons all seem to have found *The Deputy* quite a bad play. Consequently, though they must resent the fact that Hochhuth resorted to the dramatic form at all, they cannot but rejoice that (as they see it) he failed to exploit that form for anything like what it is worth. Yet even this is cold comfort, since, in the first place, the dramatic form has a special impressiveness even when handled with only moderate skill and, second, more importantly, since it is not just a form of writing that is in question but a particularly potent form of presentation: enactment before an audience. Here again, one may have a low opinion of the particular manifestation: one may fault the actors, the directors, and even the audience. But here again there are forces which remain operative when actors, director, and audience leave much to be desired. Theatre is sur-real. The little ritual of performance, given just a modicum of competence, can lend to the events represented another dimension, a more urgent reality. And, to the actual, present force of the enactment for the spectators who are there, one must add its symbolic force for those who hear about it. Putting Pius XII on stage at all is a highly charged act; and, so far from being illegitimate, a feeling of shock that he *was* put on stage is part of the game, and was in the cards from the beginning.

The Puritans were always right in their apprehensions, whatever one thinks of their ethics, and it was with their usual well-grounded fear that they always tried to stop this or that from being represented on a public stage. And the Puritans' antitype, Queen Cleopatra, agrees with them that the worst way of being exhibited for disapproval would be to be exhibited on a public stage. Once again, the feeling arises that a swindle is involved. On stage, falsehood is not merely uttered, it seems to become truth. You see Pius XII in three dimensions *actually* doing those dreadful things which, *actually*—but this second *actually* is weaker than the first—he did not do.

To the fear of the theatrical occasion add fear of the theatre as an institution. Again, those who feel the fear do know what they are afraid of. A churchman readily understands the power of the theatre because it is a power that resembles his own. Putting it brutally, both church and theatre lend themselves to demagogy. Each one at its best tries to inspire and edify but, when not at its best, is content to seduce and degrade. Men on a stage, like men in a pulpit, have their histrionic opportunities maximized, while those in the plush seats or wooden pews are placed in a position of maximum vulnerability. A maximum of eloquence and magic from those in charge, with an audience or congregation that is not allowed to answer back! Neither church nor theatre has evolved in an atmosphere of rationality, let alone of give and take.

What must be especially galling to the churchman today is that the stage sometimes has the edge over the pulpit. For one thing, the modern theatre audience is not limited to a particular congregation, but is general. It, and not the church, is truly catholic. There had been criticism of Pius XII among the Faithful, but the news had scarcely spread *beyond* the Faithful. Hochhuth was more dangerous because of his general audience, as Cardinal Spellman acknowledged in his devious way when accusing the playwright of stirring up strife between Christian and Jew. No doubt there are advantages in the church's holiness, real or assumed, but, where criticism is concerned, the greater advantage lies with harsh secularity. That the theatre may have its origin in religion, and has sometimes kept company with religion, should not prevent us from seeing how thoroughly secular an institution it still is and how inclined it is to take full advantage of its secularity. Thus the theatre takes Pius XII out of the dim candlelight of the church and turns its spotlights on him. He may never recover. Naturally, those who revered him were offended: it was their reverence that had kept him in twilight. Of course there is fearful vulgarity in a pope's becoming a topic of chitchat at Sardi's and the Algonquin, but from Hochhuth's standpoint that is the price to be paid for the right to discuss Pius with eyes no longer closed in prayer, in tones no longer hushed by awe. There is no need for a theatre of cruelty, for theatre is itself cruel . . .

If only *The Deputy* had not been a play! That is one of the two most pointed things that can be said about it. The other is: but is *The Deputy* really a play?

People putting this second question have generally had in mind that *The Deputy* is inordinately documentary. Hochhuth has unloaded bucketfuls of factual reports, and actual quotations, into his dialogue. That, we say, is not drama, but history. However, our saying so turns out to be a criticism only of particular passages. The fault which people find in the play as a whole is that it is not historical enough. They find it, on the contrary, too melodramatic. They complain that this is a stage villain of a pope, whereas the actual Pius XII had pleasingly human traits that are not shown in the play. Actually, then, their complaint is not that *The Deputy* is not a play, but that it is only a melodramatic play.

Since evidently what is being called for is an unmelodramatic *Deputy*, we are entitled to ask what such a work would be like. Presumably it would be a play in which Pius's bad traits were balanced by good traits. The laws of dramatic structure would then bring it about that Pius's antagonist, Father Fontana, would also have his good traits balanced by bad ones. At least one critic actually observed of *The Deputy* that Bernard Shaw would have given the pope a case. Now a "case" implies a good deal more than some pleasant character traits. A man might be pleasant, or even good, and still not have a "case" in the historical situation described. So, to characters of mixed good and evil, we must add—in this prescription for a *Deputy* which is a "real play"— a *theme* of mixed good and evil, a *problem* in which there is a case for both sides.

In making these technical changes in the play we would change its philosophy and remove its *raison d'être*. No affront would have been offered to Pius XII. Faults, in a context of nonfaults, only make a man the more human, and so the more amiable. If in his turn the good Father Fontana has some notable faults, the score is evened up, and Hochhuth's play has been made over into something completely innocuous, proving only what would be conceded in advance, and enunciating the world-shaking principle that none of us is perfect.

And yet the theory of drama behind the criticism of Hochhuth is a well-proven one. It is true that *Saint Joan* (for example) becomes a better play because of the weight Shaw gives to the Other Side. *Saint*

Joan does show a conflict of right with right, and a fascinating kind of conflict it is, and one which the art of drama is well suited to present.

In a sense, the play Hochhuth's critics wanted him to write had already and triumphantly been written. It is Schiller's *Don Carlos*. On the face of it, Philip is the villainous tyrant, Posa, the virtuous rebel. But Schiller then does just what, as students of the drama, we may wish him to do: he gives Philip a kind of rightness and some endearing personal traits, while he offsets the more obvious rightness of Posa's arguments with a personal arrogance which can only horrify us. Indeed, the play is in the end more damaging to Posa than to Philip, and it could be that critics of Hochhuth who have limited their demands to more sympathy for Pius really wanted no sympathy at all for Father Fontana.

I have implied that if *The Deputy* humanized Pius, and stated a case for him, then the play would be affirming something as interesting and significant as the fact that ten minus ten equals zero. But why should this be so? The statement would not apply to *Don Carlos*. There, the humanizing of Philip, and the statement of a case for him, adds to the meaning and to the dramatic tension. What is the difference?

We can get at it, I think, by asking what would happen if *Don Carlos* were rewritten on the lines of *The Deputy*. Philip would then be pure tyrant, Posa, pure idealist. Thousands of German readers and spectators have actually taken them this way, and enjoyed the play very much. It disturbed no preconceptions; on the contrary, it made a very reassuring melodrama. Polemically speaking—and we *are* speaking of polemics—Hochhuth's project is very different. He is taking a respected figure and removing every reason why we should respect him.

Is it fair to remove even objective evidence that there were things about Pius to respect? If this were a biography, it would simply be unfair. But drama is not only more selective than biography, it is selective according to different principles. It never lays claim to an interest in all of a man, but only in that part of him that is manifest in a chosen and partially fabricated Action. A playwright may start with a historical figure, but that does not absolve him from the job of putting him through the mill (or sausage machine, if you insist) of the drama. By all means, if a Shavian drama on Pius XII were planned, then a case for Pius would emerge: Shaw would even invent positive and likable traits for him, as he did for Cauchon, but the net result in a Shavian drama with this subject matter would be to excuse, at least in some measure, what Pius did. Let some Shavian playwright try it: speech is free. Meanwhile, is it not also legitimate to plan a play, not in extenuation of Pius's actions and nonactions, but in condemnation of them?

And is melodrama the best word to describe what happens if we do? I have just said that many Germans have taken *Don Carlos* as melodrama, and have enjoyed it as such. The last clause is essential.

To convert material into melodrama is to rearrange it for our delectation: it must be fun. Is *The Deputy* fun, and should it be? Was Hochhuth's aim a stirring narrative, spiced with a facile appeal to conventional notions of right and wrong? Surely we are not approaching an understanding of his enterprise by this route. Let us try another.

From what realities does Hochhuth start? Clearly, with the realities of the Nazi era and the Nazi regime. Now if he had put Hitler on stage, one can imagine how monstrous the characterization would have been. Consequently some people would have said: "This is very unfair. The Führer actually loved dogs and children. He was nice to Eva Braun. Some of his social policies brought real welfare to thousands of people." A playwright could indeed bring in enough of such items to balance the negative traits. In that way, certain demands could be met. I could argue that, even as truth, a portrait of that man conceived in hatred might be more valid than one written according to the dogma that all men are a blend of good and evil, but my point here is that the aim of a play is not portraiture, and that the choice of such material as this does not arise from the desire merely to state what went on.

It is not likely that a play would be written about Hitler in the first place except to express, not merely disapproval, but outrage. Bernard Shaw did try to represent him in the Shavian vein: the effort (in *Geneva*) has very little value or significance. Charlie Chaplin's effort (in *The Great Dictator*) has more value and significance insofar as Chaplin was outraged, but has limited value and significance in that the outrages of Hitler cannot find adequate expression in the art of Charlie Chaplin . . .

Two things stand out in our time: first, that gigantic outrages against mankind are constantly being committed and, second, that mankind is not outraged by them. As the outrages themselves increase in scope, our ability to respond to them diminishes. Have we got used to them? Have we grown bored by them? Can we tell ourselves someone invented them, and they didn't really happen? Were they at least vastly exaggerated? These questions are all active in our little brains and nervous systems, mingling with each other in a fashion logically indefensible but psycho-logically irresistible.

The crassest rationalization of all is that Outrage is a name for what others do to us, and never for what we do to them. A factor Americans haven't understood about German anti-Semitism is that the Germans at the time felt too outraged *by* the Jews to feel outraged *for* them. You will retort that they had no right to feel that way and I will retort that that is just my point, and applies to the lack of widespread outrage in America over the bombing of Hiroshima. Americans at the time were full of the horrors, real and imaginary, which the Japanese had perpetrated against Americans.

Each country, today, has a bad conscience, and particularly the great powers, but each is very concerned to disown it by the diversionary maneuver of incessant talk about the misdemeanors of others. The others may in each case have much more than a mote in their eye, yet that is no reason for denying the beam in one's own. The politicians are not concerned to cure this disease, they are concerned to exploit it, and so what would like to regard itself as a dialogue between East and West is only a recriminatory harangue. The other side is bad, and responsible for everything that is wrong. Our side (whichever our side is) is good, and even its most hideous actions are necessities imposed by the other fellow's iniquity. If you are looking for melodrama, my friends, don't look in Hochhuth's *The Deputy*, look in your morning newspaper.

Luckily for our sanity, there have been objections, and especially from men of religion and men of thought, from Pope John to Martin Buber, from Martin Luther King to Arnold Toynbee, from Bertrand Russell to Walter Lippmann. And the young people are in eruption. As for artists, Hochhuth can be taken as representative of those among them who see their task at this time to lie in what we may call declarations of conscience. *Of course,* the aim is not to show that Hitler had a human side. The reason for presenting Hitler would be to show that a human being can, to all intents and purposes, become inhuman and monstrous. That is Outrage Number One. And Outrage Number Two is that so many men were not outraged—*are* not outraged. Some worshiped Hitler. Some gave him sneaking respect. Many thought that, well, he wasn't as ineffective as a lot of other people. Some merely accepted him, whether from fear of the alternative, inertia, or completely open-minded skepticism.

What Hochhuth believes to have been the attitude of the historical Pius XII entails a particular outrage. Pius was no Nazi: his conscience might have been clearer if he had been. Pius loved reactionary, old Germany, and dreaded more than anything else atheistic, new Russia. Things he would hear about what his Germans were doing would make him nervous, but he would not let himself become their enemy like the Russians. Was he not Christ's deputy in the war against anti-Christian Communism? So Pius XII left the Jews to their fate. Auschwitz was liberated by his enemies, the Russian atheists.

For Hochhuth, Pius embodies a double offense. Politically, he falls into the trap, or remains in the rut, of imagining that all will be well if we are always and exclusively anticommunist. Morally, this representative of Jesus turns out to be a Pontius Pilate, washing his hands of the moral issue that faced him. So finally he does not represent Christ but, instead, represents all those in our time who, while refusing open, enthusiastic support to the Monster, give him an acquiescence that is really *carte blanche*. Americans who give *carte blanche* to presidents to wage unjust wars have no very solid grounds for feeling superior to Pius XII.

I have mentioned that a play was written in Pius's defense, and I have suggested that that kind of thing is doomed to failure, because all that can be brought to Pius's defense is an argument. Anyone who would write a counter-Hochhuth has already made the mistake of assuming that what *The Deputy* presents is an argument against Pius. But the real "offense" of Hochhuth is precisely that he takes for granted that Pius is indefensible and that no argument could make any difference. That is the kind of play *The Deputy* is. Of course, Hochhuth makes assumptions that not all can accept. Of course, his play is not addressed to everybody. Yet, in one sense, it *is* addressed to everybody, for it assumes that right and wrong are known to the human heart, and that if we choose to brush aside all ideology and opinion and current politics, we recognize an outrage when we see it. To make the outrage visible, Hochhuth concentrates upon it, isolates it, shows his Pope Pius as wholly outrageous. And in an unexpected way, Hochhuth bypasses the argument most readily available to him: that Pius was afraid of Hitler. Cowardice would make Pius little, but it would also make him human. This Pius is *inhuman* in that he is cold, callous, cut off from others, lacking in imagination about them. He cannot feel. He is a nonhuman human, and, in the circumstances, *of all human types the one least able to represent Jesus Christ.* To the extent that the Hochhuth portrait is thought of as the historical Pius XII it is an even more terrible indictment than Catholic spokesmen have realized.

If *Don Carlos* and *Saint Joan* are precedents, the prototype is *Antigone*. But for my present purposes we need to imagine an *Antigone* more primitive than that of Sophocles, which is, after all, a late and highly sophisticated reading. Sophocles may not, as some moderns think, have made Creon as sympathetic as Antigone herself, but he did offer him a partial sympathy, and when we do that we are on the road toward Schiller and Shaw, at the end of which road stands Anouilh with an Antigone who stands for neuroticism and a Creon who is a rather sensible chap. With Brecht's Antigone, in which the heroine is wholly right, and Creon an inhuman tyrant, we are starting out again where we may presume the story to have originated in pre-Sophoclean days.

Those who tell us that this spells melodrama rather than tragedy should not take us aback. We should, on the contrary, let them spur us on to look what happens when tragedy is not attempted. Take the question of how plays end. Tragedy and, for that matter, comedy, farce, and melodrama end with a suggestion of either pessimism or optimism. A pessimistic ending tells us that nothing can be done. An optimistic ending tells us that nothing need be attempted: since everything is already in order, we should feel reconciled to the All. It is, in fact, hard to put an ending on a play that does not have some such conclusiveness, optimistic or pessimistic. Yet an attempt—often known as the bitter ending—has been made from time to time, and it is bitter because it is not a true ending at all. We associate open-endedness with tragicomedy, and it has a special point in activist drama, polemical drama, drama of Commitment, because it says, what happens after this is up to you, the public.

A classical instance of such tragicomedy of Commitment would be Brecht's *Good Woman of Setzuan.* The fortunes of the protagonist go from bad to worse. There can be no comic denouement, but the author will not provide any final cataclysm either. As soon as the main character's position is clearly revealed as an impasse, Brecht refuses to stage a final catastrophe, and, as to denouement, asks the audience to devise one—off stage. Which is only making completely explicit what much bitter, activist tragicomedy had been doing for generations. (There is a similar explicitness to the end of *The Threepenny Opera.* John Gay had already indicated at the close of his *Beggar's Opera* that what is happening is what happens in opera, not life. Brecht's version of things is not complete till the audience understands that what happens in life is just the opposite, and that the relation of art and life, here, is that of illusion and reality, false propaganda and fact.)

And at this point, to clear up a possible misunderstanding about Brecht might well be to clear up a misunderstanding about the whole problem of drama and propaganda. The term propaganda was often applied to Brecht with no other intention than to damage him. It was inevitable, then, that those of us who came to his defense should take either the line that his work was "not propaganda" or the line that it was "more than" propaganda. And I should add that I still think the second of these lines is correct. But polemics, while always needed, always distort the problems, and one way they do so is by luring the polemicist into positions he would never take except in the heat of argument. In this way, those who took Brecht's part were often lured into implying that there is something deplorable about propaganda as such. Hence if Brecht was "more than" propaganda, it could only be "in spite of" propaganda, and even "in contradiction to" the propaganda, not just "in addition" to it.

Brecht the person and Brecht the advocate were not always at one, and some of his plays become more, rather than less, dramatic because the advocate is outdone by the person. There is a tension between where Brecht wanted his sympathies to be and where they actually were. From this tension his plays sometimes benefit. In stating this much we are on firm ground. But the ground is less firm when we imply that Brecht was well served only by his unconscious, and is only dramatic unbeknown to himself and in spite of himself. How much respect can one have for an intellectual playwright who is so much less aware of what he is doing than his critics are? And is it fair to offer Brecht the backhanded compliment implicit in this kind of criticism without first examining his work in the terms he himself proposes?

It would surely be fair to question the motives of the critics as rigorously as they have questioned the motives of Brecht. I discern a negative motive and a positive one. The negative one is to discredit the doctrinal content of Brecht's work, the positive one is to vindicate him on entirely traditional lines—and thus make of him essentially a traditional artist working in the principal accepted genres. Stage directors with this viewpoint present Brecht as a "classic" bearing witness to the unchanging human tragedy and comedy. His plays tend, however, not to get across when presented in this way, and that surely is a rather conclusive, if pragmatic, refutation of the viewpoint.

Suppose that, on the other hand, one were to apply to Brecht the theory which Rolf Zimmermann has applied to Hochhuth? Herr Zimmermann maintains* that there exists, beside the main traditions of literature, a tradition of polemic. Having its own aim, polemical theatre has its own method. The aim being to re-create the author's sense of outrage, the method is not to use "rounded," "human," equally-right-and-wrong characters, but enactors of the outrageous on the one hand and, on the other, victims of outrage and rebels against outrage. The ending will be the open one of bitter tragicomedy. A Brecht production infused with this idea does get across to its audience, as has many times been proved. I suggest, then, that it would be wise to take his plays (except for the very early ones) as in the first instance Theatre of Commitment, whatever else they may be as well.

That Brecht's plays are Theatre of Commitment but other things as well has won him approval of a sort from critics who did not share his commitment, but *The Deputy* is Theatre of Commitment and nothing else, and so Hochhuth is open to attack both by those who don't share his convictions and by those who insist on the canons of conventional drama. His play has been little praised, and yet one cannot believe that it made the impression it did solely because of its subject. The history of literature is strewn with works on big subjects that make no impression at all. It could even be said that the subject of the Nazis had become boring until Hochhuth

---

* In his essay "Drama or Pamphlet" in my critical anthology *The Storm over "The Deputy."*

came along with a play *on* that subject. But if we wish to know if Hochhuth's play is a success we have only to remind ourselves that the purpose of this kind of play is to communicate a sense of outrage. And it *has* communicated a sense of outrage. Is it not Hochhuth's sense of outrage that his opponents are upset by? Surely they didn't get as angry as they did just because they disagreed? The problem, to recapitulate, is that this is, successfully, a play. If only it were a play of ideas, one could handle it by argument. And if it were a play of ideas by Shaw, one could observe what a strong case he had put for Pius. But the author of *The Deputy* is outraged by Pius, and communicates his sense of outrage in a manner that would not seem to brook No for an answer. You have to enter into it, let your heart respond to it—or move out of its path, and be outraged *by* it.

To whom does the Theatre of Commitment address itself? Not to everyone. It has human enemies; and human beings who admire the enemies, or enjoy some kind of solidarity with them, cannot but detach themselves and walk out. An enemy does not make a good audience. What about allies? It could be said that they don't need preaching to. Yet propaganda can serve the purposes of ritual, one of which is to confirm people in their convictions and prepare them for renewed struggle. But the ideal audience for the Theatre of Commitment is, I think, neither one set of militants nor the other, but rather a mass of people in the middle, who may be vaguely sympathetic to the cause preached but are a little sluggish and sleepy about it. They may assent but they are not really committed, and the purpose of the Drama of Commitment is not to be *for* Commitment but to get people to commit themselves. Could not most of us say we belong to this audience, and does not the Theatre of Commitment have, by that token, a large enough clientele?

Yet another reason why *The Deputy* is a crucial instance of Commitment is that Hochhuth writes not only for this audience but about it. This is the play about the Nazis that is not about the Nazis but about those who were "a little sluggish and sleepy" in opposing them. The common view is that the leading Nazis bore most of the guilt, a little of which rubbed off on those who went along. Hochhuth would put far more of the guilt on the fellow travelers, and his presentation forces us to realize how much could have been done against the Nazis which was not done. Now a dramatist cannot but present individual cases, and in picking his chief individual target Hochhuth made a choice that was perhaps malicious and certainly audacious: the titular head of our soi-disant Christian civilization. But, in Germany, certainly, this Holy Father can easily stand for a lot of other fathers, the fathers of very many of Hochhuth's own generation. This character "is" many middle-aged and elderly Germans of today who claim a spotless record but who can be shown to have been no better than neutral and maybe quite a bit worse. That, though, is only to say that they are "a little sluggish and sleepy," that they are you and I, and that they and we are Hochhuth's audience.

As long as such an audience exists, and urgent reasons exist why they should be roused from their semislumber, there is a place for a literature of Commitment, and as long as certain people live in special dread of plays ("Please, God, let it not be a play!"), there is a place for a Theatre of Commitment. Any dent that any theatre can make in the world is no doubt small, but theatre people who on that account give up the effort as hopeless are generally agreeing to make no dent at all. Writing some years ago about T. S. Eliot's wish that Murder in the Cathedral might have made inroads on Nazism,* I wrote that this play or any other would have been no use against the SS and the Wehrmacht. There are times when the poet may be called upon to drop the pen and take up, if not the sword, then whatever is the most effective implement of direct action. The years 1942–45 were such times, if such times ever were. And if one were Vietnamese, one might well feel that the 1960s were also such a time. In the United States the situation is different indeed. Here the point, surely, is not more violence, but less. Here the point is to subjugate the machine and tame the beast. Here every action and word in the direction of gentleness and restraint is so much to the good. One could say the need was for civilization, just that. One could say, education. But there is an urgency which neither word suggests, and therefore one must out with it and say, there is a need for propaganda.

People tell me that America is so far gone in television, radio, and movies that the poor old stage is as obsolete as the horse and buggy. Obviously that is not true, or our priest could not have been so dismayed to find The Deputy was a play. The idea that the theatre is obsolete reflects the wish of vested interests that it may become obsolete. The theatre is a threat but would cease to be so were it swamped by the media. It represents what the powers behind the media wish to have swamped. It is the last refuge of personal association, of the simple assembly of persons with common interests at something less huge and overpowering than a stadium. A theatrical

*See page 151 above.

event is nothing more than itself: it is not simultaneously seen or heard by the nation. There is nothing to it but what each person present can see and hear; it is a self-contained human transaction.

Which is not only part of its charm, but part of its value, and is beginning to be felt as such. The young people who are in eruption in America today are not stuck in front of television sets. It is more often their parents who are to be found in that pitiful posture. The rebellious young have walked out on their parents. They are on the streets outside, playing their guitars. These are years that have even produced a theatre called Theatre in the Street.

There is, of course, nothing wrong with television. When run by human beings for human beings, that invention will be seen to have possibilities. It still won't duplicate the function of theatre. *Theatre is people present:* actors present on stage, spectators present out front, a living contact between the two groups. Everything we call theatre is in that electrico-human circuit, which neither television nor movies will ever be able to set up. Even when improved, television will be of the new, mechanized, big-scale world, like President Clark Kerr's multiversity. Certainly, theatre is old-fashioned in belonging to the old, intimate, small-scale world. More old-fashioned and also more new-fashioned, because the new generation is defecting in droves from what the middle-aged say is modern and up-to-date. There is no substitute for live human contact. Theatre has the same appeal as coffee houses have proved to have, and in fact, in New York today, there is a more lively theatre in the coffee houses than in the Broadway show shops. As William James made clear, there is something bad about all bigness in human organizations, and the anarchists are certainly on to something when they insist on holding on to the small groups, the personal meetings-together, at all costs. The theatre, accordingly, is an institution for Jamesians and anarchists, and for the Jamesian and anarchist in each of us, to hold on to.

My subject is shifting, here at the close, from Theatre of Commitment to a possible commitment which we might make to theatre. What is the connection between the two themes? A theatre on the street would not necessarily stage *The Deputy.* A coffee house theatre would not necessarily concern itself with Brecht. But there is a degree of "subversion" in the act of theatre itself. Wherever "two or three are gathered," a blow is struck against the abstract non-gatherings of the television audience as well as against the gatherings of expense-account mobs on Broadway. A blow is struck for the old and obsolete which—if we are lucky (or just persistent?)—shall be the new and modern. Subversiveness, rebellion, revolution in the theatre are not just a matter of program, much less are they to be defined in terms of a particular kind of play.

As for the particular kind of play I have chiefly been talking about, if it does not have much effect on the world, it may yet have quite a salutary effect on the theatre, always provided that the world consents to go on existing. I make no prophecies. I simply remark that, in the drama of the 1960s, the Theatre of Commitment is the principal new presence. There are reasons both political and theatrical to welcome it.

(1966)

WRITING FOR A POLITICAL THEATRE

In the sixties I wrote a good deal about political theatre. In the seventies I wrote *for* a political theatre, beginning with a political extravaganza at La Mama in New York called *The Red White and Black*. My documentary *Are You Now or Have You Ever Been* opened at Robert Brustein's Yale Rep on the day Nixon's reelection was announced in 1972: subsequently this play was performed in many parts of the world, banned in South Africa, and filmed for Showtime on television. During the seventies, serious interest in political theatre waned, and the political playwright turned to what some termed "special interests," especially feminism and gay rights. I wrote a play, *Lord Alfred's Lover*, which sought to "place" Oscar Wilde, for the first time I think, in the history of the struggle for gay rights. The piece that follows began as a talk at Columbia University to other theatre people still interested in political theatre in the eighties. Among other things, a paradox of my subject is here pointed out: as serious interest in political theatre waned, a less serious, "popular" interest grew, and showed itself on television.

> *Most wretched men*
> *Are cradled into poetry by wrong.*
> *They learn in suffering what they teach in song.*
> —Shelley

> *The criticisms [of* Heartbreak House*] are all stupid . . . because every situation in my plays has a public interest; and critics . . . are incapable of public interests.*
> —Shaw

> *Did that play of mine send out*
> *Certain men the English shot?*
> —Yeats

Clearly the bone of contention is propaganda, and since people usually disagree on the subject, let me set out from a proposition we can all agree to: bad propaganda is a bad thing. But here our difficulties start because the word "bad" in this context has two entirely different meanings which, however, are often jumbled up together. There is (a) "bad" in the sense of "poor" propaganda possibly for something good and (b) there is propaganda, poor or otherwise, for something bad. There is no scientific way of measuring either kind of badness, but it is clear that one kind concerns the means, and the other, the end. The means, here, signifies the form and the end signifies the content. Commonly, the ends and contents are settled in advance by a given audience. Thus a play founded on, and dedicated to, Catholic theology has good ends and good contents for performance in a Catholic church or in the city square of a Catholic city. Provisionally, my phrase "propaganda for something good" only means propaganda for something its audience can respect. I say "can" because it may be something the audience already respects or it may be something they can be persuaded to respect. As well as preaching to the converted, there is preaching to the heathen, and the latter takes precedence since originally there are no converted as yet. First, a faith; second, conversion to it. The word propaganda itself, as we use it, derives from its use, in the original Latin, on behalf of the Counter-Reformation. Propaganda was the propagation of the Catholic faith, which in turn was my reason for using Catholicism as the first example of a cause that can be propagandized for.

Most communities are hostile to propaganda for various causes, but none are hostile to propaganda for all causes, since each community—or the regime that dominates it—wishes to propagate what it sees as its own cause. All communities are in fact saturated with propaganda. All, one could say, are being sold a bill of goods, day in and day out. The job is done by television, radio, newspapers, billboards, by churches if any, but above all by schools and parents. The purpose of parenthood, within the nuclear family as we know it, is to drum into the resistant heads of infancy the received ideas (prejudices, assumptions, habits, etc.) of the larger group the family is part of, notably a class. Even generational revolt is not to be interpreted as rejection of what the parents have taught. Rather, it is an accusation, in the name of the values implanted in childhood, that the parents have betrayed those values.

Let me put a question: if propaganda is in fact taken for granted by all, and quite ubiquitous, how is it so many people think they are against it and shudder at the very mention of the word? The main reason would seem to be that they don't regard their own propaganda as propaganda. It's just the truth. Propaganda is what "the others" preach. Thus, in America, what Communists say is propaganda, but what the National Association of Manufacturers says, or what the Heritage Foundation says, is not propaganda, it's research, it's truth.

There is a widespread feeling that propaganda should be kept in its proper place. What its proper place is, however, has not been agreed on. It could be the convention hall, the parliament, the church, or the Union Square, the Hyde Park of a given city. But there has been a strong feeling that its proper place is not in the arts, and there has been an especially strong feeling that its proper place is not in the theatrical arts, a term we must use today to include dramatic art in motion pictures and television. This strong feeling comes through to us in two quite distinct currents of thinking. One is that of the politicians. An extreme case would be a politician like Ronald Reagan whose background is in the entertainment business. The politicians assume that entertainment should entertain, not teach, just as it should make money, not request subsidies. In the days when we used to speak of movies with a message, Humphrey Bogart said messages should be left to Western Union. From the Reaganite viewpoint propaganda is too serious for entertainment and is likely to be propaganda for Communism or something Reagan would gave that name to.

Thus the first current of thinking that runs counter to the idea of propaganda in performance arts is philistinism: the plain honest folks who just want a good time are being handed the Communist Manifesto in disguise. That was what was in the late Senator Dirksen's mind when he questioned the production by the Federal Theatre of works with such suspicious titles as *Up in Mabel's Room* and *Another Kind of Love*. The Federal Theatre, by the way, came into existence in 1936, and was shut down three years later because the Congress suspected that it was a propagandist theatre in the sense I have just been defining, suspected that it was both antientertainment and that it was anticapitalist.

But although the Everett Dirksens and Ronald Reagans have been in positions of political power, the stronger opposition to the idea of propaganda in the arts has come, I think, from people who are not in such positions—indirectly from the writers who comprise the intelligentsia and directly from the teachers who adopt and disseminate the views of the intelligentsia. Here the encounter with Communism is a little more serious than it was with Senator Dirksen.

In our lifetime, it has been the Communist movement, headed by Moscow, that has most fervently championed the idea of culture as propaganda, each art a weapon, a weapon of the working class, a weapon of world communism. In the West, it was the generation that grew up in the thirties that espoused this idea with most zeal, and it was this same generation, a little later on, that rejected it with most vehemence. Many rejected not just that particular propaganda but all propaganda—except their own propaganda against propaganda.

To come down to cases, one might say: the thirties produced Bertolt Brecht, and the fifties produced Samuel Beckett. The one said, "Change the world, it needs it"; the other, "Nothing to be done." If only life were as simple as such a contrast suggests, but what the contrast brings to my mind is the witticism of Jan Kott which I have already quoted, that for fantasy we have Bertolt Brecht, and for realism, Samuel Beckett.

Kott boldly sets aside the question what Brecht or Beckett might be propagandizing for and asks instead what the author's politics actually are in the place where, and at the time when, they have been launched. In *The Caucasian Chalk Circle* Brecht has projected a Soviet Union where competition and oppression have been replaced by pure reason. In *Waiting for Godot* Beckett has projected a world in which miserable but stoical mankind is sort of waiting for something to turn up that probably won't. Brecht's error is a bad joke that only by Kottian courtesy can be called fantasy. Beckett's reality is that of more and more people in the world with every day that passes.

Is *Waiting for Godot* propaganda? Since counterpropaganda is a form of propaganda, as counterinsurgency is a form of insurgency, one could answer this question in the affirmative, and this is to say that in our time the apolitical has become supremely political. The old state of affairs has been reversed. When Brecht grew up, political literature was a literature of opposition, a literature that threatened the establishment, the State. Today Brecht's own plays serve to stabilize Soviet domination of East Germany, and a political poet in East Germany, as in Russia, is one who supports the State. In this situation, to show oneself apolitical is an act of rebellion. I am afraid the Soviet government is correct in accusing its artistic nonsupporters of anti-State activities. It *is* anti-State to paint an abstract painting. It *is* anti-State to compose twelve-tone music. It *is* anti-State to write a poem saying that the sun is shining and that the sunshine was not produced by the Politburo.

People speak of political theatre as very special. But in the theatre anything can become political by a sudden turn of events outside the theatre. During World War I, there was a potato shortage in England, so that when the line "Let the sky rain potatoes!" came up in a Shakespeare production, the audience rose to its feet and applauded. Now that was political theatre—momentarily. And it would be political theatre if an anti-Semitic regime decided to celebrate its accession to power with a gala performance of *The Merchant of Venice*.

I would not want to define politics so broadly that all art is political. That is as unfruitful a proposition as that no art is political. Much drama that people loosely call political might better be termed social, just as what is often meant by sexual politics is no different from sexual sociology. It would be more sensible, I think, to limit the term political to works in which the question of the power structure arises. *Saint Joan* is a highly political play, while *Pygmalion*, not without political implications, is mainly social. It may of course be hard in many situations to raise the larger social issues without simultaneously bringing the political background (the power structure) to mind and into question. This, I take it, is what Carlos Fuentes is getting at when he writes:

> I do not believe that literature has an immediate, partisan role to play, but I do believe that literature is revolutionary and thus political in a deeper sense. Literature not only sustains a historical experience and continues a tradition. It also—through moral risk and formal experimentation and verbal humor—transforms the conservative horizon of the readers and helps liberate us all from the determinisms of prejudice, doctrinal rigidity, and barren repetition.

But these remarks are paradoxical. Some of them could just as well support the view that literature is conservative, and the rest are true only of a small proportion of what gets written—namely what has high merit. Most writing, most literature, most art, is only the opium of the people, is but the intellectual equivalent of our politics and economics. The *New York Post* (founded in 1801 by Alexander Hamilton) is literature, and at that the most widely read. Minds which deal in moral risk, formal experimentation, et cetera, are not represented in it, or in the most widely read fiction, or even, probably, in the most widely read poetry. As for the most widely consumed drama, that is situation comedy on television. And here I'd like to mention again the theoretical opposition which the entertainment industry offers to propaganda. In practice, *all* their entertainment is propaganda, either by directly validating the status quo, or by offering convenient evasions of it.

What is needed, perhaps, if we can still believe in changes for the better, is not propaganda for propaganda itself, but propaganda for what Fuentes is calling *literature,* and which I would call *art* in order to include all the arts. The pressure of modern life, in either its capitalist or its socialist forms, in America, Russia, and elsewhere, is toward the suppression of the very spirit of art, of the arts, and their replacement by, yes, propaganda, propaganda for whichever or whatever is the current Way of Life. Writing what the Russian government wants written in the way the Russian government wants it written, a writer becomes a hack and produces, as required, bad literature. But so does the American entertainer, though his master be not entitled the State but Private Enterprise. In both situations, the job of the hack—that is, of most writers—is to avoid moral risk, formal experimentation, and daring humor, carefully to leave in place and unthreatened the conservative horizon of the audience, and keep them unliberated from the determinisms of prejudice, doctrinal rigidity, and barren repetition. All of this is achieved both by socialist realism and by the everyday and accepted writing of our own playboys of the Western world. And, in the first instance, nothing can be done about it in either half of the world, for, in the one half, so-called "dissident" writing is usually banned and often, in the other half, the money cannot be raised to put on the real play.

In the East, the Samizdat is the one positive possibility, and it has proved a far larger one than anybody would have predicted. The West has its nooks and crannies of another sort. A play of mine, critical of certain aspects of show business, and the people in it, became stageable through money whose source was that same show business. To be specific, Los Angeles actors who earn a good living off commercial television put my play on in their spare time and made a long run of it by presenting it weekends only when their weeks were spent earning their living.

I am not implying that no good playwrights fare well under the Western system. I would say, though, that many are depoliticized and defanged by it. Thus Beckett was political and urgent in Poland, but not in America. Here the question was whether he would become chic, and until he did, he was unsuccessful. Walter Kerr, the most influential newspaper critic of the time, found nothing whatever in *Waiting for Godot* to admire. That was in the fifties. Later, what put Beckett across was snobbery, otherwise known as academic authority. The academy decreed that he was Important, and the newspapers cannot buck such a decree. He would no longer be disrespectfully mentioned by their reviewers. He became Important. By the same stroke, his sting was drawn.

There's an analogy with modernist music. Alban Berg is one of the least popular composers at the Metropolitan Opera House, but his prestige, as academically decreed, is such that they daren't fail to produce him. The auditorium doesn't have to be full, and, in an opera house, those present don't have to listen.

It was a bizarre experience for me as a longtime translator and associate of Brecht to see his *Mahagonny* at the Met in 1979. The play is, among other things, an attack on the rich, but the orchestra tickets were $50, or $100 if one wanted to be at the party afterwards. A procession defying the rich marched down the aisles at the end, and the rich who occupied the seats costing $50 and $100 applauded. Such is the neutralization of political theatre in the West.

I should add that when I saw the same work in the Staatsoper of East Berlin, although the opportunity for a clearcut attack on plutocratic

America seemed obvious, the piece was taken as pure art, that is to say, as meaningless. If we live in a world where totally apolitical art can become totally political, we also live in a world where ultrapolitical art can be totally depoliticized, either in New York or East Berlin. Either the Declaration of Independence or the Communist Manifesto can be co-opted by a theatre of the truly absurd.

I have been saying that what makes the politics of a play can be the precise moment at which it is performed and the precise place where it is performed. This is not to deny that some playscripts are of themselves much more political than others or that some address themselves overtly and primarily to politics. Those who still think the overtly political drama an out-of-the-way phenomenon must themselves have been out of the way lately, for the movies and television have been deluging us with political theatre. It has become routine to place any event in recent history, from the abdication of Edward VIII to the Watergate scandal, on screen with actors impersonating the historical characters. Invariably these presentations take sides, usually to the point of melodrama, bad guys versus good guys. At the same time, they can be quite confused and confusing—as when the filmmakers haven't realized which side they have taken or when they wish to cover up the fact that they have taken a side. Any fool can see that the four-hour television presentation of the Alger Hiss case, *Concealed Enemies,* is partial to Hiss and hostile to Whittaker Chambers; yet, if memory serves, a denial of this evident fact is written into the presentation itself.

Inevitably the docudrama, as this genre has come to be called, has come in for severe criticism. The most dubious recent example is *The Atlanta Child Murders* by Abby Mann. Here an author-director took the case of a man who is now in jail for murder and told the story so that the audience must get the impression that there had been a miscarriage of justice and that the convicted man was innocent. Had the genre been pure drama, that indeed would be that. It being docudrama, the author-director can have it both ways and, while strongly suggesting one version of the facts, also avoid affirming anything for sure.

What is unsatisfactory about docudrama is that its audience has no way of knowing where reporting leaves off and invention begins. If drama is a weapon, docudrama is a boomerang because, if the viewer is free to think that the fictions are facts, he is equally free to think that the facts are fictions. Perhaps Abby Mann would like to be to his hero what Émile Zola was to Alfred Dreyfus. But what Zola did was very different from writing a docudrama. He issued an accusation, and stood trial. If Dreyfus in the end was vindicated, it was not because any fictions had been invented in his behalf. All the fictions in the case were for use against him.

I have a solution for what I would call, not docudrama, but documentary drama, which I tried out in my play *Are You Now or Have You Ever Been*. It is that the author abide by a clear set of rules that the audience will understand, whereby no fiction will be foisted on them as fact. I don't mean I eliminated point of view or even personal prejudice. I mean I tried to make them visible so there would be no deception. The main rule I went by was to put into people's mouths only words which they had used and which indeed they had placed on the public record. No investigative reporting. No confidential sources. Just what people had said in public, and for the public, with a stenographer taking it all down for later use by a printer. Where point of view and prejudice enter in is in the choice of material: you choose what *you* think is important, or funny, or indicative of character, or what not. Still, you don't have anyone say what he did not say, nor do you adjust the context so that the meaning of a statement is distorted.

Let me give you an example of such an adjustment which I had to block. At a rehearsal I found that the director had created a very good curtain line for one sequence by importing a statement from another occasion. He had a committee chairman say something he had really said but not on that occasion, not prompted by that cue. Here the director had not understood the rules under which I was operating. He had made a passage more dramatic but by lying: by giving the public the impression the chairman came up with a response which he had not in fact come up with. Had I permitted such small adjustments the result would have been a total change in genre: aiming at documentary drama we would be headed for the bastard and dubious subgenre docudrama. I had to turn down a television offer from David Susskind's organization because the television people claimed a control of the script that would have allowed them to make such adjustments throughout.

Reverting to *The Atlanta Child Murders,* the final irony was that the real drama in the material—whatever might be the actual history of what happened in Atlanta—ran clearly contrary to what Mr. Mann had in mind. This was the drama of a black class war, in which those blacks who have risen to the dizzying heights of the middle class loathe and despise no one so much as their brothers and sisters who have failed to do this but who, on the contrary, stand there as living reminders of the past-we-have-put-behind-us. These reminders must be liquidated. Dramatically, what is available here is the tale of someone who is *guilty* of a murder which is in the logic of the situation. If Mr. Mann should opt neither for documentary nor docudrama but for drama—"realistic" by all means—this is what he would have to come up with.

Two more questions: doesn't propaganda in the arts have certain limits, and, in the past hundred years, the modernist period, have these limits not sometimes been transgressed? The answer to both questions is yes.

Modernism has been oppositional, and that has meant, among other things, that modernist playwrights have liked to think of their audience as an adversary. Peter Handke even served notice to his audience—in one play title, *Publikumsbeschimpfung*—that he was going to bawl them out. In the earlier generations of modernism, this was not explicit, but it was sometimes so strongly *implicit* that relationship with audience became a problem. To me the most interesting case in point is that of Frank Wedekind. I quote the finest appreciation of his work in English—that of Alan Best:

> Wedekind's intention is to use the artist [as a protagonist] to confront the members of his audience with the realization that their own way of life and philosophy are equally bankrupt. . . . The "unsuspecting member of the public" is thus presented with a caricature of his own situation which, Wedekind hopes, will cause him to reassess his position.

I must confess to a very personal response to these lines: I grew up with people who had such thoughts, and I still feel an attraction to them. A theatre with ideas? A theatre that presents a challenge? Is not that exactly what some of us have always been calling for?

But the claim Mr. Best rightly says Wedekind made goes much further. Envisaged is a theatre in which the audience might, as doubtless it should, reassess its position, and, if you know Wedekind's plays, you know, or guess, that the word "position" refers to the whole middle class and all its views, attitudes, and feelings. The middle-class audience is to be made to realize that its own way of life and philosophy are bankrupt.

Envisaged, then, is a kind of event that never occurs, for nowhere in history is it recorded that an audience changed its mind *about everything,* and decided that its way of life, till then acceptable, had now become unacceptable. Even evangelists, who do convert people, would never claim that much. In their congregation are many of the already converted, and those they convert on a particular occasion are individuals who "come forward" one by one. One member of an Ibsen audience once said that, when he saw *The Wild Duck,* the bottom dropped out of the universe. The universe, however, did not see *The Wild Duck,* and one can be sure that even the rest of that particular audience was at the office at nine o'clock the following morning. As to Wedekind, what really happened was that he split the public: part rejected him just because he rejected them, and part went along with him because they agreed with him already. The second group was not always large enough to pay the theatrical costs, and so the history of Wedekind's plays in the theatre is not a prosperous one.

To the world public, he is known, if at all, only through Alban Berg's opera *Lulu*. Part of the opera public, as I said, still rejects even that. But Berg changed Wedekind. Musicalization would change Wedekind anyway, for music, I think, cannot even embody the *intention* of making people find their way of life bankrupt. However that may be, those who have ears to hear will recognize that, in Berg's opera, the Lulu story ends in a deeply felt compassion not present in Wedekind's words. Any hostility between stage and auditorium is thereby banished.

But it was never really there. A truly adversary audience would either walk out or jump on stage and throw the actors out. Such scenes are not unknown to history, though playwriting was not usually the cause. When one speaks of the modern audience as being, *in general*, adversary, one only half means it. There is a story about Shaw, arch propagandist as he was, that makes my point. Someone sought to curry favor with him by declaring the audience to be a fool. Shaw retorted, "But don't treat the fool according to his folly!" Wedekind was apt to make the blunder of doing just that.

There is a snag in Shaw's position too. As Egon Friedell inimitably put it, his audience could suck off the sugar and put the pill back on the plate. Not treating the fool according to his folly meant providing the fool with an entertainment. Since Shaw never failed to do this, the intended or half-intended adversary relationship never showed itself at all. His recurring joke against Englishmen goes down best with an English audience.

A *cause célèbre* is Beaumarchais's *Mariage de Figaro*. Even today it is regarded as a politically revolutionary play in half the world, the Communist half. Forgotten is that it was directed at cynical noblemen like the Duc D'Orleans, father of King Louis Philippe, who had already concluded that the ancien régime was bankrupt. A play for cynics, then, rather than for Communards.

A play is always *for* someone, and is never really *against* its audience, because a play is *play,* and can only *play* at being against its audience. Taken as play, Peter Handke's drama worked. One remembers that the actual audience received the alleged insults with smiles. At his best, even Wedekind assumes these things, though certainly the other assumption is at work in him too and is, as it were, the official quintessence of Wedekindism.

Another *cause célèbre* is Gogol's *Revizor*. At the point where the *gorodnichy* (mayor or, rather, military governor) is fully exposed as ridiculous, he suddenly talks directly to the audience. "What are you laughing at? You are laughing at yourselves!" Doubtless Gogol felt entirely sincere as he wrote that. But it is hard for a spectator to take himself as the butt of a joke, and even if he succeeds he does not have the reaction a moralist-writer wants. Perhaps he just walks out. But this is not what generally happens. What generally happens is that if I belong to a class or group that is being attacked, I assume I am an exception to the rule and I laugh with the author (who very likely belongs to the same class or group) against the class or group.

In *Tartuffe* Molière may have wished to get at hypocrites in his audience, but what hypocrite would see himself in Tartuffe? To admit any such thing he would have to cease to be a hypocrite. *Tartuffe* is no play for hypocrites, at least not for hypocrites who have the slightest awareness of their hypocrisy. It is a play for people who preen themselves on their immunity to hypocrisy, as also to credulity, the other great vice there set forth. If *Le mariage de Figaro* was originally a play for cynics, *Tartuffe* was originally for *honnêtes hommes,* solid citizens.

Did Frank Wedekind not know all this? As an artist he must have known it in his bones, but I would take it that he fell victim to exasperation. Shaw was exasperated at the same thing—the failure to really get at the public and change it—but seldom or never put his comic art at risk. Anything for a laugh? Molière had remarked on what a business it was, making the solid citizen laugh, and this business is, in a sense, the bottom line of comedy. Shaw never overlooked that fact. He even confessed to a tendency to introduce *too many* jokes. Frank Wedekind, on the other hand, sacrificed the bottom line in an effort to force the audience to see that they themselves were laughable. This is a losing game. People would either walk out or decide Wedekind was laughing at someone else.

Bad propaganda is bad, but what propaganda could be worse than the propaganda that does not and cannot propagate? And this is a question that arises from discussion of one of the most gifted of modernist playwrights.

I have left to the last the question people always put first: what effect can such a thing as political theatre—propagandist theatre—ever hope to have? The question is always intended as a rhetorical one. We are being given to understand that, in the world of the Politburo, and the Pentagon, and General Motors, and the Republic of South Africa, what a writer has to say—even a writer for television—can have little effect. You could put on any number of plays and films saying No More War on August 31, 1939, and on September 1, Hitler's tanks would have rolled into Poland, willy-nilly. You can't hold back a bullet with a speech from Shakespeare any more than you can roll back an avalanche with your little finger. Metaphors and examples could be multiplied, and have been, because there is a point here that must be conceded.

But it is a point that should not be pushed too far, as it often was by, for example, W. H. Auden in an overreaction from youthful activism. Auden would observe that no poem kept one Jew from the gas chamber; that poetry "makes nothing happen"; that only the secret police can be unacknowledged legislators. So blatantly untrue, this last sally: Richard Wagner was clearly an unacknowledged legislator of the Third Reich. Culture in general and the arts in particular are always a factor in history. James T. Farrell said, "Naked power rules the moment, ideas rule the ages." It is a pronouncement that, as it were, brings the meeting to order. Yet it overstates and omits. It says nothing about bad ideas, or the use of good culture, including some of its good ideas, by naked power. Perhaps, like many Americans, Farrell could see education and culture only in positive terms, yet, in the 1930s, the Germans may have been the most cultured, the most highly educated nation in the world. Their culture, their whole educational system, some good ideas included, became enslaved to naked power which, in one sense, was not naked because it was clothed in ideas, the bad ideas of *Mein Kampf.* If good ideas actually ruled the ages, naked power could never succeed in grabbing hold of the moment. Things in real life are much more mixed up. Still, though one is not entitled to say culture is always a positive factor in history, one must say it is always a substantial factor, and one must, I think, reject the contention of Marxism (vulgarized Marxism?) that culture can only be a result and not a cause—a "superstructure" on an economic foundation.

It is easy to understand how writers come to feel that the sword is mightier than the pen. The man with the sword looks strong, feels strong. The man with the pen looks weak, feels weak. The individual writer, these days, tends to be overwhelmed by a feeling of impotence. What is one man among millions, particularly if he cannot find access to even thousands of readers or viewers? On one occasion, the late Jean-Paul Sartre was told that what he wrote was going to have very little effect. He agreed but said he had to write it anyway; it was his duty. That was a good reply, and leaves open the possibility that what he wrote might have repercussions later, but it is not all there is to say. Expressions of impotence, in this field, have in mind the single obvious factor that a mosquito cannot stop an elephant stampede. Cumulatively, what intellectuals and artists say and do still has an effect, if not always a good effect. We should never let self-doubt, parading as realism, go so far that it betokens sheer lack of self-respect, abnegation of one's identity. Certainly the world will invite you to be no one; but you can decline the invitation.

It is a curious and important fact that the Communist world is much more aware of the social importance of artists and intellectuals than in the so-called free world. We have all heard it said: "You American writers are free to say what you want because no one cares." What I'd like to add is that the people who don't care are making a mistake, a democratic mistake one might call it, since it is based on a refusal to accept the artists and intellectuals as an elite.

In our popular culture, stars and superstars are accepted as an elite. In academic culture, certain scientists are accepted as an elite. Artists and intellectuals as such are not accepted as an elite, though some of them are co-opted to the elite of stars and superstars. Thus a poet like Rod McKuen is assigned to an elite, but a poet like Wallace Stevens is not. Yet Wallace Stevens belonged to a real elite, because that is what the intellectual and artistic leadership of a country really is. Which is conceded when people speak of Emerson as the spiritual father of a country which has George Washington as its political father. However contemptuously an elite may have been treated, however much it may have been ignored, it remains an elite. The talk we have heard against elitism since the sixties has mostly been rather thoughtless, a mechanical application of the idea of majority rule to areas where it does not apply. There is no reason to think a democratic culture needs elites less than Washington's army needed generals.

Playwrights are artists, and like other artists should refuse to be discouraged beyond a certain point. That a political play will not turn a nation's politics around should not deter anyone from writing a political play. One writes it for two reasons other than self-expression: first, in order perhaps to have some little effect on someone somewhere sometime; and second, because politics is one of the main subject matters for writers to treat. The earliest play on record, in the West, *The Persians* by Aeschylus, is a political play, and when I saw it revived in Germany after World War II, I felt it was probably having a strong effect on the German public, if not necessarily a good one. Shakespeare's histories are political plays, and his tragedies have markedly political dimensions—something is rotten in various Denmarks. It has been said, with perhaps permissible hyperbole, that Shakespeare's histories helped win the Battle of Britain in 1940.

We should all refuse to be discouraged beyond a certain point by the fact that many political plays are flops—and deserve to be. Many plays of all kinds are flops and deserve to be. There is nothing wrong with politics as a subject; quite the contrary. There is also nothing wrong with propaganda as such. John Keats says, "We hate poetry that has a palpable design on us."* One sees what he meant, and one could instance occasions when propaganda has been unduly intrusive—bossy, so to speak. But the writers of most books of the Bible certainly had a palpable design on us, and I see nothing wrong with the palpability of such design. Artists, if anyone, have the right to show their colors and the right to wear their heart on their sleeve. *Impalpability* has its

*Letter to John Hamilton Reynolds, February 3, 1818. The subject is Wordsworth's poetry, but the following could be applied to propaganda: "Poetry should be great and unobtrusive, a thing which enters into one's soul, and does not startle it or amaze it with itself, but with its subject."

dangers. A writer who has a design on us, and pretends not to have, is attempting deception, just as much as a writer who bullies us or a writer who lies to us. The threat here is not from propaganda but from dishonesty. In politics, propaganda has so often been dishonest. But the fact that dishonesty is normal in politics does not mean it must be normal in political art, political theatre, though it wouldn't hurt to ponder the specific, often corrupting pressures under which the political artist works.

If the great, classical view of art, dating at least as far back as Aristotle, is that the main purpose is to give pleasure, in most places and at most times art has been regarded as instructive as well. Almost all theories of comedy, for example, embrace the idea that comedy ridicules bad behavior. To ridicule bad behavior is to have a conception of what *is* bad in behavior, and it is also to be recommending the *good* to one's audience. Propaganda? Doubtless the word is too blunt, too political for useful application to most comedies. Yet propaganda is implicit, and explicitness in art may sometimes be undesirable because too crude and uncalled-for: one knows this sort of explicitness from bad propagandist art. No case against good propagandist art is thereby made—good in either of the senses I cited at the beginning, good, that is, in both its means and its ends, its form and its content.

I began by declaring that bad propaganda is bad. I end affirming that good propaganda is good.

(1985)

LORD ALFRED'S LOVER

Prisoners at Auschwitz had a number tattooed on their arms, and in 1985 William F. Buckley proposed that "everyone detected with AIDS should be tattooed in the upper forearm . . . and on the buttocks." Homosexuality is a bitterly political topic. Buckley later withdrew the suggestion, but only to remove the German connection. About ten years earlier, when I received a CBS Playwriting Fellowship, I resolved to write a political play about Oscar Wilde—not another play exhibiting a picturesque personality who came to a pathetic end, but a drama showing what hit Wilde, what social forces he collided with. While I was working on this project, a then-new magazine, *Christopher Street*, asked me to write an editorial for their first issue. It is the essay that follows here. The magazine declined to print it because (I gather) it ran counter to their intention to be unflappably urbane in imitation of the *New Yorker*. So I used it as preface to *Lord Alfred's Lover*. Though it says nothing *about* that play, it tells about the material from which the play was made.

What happens now that that Love *has* dared to speak its name? Actually, several names have been spoken, and none of them provides any grounds for enthusiasm. Homosexual? A linguistic hybrid and monstrosity, as Edward Carpenter long ago pointed out. And one, as we may point out today, that can only give rise to other linguistic monstrosities, like homophobe. And more serious than the linguistics is the suggestibility of the word: no heterosexual thinks himself defined by the heterosexual label, whereas we homosexuals are considered to be defined by nothing else: we are those strange—yes, queer—people who, in bed, perform antics A, B, and C. The word gay is less clinical but hardly more flattering. While it conveys the salutary notion—to be elaborated below—that it is very important *not* to be earnest, it also, alas, comes down to us in an aura of curly blond hair, blue eyes, and prettily vacuous laughter.

Carpenter's objection to the word homosexual is that homo is Greek, while sexual is Latin; and there has been a rule against linking the two in English words. Also the Greek prefix *homo* (same) gets confused with the Latin noun *homo* (man).* The word homophobe indicates a phobia about the *same* something, and if the something is sex, one would infer a phobia about the same sex, and yet that isn't what George Weinberg meant (when he introduced the word in his book *Society and the Healthy Homosexual*). But the linguistics are again the least of it. The importance of the word homophobia has been as part of a polemic waged by Dr. Weinberg against other doctors—the ones who hate homosexuals. Hate is bad, and hating homosexuals (from our viewpoint) is worse. It is good to condemn faggot baiters, not least when these include so many members of the modern priesthood, the priesthood of psychiatrists. Our thanks to Dr. Weinberg, but a "homophile" doctor is still a doctor,** and just as liable as the "homophobe" to think of sexuality solely in terms of good and bad individual health, of more neurosis or less neurosis. The philosophy that commonly underlies this type of thinking is a form of positivism according to which wrong ideas (ideas that seem wrong to us) are just a gratuitous form of superstition. Such ideas are expected to blow away at the first breath of common sense, unless, of course, the holder of the idea is one of the Bad Guys. And homophobes are Weinberg's Bad Guys. They simply shouldn't believe such things with Weinberg out there waving the flag of Reason in their faces.

I am not going to take the position that Weinberg's flag is not that of Reason. I'm going to question the usefulness of waving it. Perhaps not even that: let Dr. Weinberg wave it, and let his opponents get slapped in the face by it, nothing is thereby lost, and maybe something is thereby gained. The masses (who view such capers on television) may thereby begin to be reeducated, and serve 'em right.

But, for us, the nonmasses, this once notorious, now almost glorious minority of the "Homosexual," the "Gay," the flag-waving cannot do a thing, least of all help us understand who and what we have been and are. It will tend, indeed, to deceive us. For (let me make a positive assertion of my own) "homophobia" is not an individual neurosis, a personal eccentricity, a strange miscalculation, an intellectual misun-

---

*In Italian the two homos are distinct: 1. *uomo*, man; 2. *omo-*, same, as with the prefix homo- in homosexual, same-sex. But this has not prevented Christian Holder, dancer and painter, from calling an art exhibit "Mondo Homo," which presumably is saying "male homosexual's world," in a phrase half Italian, half Latin, suggested by the wholly Italian *mondo cane*, a dog's world.

**My readers may welcome this further information. The M.D.s do not regard Weinberg as a doctor at all, since what he has is a Ph.D. But some of them have consented to bicker with him in public. There was, for instance, a television discussion in which Charles W. Socarides, M.D., took part.

derstanding. What we should be studying now is not individual psychology or even mental pathology but history, above all the history of ideology.

I use the word ideology here to embrace the whole complex of thoughts and organized feelings by which a social order, or a social movement, seeks to promote and maintain its existence. Protestantism is ideology to that school of historians which affirms that Protestantism arose to publicize and justify a developing capitalism.

Kate Millett has popularized the term Sexual Politics. Sex, as Zola said, is nothing if not social, so it is natural to find that doctrine on sex never exists in a social void but, on the contrary, has everything to do with promoting social trend A and opposing social trend B. There is nothing "sinister" in the alliance of certain sexual doctrines with reactionary politics: such will be found to be the sexual doctrines favorable to reactionary politics, that is all. A "homophobe" is not necessarily a Bad Guy, he is just a guy who takes his stand with a certain ideology and with the forces which created it in their own interests. And the smaller issue must be judged in terms of the larger. However bad "homophobia" might be in itself, one still has to ask the question: is it justifiable in terms of the whole—the whole society?

What happened? What has Western history been? What we are confronted with is a social order—a succession of social orders, if you will—which has made homosexuality taboo. What does that mean, exactly? What is a taboo, and why? I throw this last question out to any reader who may be able to provide a better answer than those I have been able to pick up in my occasional incursions into anthropology and psychology. What I have picked up is this: each society—or the ruling class therein—has certain intuitions as to what is bad for it, what threatens its existence. Right or wrong in the eyes of God, such intuitions are unquestionably acted upon. By hook or by crook—if not by legislation, then by custom—what is bad is placed under an absolute ban. Help is provided on the propaganda front. Banning entails exaggerating to the point of mythmaking the dangers of what is banned. Hence, treated from an "objective," i.e., external, viewpoint what is said against what is banned is always absurd: exaggeration (as in all religions) is held to be fully justified if the enemy is sin. And the enemy is always sin, since sin is what the enemy is.

Take the injection of the penis in an anus. Viewed from way outside, this act could be seen as anything from, at one extreme, totally uncalled-for (why that protuberance in that orifice? how very odd!), to, at the other extreme, totally obvious (the oddness in this consisting in the strange coincidence that *that* protuberance just fits in *that* orifice). Viewed, however, from inside a social order that has decided what it has decided, the conjecture can be viewed in only one way: as not right but wrong.

It's what "we" have decided *not* to do. Off on mythopoeic wings, we can call it anything in the book, and we will ransack the book for things to call it. People often cite the speech of the judge sentencing Oscar Wilde:

> The crime of which you have been convicted is so bad that one has to put stern restraint upon oneself to prevent oneself from describing . . . the sentiments which must rise to the breast of every man of honor who has heard the details. . . . It is no use for me to address you. People who can do these things must be dead to all sense of shame. . . . It is the worst case I have ever tried . . . that you, Wilde, have been the center of a circle of extensive corruption of the most hideous kind among young men, it is equally impossible to doubt.

Objectively speaking, this makes no sense. Wilde had not been the center of the circle at all. If there was "corruption," it was *of* him *by* the others. It was not the worst case the judge had ever tried, and there must have been many "men of honor" to whose breasts(!) the sentiments mentioned did not rise. But mythology describes what is imagined to be, and mythologizing ideology describes what one is supposed to imagine if one is not "dead to all sense of shame." Critics friendly to Wilde have reproached the judge, but for what? For not living *outside* a system of thought and feeling which he was trained to live *inside*? Why pick on Justice Wills? The judge at the previous trial, which had ended in a hung jury, had thought no differently of the crime or crimes in question. On the contrary, he said in so many words: "With regard to the gravity of the case, I think there is no worse crime than that with which the prisoners are charged." Not the crimes of Nero, one asks oneself, the crime of Judas? Would these judges have spoken differently had they lived to know the crimes of a Hitler or a Stalin? It is unlikely, since *Wilde's own attorney,* speaking of the accusation of sodomy, repeatedly described the latter as "the gravest of all offenses."

    All of which I am citing here only to make the point that when something is taboo, no words are too strong, in the view of the tabooers, to express its unacceptability: exaggeration of the facts is held to be justified in the cause of further discouragement. For, as Freud stressed, nothing is taboo that would die out of itself. It is only necessary to taboo something when everybody wants to do it—perhaps not every person ever born but people in general. It was the incest taboo that preoccupied Freud, and he held that he himself, and you, and I have indeed wanted to commit incest. No one has been more aware of the universality of homosexual wishes than the so-called homophobes. We should hand it to them. When Earl Montgomery was confronted with the Wolfenden proposal to make permissible any sexual act between consenting adults in private, he asked in the House of Lords what in

God's name he was going to do, under those rules, with a troop ship holding three thousand lusty young males? He assumed that "discipline" would go to pieces, and who can say that he was wrong and that his more "sanguine" opponents were right? The "homophobes" have often been the realists in these matters: their opponents have often been off target.

The mistake is to indulge in those discussions of ethics-in-the-void—or, as psychiatrists so often do, of individual patterns outside of a given social order, outside of all human history. To be sure, we have the right to believe it would be a good thing if Montgomery's three thousand men did "have sex" with each other, but this right of ours imposes the duty of examining the whole context of such an eventuality. We might, for example, conclude that the breakdown of "discipline" would be a good thing. Our grounds for such a conclusion could be that we are against all military discipline, all military organization: we are anarchists. Or our grounds, more moderately, and on historical more than philosophical lines, might be that we do wish to preside over the liquidation of the British Empire. In either case, the criteria lie outside psychology, mental health, sexual morality, etc.

How is it that liberal people today see the taboo on homosexuality as less and less necessary? And, as liberal folk ourselves, are we to concede that it was necessary in the past? Hard questions! Let us use as a crutch Karl Marx's idea that humanity doesn't undertake a break-through unless and until it is possible. Liberal people see the taboo on homosexuality as less and less necessary because it *is* less and less necessary. Whether the many gross injustices of history were ever "necessary" in an absolute sense is a philosophical question—ultimately, the problem of evil. Marx and others have rendered the problem a little less painful by arguing that, so long as class oppressed class, injustices were inevitable and necessary, but that they will cease to be so as we emerge from class conflict into freedom, into real democracy. Capitalism needed to oppress the workers, needed to oppress women: socialism has no such need.

It seems to me that many besides strict Marxists can learn something here. The taboo on homosexuality, absolutely necessary or not, was definitely *seen* as necessary by a whole civilization, and while no one, I think, ever succeeded in demonstrating that it *was* necessary, one can certainly piece out for oneself the logic by which the conclusion was reached—or rather the nonlogic by which the *assumption* was made.

Let us first dismiss from our minds the myth of civilization. *Homo sapiens* is not *sapiens* at all, has never yet become a civilized creature. We have the idea, but, except in individual, exceptional cases, we have not had the actuality. The various revolutions which made whole peoples feel that civilization was at hand have given place one and all to disenchantment: after October, the Gulag Archipelago. A friend of Bernard Shaw's wrote a book called *Seventy Years among Savages*, about which Shaw liked to say, "My friend had, of course, never left the British Isles."

The semicivilizations, which are what we have made, were all, as Marx rightly held, based on oppression of one class by another. Throughout human history, the welfare of some classes has been sacrificed to the welfare of others, and throughout the recorded history of the West, women of all classes were oppressed, their happiness being sacrificed, when necessary, to that of men. I say "when necessary" because obviously some women have known some happiness, but it was a happiness that could be and often was sacrificed to the happiness of others. If not the unhappiness itself, the threat of unhappiness was a constant. A slave is not always miserable, but at any moment is liable to be made miserable, and by means that are legal. The infliction of unhappiness has been institutionalized, and the slave has no right to do anything about it.

The enslavement of women is the precondition of the taboo on homosexuality. The prime factor (and motor) is domination by a certain class of men. These men assume, it would seem rightly, that a certain type of manliness is needed first to propel them to the top and second to keep them there. This manliness cannot be equated with any universalist, "religious" idea of virtue, because its function is to oppress: to conquer and to hold on. If such processes, in sheer logic, would seem to imply much violence and cruelty, history, in sheer fact, will bear out the same proposition. If manliness means to be noble and magnificent and proud, it must also entail being cunning and fierce and rapacious. Any man who comes short of the mark in these latter respects is unmanly, womanish. I use the expression "short of the mark" to stay inside the ideology I am describing. Stepping outside it, one could add that it is not just deficiencies that make trouble. A male may have a prettiness of appearance, or a gracefulness of movement, that forms no part of the prescribed pattern. What is not for us is against us. What is not good is bad, therefore very bad, therefore utterly evil . . . If history teaches anything, it is that there are no lengths to which ideology will not go.

Woman is an angel so long as she stays within the role assigned her by her oppressor. Any sign of rebellion is satanic in the strict sense of reiterating the disobedience of Satan, and there is something idiotically simple about the fact that there never was anything to the famous diabolism of woman except her occasional failure to submit to the tyranny of man.

There was usually one way in which the male who failed to be masculine in the approved style could yet prove acceptable to society, and that was by cutting his testicles off. Our semicivilization has had various uses for eunuchs—from hailing them as saints to employing them as singers. What it has not had any use for is the effeminate man with testicles. I use the word effeminate advisedly to signify the man who *is* things and *does* things that are associated with women—sewing and housekeeping, for example—and who abstains from hunting and battle.

The ultimate objection is not to sewing and housekeeping by a genital male. It is to the use he makes of his male genital. The effeminate male, though he may not be exclusively homosexual, does not wish to limit his sexual activity to women. Though in an enlightened society, if we ever achieve one, the word homosexual will probably not be a good description of anyone, it has been the right word for a sexist society to use, since this society did see a male who enjoyed sex with his own kind as being, beyond anything else he might be, "a homosexual." Incidentally, that is why such a strenuous effort is made to free any person of admitted greatness from such a "charge." It is important that we not know if Walt Whitman ever went to bed with a man because if we knew he did he would be "a homosexual," and we would not be able to picture him thereafter except as a penis entering the mouth or anus of another man (or vice versa). Next question: but wouldn't it be reasonable to suppose that the penis of Socrates often described the same trajectory? Say that again? Oh, no, no, Professor So-and-so has shown that all that stuff in the *Symposium* and the *Phaedrus* is just symbolic! Anyhow that was a very long time ago; Jesus hadn't happened yet, and the Greeks are incomprehensible anyway . . . Who says we don't have collectivism? Classical scholars, in a vast collective effort, have effectively conspired to hide what they have known from the public, a conspiracy that is only now coming to an end.

What is wrong with effeminate men? First, that they don't put their penis where they are supposed to want to put it. Second, that they put it where not just they but Sinful Men by the million do desire to put it, namely, in the mouth or anus of another man (or anywhere else on him, it makes no difference, between his thighs, on his belly, in his hand, all of which offenses are worse than murder: Oscar Wilde was not found guilty of sodomy after all but only of "gross indecency," i.e., *some* physical contact or other).

Because I am male, I see the situation of males most easily, but a little imagination makes me see the similar plight of lesbians. Lesbians have the same kinds of things "wrong" with them as effeminate men. They confuse the sex roles in dress, posture, gesture, tone of voice, etc., and then, beyond all these matters of style, which are serious enough, since life *is* life-style, lesbians don't perform the sex act that is expected of them—by the Lords of Creation, that is—but on the contrary, give expression to a natural, but taboo, tenderness for the same sex. Clearly, they should be burned at the stake, or at the very least ducked in the pond as witches.

A paradox is unfolding in my argument. A heterosexualist world decides that nonheterosexuals, though to all appearances human beings, are to be defined purely by their sexual acts: they will be deservedly diminished by such definition. What, however, that same heterosexualist world really resents about nonheterosexuals is that they refuse to limit sex to what has been its primary physical meaning: procreation. On the contrary, they completely divorce it from procreation and imply that it can have another meaning for humankind. Homosexuals "do nothing but fuck," yet their fucking is anything but "real" fucking—as defined in biological terms by the pope and Norman Mailer—it is just an elaboration of hugging, embracing, kissing, murmuring sweet nothings, or mere eye contact. God said, "Be fruitful and multiply!" but these people are using the bodies given them for that purpose for . . . well, what? Frivolous purposes, obviously. They're "balling," and liking it. What could be more revolting?

One thing: a religion that knows nothing of Eros and is still, in the twentieth century, preaching fertility. Besides, as we now realize, "Be fruitful and multiply!" is not religion, it is politics, and today a politics of catastrophe. The world stands in life-and-death need of a check in population growth. One reason that many liberal folk no longer oppose homosexual relations is probably that they no longer feel the need to promote fruitfulness and multiplication. However this may be, the taboo on homosexuality may certainly be traced to primitive times when the power of a tribe might well depend on its size and when, accordingly, an ideology that tried to steer all the semen one way had at least a rationale.

If "Be fruitful and multiply!" only suggests the Old Testament, let me bring up what happened less than a hundred years ago, in the epoch of imperialism, namely, the colonialist application of fertility worship. Its classic spokesman was an American president, Theodore Roosevelt, who believed that the white race must multiply to avoid being swamped by the nonwhite races. The declining birth rate in the West he attributed to "the capital sin against the race and against civilization—willful sterility in marriage." The "woman who flinched from childbirth," Roosevelt wrote, was on a par with the "soldier who drops his rifle and runs in battle."

> The man or woman who deliberately avoids marriage and has a heart so cold as to know no passion and a brain so shallow and selfish as to dislike

having children is in effect a criminal against the race and should be an object of contemptuous abhorrence by all healthy people.

It would seem that, in order to be the masters of reality, as they are, politicians have to be the masters of unreality as, in their rhetoric, their "oratory," they also are: the perfect blend of this reality and unreality spells success, of which Roosevelt had his share, as did his United States of America. To confine ourselves here to the unrealities (albeit unrealities of genius), isn't it interesting that Roosevelt could see the unmarried only as people having no passion at all and very little intelligence, in other words as scarcely people? Roosevelt's understanding of the human body and soul would seem to be almost nonexistent, since he assumes that people avoid marriage only from selfishness and dislike of children. Apparently, he knows no selfish people who like children. Yet if he hadn't been president he could perhaps have been pope. He certainly shared with the Vatican the bizarre illusion that decent young couples making love are really intent on, first, a pregnancy and, second, an increase in the birth rate. The lover whose mind wanders back to anything immediate in his experience our president calls a criminal against *the* race, and we know that *the* race is the Caucasian one, and so the majority of humankind, being black, brown, or yellow, can make unprocreative love without being accounted criminals. The more unprocreative *they* are, the better!

Who was it first decreed that, since indubitably penis and vagina have made contact before a baby was born, sexual pleasure is primarily if not solely Mother Nature's inducement to make babies? A bold idea indeed, not least in making no claim whatever to logic or even common sense. A billion-dollar idea that would go to the making of empires, perhaps mainly to such things. Philosophy is not the strong point of ideologues. But neither, as I said at the outset, is it meant to be. Imperialist ideology is meant to further imperialism, and nothing else. It did. If we now see it critically, that is because imperialism is in evident disarray. The victims of imperialism can no longer be invited to see their conquerors as the wave of the future, only as a wave of the past. Skepticism has arisen, and downright rebellion has occurred. Roosevelt, being no longer a material power, cannot impose himself as a spiritual power. The white race will not multiply till it overwhelms black, brown, and yellow. The "obligation" to even try for that result has vanished. Those penises have long ago gone limp, and retreated from those vaginas. Thank you so much, Mr. President, for exemption from the compulsory erection, the forced ejaculation. May I now do, not as *you* wish, but as *I* wish?

It is the most subversive question in the world: "May I now do as I wish?" Those in power—except perhaps for moments, as in Paris

1871—do not say yes to it. You wish an abortion? The answer rings out from governments capitalist or socialist: you may not have one. You wish to embrace the body of a person you are not linked to by marriage? You're not supposed to. A person of the same sex? Even less. (Qualification: liberal governments will let you *get away with it* if you agree to be furtive and treat such love as something you are ashamed of and wouldn't wish your mother, your aunt, or your daughter to know about.)

Today we are feeling that more is possible. Some of us have already claimed more. Others soon will. None of us have a bad conscience about this. We feel it's the Powers That Be that have the bad conscience these days. And when the pope has the bad conscience, the "sinner" has the good one. Fertility worship is only fertility worship. Let us be bold to say this: sexual intercourse focused on fertility is barbaric (without being primitive, the really primitive thing being to make love without even knowing a baby might result).

I am not a Leninist but will offer Lenin's *Imperialism: The Highest Stage of Capitalism* as a sufficient retort to Roosevelt's *Winning of the West*. On the sexual question, the prophets are Walt Whitman and Oscar Wilde. *Leaves of Grass* repudiates Horatio Alger and Theodore Roosevelt in advance, substituting "loafing" for "getting on," substituting enjoying and revering the environment for exploiting and destroying it. In personal relations, Whitman links sex with friendship, which may well be the most revolutionary act in nineteenth-century literature. It is certainly more important than his homosexuality as such. But woman had been on a pedestal for man, and so friendship, for the time being, could best be found with one's own sex. Whitman's implicit message to the boy scouts of America is indeed: have sex with each other! Ditto for the YMCA dormitories, and college locker rooms. All of which is still "shocking" today.

Intellectually, as witness especially "The Critic as Artist" and "The Soul of Man under Socialism," Oscar Wilde was a more sophisticated man than Walt Whitman. (The second essay may well be the main reason I am not a Leninist.) But the boldness of Wilde's main doctrine lies in its utter simplicity, its absolute lack of irony or double entendre. I refer to his hedonism—which as literary doctrine has been called aestheticism. It is the same thing as his famous—notorious?—frivolity. Just as Whitman, in the era of getting on, proposed to "loaf," so Wilde, in the era when art was respected only if it was edifying, proposed an art that was "totally useless." It would be in order for some clinician of the orthodox (i.e., heterosexual) faith to infer that this was how the two writers' homosexuality affected their thinking. Sex is not purposive and for procreation. It is self-justifying and for fun. Life is not purposive and for becoming vice president of the board. It is self-justifying and for fun. To loaf is to live. As for the art which both writers dedicated themselves to, it is, for Whitman, the celebration of life as loafing. And if Whitman, the older man, retains a little of the Upward and Onward which was the obligatory blather of his century, Wilde, in his definitive statements and restatements of his position, removes the last shred of it. One thinks of the epigrams prefaced to *The Picture of Dorian Gray*—of the epigrams throughout his writing and his talking—but one might just as well think of his masterpiece, *The Importance of Being Earnest*. On the face of it, the play is irrelevant—irrelevant to *everything*—the classic defense of irrelevance. It is amusing, by the way, that relevance should have become the word, in the 1960s, for what Wilde in the 1890s has called earnestness. Earnest people make love to the opposite sex without contraceptives and with a fixed, unsmiling look of deliberate purpose on their pale faces that tells us their sole concern is increasing the birth rate so that the institution of the family may flourish and the white race may become more numerous and races of other colors may be held in check. To be earnest is nothing if not important, and to fail to be earnest is to be "a criminal against the race." Love-making without demographic or imperial intent is at best trivial and, in its classic and classical form, the monstrous, unnameable *peccatum contra naturam*, the worst of crimes, the greatest of all offenses. Behold this Nero of family life, this Eichmann of anti-Aryanism, Mr. Oscar Wilde! He did indeed propose the most subversive of all sub-versions: to make love with a smile and no further end in view.

(1976)

IN EXTREMIS

That I lent a good deal of support to political theatre did not mean that as a critic I had to be "soft" on each contribution to it. I felt it should be held to a high standard. Perhaps I was overhard. But it would not be proper to tone these old reviews down after the fact. Indeed I should, and will, restore such original titles as could not be printed in the *New York Times*. (That is where three of these four pieces appeared, in the Sunday Arts and Leisure Section, then edited by my friend Seymour Peck, whom I used to tease with much news not "fit to print." "The Theatre of Interpretations" appeared in the *Nation*.)

OPPENHEIMER, MON AMOUR

In the program of *In the Matter of J. Robert Oppenheimer* at the Vivian Beaumont Theatre, the director writes, "The play answers no questions, rather it begs the question." I wouldn't have put it *that* strongly, but it is certainly true that the Heinar Kipphardt play seems to seal its subject off rather than open it up.

Both the author and the Lincoln Center management have stressed that this work is a play, a dramatization of Oppenheimer's "trial" by the Personnel Security Board in 1954. Our first question must be: What kind of drama results? And our first answer might be that there is always a little ginger in courtroom questions and answers, and much of *Oppenheimer* is no better and no worse than many another courtroom drama based on a significant case and put together by a theatrical pro. You could drop in on this show at any time between eight-thirty and eleven and enjoy the parry and thrust of forensic cross-questioning, and probably this is the simple base of most of the pleasure the play has provided in the various countries where it has run successfully.

But it has a second claim to interest as art: that it dramatizes issues, and issues of the greatest urgency as well as magnitude. "Guilt by association." "Where does loyalty to a brother end, and where to the state?" "Loyalty to a government, loyalty to mankind." "What kind of people are physicists?" "Can a man be taken to pieces like the mechanism of a fuse?" And there is none of these themes that does not light up for a moment or two during the evening, ignited by some vehement bit of aggression or debate, the trouble being that the play as a whole is but a series of such flickerings: the conflagration which we as theatregoers cannot but hope for never happens. In other words, there *is* no play-as-a-whole, there are at best energetic dialogues laid end to end. Too many themes spoil the broth: needed is a single theme.

Needed also is a complete Action to carry the theme. In basing his play almost solely on the transcript of the 1954 hearings, Heinar Kipphardt gave himself no opportunity to find real antagonists for Oppenheimer. The result is that the source of all evil, in the script, too often seems to be Roger Robb, counsel to the Atomic Energy Commission. Which in turn makes the actor in the role force the pace, pretending to be an instigator, where in fact the gentleman was only the rather inept servant of Admiral Lewis Strauss, who cannot be brought into the play because he did not attend the hearings. In short, this play, for which it is claimed that it dramatizes issues, *cannot* dramatize issues, since too many essential factors are excluded *ex hypothesi*, and the excluded parts are the most dramatic, being the most human. The *included* parts are the most abstract ("What is absolute loyalty?" etc.).

The nearest Kipphardt comes to providing Oppenheimer with a worthy and plausible antagonist is in his vignette of Edward Teller, strongly played at the Vivian Beaumont by Herbert Berghof. But the framework of the show requires that Teller be presented solely in formal answers to formal queries. Essentially, the episode is an exegesis of the Teller position, nothing more. As it ends, Teller and Oppenheimer confront each other. Shall we at long last get an actual encounter, a real scene? No. That wouldn't be part of a "hearing." There are no lines. After extracting as much from a glare as may be extracted from a glare, Berghof can only make his exit.

Leaving on the stage the protagonist. And does even he exist—in the theatre? On the contrary, it is not the smallest weakness in this play of many weaknesses that the title role is so passive, is brought so little in dynamic relation with other characters, a feature which is stressed in the physical production by having Oppenheimer sit on one side all the time. (At the Vivian Beaumont, when not speaking, he sits with his back to the audience.) Character, on stage, is a precipitate from action: an anvil is struck, the sparks that fly are characters. But Kipphardt wants us to accept Oppenheimer as a given quantity, like Jesus in Catholic movies, and with the same effect of pious torpor. The actor is expected to just sit there and be Oppenheimer. Obviously what he *will* do is the usual actor's job of tweedy-college-professor-with-pipe-and-prissy-voice. Not interesting; even when the patina of Joseph Wiseman's very great sophistication—body held just so, voice held one degree from plaintive quiver—is added.

I've spoken of *Oppenheimer* as, in the first instance, theatre, but I don't actually regard it as more important to write a good play than to tell the truth about J. Robert Oppenheimer. The life of Oppenheimer is far more interesting than most good plays, and I for one would gratefully accept a bad play, or a good nonplay, about him, provided it made a fascinating contribution to biography, to history. I have noted that Kipphardt's commitment to a historical document hampered him as artist: did it make him that much better a historian, and that much more reliable a student of the actual Oppenheimer? Unfortunately not. His play cannot even have the value of a movie like *Point of Order* [a documentary about McCarthy], since it shuttles between fact and fiction without letting the audience know which is which.

The claim implicit in Kipphardt's published notes is that, while small facts are shifted around a bit, no damage is done to the essential truth of history. It is, however, Kipphardt who decides what the essential truth is, and, as far as his audiences are concerned, he decides in secret: only the researcher who goes over the same ground will ever know what he discarded as inessential or what he added to the record by way of "truth" which was not actually documented as fact. Going over some of this ground myself, I find a number of the changes merely melodramatic. Kipphardt has Oppenheimer spending the night with a lady friend in a hotel where their presumably amorous conversation is recorded on tape by security officers. In fact, I believe, the "hotel" was the house of the lady's parents, who were present; and nothing was tape-recorded: security merely knew where Oppenheimer was. Again, it is strange, in a documentary style of play, to exaggerate what an arch-exaggerator like Joe McCarthy actually said, yet Kipphardt did just this in the one McCarthy excerpt in his original script. (At Lincoln Center, *echt* McCarthy has been reinstated.)

I would agree with Kipphardt that all such details fade into insignificance beside the question: What is the essential truth of the whole Oppenheimer story? The trouble, here, is that as we pass from fact to truth we also pass from knowledge to opinion: on the truth of the story there will be no agreement but only Kipphardt's opinion, my opinion, and yours, dear reader. A couple of comments may be in order.

For those who take a friendly view of Oppenheimer, the most thrilling and dramatic account to date is not the Kipphardt play but *Lawrence and Oppenheimer* by N. P. Davis.* Yet, like Kipphardt, Davis is so busy rescuing Oppenheimer from fools and knaves that he fails to draw a credible portrait of the man himself. For, quite apart from the notorious "Chevalier incident," which has never been fully clarified, Oppenheimer seems far more problematic—far less sweetly reasonable—than his liberal admirers think. This man of thought was overawed by power. In the thirties he felt the attraction of Soviet power. Offered, however, a fantastic opportunity to add to the power of Russia's chief rival, the United States, he dropped his "left-wing ideas" overboard, freely denounced ex-comrades to the security police, and agreed to see modern life paranoid-style, as a struggle for a "Free World" against Russia. This quick footwork is explained away by Davis and blandly passed over by

---

*Later, there came along a rival to Davis in Philip M. Stern (*The Oppenheimer Case*), 1971.

Kipphardt. The latter does not even notice that Oppenheimer's approach to the Security Board was one of extreme servility throughout. While considerably heightening the malevolence of Roger Robb, Kipphardt protects his audience from the knowledge that Oppenheimer presented to Robb nothing other than the classic Eichmann line of defense: "I was not in a policy-making position at Los Alamos. I would have done anything I was asked to do."

It is therefore quite possible that if other dramatists write about Oppenheimer they will completely reverse the liberal image presented by Kipphardt and Davis and follow in the wake of Haakon Chevalier's two books on the subject. In one of these Chevalier states that Oppenheimer was a sort of Greek tragic hero: tremendous but with a fatal moral flaw. The flaw he sees as pride which finally becomes megalomania. In both books Chevalier maintains that the older Oppenheimer was power-crazed, corrupt, ruthless, totally dehumanized.

But this isn't convincing either. The liberal interpretation and this illiberal one seem to me polar opposites and both equally incredible. Yet both parties have something. Both parties may have a great deal. Oppenheimer was not only a very gifted but a very big man—much room in him for good *and* evil. He was not the liberal that Kipphardt and Davis make him: he passed from the illiberalism of Stalin to that of the Congress of Cultural Freedom without a qualm. But he was not dehumanized, even at the end. He remained human-all-too-human, especially if we bear in mind that the human, though not always amiable, is always contradictory.

Oppenheimer's stature is not in question, but do we have a playwright big enough to depict him? While the German playwright Kipphardt may not have achieved a masterpiece here, he has at least produced a lively, thought-provoking drama. It is depressing to think that no American dramatist has tackled the subject at all, and it is even more depressing to think what some of them would do with it if they did.

A bizarre feature of the New York production is that some of the characters have their real names (Oppenheimer, Teller, et al.) whereas others have fictitious names. It seems that the real names were removed on the advice of lawyers, libel suits being feared. This raises several issues. One is whether the legal advice was well grounded or overfussy. If it is well grounded, then the laws obviously need changing to permit documentary drama to exist. As to the present, pragmatic solution it is thoroughly unsatisfactory. If Edward Teller can be presented under his own name as a heel, why should a very engaging version of my Columbia colleague Isidor Rabi be called "Jacob Lehmann of M.I.T."? (These are all lawyers' games anyway, as the whole transcript of the "trial" was published, and the published text of the play—Hill and Wang, 1969—uses all the real names save one.)

(1969)

THE THEATRE OF INTERPRETATIONS

Against the positivism which stops before phenomena, saying "there are only facts," I should say: no, it is precisely facts that do not exist, only interpretations.

—Nietzsche

Clearly the outstanding fact about "the theatre of fact" is that it is vehemently suspected of propagating nonfact, even lies. Rolf Hochhuth is the *cause célèbre*. Both his plays were based on factual propositions which most people utterly reject: in the one case that Pius XII acquiesced in attempted genocide, in the other that Churchill brought about the death of Władysław Sikorski. A recent play by Conor Cruise O'Brien deals with an alleged crime that stands midway between these other alleged crimes of Pius and Churchill: O'Brien believes that Dag Hammarskjöld and Andrew Cordier,* while they did not bring about the murder of Patrice Lumumba, were worse than acquiescent in it, since they could and should have prevented it but (according to *Murderous Angels*) deliberately and purposefully refrained from doing so.

Our most natural expectation of a documentary theatre is that it would either translate the history books into stage terms, or, dealing with very recent times, that it would remind us of what we know we lived through. Actually, the playwrights, if dealing with earlier history, are revisionist and rebel historians of what the profession could only regard as an extreme sort. If dealing with recent years, they remind us of nothing but charge that we never knew the truth and regarded Pius, Churchill, Hammarskjöld, and Cordier as men who not only did not

---

*Reference is to the mimeographed script in which I first studied *Murderous Angels*. In the published version (Little, Brown, 1968) Cordier's name occurs only once, and only as "Andy" (p. 162). In the version produced on Broadway in 1971, it did not occur at all.

stand for murder but couldn't conceivably stand for it: not being that kind of person. The gist is, then, (a) that the history books are wrong and (b) that the men whom we idealists have most admired were not themselves idealists but at best ruthless realists, matching Hitler's crimes with their own (Churchill), at worst megalomaniacs (Hammarskjöld), schemers (Cordier), or organization men (Pius). Implicitly the plays call on us to (a) see history in terms quite other than those taught in the schools and (b) repudiate the idols of the Establishment: the un-usually holy pope, the gallant spokesman for anti-Nazi heroism, the religious poet who raised high the banner of the United Nations. And why not? That was exactly "where the action was" in the 1960s, and the force of any type of historical drama resides in its topicality: it must quiver with the life not of the era depicted but of the period of the performance.

The Deputy was successful. Which is not to say it was universally acceptable. This type of play will be unacceptable to those who are its target, but it can be held unsuccessful only if it misses the target—that is to say, if it can be shown to be mendacious or otherwise unsound. Marginal errors or dubieties will not wreck them. Central ones are another matter, and here Soldiers was in trouble. Hochhuth was unable to make even his best-disposed readers and spectators share his belief that Churchill was guilty as charged. That Hochhuth tried to make the crime less incredible by arguing that it was tragically defensible only compounded his problem. For, with this, Soldiers just became confusing and confused. It is, indeed, one of those out-and-out failures which no ingenuity can redeem: for every device or idea to which the author has recourse only reveals itself as ingenuity—in the one lost cause. Seldom has so much intelligence produced such a stupid result. My only emotion upon seeing Soldiers was distress at the thought that the author of The Deputy could come to this. I suppose the case is instructive. The two plays are very obviously of the same authorship. The Deputy has some of the shortcomings of Soldiers, especially a Schillerian type of dialogue unrelieved, as in Schiller himself, by humor, but lacking Schiller's sheen and poetry. Soldiers has none of The Deputy's merits. Hochhuth's talent is for shared outrage. The material of The Deputy offered him a foothold, the material of Soldiers did not.

O'Brien's play stands midway between the two Hochhuth plays in yet another respect: its main accusation is more firmly grounded than that of Soldiers but less firmly so than that of The Deputy. I speak here not for historians but for spectators. When we see The Deputy, whatever we may be unsure of, we are sure that Pius XII did stand idly by when he could at least have attempted to do something. When O'Brien urges the complicity of Hammarskjöld and Cordier, we receive his presen-tation as an opinion, a sort of prosecutor's brief, and, however much we may be taken with its wit and thrust, which are considerable, we remain willing to listen to other reconstructions of the evidence.

The *New Yorker* has raised the question: What legal recourse have the villains of such plays? It seems that libel actions have been threatened in some cases. Faced with such threats, Lincoln Center changed the names of some characters in the Oppenheimer play (though not all of these were villains). People can hardly be pleased to find themselves badly thought of by a playwright, but it would be a gross infringement of freedom of speech to prevent playwrights from thinking badly of people. Yet replacing one name with another is a transparent trick, and I am surprised that most of the aggrieved have settled for it. Probably many in the future will not—a pilot involved in the crash that killed Sikorski is already suing Hochhuth in London. * What seems to be needed is a loosening of the libel laws as they apply to the stage. What the journalist can say in an editorial or article—possibly even what Drew Pearson can say in a column—the playwright too must be permitted to say.

I am assuming that the best corrective for untruth on stage will not be litigation but criticism: that of the dramatic critic and that of playgoers in general. If what a playwright says is truly scandalous, the proper retort is in the scandal itself, as it is talked about and as it finds its way into print. By all means, let the admirers of Pius XII present their case. If some argue that when mud is slung some of it always sticks, one has to reply that this consideration cannot justify a ban on mud-slinging. That argument is not a universal truth, anyway. Much mud was slung at Joan of Arc (by churchmen, as it happens), but none of it has stuck.

The documentary play is a little trickier than it looks. That a play is documentary at all means that it surprises and probably appalls its audience with material of which it can and indeed must be said, "Yes, and this actually happened." Hence it was nothing less than cheating when a fictitious episode was inserted into an otherwise "factual" Pittsburgh Playhouse presentation of HUAC proceedings. People left the theatre thinking certain things had really happened which hadn't. That is how the theatre becomes an *un*educational institution!

In this country, the producers of *In the Matter of J. Robert Oppenheimer* stressed that the dialogue was spiced with fiction. For their aim was to forestall libel suits. In Europe, everyone had thought that "it was all true," and one would have had to do a good deal of research to learn that Kipphardt gave a twist of his own to almost everything. Peter Weiss's *Investigation* kept pretty close to the printed records but was

---

*May 4, 1972: the *New York Times* announced that Edward Prchal, pilot of the plane that crashed on take-off from Gibraltar, killing Sikorski, has been awarded $130,000 in damages.

criticized for a certain kind of editing (the word "Jew" kept being replaced).

Would it be a solution to some of these problems if the dramatist did not add any words at all of his own? That he adopted such a course is stressed by Donald Freed in his recent play *The United States vs. Julius and Ethel Rosenberg.* * "Every word you will hear or see on this stage is a documented quotation," he tells his audience. They could well ask what difference it makes, since the principle of selectivity leaves Freed with so many options still open. He has a picture in mind, and he picks the quotations that support it. Theatre of fact in a world where the facts are so many and so various leaves elbowroom for some very large elbows, and selection is not all, there is also the little matter of ordering the material, both as to juxtaposition (montage) and cross-reference. Cross-reference is one form of repetition. There are others, the simplest of which—immediate simple repetition—can have a remarkable effect. Freed repeats anything that takes his fancy. "Un bel dí." "The Battle Hymn of the Republic." Strong stuff that, repeated at crucial points of the evening. Freed has noticed that Joe McCarthy used to say, "I have here in my hand a list of . . . ," giving various nouns and statistics at various times, so in the play he has McCarthy repeat the phrase half a dozen times *without interruption*. Now, a single beat of a drum is one thing; repeat it a single time, a little is added; repeat it a few times and the phenomenon is quite different; repeat it many times and all hell has broken loose. This is the principle involved in repetition of words too; and can easily nullify the principle implied in "Every word you will hear or see on this stage is a documented quotation."

What is the moral? That we can do without documentary drama altogether? That Freed should have presented his material with less manipulation? Or with more—introducing *un*documented material? Well, to begin with, it is a matter of indifference whether material is "documented" if one does not know the value of the documents concerned. Anything is documented that comes from a book, even a bad book. Next, the main question is not whether a speech is documented (in any sense) but whether the audience is on firm ground because it knows what it is getting. The fiction in *The Deputy* is acceptable because it is not taken for nonfiction: to get Hochhuth's message we don't have to believe that there was a Father Fontana who confronted the pope. It follows that there is no special virtue in the plea that all such fictions have been eliminated, especially when we begin to realize how much artifice there can be in cutting, rearrangement, repetition, etc. But, in turn, a work in which every word is a quotation could be valid on the grounds on which we must judge all documentary drama, such as honesty

*Later called *Inquest*.

and intelligibility. In the case of Freed, I have in effect argued that there is dishonesty (no doubt unconscious) in what is evidently claimed in the way of authenticity. Freed is also unintelligible in the sense that he does not really tell the story but takes for granted that we know it, or even that, having our hearts in the right place, we can guess it: So-and-So *must* be innocent, or So-and-So *must* be guilty, these things follow from correct ideology. All of which is an evasion because this way the playwright shirks his obligation to tell the story and create the participants. Instead, we see marionettes dangling on the string of our present discontents.

To tell the story and create the participants. Am I right in assuming that these are things the playwright has to do? Peter Weiss has suggested, on the contrary, that it is permissible for the documentary playwright to "quote" characters rather than create them. He himself, presenting the Lyndon Johnson cabinet in his *Vietnam Discourse,* does not ask the actors to do clever, lifelike impersonations, let alone caricatures à la *Macbird,* but merely "cites" these people. I have not seen *Vietnam Discourse* staged, but I hear from admirers of Peter Weiss that it is his least theatrical effort so far.

O'Brien is also in trouble—or at least in problems—in this department, as I have reason to know. Herbert Berghof wanted me to direct *Murderous Angels* with himself as Hammarskjöld. I asked O'Brien if it could be more a play, especially in certain parts. Could Hammarskjöld be given scenes in which O'Brien's tragicomic sense of him would be more fully realized on stage? For it seemed to me that, while the author's view of Hammarskjöld was clearly stated, little was done to enable Berghof to walk on and *be* such a person. O'Brien in effect asked me to accept his stage figures as Weissian "citations," and I, for my part, would have been glad to attempt a sort of political spectacle, influenced by the Living Newspaper and Piscator, in which character is subordinated to documentation. News clips. The UN on television, etc. I could even have done a little boasting about my use of "multimedia," but, even had the rights remained available,* Berghof really did not wish to play a citation, he wished to play a man. Was he wrong? In the essay "The Theatre of Commitment" above, I myself argued the case for certain political and polemical simplifications. These included a two-dimensional form of character—political caricature, if you will, but not necessarily comic—in which the playwright forgoes psychology (*full* characterization) in order to channel outrage through an expressive stage figure. An example of such a figure is Hochhuth's Pius XII. It does not provide a rounded picture of the actual man. It does drama-

*They went, first, to the National Theatre in London and, later, to the Mark Taper in Los Angeles and the Phoenix in New York (1972).

tize—or, if you prefer, theatricalize—what Hochhuth believes to be Pius's role in World War II, and I would have no complaint against Kipphardt's Oppenheimer or Freed's Rosenberg pair or O'Brien's Hammarskjöld if as much could be said of them. But, in all three instances, the theatregoer can only feel frustrated. The material exudes drama, and it should be remarked that none of the three plays could have any trouble holding an audience. (A hint for the young: in this genre you can hold your audience without being much of a playwright.) Yet in each play we long for scenes that never take place. Shouldn't Oppenheimer be confronted by Admiral Strauss, Hammarskjöld by Lumumba? If not, surely there should be *some* confrontation which brings action and character into dramatic focus? Of course, our authors have alibis. These are documentary plays, and such confrontations could not be documented. Even so, when told what the Rosenbergs did not do (commit espionage), couldn't we, this being drama, be shown what they did do? The point applies equally to the Oppenheimer play. Oppenheimer is also shown as "not a spy." But what is he? What was he actually up to in Los Alamos and earlier? Here the author will cite another alibi. His play is based on the "trial" record, and so *cannot* show Oppenheimer before 1954. The Rosenberg play cannot show what their "record" doesn't show: the life they did lead, the kind of people they actually were. But such alibis only raise the question whether the decision to be documentary in this way was a shrewd one. O'Brien, to do him credit, leans on no such alibis but argues in his preface for certain freedoms à la Hochhuth. (His whole play is a *Deputy* with a Protestant "pope"—an interesting point, considering that he is of Catholic background, Hochhuth of Protestant background.) But *Murderous Angels* would be a better play—would be "more a play" if the author were freer, if he would let go, if he would let *his* Hammarskjöld come into being—by natural childbirth, as it were. * In the plays of Kipphardt and Freed, certainly, one feels the absence not only of full characterization but also of any effective two-dimensional protagonists. The final paradox of their theatre of fact is that their protagonists are balloons inflated with liberal legend and liberal sentimentality.

(1969)

*Seeing the play in the New York production of 1971, I was struck by the *un*natural birth of a certain sexism in it. We were to admire Lumumba the more because he was a womanizer. We were to think even less of Hammarskjöld because he was a homosexual. Sexism rears its head high in an assumption, clearly made by O'Brien, that warm, human feelings flow naturally in the veins of a heterosexual, whereas a homosexual is a cold fish. The second part of this proposition effectively prevents O'Brien from dramatizing the relationship between Hammarskjöld and his black lover. The overall structure is, of course, mechanical as well as sexist: hetero hero with white mistress *versus* homo hero with black lover in a play subtitled "a political tragedy and comedy in black and white."

MOTHER CHURCH FUCKER

I probably missed about a third of the words in Leonard Bernstein's *Mass,* as revived at the Metropolitan Opera House, either because the voices were amplified too much or because they were drowned out by the over-many things going on at the same time. Of the other two thirds, the good ones were all quotes, and most of these were in Latin—I hope Mother Church gets a share of the royalties.

Whatever Leonard Bernstein's status as a composer, as a writer he rates at best with Kahlil Gibran, but is not going to prove as popular, even though his method is based on that of really popular poets of our place and time such as Oscar Hammerstein II. The "death of God" is here recorded in the double rhymes of the Broadway supermusical. "When my spirit falters / On decaying altars . . . " My memory (from which I quote) may be bad but could not be more uninspired than Mr. Bernstein's Muse. Nihilistic, Weatherman-type delight in destruction is re-created in words like these: "Wasn't it smashing / To see it all come crashing / Right down to the floor?"

Dismissing the individual lines of the piece as subliterate rubbish, would it be possible to make a case for the overarching design of it? There must be something to the form of a Catholic Mass: it has had the longest run of all history—nearly two thousand years. Mr. Bernstein may be said to have known a good thing when he saw it, as could have been said earlier of Cecil B. deMille when first he looked into the Holy Bible, the trouble being that the Mass was not intended as drama, nor yet as "theatre piece." There has been a great deal of teaching in our schools to the effect that theatre and ritual are one. Nevertheless they are not one, since there is a broad contrast between persons taking part in worship and persons looking on at a show. The Catholic Mass is a show only to Protestants and other heretics—including, alas, Mr. Bernstein. True, he got the better of those few stuffy priests who complained in the papers that he wasn't respectful enough. He is more than respectful, he is deferential, he is servile, he is abject and very eager to kiss much more of them than their ring finger. He is nonetheless caught in the fallacies of the participatory theatre even when, as at the Met, the thing is not carried to the length of hugging and kissing the audience. For this Mass, unlike the one in the church on the corner, is gawked at by persons who have paid, not to worship or otherwise participate, but to gawk. Now people who are being watched change their deportment accordingly and, under professional circumstances, the changed deportment is called acting. A priest offering you the Host can be regarded as an actor by unbelievers. To the believer what he offers is not histrionic prowess but service in a practical matter—handing across the body and blood of Jesus.

The priests I saw quoted in the press seemed unaware that this *Mass* is vulnerable in a much more vital spot: a Catholic Mass is falsified precisely in becoming theatre. Which in turn means that faulting Mr. Bernstein as poet is insufficient criticism, for, even if he were Yeats and Eliot combined, his present enterprise would still be dubious, if not doomed. When we read that our Christian forefathers hated the theatre and sounded off against playacting, we should realize that they had a very strong point. And such forefathers include not only New England Puritans but Catholics as far back as Saint Augustine.

On the other hand, it would be possible for a dramatist—stopping short of the re-creation in the theatre of an actual Mass—to use features of that ritual in a work whose rationale lies elsewhere, and it is possible to descry in the Bernstein *Mass* the hazy outline of such a work. The pattern is that of a certain kind of group therapy session. A bunch of people come together for an evening. They sit cross-legged in a circle on the carpet. They get acquainted by chatting, maybe even by singing a little. As time goes by, the conversation becomes animated, even quarrelsome. Everyone's aggressions come out. They are supposed to—and people have no inhibitions, now, about their language or their gestures. Angry exchanges are going on all around the room. Sometimes they are "physicalized." Fistfights break out on one side, desire on another, it's a mix of brawl and orgy and for a while is allowed to run its course as such. But there is a controlling hand behind the activities, that of someone who is being paid to deliver therapy. He, she, or they stop the brawling at a certain point. Everyone subsides, panting, like boxers when the bell rings. He, she, or they deliver little pep talks, inviting each paying guest to embrace and hold a neighbor or two. I myself was at one such session where we all held on to us all (if you can figure how that might be done). Whereupon the blessing is pronounced, the session breaks up, and each participant forks out twenty dollars.

Leonard Bernstein is one up on the group therapists in that he offers a bargain rate. Orchestra seats, the night I was at the Met, went for a mere $17.50. But otherwise there really wasn't much difference. Even the presence of an audience can be paralleled in some forms of group therapy—psychodrama at the Moreno Institute, for example. The rhythmic structure is the essential thing. And its attendant themes. The movement is from sociability to warmth. Then the warmth gets *too* warm, and aggressions emerge. As the celebrant of Bernstein's *Mass* prepares to throw the sacred insignia of his office to the ground, the people run amok—the scene is reminiscent of Moses' descent from Mount Sinai in biblical movies. The rhythm up to this point is natural enough, and easily paralleled all through the history of music and drama. It is the culmination that is less universal and (depending on your purpose, of course) less acceptable. This culmination consists of a stoppage of conflict which is arbitrary, not organic, and an equally arbitrary tacking-on-at-the-end of Love Love Love Love Love as a solution that may not be questioned. To be *for* love is, after all, just to be "against sin." You better believe it.

And you do; but that doesn't render the theme any less hard to handle, and it is the paradox of art that what is easiest to believe is the hardest to make believable: it is believable in good art and unbelievable in bad. *Mass* reaches a, for the moment, new low in unbelievability. One cannot even be interested in it as art; adverse criticism of Mr. Bernstein the dramatist (or theatre-piece maker) is too easy. But one should criticize that which he is part of, for much of *that* continues to be accepted even in circles where *Mass* was rejected when it first came out a year ago.

In the theatre, what Bernstein is part of, as I have intimated, is musical comedy, which inherited from Victorian melodrama the arbitrary happy ending and the phony Solution through Love Love Love Love Love. But Bernstein is part of more than the theatre, he is part of liberal America, and this in a specific phase, aptly signalized by the original occasion of the *Mass*, the opening of a Kennedy cultural center in Washington. Like Bernstein, John F. Kennedy was talented, charming, and energetic on that grand, frenetic scale that foreigners call "American." Their good looks were somewhat in the same style when both were young, despite extreme differences of racial background. And their boundless ambition had the same way of looking idealistic.

Kennedy differed from Bernstein in being one of the chief architects of the war in Vietnam, but there is generally and maybe perforce a wide gap, in politics, between practice and theory, and so between the Lost Leader and Leonard Bernstein, his posthumous poet laureate. For this Bernstein is, by virtue of his *Mass*, more than Robert Frost could ever have been, even had he continued to write poems in honor of Kennedy. Frost adorned that regime with glories brought from other climes and times. *Mass,* insofar as it breaks through to expression of any kind, expresses Kennedy liberalism, that is to say, the public relations pitch of this liberalism, as against its real meaning. The best word, then, for what Bernstein proffers is *ideology,* with the Marxist implication that its function is to hide the real meaning. Vietnam? Oh, that's bad. It has got the younger generation really riled up. To the point where they are addressing *us* (the public at *Mass*) in these words, and again I quote, if again from memory: "You people of power / Your hour is now!"

I feel there must have been a few more lines like this that some people heard though I did not, for the word circulated last year that, in presenting *Mass* to surviving architects of the Vietnam War in Washington, Bernstein had in effect indicted them as war criminals and threatened them with revolution. But this was a conclusion that logicians would describe as excluded by the premises.

It is at this stage in our exposition that the concrete, present function of the hoary old melodramatic ending reveals itself in all its ignominy. Yes, the war is bad, and the mood of the students is ugly but lo! but list! who comes here? Well, dear old Love comes here. Naturally, if not organically. Dear *young* love. It is a choir boy who acts as *deus ex machina.* "A little child shall lead them," if sent out on stage by the stagy and sentimental Bernstein. And shall hug them. And shall end up on their laps. Go in peace; the group therapy session is over.

And this is peace—for Vietnam? I wouldn't say *Mass* raises no questions. In my mind it raised the question: is the well-heeled, educated, hip, and oh-so-cultured liberalism of upper-class America today any better than Spiro Agnew says it is? It is not worth $17.50. Is it worth a dime?

(1972)

WERE YOU THERE WHEN THEY WENT DOWN ON MY LORD?

There is a line in the Bible which may be regarded as the very foundation stone of Catholic Christianity: "This is my body, take, eat . . . " It has turned up at least three times in the avant-garde theatre of recent years, and every time it referred to fellatio.

And that's "where we're at" in this year of that same Lord, 1972. Audacious, huh? Audacious once upon a time but, in 1972, boring. Quite a feat on the part of our culture: to make *that* boring. But I'd put nothing past us. Think of the savage doings shown nightly on the seven o'clock news. All boring, now. If one is having dinner at the time, the fork does not so much as pause between the plate and the mouth. So, Lieutenant Calley slaughtered all those little men? Pass me the chocolate sauce.

In his play *And They Put Handcuffs on the Flowers*, at the Mercer Arts Center, Fernando Arrabal does not go further than Calley, which, let's hope, is impossible, but he does try hard to go further than his fellow playwrights. In the previous shows I mentioned, the fellatio—though invoking Jesus' memory—was at least not performed on Jesus' body. In Arrabal's opus, it is; and while He's on His cross at that (singing a bit of Italian opera at the time, well, naturally).

Nor, as they say, is that all. For me this show is, as they also say, "literally unique," since it is really and truly the only time I've ever seen anyone eat his own testicles. Seeming to, that is. And seeming to get them down too. And, except when escorting children to the bathroom, I don't expect to see urine pouring out of a penis. I did actually see this at the Mercer Arts Center and—again, *naturally*—the owner of the penis seemed at the time to have just been strangled.

Such is Arrabal's account of life in the jails of his native Spain, and it has been called stunning, shattering and unforgettable, powerful, devastating, and profound, harrowing, brilliant, and inspired, by men who write on plays for a living: "Deeply beautiful." "The work of a poet." Well, okay, but may I draw the line when one of these colleagues adds: "For the love of mankind, see it"? For one thing, that isn't why *he* saw it. He saw it to get paid by *Cue*, just as I saw it to get paid by the *New York Times*. But you out there, you, the toiling millions who read this paper and do not get paid to see plays, can you reasonably be asked to pay your $5.50 for just this reason? Maybe if you don't love mankind *all that much*, you might think $5.50 and a visit to the Mercer Arts Center about fit the case. If you love mankind more than that, you'd want to *do* more than that. You might block the aisles in St. Patrick's Cathedral as some stalwart sisters have been doing lately. You might risk going to jail. My question is whether you would go to a *play* about jail. From that motive.

Some evidence I have. For some of you were present the night I received my thirty pieces of silver from the *Times* to review Arrabal. When the Lord was being "molested," you looked nervously to left and right to see how I and the others were taking it, and when you found that we were not, after all, stunned, shattered, devastated, and harrowed, you were so relieved: You grinned a little sheepishly. It was just a play, wasn't it? That guy didn't *really* swallow his testicles, and nothing really happened to that Christ, who never even got His loincloth off. Which is just fine with me. I was brought up on theatrical conventions— on the assumption, that is, that the theatre does have conventions: on stage, you don't always do things, you often just pretend to do them.

One problem area for Arrabal, who is also the director of *And They Put Handcuffs on the Flowers*, is uncertainty of convention. He uses *some* conventions (unremovable loincloths, for instance) but then, at other times, proceeds as if all conventions were being "courageously" abandoned (as when an actor is asked to prove that his penis is what his urine flows through). Now uncertainty of convention always produces uncertainty of effect. The image is neither focused nor deliberately out of focus, it is just unclear, it is just what it should *not* be. As against a masterpiece where (by definition) everything is just *as it should be*.

Arrabal says he'd like his play to be a shout. It *is* a shout; and that's the trouble. He is like some debater who, whenever he's in difficulties, raises his voice. Or like many of the rock groups which, when they have no music to offer, offer earsplitting noise. We live in an insensitive time, and we make ourselves more insensitive by the things we do to ourselves. Our pop music is too loud—which is the way to drown out conversation, to get rid of other people and ultimately to get rid of ourselves. Suicide would be better. Rock stars regularly commit it.

Arrabal uses the word "shout" symbolically, and so do I. There are louder shows in town, measured in decibels, but not measured in stridency of soul. Inevitably the result is self-defeating. Like sound in the literal sense, spiritual noise can be so loud one cannot listen. One gets to a point where one cannot even hear it, but just decides to ignore and live with it, the way one holds a conversation in the subway without hearing the din of the trains. Thus it is that our attention—which is what a writer, above all a writer like Arrabal, supremely wants from us—is something we do not and cannot give.

All of which is the more dismaying because of Arrabal's subject. Political prisoners in Generalissimo Franco's jails are brothers to whom our hearts go out with particular love. In a work of art they can easily stand, too, for other brothers in other jails. The conscious purpose of Arrabal must have been to make us feel this. But either he simply cannot, or there is an unconscious purpose that gets in his way. One could not believe that this play was written *by* one of the brothers. The viewpoint seems rather that of a visitor to the jail—a very shockable, middle-class, "aesthetic" visitor at that. True, his kind of shock makes a valid subject, and one that has this much to be said for it: it can be shared by the guilt-ridden, liberal middle class which patronizes the Off-Broadway theatre.

But even this lesser drama is not really created, for *all* drama is effectively trampled underfoot by Arrabal's elephantine dramaturgy. When in doubt, and he must have been in doubt nearly all the time, he reaches for a "daring" effect, a "shocking" exaggeration; and this is so very, very boring. The aim, a work of art expressing brotherly love; the product, a monstrosity conveying an impression of a poet-narcissist. Alas!

The subject itself goes virtually untouched. Arrabal hardly begins to show what prison is all about. His vignettes of the ruling class are the clichés of agitprop—this phrase indeed almost flatters them. Who and what put these men in jail? Not a living word! Everything is reduced to the grand guignol melodrama of monstrous torturers and innocent victims. That our brothers have other qualities besides innocence (and aren't always innocent in the sense assumed) is something this would-be revolutionary playwright seems not to have told himself.

There is a fatal ambiguity. Arrabal wants to say: prison is obscene, therefore bad. But he himself suffers from a small-boy fascination with obscenity: for him it isn't so much bad, finally, as it is alluring, even necessary to his sense of fun, his sense of being an Artist.

In the window of a porno bookstore on 42d Street the other day, I saw the jacket of what I suppose was a juicy novel about Auschwitz and the high jinks there. It showed a Jewish boy kneeling before an SS guard, and it was entitled *Go Down, Aaron.* Arrabal and his admirers no doubt despise that sort of thing. The question is: do they have the right to? We are confronted these days with a pretentious *pornography of the avant-garde* which is defended, in court and elsewhere, by the argument that it cannot really be pornography *because* it is avant-garde. I couldn't care less about either the scientific or the legal definition of pornography, but there *is* something at stake, namely our right to be offended and disgusted—nay, on occasion, our obligation to be so.

I began by saying that the avant-garde "daring" no longer packs a punch. One would be too charitable, however, to say that it is inoffensive. The person who cannot be offended and disgusted by anything—or even by anything labeled avant-garde art—is no longer a person. At this point our avant-garde friends will put in: "but you're *supposed* to be offended and disgusted." The question here is: with whom? And I'm afraid that in this instance we have to be offended and disgusted with Arrabal.

There was something I noticed about my fellow spectators other than their tendency to smile nervously at the horrors. It was that they seemed inhibited, even intimidated. They would have liked, I think, to protest the play, but this would have exposed them to ridicule on the dual grounds that they are reactionary and that they are philistine.

It is time to say that the emperor of the avant-garde is naked. It would be appropriate if radical Catholic groups disrupted the Arrabal play. That will be hard, not only because of the inhibitions and intimidations just mentioned, but because Arrabal tries to forestall any such objections by the device of getting it in first. The audience is humiliated from the moment it is denied numbered seats and is ushered, in a mass, into an unlit auditorium. Later (as I am sure you would guess) individual spectators are picked on and bawled out—the usual arrogant brainwashings of our fake activist theatre. But theatrical totalitarianism is another thing it would be good to launch a protest against. And, as I say, to disrupt. Let those who call for audience participation take note that, when finally the audience does participate, it may take action against *them.*

Not necessarily in the style of avenging furies. That would itself be Arrabalian. His show deserves a better fate than that, if only because, despite any impression I may have given to the contrary, it is not all bad. It has moments of beauty, as for example in a lyric exhibition, at one point, of naked lovers, seen very simply, quietly, motionlessly, without the usual gothic contortions or hyperesthetic hysterics. It has actors of such distinction that they are often worth watching without respect to their plight in this play: Ron Faber and Peter Maloney, in particular, are flowers who manage at times to get their handcuffs off.

The show should be disrupted, not by Weathermen but by nuns, perhaps the same nuns who disrupted the services in St. Patrick's. Such an occasion would be civilized—unlike the play disrupted—and very educational for the audience, the actors and, above all, the author-director.

(1972)

IN MEMORIAM

Obituaries are mostly written by professionals in that line of journalism but, if a writer has lived to be sixty, he is probably asked to write about his contemporaries when they die. I have accepted such invitations four times, though the invitation to write on one of them did not come till years after his death. Three of the results follow here; the other is in my *Brecht Memoir*. The point in each case was not just that a good man had gone and I was glad to honor him. The points were two: first, without being intimate with the good man, I did know him, and have my own perspective on him, and, second, I had been in at least argumentative and at most quarrelsome relationship with the good man—after the fight *with* him was over I still had to fight with myself *about* him. Of Brecht I have said that I sometimes hated him, which has permitted people to speak of my love-hate for the poet. They are wrong. Love-hate—ambivalence—was not what was involved. Rather, disagreement. Distance. Not all tangling with another human being is a Strindbergian war to the knife. I have experienced it as a striving to get closer when feeling very far apart. Closeness achieved too easily becomes a facile euphoria. The *agon* (antagonism, but not necessarily hate) may well represent the terms set for authentic encounter. The leitmotiv of my four In Memoriams is love.

STARK YOUNG (1881–1963)

The aesthetic principles are at bottom such axioms as that a note sounds good with its third and fifth, or that potatoes need salt.

All intellectual work is the same—the artist feeds the public on his own bleeding insides.

There is in the living act of perception always something that glimmers and twinkles and will not be caught, and for which reflection comes too late.

We long for sympathy, for a purely personal communication first with the soul of the world, and then with the soul of our fellows.

—William James

THE ARTIST AS CRITIC

A man who has written novels, poems, and plays probably will not wish to be remembered chiefly as a critic. That is to be considered a success in a secondary pursuit and a failure in the primary ones. But is criticism secondary except in the sense that it is dependent on the others: one criticizes novels, poems, and plays? Is it easier to criticize well than to write a good novel, poem, or play? Doubtless the answer to this question varies with the individual but one cannot answer with a blanket yes. It is hard to write good criticism. Is the result less interesting for the reader? No. Nothing could be more interesting to avid readers than a page of criticism by a Samuel Johnson, a Matthew Arnold, a T. S. Eliot, an Edmund Wilson. Finally, is criticism less *important* than the literature it criticizes? Oh, dear! What I think we should do with this question is reject it. Though conceding that criticism is, if you will, a parasite upon what it criticizes, as the mistletoe upon the oak, one need not declare the result inferior. If it has less of quality A, it has more of quality B. The oak may be the king of the forest, yet it is the mistletoe that one kisses under at Christmas. (What would it mean to say: oak is better than mistletoe?)

All of this is a preamble to saying that the crown of Stark Young's creation—as of Edmund Wilson's, who also wrote poems, novels, and plays—is his critical prose.

When I was young, we asked each other whether a given literary critic was a Marxist or a Freudian. Recently I was asked to contribute to a symposium in which critics would declare an allegiance to more modern schools of thought such as structuralism and semiotics. Following any of these trails, and others comparable, what one encounters is a claim, explicit or not, that by a given method, as like as not called methodology, literature can be rescued from mere connoisseurs and belletrists, from mere appreciators, and recorders of personal impressions: literature can now be understood and in depth.

I said I wouldn't wish to contribute to that symposium except possibly to express a dissent. I didn't see criticism being saved by any *ism* whatsoever: I would rather see criticism uncommitted to all isms whatsoever. Good criticism, I went on, is a matter of the critic's talent, not his philosophy, it is wholly a matter of his intelligence and his sensibility. A "correct" approach, embracing a wider, perhaps more scientific comprehension of aesthetics, might seem to offer an entrée into the arts even for those lacking in intelligence and sensibility. You may not respond much to Beethoven's last quartets—your receiving apparatus may be too crude, too closed off—but don't worry, we can give you a vocabulary by which you can explain those quartets as they were never explained before. This way you fill up pages, use opaque language, make a big intellectual impression, but you will be evading the main issues . . .

I realized while I was giving this little lecture that my models, among my older contemporaries, were indeed Edmund Wilson and Stark Young, and that I was on guard against not only certain recent developments in France but against, say, T. W. Adorno's philosophic criticism in Germany, even though there are fine personal perceptions buried in Adorno's tortured super-bureaucratic prose. I resist the tendency in recent years to replace criticism by theory. One could easily name living scholars who were better critics before they had a philosophy of criticism—that is, when they were educated young people who responded to the arts using nothing more than a traditional vocabulary and nothing other than the traditional stock of words and notions in the field.

Criticism may often be in a parlous state but it has never yet been rescued from that state by a philosophy of aesthetics, nor yet by semantic adjustments, however subtle. A new phrase—Significant Form—or whatever—may send a few shivers down a few spines, but is not really an eye-opener. Nothing a critic has can open your eyes except his own eyes: he says, look! and you look. Which sounds gratuitous but is not. For you had failed to look, or had not looked with sufficient concentration and discrimination. A good critic will get you to do so.

When I ask that the traditional vocabulary be used, I mean that criticism is intended for the nonspecialist. It is good talk committed to the printed page. Presumed is a circle of talkers—the artist's audience. What they speak is English as it is spoken: English as it is not spoken is no more appropriate than, say, a language of symbols, like the pluses and minuses, A's and B's, X's and Y's, of a *Principia Mathematica.*

Even a critic is a person. No: especially a critic is a person, and the voice of a person must be heard in all his work. Conversely, all criticism in which a human voice is not heard is bad criticism.

Question: Isn't it possible that criticism might become too personal—in the sense that the person indulges himself, asks for overparticular attention, preens, poses for the cameras, overinsists that attention be paid to him?

Answer: Oh, what an unfair question! How could one answer it except in the affirmative? But this affirmative answer is so uninteresting!

May I advocate a style for criticism, however serious, that is not too far from the spoken word? An argument has been made for obscurity in modern literature. But when this literature is discussed by an Edmund Wilson it becomes less obscure. That is why he took pen to paper: to explain the more unknown by the less unknown. The more grandiose and doctrinaire school of modern criticism explains the unknown by the more unknown. Proust is difficult, God knows, but criticism of Proust can be even more difficult! My argument is that this is a reason for not reading such criticism.

Good criticism results from no lazy or easygoing process or mentality, but its purpose *is* to make life—the life of the student of the arts— easier. If it fails, the student is justified in taking leave of the critic and having another go at Proust . . .

Stark Young's theatre criticism rests on two principles: (1) the autonomy of art and each work of art; (2) the autonomy of each of the arts, including the theatre art.

1. How can one square the statement that Stark Young stood for the autonomy of art with the notion, the knowledge, that he was famously a "Southern" critic? Edmund Wilson called him an unrecon-

structed Southerner, and the phrase is accurate, even in the extreme view of that time as to what "Southerner" meant: it meant of course a white Southerner who still saw himself as a Confederate soldier. If Stark Young was that kind of Southerner, would it not follow that his criticism showed a bias? Did he not favor works that such a Southerner would sympathize with? Did he not view other works with disfavor? To which one must answer, yes, every critic's work reveals certain biases, and Young's is no exception. One will see him fail to bring the same sympathy to plays with one background that he brings to plays of another background. No critic is God. Still, the effort was to see each work of art in artistic terms. In intention if not always in practice, Stark Young gave every work a fair inning, a fair chance to be a work of art. Was he an aesthete? No, not if that word means art for art's sake. Stark Young would have been quick to observe that art was for life's sake. Only it must be art. And the critic's first duty is to report if a given work *is* art—if what was to be expressed has in fact been expressed and that in the terms of the particular art concerned. In other words, art is valid, is self-justified, doesn't have to justify itself by nonartistic criteria—whether those of a pope or of a commissar, whether those of Jerry Falwell or of the *New Republic*'s editorial board. Each artist should be happy, should feel privileged, to serve art itself. (Yes, art is serving something. Art is serving life. I shall come back to that later.)

What of Dante? Was he not serving the Christian religion? That, too; but not that instead. He could so easily have served the Christian religion without writing *The Divine Comedy*! If in the service of *that* religion, he created *this* poem, one asks first: has the poem been created? Is it a *poem* and not just a Christian message with aesthetic trimmings? The consensus is that, yes, it *is* a poem, and among those agreeing to this consensus are persons who do not serve that religion, persons who are not Christians. Catholicism, pragmatically speaking, is not as universal as art: for Dante has a range that goes beyond that of his Church. The human race does not accept a single theology, but it seems likely that it does recognize as universal certain principles of art. In that sense, art is the true catholicism.

Art is autonomous, which is to say it is not to be judged as theology, philosophy, sociology, psychology, or whatnot. Each work of art is autonomous, which is to say it must not be judged by preexistent standards—"all good plays have three acts, therefore this play with two acts is bad"—but as it *turns out* to be, with the effects it *turns out* to have. Necessarily, then, it must be judged in terms of its internal relations—the relations of its parts. In taking this position already in the 1920s, was not Stark Young the father of what in the thirties and forties came to be called the New Criticism, of which the worthiest as well as best-known monument is the college textbook *Understanding Poetry* by Cleanth Brooks and Robert Penn Warren?

In time the New Criticism was deluged with objections on historical grounds. Critics pointed out again and again that it was wrong to wrest works of art from their historical context and tell students they need only look at the poem on the page before them. But there's a misunderstanding here. This New Criticism did not presuppose ignorance of history. Rather it presupposed an educated reader who knew his history. What *was* being maintained was that nothing of history or any other subject could make a poem worth reading, could justify a poem's existence. To be justified, it had to exist as itself: in terms of the relation of its parts, in terms of what was there on the page, just as a piece of music had to justify itself to your ear, had to create an existence for itself by being listened to, not by being enlarged upon cerebrally and culturally, not by being related to its background, these latter processes not to be excluded but only to be postponed. You can relate a poem to its background once it has registered with you as a poem. Otherwise a bad poem, an unrealized poem, might be of more service than a good one. And indeed if one is going to rifle literature for information, why couldn't bad works of art prove more relevant and helpful than good ones? Let's not confuse the possible documentary value of bad art with the history of good art. The history of good art can only be written by historians who appreciate the *goodness*, which is to say they have experienced it. Otherwise what you will get is the history of music by persons who have never listened to any of it. Such history is not unthinkable: it is quite easy to put together lots of information about Beethoven, or the sonata form, without doing any listening, even of the most external sort. And what I'm calling "external" listening isn't of much worth either. The listening that great music deserves and requires is "internal"—i.e., it makes a demand upon the inner man, the whole man, it is a listening not only with the ear, but with the brain, and not only with the brain but with the heart.

Very well then, one must learn to look at a single work of art and observe, and respond to, all its internal relationships. This formulation perhaps suggests merely mechanical relations, or correspondence to existing customs, hardening as they do into formulae and rules. To observe which lines rhyme with which in a sonnet is certainly to observe internal relations, but it is not art criticism: it is only mechanical measurement. It proves nothing artistically, as bad sonnets have the same rhyme scheme as good. Traditional French schoolteachers indulged a good deal in these mere mechanics: they set forth the customary modes of famous works, and exhibited the particular work only to exemplify the general rule. Thus a reader can observe that dramas have a climax two thirds of the way through, and can then give instances. If the pupil of such a teacher becomes a drama critic on a newspaper, he may well end up complaining that so-and-so's new play does not have its climax two thirds of the way through. Routine criticism, bad criticism, comes about that way: approving or disapproving according to received doctrine or habitual formula.

But what the critic really needs to do is enter into the *life* of a work of art: only then can he hope to say if the real job has been done. What is the real job? Stark Young had an answer that is shocking in its simplicity. He said that the artist has some idea: the critic must, first, find out what it is and, second, estimate if it has been fully expressed in terms of the art in question—in pigment for a painter, in sound for a musician, in words only for a lyric poet, in theatre for the artists who make theatre. And here we must pause to note that in using an ordinary word, the word Idea, Stark Young has invited misunderstanding. Read on and you will learn that he is not talking of what is called the drama of ideas, he is not talking of the Platonic Idea (though that indeed is never far from his mind), he is using the word Idea to indicate that singleness of intention in the mind which will draw all else with it. In this sense, the painter of an entirely abstract painting may be said to have an idea. Likewise the composer of a fugue.

Here the word Singleness is just as important as the word Idea. A work of art is anything but a bundle of ideas. The last thing an artist tries to do in one work of art is toss in all the ideas he's got. Indeed, two ideas have often proved one too many, because, unless the one is subordinated to the other, they will merely compete for attention, cause confusion, prevent the work from being truly single, from having that *unum necessarium* which is Unity itself. And Stark Young will call on Plotinus and Augustine to endorse him here, for the doctrine of Unity is his holy of holies. If it is also a commonplace, so much the better: art can be universal because it is universally agreed that a work of art must be a Unity, and therefore that any defect in this regard will be grounds for dissatisfaction and complaint. But again one must note the futility of judging by externals. *Unity cannot be established by Unities.* Or by any external requirement. Conversely, a play by Shakespeare, brazenly disregarding the Unities, may have unity, indeed would not be a Shakespearean masterpiece if it did not.

A *single idea, then, expressed in a single, a unified work:* this is what we are to demand. But what does it mean *expressed?* Fulfilled. In the medium concerned. The idea seeks out that medium as the appropriate one, and the medium in turn successfully offers itself as the appointed realization. Thus was stone the medium in which Rodin could realize this idea and that.

2. The autonomy of each of the arts, the autonomy of the theatre art. Each art, Stark Young liked to say, should be doing what it *alone* can do. Not duplication, but differing uniquenesses, is what the gods have offered us. So the true philosopher would contemplate what stone has expressed for Rodin, paint for Cézanne, music for Bach, and so on.

What of the theatre art? People of my background have tended to see it as literature wired for sound and latterly wired also for the television screen. In other words, performance tended to be viewed, by literary people at least, as just a transmission apparatus like a telephone. Bernard Shaw, for instance, viewed movies as merely a way to reach a wider audience, not as the adaptation of his work to the ways and means of another art.

When I first heard of Stark Young, he was on the staff of a magazine called *Theatre Arts,* and what most of us imbibed from that monthly magazine was the view that theatre wasn't just one art, literature, it was several: it was music, it was stage design, it was acting and directing. One art was added to another. The various arts were piled one on another. A rich potpourri! This, however, is not the doctrine of Stark Young.

Equality was not a favorite notion for him, and certainly he did not preach that, in theatre, the various arts were equal. What he did say is continuous with the theory I have been expounding. If each art is unique, then theatre is not literature. But if theatre is unique, then it has a character of its own: is one thing, not several things. Those several arts have to be combined in a unity, and, if this is not a union of equals, then some sort of ranking order will be discerned—*dis*order being inconsistent with the overall principle of unity. In this ranking order Stark Young puts the playwright first. Second comes the actor, and in one respect he is first: he comes at the spectator first, is that which the audience confronts *in the first instance.* To the extent that some plays are actor proof, the director too might move into first position. To the extent that a play is weak, but susceptible of rare spectacle, the set designer and costumer might, exceptionally, move into first position . . .

Now here comes an essential part of the theory which perhaps even today has not been fully absorbed, though it follows quite smoothly from Stark Young's premises. Although the playwright is the mastermind of dramatic theatre, the actor is not a telephone transmitting his dialogue, nor yet a semaphorist signaling his gestures. He is a person. He is an artist, and as such a maker of art, a creator of something new. True, this something new can be, should be, an interpretation of what the playwright has written. But an interpretation that is also a work of art is itself unique, therefore different from, distinct from, what it interprets. Again the principle of the single idea applies. The actor of Hamlet does not merely add one line to another, "interpreting" each line as he goes along, thus arriving at The Interpretation by aggregation. That would only be improvisation. The actor has studied the role. He has absorbed it as he *can,* that is to say, as he *is.* It is rash, as Stark Young often pointed out, to say: this actor *became* Hamlet. No, he remained himself. Only a god like Proteus becomes someone else. A human being establishes points of contact: finds what, in his own personality, can be used to express what Shakespeare has written. What Proteus would come up with one might call the Platonic idea of the role. But of the human actor one cannot even say that he should get as near this as he can, for that is not how your human actor works. He is not a dybbuk climbing inside someone. He is an artist making . . . *something new.* Something new that he hopes the author might endorse if he were around but which in any case must be a dovetailing of Shakespeare's unique piece of writing with his own unique personality and unique artistry. "Dovetailing" is an ill phrase if what it suggests is pastiche. The final result must be single. The actor cannot invade and annex Hamlet, but he has an idea of Hamlet and he can express it. Ideally speaking. And this, not mere subordination to Shakespeare, *is* the ideal. If less is achieved, it will be for the critic to point out that the idea is but imperfectly expressed or, worse still, that the actor's idea is itself unworthy, misleading, even dead wrong.

So what is required of the theatre critic? The perspicacity to read the idea in the performance, and the tact to sense if it is fully expressed and in what details, by what means, by what surprising line-readings, by what unpredicted movements. What the critic must not do is accept or reject these movements, these line-readings, on their own—as being traditional or the reverse, as being handsome or brilliant or the reverse. He must see them, feel them, as part of a pattern, the pattern that expresses (if all is well) the pervasive idea.

I am restating what I have taken to be the two main principles of Stark Young's theatre criticism. In essence they are traditional, even perennial, nor are they unduly complex. Nonetheless they remain beyond the grasp of most dramatic critics, who seem incapable of the discipline required, the intellectual labor required, and instead blurt out their immediate reactions to the separate parts of the theatre occasion. They register only a brute response to each moment, or perhaps only to certain moments, the moments when they are awake. And since such waking moments follow minutes of somnolence, one senses the lack of connection with what has been going on. Our critics are accustomed to let themselves be as passive as the most helpless, hapless spectator. "Show me!" "Entertain me!" Alas, extreme passivity simply inhibits all real artistic experience. When Walt Whitman said that for great art you need great audiences, he meant, I should think, that the spectators ought to be artists too, people willingly a part of the artistic experience, bringing to the event eagerness, curiosity, intelligence . . . The ideal spectators I find myself dreaming of here would of course all be critics. Criticism doesn't have to be written down. What, following in Stark Young's footsteps, I've been defining as the critic's attitude is only the ideal spectator's attitude. I'm dreaming of a wakeful, alert audience that would grasp an idea and figure if it was being properly expressed.

The Artist as Man

I had not followed Stark Young's career at the *New Republic* before World War II—I was too young for that—but I picked up the books on theatre that he had brought out in the twenties and mentioned them in glowing terms in my first book on theatre, *The Playwright as Thinker*, 1946. Stark Young was to retire from the *New Republic* in 1947, but he wrote a long review of my book a few months before that happened. Rereading it today I find him in two minds about the younger critic: I couldn't have been that good if I was also that bad! On the one hand, he says the book is "worth reading," nay, "excellent," and "manages to say a surprising lot, and amid so much knowledge, scope and even prophecy, to omit vast quantities of nonsense and vapor." On the other hand, he pushes it away as minor and external to its real subject, which is art. In an attempt to sum up, he says that the book has range, and that he can't do justice to it, the book is so ambitious, but he does think he has found its weak spot:

> The bright shortcoming in the book is the author's lack of knowledge of the theatre. . . . I gather from the text that his presence at some theatre occasion would be worth little, though he might be good, taking the play as itself solely, on the future or the past for it. You can tell, from what he says about various plays, that he has never seen them produced. . . . There are many moments in great drama where the actor's voice would be the final test of the moment's power, but Mr. Bentley does not know that.

Stung by these comments, I was determined to prove that I did know—or would get to know—the theatre. Hitherto—Stark Young had guessed right—I had done hardly any theatre criticism: I was too busy studying for a Ph.D. in comparative literature. But I was now able to get myself invited to write a mini-manifesto about theatre and its critics on the occasion of a visit to New York of the Old Vic of London. It contains a long paragraph about Stark Young in which *I* am in two minds about *him*. In his review of me, he had stressed my youth, and in this retort of mine I find him old and tired and nostalgic. He is living with the theatre's past whereas one must think of its future and, if one writes on it, live with its present, etc., etc. On the other side, I find him worth reading and the best dramatic critic around.

It was this piece, entitled "The Old Vic, the Old Critics, and the New Generation," that brought me the first of those letters from Stark Young that would much later find their place in John Pilkington's two-volume *Stark Young: A Life in the Arts*. It was a long letter with many interesting and characteristic things in it, yet what has stuck more clearly in my memory is that Stark Young had cut out paragraphs of my piece and scribbled on them. One scrawl read "two times two is four"—this was written on top of my excoriation of the Broadway critics. He didn't disagree with my diatribe, but to him such things were not worth bothering about. In his review of *The Playwright*, he had agreed with my refutation of some argument or other by Allardyce Nicoll, but had made it clear he didn't think Allardyce Nicoll worth refuting. Here you may sense the distance between the veteran artist who had fled academia three decades earlier, and the young assistant professor who considered himself rather bold in taking on the leading academic in his field. Nicoll was at the time dean of the Yale School of Drama.

The important thing for me was that Stark Young's letter brought us face to face for the first time. After which acquaintance grew to friendship. Professionally, we now became a mutual admiration society. I dedicated a book to him, and he did something more unusual: in a reissue of a book of his, he deleted the name of the original dedicatee and replaced it with mine.

Of the private Stark Young I don't wish to say much more than that he is still in the shadows. He withheld a large and central part of himself both from his novels and from his letters. It was my privilege to make contact with that private life and at least glimpse some of its joys and its agonies, its triumphs and its failures, its realizations and its errors.

But there is a point I wish to make about Stark Young's work which is intimately related with the self which he kept hidden. I disagree with those who find Stark Young precious, overelegant, dandified. They would have a real point only if the elegance of his writing was a self-contained thing, if his work was all surface and gave no sense of what was under that surface. Even without knowing his life, I think you can gather something else from the writing, and especially from the best of it. The qualities he achieved in his prose are a triumph over equal and opposite qualities in life, and indeed, if one is to understand Stark Young, I think one will do so *in terms of opposites*. What he thought of the world you could figure by reversing what he says about high art or what he himself makes by way of high art. Why the enormous emphasis on beauty and soul? Because this world is ugly and soulless. Why the passionate love of intellectual clarity, of spiritual simplicity? Why the predilection for high style, why the consistent attempt to achieve it? Because the world is a mess, a chaos, complex and untidy beyond all comprehension, because our life and work are styleless, undistinguished, paltry.

It has been said of Ernest Hemingway that his prose at its best seems written in the state of tension of someone with only hours to live, and indeed we now understand that Hemingway lived for years with such a sword hanging over him, a sword his father had already used, and which, alas, Ernest would use long before he had lived out his time. In Stark Young's work, I don't feel it is death who waits in the wings, I think it is pain, psychic pain, unbearable anxiety threatening to overpower and overwhelm with its manic message: CHAOS IS COME AGAIN.

And so qualities that keep us from being hurt are the qualities that above all else are sought after. *"Qualities that keep us from being hurt."* I have taken the phrase from Stark Young. From the heart of Stark Young. What is there is a sense of hurt. I must report that this is what I felt in the man I met and then learned to know and then learned to love. The beauty he sought to create, like the beauty he doted on in Italy and Greece, in the Old South or in the furnishings of his New York apartment, was what he turned to for help: his life belt. The key to his character, if there is a single key to so large, subtle, and mysterious an entity, is what he turned *from,* what he averted his gaze from, what he fled from in something akin to panic.

Back in the years that have been called the Red Decade, Stark Young would sometimes be spoken of as an escapist. The implication that he escaped all reality is false, yet the movement of his will and imagination—and these do move in one direction or another, at one speed or another—is quite accurately described as flight, as at least attempted escape. For Stark Young, the heart of darkness was not out there on an alien continent at the end of a long journey. It was here in Mississippi, it was there in New York, it was universally *of our time,* it was *now.* Which begins to explain why Stark couldn't help making any previous age something of a Blessed Isle: after all, he had fled to it in search, if not of final bliss, at least of relief—release from intolerable pain.

If there is any point in John Pilkington's presentation of Stark Young where I venture a partial dissent, it is where he connects him with "Christian humanism." I did not find Stark religious. He fled so fast, the hound of heaven couldn't catch up with him. Instead of religion he had two things. The first was Art—all the arts—which he embraced with the fervor which the religious give to God. "A life in the arts," yes. Stark Young dwelt with beauty as a saint dwells with goodness . . . The second thing was Love, and not of God, but of people. In no one I have ever met was the life of the affections more spontaneous and abundant. How he loved to love! In an age when we consider the critic cold, and the intellectual withdrawn, he was the warmest and most outgoing of men. Is that Southern courtesy? I would say it is much more than courtesy, it is *hospitality* in its elemental form: making people feel at home because your arms are open to them and you want them: you love them. Stark Young had a genius for loving which made it easy for him to include ever new people in the circle of the beloved. But three persons were privileged beyond the others: his sister Julia, his nephew Stark, and his lover William McKnight Bowman. The published letters bear eloquent and lovely witness to the first two of these loves. In view of the mores of those times, the third had to be hidden but, if you would understand Stark Young, make due allowance for it. If I have placed a primary stress on what he fled from, I would also call your attention to what he fled to: to beauty and to a love that was not supernatural but for him . . . natural. In the years I knew him (and many more) he was, so to say, monogamously homosexual.

Escapism was a dirty word because it implied the escaping of all the realities. Stark Young did exclude a lot. I think he felt he had to, to keep sane. His friends sometimes wished to reform him, correct his opinions, fill in the gaps in his knowledge. For it wasn't just modern philistinism he rejected. He rejected most of modern art and literature. There was an impulse there to reject the whole modern age. And upon mature consideration one sees this as itself a modern phenomenon. Stark Young was not a character in his own best-selling "Southern" novel, *So Red the Rose*. On the contrary! He fled *in fantasy* to that world, and the vehemence of the flight gives it its glamour, its intensity, without in my view concealing that the novel is itself, for all the many pure facts inserted therein, a fantasy. If I were to suggest a theory of Stark Young's life and work, it would be that his direct treatments of reality—his novels and plays—often tended too much toward fantasy. Where he was absolutely real, where he was firmly in command of reality, was in his treatment of those "fantasies" which we call the arts, and particularly that super-fantasy the theatre art.

Let me add one more thing to my account of his philosophy of theatre. Had he really been an escapist, an aesthete in the usual sense, he would have made the theatre into an ivory tower, into that castle of Axel in which it was said, "As for living our servants will do that for us." But Stark Young was no more of an aesthete than he was an ascetic. He believed in living up to the hilt. And he did live up to the hilt: one feared for him, so eagerly and totally did he give of himself. Therein lay both his strength and his vulnerability. He did not live apart: he lived on East 57th Street, New York City. He did not wish a life apart for art, either. Art was not, I repeat, for art's sake, it was for life's sake. It had a purpose: to improve the quality of living.

In that masterpiece, *The Theatre*, where the topic is the director, Stark Young wrote:

The glory of the theatre is that it comes so close to human life that it breaks up into all our channels of response and expression: all are alive together and through all the whole sum appears. This insight into the revealing power of each of these theatre mediums amounts after all only to the director's being alive in it. Through these diverse avenues he seeks life for what he desires to create, exactly as in our daily experience we look at one thing and listen to another, or as we fling ourselves on words, on song or color, or rhythm, action, ideas—sowing ourselves on every wind—in order to create ourselves in terms of living.

Certainly this man *created himself* not in terms of art only but in terms of living. He flung himself on words, on song, on color, on rhythm, action, ideas. He sowed himself on every wind.

(1981)

HAROLD CLURMAN (1902–80)

He was widely and rightly known as a ladies' man. He dressed for the ladies: black, patent-leather shoes, a smart blue suit—white collar and dark, silk tie—a tiny ribbon in his buttonhole which the girls would learn (the ladies already knew) was the Légion d'honneur. Modern and dashing back in the time of the *Smart Set,* his style in courtship came to seem, well, courtly, and women (as against ladies and girls) came to smile at it or even sneer, which couldn't have bothered Harold less, as it was not women he loved but ladies and, even more, girls.

People generally "place" Harold Clurman in the thirties because of the Group Theatre and his book about it, *The Fervent Years,* but he was formed in the twenties and should be thought of as a spiritual contemporary of H. L. Mencken and George Jean Nathan, even if politically he veered left and they veered right. In the "fervent" (i.e., puritanic, in the Wildean sense "earnest") years and beyond, Harold remained carefree, even frivolous, a *bon vivant.* That he might spend the afternoon dictating a *Nation* review to a tape recorder or dashing off a short book on Ibsen never prevented him from attending the Broadway opening of the evening or from showing up as usual at the Russian Tea Room by midnight, only two tables away from Andy Warhol.

There was something frivolous, too, about Harold's "fervor" on public occasions—addressing a meeting or a class or being interviewed by Dick Cavett. Some people talk modest but then want you to accept them as the biggest ego since Napoleon. Harold *was* modest but loved to talk extremely immodest. He'd let himself get carried away, or seem to get carried away, raise his voice both in pitch and volume, talk faster and faster—a pity, sometimes, since no one else could get in a word edgewise. One listened to him, one didn't discuss with him. Interesting to learn from Aaron Copland that he was originally shy and tongue-tied. Unoriginally, as re-created by himself, the ultimate Clurman was always (in case Hitler is listening from Venezuela) the bright Jewish boy of the class whose gifts started with, if they didn't end with, a fabulous gift of gab.

Was he a great director? I don't know. I did not see the work that made him famous in the thirties, and some of his later work, which I did see, seemed to be there to prove he could match Broadway directors at their own game. But the Clurman handling of Julie Harris and Ethel Waters in *Member of the Wedding* is still luminous in my memory after thirty years. No doubt my readers (most of them) are too young to know that relationships back then were between guys (remember them?) and dolls (you *don't* remember them). A relationship between females with a great gap of age between them, not to mention what America made the gap of gaps, that of pigmentation . . . well, it took Harold to take all that in stride, to take both the little white girl and the older black "servant" as full human beings, and to imbue them with his own human fullness.

Then there's the case, the continuing, perennial case of Lillian Hellman. Her thirties plays were just that and really won't move forward from the thirties. That was the problem with the recent revival of *Watch on the Rhine*, not any fault of the actors. *Children's Hour* . . . forget it: everyone else has. But Hellman has shown, in her varied, various memoirs, that there was much more to her. What I want, need to say here is that Harold proved this years ago with his Broadway (Broadway!) production of *Autumn Garden*. He did the play as if it was, not Mike Gold, but Anton Chekhov. Result (since Hellman's writing did lend a hand at times): it *was* Chekhov, with legitimate variations American, Southern, feminist, and oh dear yes, Left.

As director, Harold is exemplary, being the answer to the big directors of today, especially the big "avant-garde" directors, who oust the playwright from his traditional centrality. Harold directed playwrights whom he could regard as the older, not the younger, brother: it was their play, not his, and, because of his intelligence, his sensibility, his talent, he did not come out of these encounters bruised. He was bigger than those I have just called big.

Extremely gregarious—Stella Adler says Harold felt no theatrical event was complete without him—he endured much more than his share of loneliness. By this I don't only mean that he must have *felt* lonely—going home, often alone, from the Russian Tea Room at 3 A.M.—but that, historically, he was, in later years, the sixties, the seventies, an isolated figure, a member, perhaps, of an obsolete though majestic species. I can't define this species here except to say Harold had a foot in two camps and felt no hostility to either: he was as much at home on Broadway as on East 4th Street, in the *New York Times* as in the *Nation,* in the company of George Abbott as in that of Hanns Eisler—in the company of Walter Kerr as in that of Eric Bentley.

The last-named used to resent him sometimes: he refused to reject much that I had rejected, not just aesthetically but politically. He was a man of the Left, of the *Nation* as against the nation, but rather indiscriminately. In the fifties he may have been the only person around who wouldn't take sides on Communism and anticommunism. He was the only person still talking both to Bert Brecht and Elia Kazan (and of course to all lesser Brechts and Kazans), the only one, anyway, who knew what the antagonisms were all about and, in his own way, cared.

In the end, though, any resentment I may have felt was swallowed up in admiration for this broad, humane, conciliatory spirit, and affection for him. I did not know Harold very well and I have not learned to love many people. It says something—perhaps everything—about *him* that, even so, I came to love him.

(1980)

JULIAN BECK (1925–85)

Julian Beck died of cancer on September 14th. The illness had been long drawn out and painful. His life had not been an easy one, even before. On the contrary. And yet I see it, intending no irony, as a success story. For, with the sixty years granted to him, Julian did exactly what he wanted to do.

To be sure, that is not the same as achieving what he wanted to achieve. He wanted to transform the world. In this autumn of 1985 it stands untransformed—or, worse, transformed in just the opposite way from what Julian wished. The point is that he was not deterred by the strong possibility of total failure. To be so deterred (as he saw things) would simply be to fail. He had faith in the possibility of total success. He was utopian. Quite consciously and gladly: which meant that there was a paradise accessible, not just externally and at the end of time but, in his heart, and today—"paradise now."

He did what he wanted to do: with his wife Judith Malina he created the Living Theatre, which, if it was not a new macrocosm, was a new microcosm. Not an ivory tower, however: a headquarters of revolution, a guerrilla theatre, though a pacifist one. This is not the place to write the history of the Living Theatre. It has already been written; and will be written again. All I can hope to do is report an experience of that theatre and of Julian.

We knew each other—not well, but we were well aware of each other—for about thirty-six years. There was a moment, at lunch in the Hans Jaeger restaurant in Yorkville in 1951, when Julian and I almost joined forces. As Judith reported in her diary: "Eric Bentley . . . wishes to direct a play for the Living Theatre if he likes the early work." Instead our lives took different paths, intersecting, sometimes in strife, over the course of the decades.

Nineteen sixty-two marked the Battle of Brecht. *A Man's a Man* was a topical play at the time of the Cuban missile crisis, and I planned to put it on. So did the Living Theatre. And there were two productions, opening in New York on successive nights. A good idea, really: it should be tried with other plays. But the two production outfits did battle with each other. The curious can consult the files of the *Village Voice* (which took the side of the Living Theatre against me and mine).

The next clash came in 1968, when the *New York Times* stuck this title on a piece of mine: "I Reject the Living Theatre." The piece said that the Living Theatre was making us all a "take-it-or-leave-it" offer, and I was gonna leave it. The topic, of course, was tactics. I thought that the Living Theatre's tactics were going to "turn off" the very people they wanted to "turn on." And this was a practical and political matter. The aim was to stop the Vietnam War. Enacting "paradise now"— orgasms for all who could manage them on the stage of the Brooklyn Academy—did not seem to me to be the way. Especially as, along with the "love" being so lavishly offered, there came—it wasn't quite clear how or why—much ill will and even hate. In this period I refused to speak at a meeting of "Theatre for Ideas" because I got word that the Living Theatre was going to break it up. (The Living Theatre did so.) And yet it was in this same period of maximum discord that I formed a positive relationship with the Becks.

Meanwhile my *Times* piece had brought me fan mail I could have done without: "With friends like that, who needs . . .?" One letter made me think. It was from a respected colleague who said I was right— but then the Living Theatre did have certain technical and aesthetic virtues I hadn't mentioned. *Touché.* But how about the implication that the Living Theatre was to be vindicated by the ordinary aesthetic standards—there was "good theatre" here and there, they did know their job, even had a little originality, et cetera? To think in this way would be to reject, not just their tactics, but their whole *raison d'être*: the connection, declared in the word "living," which they wished to make between theatre and life.

I was beginning to regret, not what I had said in the *Times,* but that I had said it in the *Times,* which is no place for what should be the intramural debates of radicals. The answer, I thought, was to get together with the Becks and have it all out face to face. I believe they arrived at the same idea independently. We certainly got together, and something even better than "having it all out" took place: a meeting of hearts and minds. I'd say it was at this meeting that we really became friends for life, an item essential to the story I'm telling. Some of the Love the Living Theatre had been offering in the theatre had seemed to me abstract or ambivalent—and definitely had a capital L. To know Julian and Judith was to learn that concrete love—with a small l—was at the center of their lives and work. This is what eternally separates them from show business or any other business.

Julian, by the way, had first-rate qualifications as a professional. He was one of the best stage designers of his time, and could have made a name as a painter, if that had been what he wanted. He was a good writer, both as poet (*Twenty-One Songs of the Revolution*) and as drama theorist and chronicler (*The Life of the Theatre*). He was a fine director, and as an actor was still growing in his fifties. In Paolo Pasolini's film *Oedipus*, though Julian's voice was unhappily not used, his performance still stood out magnificently from the rest. I have not seen the film he made in Italy about a rabbi who is being tortured by the Spanish Inquisition (*Destruction of Hope*, based on a story by Villiers de l'Isle Adam), but the stills I have seen reveal a noble intensity.

You could guess from such photos that Julian was an actor, and a pro at that. But you could also guess he was more. By the time people are forty, as Camus said, they have the face they deserve. When one says Julian was beautiful, one is not congratulating him on good looks. One is not talking aesthetics; one is talking existence. And even the confrontation of nonexistence: Julian was never more beautiful than at sixty, looking death in the eye. Suffering was there. The well-shaped cheekbones and skull seemed almost to come through the skin, but there was also the nobility of victory over suffering and the old glint in his eye that betokened his interest in *you*—the person he was looking at, feeling interested in, concerned for. He was not a saint, and wouldn't want to be called one. But there was a spiritual purity about him all the same. To be with him was to breathe mountain air. I have derived that particular lift, that exhilaration, from only one other person, someone Julian respected: the writer Barbara Deming. He resembled Barbara, spiritually speaking, more than he resembled anyone in the theatre.

He didn't get the kind of death anyone could want but he had had the life he wanted. The world had not been changed yet he had done all a man can do to change it. So, to that extent, it had, too, been changed. How Julian changed himself! Look back from the photos of the dying hero of 1984–85 (again: no irony) to photos of Julian the rich boy of the forties. Now *there's* a transformation! And how could he transform himself in such a way without transforming others? Others were indeed transformed, and even those he casually touched—either directly or from stage or screen—were permanently affected. For, as he himself put it: "I cut the curtains of deception, beautiful, so that we can go through together where no one can go through alone."

When such a life has been lived, who dares say theatre is just a business? Who dares say it is just an art?

(1985)

CRITICAL QUESTIONS

HOW TRANSLATE A PLAY?

In the early forties I was studying German and wanted to translate German poetry. I translated some of it before I was competent to do so. Indeed I never regarded myself as a *Germanist*, who could publish a translation without having it checked by someone who knew more German. It was not linguistic expertise but interest in certain authors that drew me into the often thankless work. Translation in the end proved to have another kind of importance for me: as a step toward free adaptation, which was in its turn a step toward playwriting. Adding my own lyrics to plays by others was the step I took before taking on a whole play as my own. A career of this sort put me, as translator, at a disadvantage in some ways. That it may also have given me a clearer view of certain things is the assumption of the piece that follows.

> *It is a pretty poem, Mr. Pope, but you must not call it Homer.*
> —Richard Bentley on Pope's *Iliad*

A great deal has been published lately about translation in the theatre, so, in all this literature, I ought not to have been surprised to find a not wholly favorable reference to my own work—"the often inspired (if at times too free) Brecht texts of Eric Bentley."

Too free for whom? Just this critic? Everyone? Too free just here and there? Everywhere? Let me open up some broader questions. The first is that of inevitable imperfection. Your perfect translation could only be made by God because only He would know both languages perfectly and have a perfect gift of expression in the language translated into, so that everything in the translation would work on readers or spectators exactly as the original worked on them. For such is the ideal goal, though, to reach it, God might have to perform other miracles, since in transferring a work from one country to another, and/or from one era to another, there are obstacles other than the purely linguistic . . .

The merely human translator is seldom even bilingual to the fullest extent. If, for example, he has been brought up in the one country and has then moved to the other, the *way* he knows the second language will be very different from the way he knows the first. The second language will carry no childhood associations, nor will it carry the signs of having been learned in the natural, organic way in which infants learn languages. As for the first language, he will probably speak it as it was spoken by the previous generation. He will lose contact with its development and thus with its living reality at the later moment.

Of course, there are millions of people in the world who habitually use two languages. It is another question whether they use either of them well and, even if they do, they may still not make good translators. Well as they are acquainted with the language translated into, they may not write it well, either in a general sense or—which is our interest here—in a theatrical sense. Translating for the stage one must translate into language that passes (what used to be) the footlights. One must be able to create what Jean Cocteau called poetry *of,* as against poetry merely *in,* the theatre. One must have a histrionic sensibility.

The language translated into. I stress *that* language because, of the two languages in question, that is, for the translator, the more important one. He is writer first, scholar-linguist second. This is clearest in the theatre. If the play is not in the language it's supposed to be in, there's no play. That the translator may have perpetrated some howlers is a secondary matter. All the best people perpetrate howlers. Those who believe the English Bible was written by God must believe that even God perpetrates howlers, because there are quite a few in the only translation that's really great, the King James Version.

I am told that the same is true of John Florio's Montaigne. Perhaps the best translations are the ones with the most mistakes? No reason why not. The primary criterion is what a text amounts to in the language it is (now) in. Florio and King James's clergymen made great books— as well as lots of mistakes. We have translators today who make few mistakes, perhaps none, and who make bad books, bad plays.

It's always a matter of what a given context needs. At a certain point, a scene in a play may be in desperate need of a joke. The audience *has* to be made to laugh at all costs. Good. The playwright has brought it off. What shall the poor translator do when he finds his accurate rendering isn't funny? Give a little lecture on the obligation of accuracy? Shall all those years of study go for nothing? They'd better. At *this* moment, he has to be Woody Allen, not Ralph Manheim.

But humor is only the extreme case. What applies to the funny applies also to the beautiful—or, for that matter, the ugly. No use to come up with what the dictionary, backed by the Académie Française, says is exact. What you have to come up with is the quality that has the desired effect. Make the audience laugh. Make them cry. Make them see a point clearly. Make them see stars. Make them feel good. Make them feel sick. But make them.

In his Molière translations the poet Richard Wilbur has come close to producing (so far as I can judge) the same effect that the French produces on a Frenchman. But even he can't get all the way there. Language itself imposes barriers no human being can overleap. Take rhyme. Poets in both French and English have used rhymes. The problem lies in the fact that English poets have used rhymes differently. It was, I think, impossible for Wilbur to write all those rhymes without making most of them sound clever. "Why, he's even funnier than Molière," I have heard offered him as a compliment, whereas the fact is that rhyming couplets, in English, as not in French, have wit built into them. I know a vast attempt was made, at one time, to write heroic tragedies in English rhyming couplets. It failed. Failing also to be funny, those couplets just sound *silly*, and thus it comes about that while Wilbur can be surprisingly close to Molière, he is often unsurprisingly closer to W. S. Gilbert.

A perfect translation of a work of art cannot be made by human hands because one language does not offer exact *aesthetic* equivalents of another. You can translate science, but you can't translate poetry. Poetry *is* (Frost said it) *what gets lost in the translation,* and under the heading "poetry" I'm placing the whole aesthetic dimension: everything that makes for "effect," an effect of beauty, ugliness, delicacy, indelicacy, funniness, lugubriousness . . . and on and on. Rhythm alone erects terrible barriers. Rhythmically, Shakespeare can sound rather like Shakespeare in German. But in French? I enjoyed Jean-Louis Barrault's *Hamlet.* It was probably the first time I could readily follow what was going on in that play. Yet this was because it was not William Shakespeare but André Gide.

Still, we try, we translators, and we are proud if we think we do even half as well as, say, King James's clergymen, for surely the Bible has been enjoyed as literature by persons with no Hebrew and no Greek, and we can't give *all* the credit to the translators. Stubbornly, we insist on assuming that some of the beauty of those Psalms has *come through from* the original, and that Robert Frost must have been partly wrong.

This is not to deny that there may also be works where a major part of the poetic work has been done by the translator. Scholars who know Persian tell us that there's more Edward Fitzgerald than Omar

Khayyam in that famous *Rubaiyat*. In which case, we should count it a great English poem, not a great translation. Robert Lowell has made what he calls "imitations" of originals he felt could not be "translated." In Lowell's sense, Fitzgerald's is a Victorian "imitation" of his medieval original.

Finally, then, I come to the liberties I've sometimes taken with Brecht. Did I have an acceptable alternative? Other translations I've read do not always convince me that I had. But let's go further into this.

In the theatre, we meet with at least four different phenomena all (by someone or other) called translations: (1) The rendering that is so meanly literal that Arthur Miller has used the expression Pidgin English to describe its vocabulary and style. (Translations made in language classes to show the teacher one has used the dictionary properly are in this territory.) (2) The rendering that is in correct and cogent English but otherwise sticks as close to the original as possible. (3) The adaptation. This can have (2) as its basis but then take such liberties as: making cuts and interpolations and changing the style and/or tone. (4) The variation. This verges on an original play merely "based on" a foreign one. I have introduced the term to describe such plays of my own when part of their point is an interplay between the old conception and the new. The *thing* existed long before I used the *term* as the title of my *Kleist Variations*. *Threepenny Opera* is a variation of *Beggar's Opera*. Unconsciously perhaps, Fitzgerald's poem is a "variation" on Omar's. Peter Brook's *Carmen* is not, as has been claimed, a return to Prosper Mérimée's story: it is Peter Brook's "variation" on the Bizet opera.

A discovery I made in working on Brecht was that not all his plays lend themselves to the same kind of treatment at the hands of a translator. In my view, *Chalk Circle* lends itself to close translation (2) but *Good Woman of Setzuan* does not—and therefore some of the expedients of (3) become allowable, if not mandatory. I can't imagine anybody finds me too free in my treatment of the one, but I know some find me guilty of it in my treatment of the other. Let me give my side.

In the library you can find two word-for-word translations of *Good Woman*. My name is on one of them, so perhaps that entitles me to say without undue competitiveness that neither of them reads well in English. And what reads badly *plays* even worse. German is often wordier (lengthier) than English, and especially in *Good Woman* Brecht seems to me to have given way to a kind of verbosity (volubility?) which is possible in one language but not in another. After having worked with a colleague on a "literal" version (published by the University of Minnesota Press in 1948), I later went back to the German on my own and made a much shorter text. The original intention was not to abridge, though eventually whole passages did get cut. The intention was to say everything as snappily as we'd say it in English, not as elaborately as many things are said by many persons in German. A three-hour play thereby became something like a two-hour play, and I would argue that this happened organically, and on an aesthetic principle, not because we had to fit a two-hour schedule or were fearful that our audience had a short attention span. Critics may, of course, question either my premise, or the merit of the result, or both, but I was dependent on my own judgment, that of my colleagues, and of course on experience with audiences.

Sooner or later, someone is going to compare the lyrics in three established versions of *Threepenny:* mine,* Marc Blitzstein's, and the Willett-Manheim. For they represent three distinct approaches. Take your pick:
A. Willett-Manheim—unfree, get everything in, never mind if it's a good lyric.
B. Blitzstein—very free, leave out what's not easy or politic to leave in, make it a good Blitzstein lyric.
C. Bentley—middle of the road, not too strict, not too free, trying to make a lyric that sounds good with the music and that sounds Brechtian.
I naturally think there's a case for C; I also think there is a case for B; in practice, there wasn't much of a case for A, as you couldn't tell what they were singing about and had to look it up in the book. (If you don't believe me, try to figure out the words in the recorded version of the Lincoln Center production.)

Blitzstein and I used to quarrel. There was sibling rivalry, and both the brothers wanted to own Dad (Brecht). But we agreed on a fundamental point, and I recommend it *an die Nachgeborenen,* to those who come after. We agreed that the place to translate Brecht songs is at the piano. The translator has to sing them—with their accompaniment. It's the only way—the only way known to Blitzstein and Bentley anyhow—to get them right. Goethe had said one must "never read, always sing" his songs, and Brecht is the most musical—in that sense, the least literary—poet since Goethe.

Anyone who looks up my early critical writings will find I used to attack all the freer translations, especially the Broadway adaptations I was called on to review. I still loathe such an effort as S. N. Behrman's free version of one of my favorite French plays, *Amphitryon 38.* This was why I led off with Brecht translations, in the forties, which stuck close to the original. The freedoms my critics speak of are all of later date—post–1960, in fact. It began with *A Man's a*

*The lyrics are "mine." The book was translated by my friend the late Desmond I. Vesey.

Man. Those of us who were putting it on in the America of the Cuban missile crisis wanted to update it somewhat. As theatre people, we also wanted more songs in it. We could perhaps have imported songs from other Brecht plays. I took the more arrogant step of writing in some lyrics of my own. The fact was that my interest was spreading out from translating to other things, notably songwriting and playwriting. I'll add that I did not continue to make Brecht the victim of my venturesomeness. From *A Man's a Man* on 42d Street, I went to *Orpheus in the Underworld* at City Center, keeping all the old music but writing a new libretto—a free adaptation or, if I may be permitted, "variation," of the old one . . .

Any foreign play that's worth the trouble should be around in more than one form: specifically, in a reasonably close, strict, scholarly translation, that leaves no passages out, and writes no passages in, *and* in at least one freer version with certain more ambitious ends in view— in one case, to get at certain subtleties in the original that are missed in the more literal text, in another to make a text more theatrical and "public," in another ("variations," yet) actually to add something in significant counterpoint to what was there before. I have already made it clear that a reader who finds my later version of *Good Woman* too free can hunt up the earlier, unfree version in the library. I was also at pains to bring out *A Man's a Man* in two different versions, one close to the German, one less close. Couldn't this procedure be adopted more often? The publishers' answer is, "No, it costs too much." I tested this recently when the University of Minnesota Press asked me to endorse Geoffrey Hill's free adaptation of Ibsen's *Brand.* I said, "I will if you print a literal version on opposite pages so the reader can see what your poet added and subtracted." They wouldn't; so I didn't.

Not so incidentally, the literal version I wanted printed on opposite pages was the text the adaptation had been made from. The National Theatre of Great Britain has persuaded Geoffrey Hill and other professional writers to translate from languages they do not know. What I was proposing was that readers of *Brand* should see how the arrangement works to the extent that they can do so without also knowing Dano-Norwegian, but I received the impression that even a university press does not wish people to be aware of such problems. For my part, I couldn't ask students to read such an adaptation at all if there was no way in which they could check it against the original or a closer English rendering. Naturally, I apply this principle to my own work. Students of Kleist cannot find what they need in my *Kleist Variations.* They must read either the German original or a close translation thereof.

I myself have translated from a language I don't know, or don't know adequately, namely, Russian. I relied on friends who know Russian better and also on the translations (acknowledged) of Constance Garnett. Though I am therefore in no position to condemn the practice without qualification, I am more than willing to condemn it *with* qualification. Although a competent colleague can explain to an adapter what is concealed in a subtle word or phrase of the original, he cannot make him feel what he would feel if he knew the other language. Granted there is guesswork (intuition) in translation anyway, a lack of firsthand knowledge in the adapter heightens the degree of guesswork and may turn sound intuition into mere whistling in the dark. Thus when I confront the poetic or humorous use of a word in German or Italian or French I am aware of being on much firmer ground than when I weigh such use by Chekhov—whatever Constance Garnett says or whatever my colleagues in the Russian department tell me. That the National Theatre habitually hires playwrights to convert literal translations into literate (and therefore playable) translations is not something I see as progress. It would be better if they used their money to teach young writers foreign languages.

I close with a note on skulduggery in this field. A producer who wants to avoid paying royalties to translators can take out five versions of an Ibsen or a Chekhov from the library and put them, as it were, in the blender. He or one of his flunkies can then claim credit as translator and/or adapter. Royalties may even be paid (yes, even by a producer to himself). The Ibsen translator Rolf Fjelde calls this now widespread abuse larceny by pastiche. It cannot be stopped by the police. The law courts can certainly not render any service if the translations ransacked are in the public domain, and probably not even if they are copyrighted. It will stop when producers cease to regard the translator as an eminently removable middle man and accept him as the peer of other artists in the theatre.

To have recourse to earlier translations is not, by the way, something an artist must refuse to do. Artist-translators of the Bible have done it ever since the sixteenth century. The offense in "larceny by pastiche" is the assumption that a good version of a play can be knocked together by a nonartist whose concentration is on (a) hiding his sources and (b) making, or at least saving, money.

(1985)

SPANISH DRAMA:
UNIQUE OR UNIVERSAL?

If I differed from many of my academic colleagues about acting, I also differed with many of them about the peculiarity and apparent impenetrability of various foreign literatures. An article about Spanish drama in the *Hispanic Review*, 1959, provided the cue I needed. Its title must suffice to suggest here what it said: "The Uniqueness of the Comedia." The author was Professor Arnold G. Reichenberger.

Only an Anglo-Saxon can understand Browning.
> —William Lyon Phelps (apocryphal)

"A Chinese novel?" said I, "that must look strange enough." "Not so much as you might think," said Goethe, "these Chinese think, act and feel almost exactly like us."
> —*Conversations with Eckermann*

I do not mean liberty to read into a play of Shakespeare's whatever feeling or idea a modern reader may loosely and accidentally associate with its subject. . . . But I do mean that anything which may be found in that art, even if it is only the modern reader who can find it there, may legitimately be taken as its meaning.
> —Lascelles Abercrombie, "A Plea for the Liberty of Interpreting,"
> *Proceedings of the British Academy*, 1930

L'oeuvre dramatique n'a que la valeur et le sens que chaque génération de lecteurs ou de spectateurs lui prête. . . . Quel serait l'effet et le sort du drame sans la collaboration active des spectateurs, sans le développement,

*l'interprétation et le sens qu'ils doivent lui donner? . . . L'oeuvre théâtrale
du passé qui triomphe dans l'actualité devient une oeuvre de notre temps
grâce à une adaptation inévitable.*
    —Auréliu Weiss, *Le destin des grandes oeuvres dramatiques*

Because I have a lot to learn from Mr. Reichenberger about Spain
and the *Comedia*, because I have learned a good deal from this very
article of his, I shall seem churlish to attack the critical principles which
he is championing—or which he takes for granted. Yet no apology is
called for, since, if I am wrong, my wrongness will stand revealed and
Mr. Reichenberger will be strengthened by the contest, while, if I am
right, I am helping him to emerge from a prison in which his better
thoughts and impulses now lie shackled by false assumptions.

Mr. Reichenberger believes in something called objective literary
scholarship, whose "task is to discover the internal laws, or . . . the
'structure,' of the art form and to explain it on the basis of its own
concepts." But how objective is it to accept no outside referent? All
that can be tested by the method proposed is consistency: a practice
can be found consistent with a theory. But since the theory is only
what is implicit in the practice, inconsistency would be impossible.
The reasoning is circular. What business have we talking about *laws* in
this context anyway? What business have we pretending that an art
form can be *explained?* In my opinion, both words—and the word *objective* too—claim too much.

What *does* the literary scholar have to offer his pupils? Historical
facts which may make it inconceivable that the poet intended what he
seems to the uninstructed reader of today to mean and perhaps probable
that he meant X, Y, or Z instead. None would deny that—given the
worth of literature itself—the literary scholar is needed. It may even
be proper that the beginning student be given training in such scholarship and, for the time being, nothing else.

The question is whether he should go all the way with it, "all the
way" signifying this assumption: that the aim of literary study is to get
back to experiencing the work as it was "originally" experienced. High
authorities can be cited:

> A perfect judge will read each work of wit
> With the same spirit that its author writ.

But what is Alexander Pope saying? He does not say with the same
intent that its author writ, but allows for a difference between intention
and execution. And even the word *spirit* brings in a conception that
goes far beyond collectible facts. Scholars can dig out many things
about an author but are not likely to stumble upon his spirit. At this
point, what is usually invoked is not knowledge but historical imagi-

nation. And there is the rub. For imagination works in two directions at once. It is conceivable that by imagination we can get closer to the actual spirit of Alexander Pope. But it is not conceivable that our imagination can limit itself to this function and desist from doing what imagination is apt to do: namely, to imagine. Life is a dream. Every hour of every day life is attended by fantasy.

Just because the historian cannot, like the scientist, exclude fantasy but draws on imagination, he inevitably takes the rough with the smooth. Is it not notorious that the great histories from Thucydides to Gibbon and beyond are personal poems, *Wahrheit—und Dichtung?*

A perfect judge . . .

The conclusion is obvious: there will never be a perfect judge. To this it will be retorted: "Let us at least get as near perfection as we can." But we are going in two directions at once. Adding historical knowledge and imagination, we also add fantasy. This is in the nature of things. We concede it when we say an audience must bring something to a play, but we seldom realize *how much* an audience brings, and how little of it the "objective scholar" would approve of.

Literature is never going to be understood the way the "objective" scholars have supposed it could be. And quite often literature has not really been relished by them: it has only been accepted as a white-collar labor. "Literary scholarship is carried on by individuals, who do not live in a vacuum and are conditioned by esthetic preferences of their own and by those of their generation and environment." If only Mr. Reichenberger didn't regret this! He is glad that Lope de Vega belonged to his generation and environment, but he is not glad that Reichenberger belongs to his! And if he cannot manage to live in a vacuum, he will manufacture a substitute: namely what purports to be the correct and certified version of the seventeenth century. But if this is the scholar's temperament, then it is the opposite of the literary temperament, which is characterized by delight in myth and a readiness to move easily between *Wahrheit* and *Dichtung.* You can move the more easily between them if you know you don't know which is which.

A remark may be added about those scholars who might make the strongest claim to enter into the very spirit of some bygone age and so offer us in their works the nearest that mortals can attain to the objective truth about that age. The angle of vision remains that of the age in which they live. Most familiar is the spectacle of the ardent medievalist who lives in the shadow of the skyscrapers of Manhattan or Chicago. His scholarship is apt to be a sort of pastoral poetry written, as such poetry characteristically was, by a court poet—or Yeats's "Lake Isle of Innisfree," written in the British metropolis. Medievalism is the kind of *ism* that the modern metropolis breeds in a certain kind of thoughtful mind. But medievalism is unmedieval. The Middle Ages had no concept of a Middle Ages and consequently could not have been in love with the Middle Ages.

I do not know if Mr. Reichenberger is in love with the Spanish "Golden Age." He is certainly deferential to it in a way in which he is not deferential to the twentieth century. Everything in the seventeenth century has to be accepted: whatever was, was right. And this is indeed implied by modern historical scholars in general when it comes to their chosen period. Today, they may be voting, like you or me, on the anticonservative side, but woe betide any of their students who questions the conservatism of whatever is "their period"!

And this posture not only differentiates the nostalgic scholar from the human beings who had the comparatively ungrateful job of actually *living* in "the period" but contains a serious and silly error: the idea that only we are wrong. Oh, those sermons in graduate classes on the limitations of modern individualism! If we believe that anti-Semitism is wrong in the twentieth century, what besides snobbery or stupidity can induce us to believe it was somehow legitimate in Shakespeare's time? All that historians can show is that anti-Semitism belonged to a pattern, and we may expect that historians of the future will show that it belonged to a pattern in Hitler's Germany just as much as in Shakespeare's England. Patterns are not holy, except to idiot sociologists. What is needed for the understanding of such a phenomenon is not respect for the past but disrespect for sin—or, to be more modern about it, such a conception as mass neurosis. William Faulkner has well said of the South in recent times that it is crucified on a black cross. Involved is what psychologists call neurosis and what theologians call sin on a vast, on a *social* scale. *Only in our day?* When Protestants burnt Catholics and vice versa, that was all right when "properly understood"? Heaven save us from proper understanding! Simple conscience and high orthodox principle would surely be a better guide.

As for the Spanish question, some historians are Spaniards, and eagerly apply to their country the phony alibi of the "pattern" and the feeble historicist assumption that to know all is to forgive all. To stress the Inquisition, they assert, is to spread a "leyenda negra"—a black legend. As if the history of other countries were, in general, much whiter, even down into the mid-twentieth century!

The seventeenth century was a century of great culture. It was also a century of fanaticism and barbarism, a century in which Cromwell treated Catholics like cattle in the stockyards, a century in which cities and populations were laid waste in Germany as in any twentieth-century quarrel over high ideals. To establish, therefore, as Mr. Reichenberger does, that honor was a high ideal in Spain is not to provide Spain with a sufficient testimonial. Of course, honor was a high ideal; but that did not stop it from functioning in a low way, as it is the classic function of high ideals to do.

Mr. Reichenberger actually does *not* disclose the laws of an art form. He states that a given group of artists held a given set of opinions and most notably that they believed in Honor and the Catholic Faith. Very true. But then, without any argument, he proceeds to assume that these opinions stand like a wall between the great Spanish playwrights and a modern, non-Spanish public. The next step in the argument is that this wall can be surmounted with the aid of historical scholarship, provided one concedes that the *Comedia* is not an expression of individual poets but precisely of history, of Spain at that time.

Skeptical as he is of individual taste, Professor Reichenberger has no misgivings about the ability of the individual historian—in this case himself—to sum up whole schools of drama in a few formulas unaccompanied with provisos and perhapses. He wishes us to be very chary of easy generalizations about Spanish drama, but he makes his own easy generalizations about Greek drama, Elizabethan drama, and the genre of tragedy. Any questioning of these generalizations would be a threat to his main thesis: the *Comedia* is unique. For he is as eager to show that this general thing, a genre, is unique, as to show that the particular thing, the play, is not unique.

Some of his assumptions are arbitrary, as, for instance, that what we all want today is tragedy, so much so that we reject a nontragic school of dramaturgy out of hand. I have been hearing just the contrary all my life. I have been told by a succession of teachers that what I *should* want is tragedy, though what in my weak, decadent, modern way I *do* want is the optimistic drama of ideas. We have even been told something of the kind in an editorial in *Life* magazine. So, in fact, a case could be made for the proposition that the Spanish *Comedia* is just what the doctor ordered. T. S. Eliot can make Dante sound far superior to Shakespeare. And the Christian optimism of Dante has had a vogue.

Has the Spanish drama really been less current in English-speaking countries than the classical drama of France? Perhaps it has—but, if so, this is surely because until recently a certain class of people knew Molière and Racine *in the original*. The same is true of the Greek drama. Conversely, the present relative currency of Greek drama is to be credited to the translators, of whom the twentieth century has borne an excellent crop. The process of translating the Spanish playwrights has barely begun—translating them, I mean, into English literature, not into barbarous translationese. But it *has* begun and lo! *Life Is a Dream* becomes an item for the national radio in England and for the Edinburgh Festival in Scotland.

What do the people who enjoy these plays in the translations of Roy Campbell, Edwin Honig, and other poets find in them? Honor and

Faith? Well, yes and no. I would not contest what Mr. Reichenberger finds to be the content of the Spanish plays. It is not about plays that I differ with him so much as about the way people's minds work. He assumes that we either relearn the old Honor and Faith by historical study or fail to get anything out of the plays altogether. I, on the other hand, doubt that such relearning is what is primarily needed. I agree that such relearning is indispensable if one is ever to know anything about the seventeenth century. On the other hand, if a person is un-responsive to dramatic art, no amount of historical erudition will help.

What is responsiveness? It is not a *separate* faculty. One's respon-siveness depends on memories and associations. How then does one respond to an unfamiliar stimulus? By a kind of spontaneous and in-stantaneous process of comparison, of analogy. If one had never seen orange, but had seen yellow, one would respond to orange as "something yellowish." Correspondingly, if one sees *Antigone*, but does not know about Greek burial rites and their meaning, one knows some other burial rites, one knows that the dead may be revered: the sentiment is there, if not the doctrine. Now, since historical learning will only provide doctrines and not sentiments, it follows that the spontaneous associations of the human mind are of more use to the reader of *Antigone* than historical scholarship.

It is a matter of equivalences. A great deal changes, and it is the business of historians to say what, but the same sentiment endures, though attached later to another object. Unless things—within us as well as without—were to be turned quite topsy-turvy, there will always be such equivalences between one historical situation and another. One does not need to be a Catholic to enter into a great Catholic poem. One only needs to be able to enter into the sentiment of faith. The Jewish faith would do, as would the Moslem or the Hindu. One does not even need to possess faith in *any* of these theologies. One only need be able, in Coleridge's phrase, to suspend disbelief, to enter, emotionally and for the moment, into the believing attitude. That makes no greater a demand upon us than entering into many another attitude with or without religious connotation. The only attitude that would not do would be faith—if one could not get rid of it even for a moment—in a religion which takes an entirely different direction, such as Hitlerism. The Christianity which Mr. Reichenberger makes such heavy weather of is the easiest thing in the world for a Western audience to accept—in fantasy, that is.

As for honor, I am shocked that Mr. Reichenberger thinks it so discredited and remote. Where did he grow up? Honor is the God of Madison Avenue and Capitol Hill, for in both places reputation is everything. That this is honor in a degenerate form is true but not relevant here, for it appears in the same degenerate form in Spanish literature of the same period, namely, the present: García Lorca's *Bernarda Alba* offers just the same critique of it that you or I would. But honor of the noblest kind is still a principal subject of literature, as surely it always will be. For Joseph Conrad it was perhaps the only subject. And incidentally, Mr. Reichenberger will find that many authors neither Spanish nor of the seventeenth century write about a single subject—even some of those he names as doing the opposite (Corneille, Racine, Schiller).

True, the Spaniards went further with the idea of honor. Morally speaking, they went too far. Mr. Reichenberger concedes this, if with a wry shake of the head, when he sides for a moment with Montaigne's self-reliance. But Montaigne wasn't a Spaniard and so, according to the scholar's code, cannot be called as a witness against Calderón. If, however, one can, as I have suggested, drop this favoritizing of the past, and be as merciless to one's ancestors as one is to one's parents and children, one can state without embarrassment that Spain suffered in "our period" from a collective neurosis. Just as goodness too much appreciated leads to pride, the worst form of badness, so any virtue pressed too far turns to its opposite. The punctiliously honorable man of the *drama de honor* spreads dishonor everywhere.

Mr. Reichenberger probably won't agree that this is so. But it is interesting that at least one distinguished colleague of his, A. A. Parker, who agrees with him at most of the points where I have disagreed, is on my side here. I cite this fact not to relieve my loneliness but to cast further doubt on the rightness of Mr. Reichenberger's view of the *Comedia*. He asks us not to look for modern views in the *Comedia*, and indeed not to look for even a conflict of views. Rigidity of ideology is its diagnostic. Hearing this, the innocent reader would expect to find Calderón dogmatic, simplistic, doctrinaire. Perhaps Mr. Reichenberger does find him so. And perhaps A. A. Parker finds him so. All very well, provided they agree as to what the dogma, the simplicity, and the doctrine are. Is Calderón the champion of the code of honor in its narrowest form? Or the opposite? Experts can be quoted for either extreme position and for many positions in between. And I was fascinated recently to find, from a survey of opinion among modern experts on Lope, that our Hispanist friends haven't the slightest idea what any of Lope's plays means. To be sure, each one states a position, and refutes all the others, but the impression given is of total uncertainty.

This is very heartening. It means, for one thing, that Mr. Reichenberger's thesis is absolutely untrue. We are *not* confronted with writing that is too unambiguous for modern taste but with a body of work whose ambiguities are still so far from complete discovery that each explorer, finding something, thinks he has found everything, like Christopher Columbus.

A kind of art which can be *explained,* which operates according to *laws,* which in turn are *understood* by objective scholarship, a kind of art which gives expression to a place and an epoch without possessing individuality or reflecting the individuality of its creators—the *Comedia,* as described by Mr. Reichenberger, is a monstrosity. Does he mean that the plays aren't very good? I see no reason to formulate such a curiously self-defeating form of defense. The word "unique" is no doubt a rash one, but if Mr. Reichenberger can apply it to the whole class, I might be permitted to apply it to superb instances of the class such as *Fuenteovejuna, La vida es sueño,* and *El condenado por desconfiado.* Mr. Reichenberger speaks as if there were something peculiarly Spanish about a work of art belonging to a community, or, for that matter, to a strict genre. There isn't. That a sonnet is a strict sonnet is not to say it lacks individuality, or does not bear the marks of its author's personality.

It is confusing to pretend that the plays of the Spanish masters seem to be the work of the community only. Every dramatist, as John Millington Synge said, has the people for his collaborator. It is another thing to suggest that there can be a great form of drama in which the people does not have the dramatist for its collaborator. Is the medieval drama an instance? There the question would be: how much of it is great? And are the Spanish masterpieces comparable? Again, the Chartres cathedral is a great work of collective authorship, but each little statue on its walls bears the stamp of an individual craftsman: there is no analogy here to a play by Lope. On the contrary, far more convincing, in my view, than Mr. Reichenberger's generalizations is such an analysis of one Spanish play as Joaquín Casalduero's essay on *Fuenteovejuna,* of which the thesis is that the play is an individual masterpiece by an author of marked individuality.

Could it be that Mr. Reichenberger's essay does not even represent "objective" scholarship but, rather, the "subjective" opinion of a certain group at a certain time? I seem to have heard a lot of it before in college lectures, not on the Spanish playwrights, but on Shakespeare and Molière. The portrait of Lope that emerges from Mr. Reichenberger's analysis is exactly what was taught about Shakespeare and Molière a generation ago: they too were "geniuses of conformity" without an independent idea in their heads, men lacking in critical and philosophic power, et cetera. I have nothing against the last generation, nor do I harbor the illusion that the present one is any better: this portrait was a feeble thing then and remains so now. It is not plausible as applied to Lope, any more than to Shakespeare or Molière, as it does not correspond to any coherent and comprehensive idea of an artist of (Mr. Reichenberger's phrase) "unsurpassed creative powers." It is true, though not news, that the great classic artists were not liberals, and it would be surprising to find them liberal in ages when liberalism did not exist.

Nonetheless, the conflicts of the age appear in the drama dramatically—that is, with sympathy for both sides, involvement with both sides, appreciation of both sides. Balzac, too, was a "conformist," but that did not prevent him from being admired by Karl Marx for his keen presentation of both sides in a social struggle. The phrase "genius of conformity" may cover *Henry V*, but it is inept as a description of *Timon of Athens, Antony and Cleopatra,* or *The Tempest.* As for Lope, let us take his *Henry V: Fuenteovejuna.* As Shakespeare pays homage to the Plantagenets and Tudors, so Lope pays it to the Catholic princes. But the "genius" of the two great playwrights could scarcely be said to consist in this "conformism." Plenty of other writers shared the conformism without writing these plays. Easy enough to appeal the dispute of Fuenteovejuna to the king in the last scene: the playwright's achievement is to have written the play that largely precedes this scene. The life of this play arises from a conflict in which the king plays no part: a conflict between peasants and overlords. In that sense, the Marxists, who have presented this play as a left-wing document, did seize on its actual dramatic center. And the classic drama lives in us, as I have said, by the equivalences we find with life as we know it. The trouble with the usual Marxist presentation of *Fuenteovejuna* was that the equivalence or analogy broke down precisely where, dramatically, it would have to culminate: in the final scene. The Marxists can only rebuild this cathedral by leaving out the spire. But it is quite conceivable that social situations will arise in which a class struggle will be referred by the two classes to a higher tribunal. At that moment *Fuenteovejuna* will show itself as topical and a masterpiece.

Incidentally, there is an inner contradiction in Mr. Reichenberger's account of the Faith. *The* faith here is Christianity. That each individual is unique is Christian doctrine, and it has never been held to exclude playwrights. If a playwright has a unique individuality, is it not bound to show itself in so highly organized and emotional an entity as a play that he writes?

Spaniards, are they human? That the human beings of one nationality are different in some ways from human beings of another is universally agreed. But the view that they are *fundamentally* different is, from the Christian and most other viewpoints, a heresy. Surely no one who believes in the Faith can accept what Mr. Reichenberger *says* about the Faith? Conversely, if Spaniards are human beings, a writer of "unsurpassed creative powers" will find their universal humanity and communicate it to any human being who cares to read him.

What about Cervantes? One has never heard these excuses and alibis urged in *his* defense. Did he not live in 1600? Was he not really a Spaniard? Was he an unbeliever? Did he cast a cold eye on honor?

Those who might be inclined to answer Yes to this last question should reread *La Numancia.*

There is a wise passage about the problem of art and history in Karl Marx's introduction to the *Critique of Political Economy.* "Is Achilles conceivable," asks Marx, "in an era of powder and lead? Or for that matter *The Iliad* in general—in these days of the printing press and press jacks? Do not song and legend and muse necessarily lose their meaning in the age of the Press? *The difficulty, however, is not that Greek art and epic are connected with certain forms of social development, but rather that they still give us aesthetic satisfaction today, that, in a sense, they act as a norm, as an unattainable paragon.*"

The plays of Lope and Calderón, Cervantes and Tirso de Molina, read in Spanish or in a good modern poet's translation, give us satisfaction today, even though we have not spent decades or even solid years in the study of Spain or the "Golden Age." Mr. Reichenberger can retort that we are misunderstanding the plays. To which we, in turn, can retort: better a delightful misunderstanding than a dull comprehension, and we might cite intelligent men who defend misunderstanding as such. "I am convinced," writes the playwright Henri de Montherlant—who incidentally adapted Vélez de Guevara's *Amar después de morir*—"I am convinced that works that last only last by misunderstandings, by all the literature which posterity surrounds them with, a literature in which the actual intentions of authors end up getting drowned. . . . This deformation takes place in front of their very eyes, so to speak, by the sprouting of a legend as to both their person and their views. . . . It is by errors that works survive."

Though it is good to have ideas stated with this degree of clarity and impudence, Montherlant concedes far too much, since his wording suggests that the vicissitudes of a work of art in its journey through time are arbitrary and accidental. In that case, it would be pointless even to discuss, say, *Hamlet;* for, since it can be "misunderstood" at will, it means whatever you want it to mean. Actually, the succeeding interpretations of *Hamlet* follow a recognizable pattern. And a wide variety of interpretations is legitimate, not because "misunderstanding" is legitimate, but because each generation's *understanding* is legitimate—and different.

One hypothesis is that a work has many facets and that each generation sees different facets, but this metaphor does not provide an adequate description of what happens. The fundamental factor is the high degree of subjectivity—the large contribution of the reader or spectator—in the process by which it is decided what a work of art is and says. This subjectivity is regrettable only from the point of view of those who demand that life be simple, explainable, reducible to laws, completely understandable, and fit to be handled by objective schol-arship. Mr. Reichenberger might deny that he makes any such demand. Nonetheless, he declines to make use of any other assumptions.

What is a great play? By its greatness it is individual. In order to *be* great it is produced by an individual. But society—the class, the whole people, the nation—is this individual's collaborator. And society is in flux, is part of history. Society is not only the coauthor but the audience, and, as audience, responds and interprets. When a work has been communicated to even one person it begins to take on a life that is independent of its author and part of which he would not have foreseen. More so, when it has been communicated to thousands of persons. Very likely there is a consensus among these thousands as to what a given work is and means. But very likely their children or their grandchildren do not agree with them. The question is often raised: who is right, the contemporary audience or the later one? And here a paradox about literary scholars unfolds. As we have seen, their proposal for the understanding of a Lope de Vega is to get back to the "original" response. Yet the very scholar who spends his life on this kind of work, when he speaks of Hemingway or Salinger, will declare that only pos-terity can judge what merit they have. The contradiction implies what might in charity be called modesty but is more probably self-contempt. In both instances, the scholar avoids paying attention to his own spon-taneous responses, in one case shifting the responsibility to his ancestors, in the other to his descendants. Disbelieving in the Now, he commits himself to the Never.

Montherlant champions misunderstanding, and Reichenberger de-plores it. Both beg the question by postulating that works of art could be understood in some such complete and objective way as, say, one can understand how a watch is put together. Granted that the work of art has objective existence, only God understands it objectively. We others do not have a choice between understanding and misunderstand-ing, we have a choice between a variety of partial understandings. And it is not that we are seeing an object minus some of its parts, as when we see something three-dimensional from one side, but that our means of apprehension are such that we supply some of the parts ourselves in fantasy. The audience "brings something" to a play. Ugliness, as well as beauty, lies—in part—in the eye of the beholder.

A play is not, in my view, whatever by sheer misunderstanding you may care to make it nor what, with the aid of erudition, you may argue it must have been "originally." Its existence is objective but not con-stant. It cannot be caught nestling between the pages of the script or strutting upon the stage of a theatre. What one has access to are thoughts and feelings of one's own, and nothing else. These thoughts and feelings are modified by thoughts and feelings about other people's thoughts and feelings. One may know something of what the play was for other persons. One may come across facts that change one's attitude. But one will never arrive at the act that the author performed in its nakedness. Always the admixture of other people's subjectivity (if one informs oneself about it) and always, without any *ifs* at all, the admixture of one's own subjectivity!

If all, or most, of this is true, it is a mistake to resent and resist the subjective element. The correct attitude to a work of art is not to withhold oneself in the name of objectivity but to give oneself as completely as possible. What is most deeply wrong with Mr. Reichenberger's theory is his *attitude* to works of art, which seems to be that of a musician who would accumulate knowledge about the technique and historical setting of a sonata and then omit to listen to it. No wonder such a musician discounts the listening of a person who knows little of the technique and setting!

Would it be malicious to suggest that Mr. Reichenberger wants to keep the *Comedia* for himself and for those arch *comediantes*, the teachers in our departments of Spanish? Every profession is, as Shaw said, a conspiracy against the public, and the form a scholars' conspiracy takes is that of an attempt to monopolize the subject matter of scholarship. The professor who teaches Shakespeare regards Shakespeare as his alone, and, if he is capable of it, writes a book in which it is revealed that his research has led to the discovery of what Shakespeare really meant. * Foreign playwrights are imprisoned by the foreign departments. They can be prevented from escaping if people are persuaded (a) that playwrights can be "understood" but that (b) they can be "understood" only by means of historical scholarship.

But persons whom this message has not reached may wander into a bookstore, buy a book of classic Spanish plays, and enjoy them. Is their enjoyment based on pure misunderstanding? If so, one might cry, in the spirit of Montherlant: *Vive le malentendu!* Misunderstanding will certainly creep in, but it would be a mistake to assume that historical scholars, once they interpret, interpret less wildly than others. What seems to me the most extravagant of all interpretations of *Hamlet* was written, not by a psychoanalyst, but by a textual scholar (W. W. Greg). * * But, upon the whole, the intelligent bookbuyer's reading of a classic play will not be classifiable as a *misreading*. One needs to understand, as I have stressed, what all reading is like: a contribution is *always* made by the reader. But ask the same scholar who is so skeptical of the common reader's claims a question or two about something more serious:

*E.g., *Shakespeare's Heroes* by Lily Bess Campbell.
* *"Hamlet's Hallucination," *Modern Language Review* (October 1917): the ghost's account of the murder is untrue, the ghost is Hamlet's hallucination . . .

his religion. It will transpire, I hazard, that he is a member of the Episcopalian Church and that he has derived all his most cherished beliefs from the King James Bible. Does he know Aramaic? Greek? Hebrew? Does he examine the words of Moses or Paul in the language they spoke and in the knowledge of the place and the time? Of course not. But that he claims in some sense to understand Christianity is implied by the fact that he accepts it. He, the common reader, does not hesitate to take the words to mean what they seem to mean, even after translation, transplantation, and the passage of millennia have done their worst. And when he enjoys the Song of Songs and finds comfort in the Psalms of David, while he may attribute some of the satisfaction to himself, some to the translator, some to the passage of time, he confidently assumes that the author may justly claim a large part of the credit.

If it were not so, what would happen to religion? If it were not so, what would happen to culture? The essence of culture is continuity. Our heritage, having been inherited, does not have to be dug up. The kind of scholar I have been criticizing should leave literature for ar-cheology. Culture exists, not for specialists, but for common readers. I use this phrase in its classic sense, which did not refer to semiliterate readers, but to the cultivated general reader, the person the poet wishes to be read by, though not the person he is professionally studied by. Common readers have something *in* common. A periodical like the *Atlantic Monthly*—not recently but in the nineteenth century—appealed to, and helped to hold together, a body of common readers. Their reading has a certain range, the greatest possible range for persons who also have lives to lead. If we are going to tell these people that, unless they devote all their reading time to one of the two dozen fields they have explored up to now, we are destroying such cultural community as existed and substituting groups of specialists. In the future there can be no communication because A only knows Shakespeare, while B only knows Lope de Vega. However, the voice that has suggested that this must be our fate is not the voice of reason: it is the voice of vested interests.

(1961, 1970)

WHAT IS THEATRE?

IS THE DRAMA AN EXTINCT SPECIES?

That this piece was published in *Partisan Review* in 1954, and thereafter in books of mine, is of less interest than the fact that it had been rejected by the *New York Times Magazine*, which commissioned it. The *Times* plays a very large part in fixing the status of people, not least artistic people. It therefore tends to exclude writing—even by writers it has asked to write—which ignores its determinations, this kind of exclusion being what we have in America instead of censorship. Did my treatment of American drama here make me un-American? Not quite. Charlie Chaplin was Anglo-American like myself, and another person I named a playwright in this period was one hundred percent American: Martha Graham. But I did think it might be necessary to look outside the drama for the highest dramatic talent.

Nobody disputes that something is wrong. People have been saying that it's because the theatre is badly organized, and other people have been replying: not at all, it's simply that there's a dearth of good plays. There being a good deal of truth on both sides, it may be wise to sort out some of the points.

To begin with "good plays." One is concerned with two orders of merit not always clearly enough distinguished: talent and genius. Genius lies to a great extent outside any useful discussion because nothing we can say or do will produce it. It comes uncalled-for or not at all. What can be discussed is the welcome we give it. And the sad fact is that we welcome it too little and too late. We welcome it when it is safe to do so, when it is practically impossible not to do so. The great modern example is Bernard Shaw. To have welcomed him in the 1890s, when he was "dangerous," would have been enterprising. To accept him after 1910, as the theatre mostly did, was to accept the accepted. By that time the public had learned how to ward off Shaw's blows: critics thought him a clown, admirers thought him a classic; whichever way you look at it, he was through.

Since the death of Shaw, how many geniuses are left in the field? Readers will agree that they are few, even if they don't accept my nominations. And among the few I should have liked to nominate some are not accurately defined as playwrights. Charlie Chaplin and Eduardo De Filippo, though they have taken on the dramatist's tasks and performed them admirably, achieve greatness in the composite capacity of actor-playwright, a special and perhaps indissoluble union of actor, role, and author. I am left, it seems to me, with but two names: Bertolt Brecht and Sean O'Casey. Yet even two are enough to make us modify the proposition that there are no new plays for us to do. The plays are there. The question is why we don't do them. The answer cannot lie wholly in their authors' politics, which are (for present purposes) not very different from Shaw's. It lies, rather, in Time: Brecht and O'Casey are now where Shaw was before 1910. When they have "dated," Broadway will announce that they are "timely."

Genius, notoriously, is tardily recognized in all the arts. One cannot be surprised at this. One's surprise should rather be reserved for the fact that there is genius in the offing at all. If economic history goes slump-boom, slump-boom, the history of playwriting, one is tempted to say, goes slump-slump-slump. The dramatic critic is not called upon to explain why at any given moment there are no great playwrights. Empirical reasoning would more probably lead him to argue that there never could be a great playwright, just as empirical reasoning would lead a moralist to argue that there could never be a saint. You are not surprised to find money changers in the temple; the surprising sight is Christ with a whip. One is amazed at Shakespeare and Ibsen; Thomas Dekker and Henry Arthur Jones one takes for granted.

However—or rather, consequently—it is much more with the Dekkers and Joneses that we must be concerned. They, if anyone, are our regular standbys: their presence is not just an occasional blessing, it is something we require; it belongs to the minimum demands of theatre. In a world of two billion inhabitants it is fair to assume that there are always thousands of them. This means that if we can justly complain of a dearth of plays we are not so much protesting that very little genius exists as implying that talent, though it exists, is being deflected into other channels. The Dekkers and Joneses exist but are not writing plays.

So much the better for them. It is all too likely that the artistic impulse—the dramatic impulse particularly—can best find satisfaction today outside the arts altogether. There is the drama of science; and even the drama of politics need not be contemptible. Among our young people I find the artistic temperament, characterized by moral sensibility and vital energy, in undergraduates who will be chemists, lawyers, and doctors, more than in graduate students who will be professionally occupied with the arts. Those in whom the need for literary expression is irrepressible write fiction or poetry, in either of which modes they can work unbullied by boobs, and in one of which they might even make a living. (Sometimes I think all our poetic and fictional talent today is dramatic talent scared away by the idiocy of the theatre. Certainly, if Ernest Hemingway or Robert Penn Warren could devote ten years to theatrical work he would write even the best of our playwrights off the stage.)

Nor can anyone pretend that television and the movies attract only the less gifted. The time has gone by, if it ever existed, when the average film is inferior to the average play. Indeed, certain stage forms have been superseded and rendered obsolete by the movies. Once *The Prisoner of Zenda* has been on the screen, you would never want to see it on the stage. Pictures like *The Treasure of the Sierra Madre* and *High Noon* transcend all the theatre's efforts to present adventure. I can explain the drama critics' enthusiasm for the current thriller *Dial M for Murder* only on the assumption that they don't go to the movies.

In short, playwriting talent has been deflected along with the theatre public into television, the movies, poetry, the novel, or out of the arts altogether, with the result that (to coin a phrase) "there is no American drama." There is a lack not only of Shakespeares and O'Caseys but also of Dekkers and Joneses. In America playwriting is not yet a profession.

Playwriting may be said to be a profession when playwrights of high average talent are given their chance, their chance being production by performers who also constitute a profession. The American theatre does not offer playwrights this chance. A play cannot be produced on Broadway unless its producers think it is likely to run for a year. Plays of "mere promise" are excluded; the theatre is a place where promises are not kept. Though there is a place for the playwright to "succeed," there is no place for him to begin or to develop.

It has been said, "Without *Titus Andronicus*, no *Hamlet*." Yet if a Shakespeare came along today, what would happen? Either *Titus* would never get produced at all; or it would be a flop and drive the Bard to drink, teaching, and television; or it would be a hit, and the poet would spend an anxious lifetime writing twenty more *Tituses*.

A profession of playwrights, I have intimated, presupposes a profession of actors. Despite Actors' Equity Association, there is no such profession, there are merely some arrangements to stop employers' running off with their workers' wages. An adequate definition of an acting profession would include what the French understand by métier—a standard of workmanship that you achieve by joining the group and by practice; as with playwrights, the lack is apprenticeship in the beginning and continuity later. You do not know what the art of acting is capable of unless you have seen an ensemble of players who have worked together, year in, year out.

In the matter of acting, America has much to learn from some other countries—notably, France, Germany, and Russia. (I don't know enough about the Orient to justify any Eastern representation.) In the matter of playwriting, I know of but one country where things are, perhaps, in a healthier state than here, and that is France. Only in Paris, it seems to me, have we today the impression that playwriting is a profession. A literate play stands the same chance of professional performance that, with us, a novel stands of publication. There is consequently a large band of playwrights who in Paris are regular and commercial and over here are (or would be) avant-garde: for example, Marcel Achard, Jean Anouilh, André Obey, Armand Salacrou. There is also an overlap with poetry and the novel as the names of Jean Cocteau, François Mauriac, Henri de Montherlant, and Sartre testify. Even the most "unplayable" poet is played: I saw *Le soulier de satin* and *Partage de midi* lavishly staged in two of the largest theatres.

In England an "unpopular" poet like M. Claudel might well be broadcast on the Third Programme; he'd never reach the West End stage unless he were willing, like Mr. Eliot in *The Cocktail Party,* to reach it on its own terms. Shakespeare continues to use up the best energies of English theatre. London produces him and ignores Mr. O'Casey today, exactly as it produced him and ignored Shaw in the nineties. Italy, ever as poor in drama as she is rich in theatricality, is finding that a profession of playwrights cannot be legislated into existence even with the help of subsidies. Germany is the living proof that a well-organized and decentralized repertory system does not necessarily, or at any rate immediately, produce its own dramatists. It is amazing to think for how little time the German theatres were not playing. Goebbels closed them when he proclaimed total mobilization in 1944. By 1945 most of them were destroyed by bombs anyway. But the actors were at work again as soon as the war ended. Since then the old buildings have been repaired or new ones built. That there are no new playwrights only proves that there is a deeper damage than that of air raids. Somewhere a nerve had been cut.

Soviet Russia I do not know firsthand. Russian movies suggest directly, reports of reliable witnesses suggest indirectly, that the Russians still have the greatest profession of actors in the world. What one knows of their playwrights is less pleasant. If the degree of organization were the criterion, I imagine the Russian playwrights are the most "professional" in the world. But if the criterion is organization at all, it is organization to a certain end, namely, enabling playwrights to grow to their full stature. Russia offsets the gift of a fabulous theatre and a good living with a heavy price in censorial restrictions. To the observation that Shakespeare also worked under a censorship, I can only reply that it is open to anyone to compare Elizabethan with Soviet censorship, both as to the regulations and their enforcement. In such a comparison, the queen, and even the Puritan city fathers with whom she had little in common, will make a good showing. If some of the Puritans would have been as strict as Stalin, had they had the opportunity, it remains important that they did not have the opportunity.

A comparison of the two epochs and regimes could not be made at all except that we still tend to think of censorship in an old-fashioned way. We think of particular acts of censorship, the striking out of a forbidden word, the banning of a single book. We have barely realized that a greater efficiency in censorship has brought in its train a new mentality both in the censors and their victims. I have in mind not only the more macabre horrors of the situation but also the prosaic dullness of Soviet intellectuals. It resembles all too closely the dullness of the bourgeoisie against which all left-wing movements, as far as the intelligentsia is concerned, were a revolt.

Not long ago, two American playwrights said in the *New York Times* that the American drama was threatened by the totalitarian mentality—in this case represented by the anti-red Senator McCarthy. One of them—Arthur Miller—seemed to feel that the American playwright could no longer speak freely, the other—oddly enough, James Thurber—that he could no longer even breathe freely—freely enough to relax and be funny. *Both statements have value as warnings; I cannot see that they have as yet much substance in fact. Satiric or other comedy may presuppose more freedom than at present exists in Russia; I cannot see—thinking of Aristophanes and Molière—that it presupposes more freedom than at present exists in America, even granting a harsh estimate of how much that is. * *And in what sense have our playwrights lost their freedom of speech? It would, I suppose, be impossible for a Communist playwright to find backers for an openly Communist play, just as it would have been impossible for a Fascist playwright to find

---

*"The constant open season on writers has seriously depressed literature in America. It has taken the exuberance and gaiety out of the theatre. . . . Playwrights may come out of hiding and start working happily again if they hear the old reassuring sound of America laughing; but if the subpoenas for Hellman and Odets are the beginning of an endless probe of Broadway, then the American theatre cannot be saved and will die."—James Thurber in "Dark Suspicions," *New York Times,* July 27, 1952.

* *Heine said: "It is certainly a mistake to attribute the sterility of the German Thalia to the lack of free air; or, if I may be allowed the frivolous word, to the lack of political freedom. That which is called political freedom is in no wise necessary to the prosperity of comedy. If one recalls Venice, where, in spite of the leaden chambers and the secret drownings, Goldoni and Gozzi created their masterpieces; or Spain, where, despite the absolutist axe and the orthodox stake, those delightful cloak and dagger pieces were devised."—*The French Stage.*

backers for an openly Fascist play at any time between 1930 and 1945. Even so, the only Communist play I know of during the past few years (Howard Fast's *Thirty Pieces of Silver*) had a small New York production and full-scale productions in Iron Curtain countries which presumably pay royalties. Is the present plea for freedom of speech a plea for any opinions other than Communist opinions? Or is the complaint that any unorthodox opinion is dubbed Communist? If that's it, the unjustly accused playwright deserves our sympathy and help, like the unjustly accused actor and professor. What I cannot see is how dramaturgy suffers.

A radical playwright, in any case, can't have it both ways: he can't make his living by flinging accusations at established society and then scold society for taking his living away if it flings some accusations back. In the past, it has been very safe on Broadway to hold dangerous views, and the result has been a spate of easy virtue. The only playwright who could not have got his plays on would have been the antiliberal. On the Negro question, for example, Broadway has its own strict orthodoxy. The Broadway radical has been in fact one of the more pampered members of the community. Though an unpampered radical said, when a play of his was rejected, "Well, I don't expect them to pay for their own liquidation," the pampered ones may be defined as those who expect just that.

In any event, we must look at a much longer span of time than Mr. Miller and Mr. Thurber were considering. The impression we have of "decline" over a period of five or even ten years is reversed as soon as one play we like comes along. I agree that *The Male Animal* is better than the comedies of recent seasons, but there may be a better one than *The Male Animal* at any moment (by Mr. Thurber, for example). Pondering the American theatre since 1900, one is bound to long for plays better than any on the whole record. Before 1918, after all, the American drama was almost moronic. The improvement in the twenties was so great it rather naturally went to everyone's head. O'Neill was thought to have superseded Ibsen and to be comparable, rather, to Shakespeare and Aeschylus. I respect several of the critics who carried on in this way and I have been relieved to discover that, when challenged, they retract their hyperboles and hence call for no refutation from the rest of us. There was no Elizabethan Age, there were not even any Shaws, Chekhovs, and Strindbergs, but there were the Provincetown, the Guild, the Group Theatre, the Mercury, the Federal Theatre. At last there were some playwrights, even if there could not, all at once, be a profession of playwriting. There were theatres with the idea of continuity in them. From this germ, if at all, must grow an acting profession.

And now what? Circumstances continue to be against the playwright. Production in New York grows more and more expensive, public abasement before the eight daily reporters more and more abject. The administration of Eisenhower is not likely to restore a Federal Theatre, which even a Democratic Congress let fall. The American National Theatre and Academy is interested, I am told, in decentralizing the theatre and depriving New York of its monopoly. Whether its leaders know how this can be done, or whether, if so, they can do it, is another matter. However, it is probably worthwhile to support ANTA; not knowing what "the one thing necessary" is, we must perforce try every-thing. Every effort in the direction of a professional theatre, a theatre with continuity, must be backed up.

Can our efforts succeed? The facts wouldn't lead one to expect so, nor have I (or other people, apparently) a convincing overall plan for the conquest of the facts. I console myself, on the other hand, with the reflection that drama—drama of talent, let alone drama of genius— has not come in the past by prescription, nor was it predictable. The professions of playwriting and acting which Shakespeare entered as a young man had not existed much more than a generation before him. Dramatic history can be swift, especially when the preparations have been made; and the activity of 1900–1950 in America might certainly be regarded as preparatory. What is more, if drama died easy, it would already be dead. The art has a powerful hold on quite a number of people, among whom I count myself. And if now I seem to be working up an optimistic peroration, I would ask: what *can* I think? If you were a pterodactyl of the decadence, no one could expect you to talk in the tone of retrospective biology. Your business would be to die; and you can die with all the more dignity if you think you're not going to die at all.

(1953–54)

WHAT IS THEATRE?

What Is Theatre? is the title of one of my critical books and might well be the title of many others. The essay appearing here was originally a talk at the University of Virginia during my time as New Republic drama critic. I had already received a Guggenheim Fellowship to write a What Is Theatre? that would not appear for another ten years or so (under the title The Life of the Drama). My talk in Virginia was both interim report and first draft. It reflects my fieldwork of that period, which consisted mostly of theatregoing in New York.

To write theatre reviews is worse than walking on eggs; it is to walk on live bodies and make them bleed. The critic's comments may be far less harsh than those that are heard at every cocktail party in New York. But, while the partygoers only commit the venial sin of stabbing their fellow men in the back, and their victims will never find out who did it, the critic commits the unpardonable crime of striking right between the eyes and taking the responsibility in public. His victims know whom to hate and receive abundant sympathy to their faces from those who, behind their backs, agree with the critic. I sometimes feel that theatre reviewing is the art of making enemies and failing to influence people.

Nonetheless, I have gone on reviewing in the only way I know how. To those who consider it an entirely pointless or wrong way I can say nothing, but I should like to remonstrate with those who remonstrate with me for being what they consider unnecessarily harsh and high-handed, who write letters asking if I never, never realize that I might be mistaken, and try to get under my moral guard by demanding which do I want to do, *encourage* people, or *discourage* them, help theatre or hinder it? For the fact that a critic may be wrong (just like the critics of a critic) is no reason for him, especially as he thinks, poor man, that he is right, not to express his views as clearly as he can or even to abstain, in so doing, from the practice of all the arts of persuasion, which include every kind of civilized aggression from gentle irony to clamorous invective.

It is understandable that, in moments of anger or wounded feelings, any one of us should call on heaven or the government forthwith and forever to abolish criticism. Naturally, each one of us taken separately, and speaking strictly for himself, does not want to be criticized: he wants to be praised. "For myself, praise; for the other two billion inhabitants of the world, criticism"—it isn't a practical proposition, so the thwarted egoist reluctantly agrees to let everyone else be praised too. To an extraordinary extent, the frustrated artist Goebbels did substitute eulogy for criticism in Germany. And in America there is a current of anti-intellectualism which can grow, whenever we don't watch it, into an irresistible tide. That is why I feel that the energy of men of good will is less well spent asking critics not to criticize than it would be in asking the community at large to hold on to its critics in the face of totalitarianism and the psychology of what David Riesman calls an "other-directed"* generation.

This applies, also, to the question of discouragement. Certainly, I, like anyone else, am discouraged, sometimes very painfully so, when my work is unfavorably criticized. I am afraid I take criticism seriously. Suppose there were no serious criticism. Then the praise of so-called critics could not be taken seriously, and by that token could not be encouraging. When all plays are praised, a good review will mean precisely nothing; some reviews are encouraging only because others are not. Criticized artists learn to take the rough with the smooth, and my experience in this field gives me the impression that the generality of them have done so. Those who cannot "take it" are most commonly not those who are starved for want of a little recognition but those who have been spoiled with overpraise. Our culture oversells every product. Reputations are never simply high, they are hopelessly overinflated. One of a critic's jobs is to prick balloons.

---

*". . . a social character whose conformity is insured by their tendency to be sensitized to the expectations and preferences of others." "What is common to all the other-directed people is that their contemporaries are the source of direction for the individual." "While all people want and need to be liked by some of the people some of the time, it is only the modern other-directed types who make this their chief source of direction and chief area of sensitivity." "The other-directed person, though he has his eye very much on the Joneses, aims to keep up with them not so much in external details as in the quality of his inner experience."—*The Lonely Crowd: A Study of the Changing American Character*, by David Riesman.

We believe in freedom of discussion, but do we believe in discussion? In the theatre, the phenomenon is almost unheard-of, for one cannot describe as discussion either the ballyhoo of the publicity men or that grandiose gab by which certain theatre people try to make their next show sound like the second coming of the Lord. Yet criticism is discussion before it is either praise or condemnation.

I am sometimes thought to be so much in love with French and German theatre that I automatically dislike anything English or American. But countries are no more equal theatrically than, say, in their military establishments. Certain German cities and one French city have theatrical traditions that are not rivaled in many other places, certainly not in London or New York. We should be able to face a fact like that without contemplating suicide—or even emigration.

Take this matter of criticism *qua* discussion. When a Mauriac or a Sartre brings out a new play in Paris, it is discussed. Catholics present the Catholic point of view, Communists present the Communist point of view, every school of opinion presents its credentials. In New York, on the other hand, we like to "keep our religion out of it"—a Catholic critic would blush if anyone discovered that he went to church. We also like to "keep our politics out of it." And, consequently, there is a single political orthodoxy on Broadway, a liberalism so hazy and insubstantial that it can be shared by Communists and Republicans; and we go to political plays to make such epoch-making discoveries as that we like Negroes, dislike anti-Semites, and wish our country both to win the war and be nice to the natives.

We do have controversial plays, but not even the author expects there to be any controversy about them: he is only affronted that anyone should not find his work to be all that is noble and of good report. *The Crucible*, one of the most controversial plays of this decade, aroused very little controversy. As far as the New York press is concerned, I don't recall that anyone took issue with Mr. Miller except an editorial writer in the *Post*. And when Herman Wouk sailed into Broadway on the Caine, with some very high explosive politics in the cargo, one columnist, Mr. Arthur Schlesinger, said something about it, also in the *Post*. But, both times, the *Post*'s dramatic critic was keeping his fingers out of politics—and out of discussion.

This season (1955–56) we have had, in Anouilh's *The Lark*, a presentation of the trial of Joan of Arc wanton enough in its anti-Catholic bias to make any fair-minded non-Catholic join the faithful, if not in protest, at least in debate. Yet, though the Catholic bishop of Worcester saw the point, a large part of the Catholic public has accepted the play, being so secularized that it doesn't know the enemy when it sees him; like so many other sections of the population, it is in no position to discuss the issues. And the issues were not discussed except in the cloisters of *Commonweal* and the *New Republic*.

"We don't discuss it" used to be something parents said about sex. Now that sex is discussed more than anything else, perhaps we should expect various other subjects to become unmentionable. Will theatre be one of them? Will playwriting be something one does behind barred doors and prefers not to talk about? That wouldn't really be any worse than the present situation, in which discussion is limited to the oohing and aahing of routine eulogy and the tsk tsk tsk of routine disparagement. The proudest task dramatic criticism could propose for itself in this place at this time would be to replace animal noises with rational discourse.

But before this can be done, we need to examine our preconceptions. If so much of my criticism, or yours, is complaint that artists have missed the target, we have obviously been making assumptions as to what the target is. Destructive criticism, in fact, is justified only as springing from love of the object missed just as surely as eulogy is justified by love of the object attained. Even if our aim is only to criticize the critic, we need to know what the object is that he loves and precisely what it is *about* this object that inspires such love.

In the rest of this essay I am going to state, as fully as I can in the space, what it is about theatre that I respect, admire, and love. Possibly this procedure will confer some incidental benefits. Not least because we cannot remove a critic's prejudices, it is good to be able to see exactly what they are. Though, in the light of this confession, some of my judgments may seem less plausible than ever, it is my hope that others may begin to acquire a certain plausibility and that what appeared unnecessarily harsh and high-handed may be, at least partly, justified by the thought, the sentiment, or the attitude behind it.

What is the essence of theatre and its interest for us? What is the heart of the matter? Many, we know, have been stagestruck, but what was it, exactly, that struck them? Many have been more than stagestruck: they have emerged from the trance and given a lifetime of backbreaking labor to this singular institution. Many have suffered bitter poverty on its account, and bitterer humiliation, for worse than the constant economic hardships of theatre are the equally constant blows inflicted on everyone's self-respect. What is this art that exacts so high a price? Many have written about it, enthusiastically announcing their own view of it and opposing all other views witheringly, banteringly, or even inarticulately. What is the *it* that arouses their enthusiasm, and the misconception of which makes them so scornful, so skittish, or so hesitant?

Well, there's something about the theatre, one starts to say, before becoming uncomfortably aware how little one is adding to the store of knowledge.

> There's something about a soldier
> There's something about a soldier
> There's something about a soldier that is fine, fine, fine.

And if we cannot quite say why, let us at least try to say what.

To begin with, the theatre is a place. This place, in all known forms, sets up such a vibration in those who frequent it that certain properties roughly suggested by the term magic are invariably attributed to the building itself. In our epoch, for example, how many journalists, and even college freshmen, have mentioned the expectant lull when the lights dim, and the thrill when the curtain rises! This, you say, may be partly a matter of audience psychology. It remains true that the paraphernalia of the theatre has of itself remarkable suggestive power. Even when no audience is present, even when the stage is bare of scenery and the brick wall at the rear is exposed, the curious machine retains an insidious attraction. No more than a human being does a theatre necessarily lose its fascination by taking its clothes off. Pirandello obviously had been struck by that fact before he wrote *Six Characters in Search of an Author*; and also by the fact that the procedures of theatre carry a similar "magic." Rationally speaking, the rehearsal doings of actors and stage staff alike are either so sensible as to be rather dull or so foolish and anachronistic as to be contemptible. To know how the dullness and contemptibility are avoided and transcended would be to have solved the mystery of the theatre as a place.

If there is something about the place, there is something, too, about its inhabitants, the actors. I have not spoken of the merits of one building as against another, nor do I have in mind the merits of one actor as against another. There is something about the actor as such, about the mere fact of impersonation: there is a "magic" to this too. Various accounts have been given of the origin of such activity; various theories have been advanced to explain its continued and universal appeal. The fact itself is unequivocal. A child loves to dress up in grandmother's bonnet and feathers. Grown-ups go to carnivals and fancy-dress balls. To give the greatest possible effect to his story, the raconteur adds mimicry to narrative. Some primitive people believe that they can appease the gods by dressing up in certain ways; some nonprimitive people believe they can cure neuroses by a form of charade or group impersonation which they have christened psychodrama. A famous young actor was recently quoted by the *New York Times* as saying, "To me acting is the most logical way for people's neuroses to manifest themselves." I see no reason to believe him and several reasons for disbelieving him, yet I'm sure his heart was in the right place. He wanted to say something definitive when all he really sensed was that there's something about an actor.

There is something about an audience—that is, about a group of people in close physical proximity, with their faces all pointing one way, and their attention—their eyes, ears, hearts and minds—focused upon a single object. There is something about ceasing to be merely an *I* and becoming, under such circumstances, in this *place,* before that *actor,* a part of a *we.* There is something about the coziness and sociability*of the whole physical setup. And possibly—though one hesitates to believe it—there is something about its uncoziness, unsociability, and positive discomfort. The lack of knee room, the pest of people pushing past and, in New York, the ban on smoking, the absence of bars, the shortage of lobby space—such things lend weight to the occasion. Again, whatever the explanation, the fact is familiar: an experience is changed by being shared in such company in such a manner.

The extreme and notorious cases of audience psychology are cases of hysterics and swooning and the premature delivery of babies. But if we judge theatre merely by the *degree* of effect, then the best theatrical entertainment is a revivalist meeting or a political rally. In dramatic art proper, we are more concerned with moderate responses—with the fact, for example, that the joke *I* imperceptibly smile at alone in my study, *we* perceptibly grin at, we perhaps all "roar" at, in the theatre.

What's the matter, are we drunk? Boastful—wishing to show off our sociability? Polite—as one would laugh more loudly at a joke made by the president of the board? The less respectable motives no doubt enter in, as we are so directly under the noses of our fellow men, so mercilessly exposed and therefore bound to be on our "best" behavior; but is it not chiefly the atmosphere of a full theatre, the psychology of *we,* that has put us at our ease, and caused a great deal of good feeling to pour out of us that normally we would suppress? That is, if we felt it in the first place; for much of the good feeling is created by the occasion, by the psychology of *we.* Or perhaps, more accurately still, while initiated by the *actor* and the *place,* such feeling is constantly *increased* by the occasion, by the psychology of *we.* One speaks of "infectious enthusiasm," and the enjoyment of an audience is a positive contagion. The Puritans were wrong to call the theatre a scarlet woman;

*"The New York theatre-goer . . . can step into almost any theatre lobby with that sense of virtuous expectation, of responsibility and enlightenment, that the drama peculiarly awakes and that makes the theatre for New York what the café is for Paris, a pleasure and also a pride, a habit and a ritual, a diversion and a duty. To the extent that America has any communal life at all, it is centered in the New York theatre; here is the last refuge of sociability and humanism."—*Sights and Spectacles,* by Mary McCarthy.

they would have been less wrong had they called theatregoing a scarlet fever. We acknowledge freely enough, I believe, that men go to football matches to share the orgiastic experience of communal waving, shoving, cheering, and yelling. The orgiastic character of theatregoing is no longer overt, but surely it is one of the first things to take into account if we try to explain why anyone would pass up all the alternatives—especially television at home and the movies on the corner—and go through hail and snow to an expensive but uncomfortable seat in an inconvenient building called a legitimate theatre. Fine word, "legitimate"! To think of the little thrillers they put on there, that would yield in the movies a nonstop feature of at most ninety minutes, and on television at most an hour program with interspersed commercials! In what one is tempted to call this bastard of a legitimate theatre such items are stretched out for over two hours by the surely illegitimate device of lengthy intermissions during which there is no bar or restaurant to go to and only a grossly overcrowded lobby to smoke in.

What assets has the theatre got, to offset its appalling liabilities? Clearly, the *place*, the *actor*, and the psychology of *we*. "But the movies have all three," counters someone. "For how could you have a film without a place to show it in, actors to play in it, and a crowd to see it?" Ah yes, but there is a "short" in that electrical system. No current flows from celluloid to audience—or, at any rate, no current flows from audience to celluloid. In the movie theatre, we can watch a story and we can admire many things that actors do, but we cannot be caught up in a flow of living feeling that passes from actor to audience and from the audience back again to the actor. In the movies, Shirley Booth may smile, and you may smile back at her; but she can scarcely catch your returning smile and toss it back again or change it and give it back in the form of a sob or a catch in the throat. Yet such are the dynamics of theatre. And, rightly or wrongly, there are people who undertake the trip to the Broadway theatre, through the worst bottleneck of traffic in the world, just to exchange smiles or tears with Miss Booth. Personally, I demand a little more. But if we want to know what theatre is, we should know what is "the least of it"—the minimum condition under which it can be said to exist.

What, by contrast, is the most that theatre could ever hope to offer? Or, at any rate, what is the most it ever *has* offered? To keep this essay within bounds I shall forget about dance, pantomime, and song, and concentrate on the art which can advance the best claim to be the principal theatre art: the drama.

Histories of the drama customarily trace a development from what are called primitive beginnings to the great periods of flowering. But there is something misleading in the procedure, because, in the so-called primitive phases, art frequently shows what is called sophistication and, occasionally, far from remaining content with minimum demands, reaches out toward the maximum satisfaction. An instance is the art of tragedy at the moment of its very inception, as conjecturally established by Jane Harrison:

> We are apt to forget that from the *epos*, the narrative, to the *drama*, the enactment, is a momentous step, one, so far as we know, not taken in Greece till after centuries of epic achievement, and then taken suddenly, almost in the dark, and irrevocably. All we really know of this momentous step is that it was taken some time in the sixth century B.C. and taken in connection with the worship of Dionysos. Surely it is at least possible that the real impulse to the drama lay not wholly in "goat-songs" and "circular dancing places" but also in the cardinal, the essentially dramatic, conviction of the religion of Dionysos, that the worshipper can not only worship, but can become, can *be*, his god. *

Perhaps this passage suggests too much. If some historians write of the later drama as if it were all but a falling away from Greek tragedy, Miss Harrison likes to hint that even Greek tragedy might be a falling away from that first sublime instant when the worshiper of Dionysus became god. To me, the value of her idea is that it sets a standard: after this, for example, we know what to expect of a tragic hero. Aristotle's dry, accurate statement that a hero must be above life size takes on larger significance. Our eyes are opened both to the god-seeking and the blasphemy in tragic heroes from Oedipus to Halvard Solness. And we sense how painful has been the loss when playwrights eschew this god-seeking and blasphemy because neither they nor their culture believe in heroes.

The origins of comedy also call to mind the highest claims that the drama can make for itself. For, though the exact circumstances are even less certain than those of the origins of tragedy, there is some agreement that comedy derives from sheer celebration of fertility—of what Bernard Shaw called the Life Force, and what modern culture in general blithely nails down in that most outrageous of its simplifications, the word Sex. If in tragedy we feel that we can be god, in comedy our identification is with the spring, the seeds, the crops to come. A feeling of oneness with nature is at the bottom of it, a profound and dedicated acceptance of life, and of sexuality as central to life—an acceptance just as sadly lacking in modern culture as genuine hero worship. No wonder our cleverer men, from Carlyle to D. H. Lawrence, plead with us to try and recapture the ancient wisdom, the ancient ecstatic attachments!

Yet, though the very origins suggest what the maximum achievement of the drama might be, it remains (*pace* Miss Harrison) for history and culture and individual genius to furnish the proof: in the fullness

---

*Prolegomena to the Study of Greek Religion.

of time comes such a tragedy as *Hamlet,* such a comedy as *Le misanthrope.* What has been added to the moment of ecstatic identification with the god, the hour of the celebration of sexual energy? In a word, that which separates man from the beasts, and that which it was the glory of Greece to display to the world in all its dignity and power: intellect, mind, reason. *Le misanthrope* is chiefly words. The old comic rhythms are at work but are given no direct corporeal expression. Comedy has been elevated into the realm of the spirit. And Hamlet is surely the first protagonist in world drama whom one would call an "intellectual." These are extreme cases. Yet the point is equally well illustrated by, say, *The Birds* and the *Oresteia.* Though Aristophanes' play wears its masquerade origin on its sleeve—for it was traditional to use animal disguises—just as surely as the plays of Molière and Shakespeare it represents the transformation of the drama by intellect. Doubtless there is no gain without some loss, and it is a pity that Aristophanes' birds and beasts retain no magic from any primeval past; the gain is that the art of drama is now something that the master spirits of the age can devote themselves to. And, though there are still people who see Aeschylus as barely emerging from the murk of superstition, the *Oresteia,* no less than the philosophy of Aristotle or Plato, is the very symbol of Hellas and its victories of mind over matter, law over lawlessness, civilization over barbarism.

Pericles referred to Greek recreations as "provision for the spirit," and it is worth stressing the spiritual and intellectual side, because in our time the other side is so grossly overstressed, most of all by writers on theatre. But I am far from wishing simply to swing to the other extreme from those who represent the drama to be primitive. The achievement of all great drama is precisely the spanning of *both* sides of man's nature, the spiritual and the physical, the intellectual and the emotional.

However high in the air of the spirit the branches of the drama may rise, the tree still has its primitive roots, even if, as I said at the outset, our view of the primitive is a little arbitrary. The latest and most erudite study of *Twelfth Night*—by Leslie Hotson—shows that play to be a none too distant relative of fertility ritual. Deeply steeped in Christianity as he is, Shakespeare delights to celebrate in his comedies something that pagans as well as Christians have always delighted to celebrate: fruitful marriage. *As You Like It* culminates in a "wedlock hymn":

> Wedding is great Juno's crown
> Oh, blessed bond of board and bed!
> 'Tis Hymen peoples every town,
> High wedlock then to be honorèd.

A *Midsummer Night's Dream* ends with Oberon's promise that the wedding night of all three couples will have results:

> To the best bridebed will we
> Which by us shall blessèd be
> And the issue there create
> Ever shall be fortunate!

And *The Tempest* has a little wedding masque at its very center:

> Honor, riches, marriage blessing
> Long continuance and increasing,
> Hourly joys be still upon you!
> Juno sings her blessings on you.
> Earth's increase, foison plenty,
> Barns and garners never empty,
> Vines with clustering bunches growing,
> Plants with goodly burden bowing,
> Spring come to you at the farthest
> In the very end of harvest!

One of Shakespeare's first comedies, *Love's Labor's Lost,* is about the futility of attempting to thwart nature by a life of celibacy, and it ends with two of the loveliest invocations of seasonal myth in literature, the winter and spring songs. In one of the last comedies, *A Winter's Tale,* seasonal myth is not merely invoked at the end, it is pervasive. Starting from the modest but clear hint of the title, the play says everything there is to say about winter and spring, taken both literally and figuratively; and the fourth act is Shakespeare's paean to springtime, to the fact of coming into this world, and hence to the process by which we come into it. Reaching for a hyperbole to indicate that he will not break faith, Florizel says that, if he does,

> Let Nature crush the sides o' the earth together
> And mar the seeds within!

In other words, the destruction of the seeds of life, the creation of infertility, is the ultimate horror.

If the comedies were written in celebration of fertility, the tragedies were written out of a sense of the horror of infertility, or rather, one might say, but for the present-day associations of the word, of contraception. The extent of Lady Macbeth's villainy is measured by the statement that—if worst comes to worst—she would be prepared to murder the baby at her breast (act 1, scene 7, ll. 54–59); and the farthest reach of her husband's wickedness is not the murder of king or friend but of Macduff's little children. Commentators have been puzzled by Macduff's first remark after the terrible news has sunk in: "He has no children." Some have not wanted to take the "he" as Macbeth at all; others have wished to limit the sense to "he has no children for me to take revenge on." But surely the speech is one of those supremely dramatic utterances that leap out of a situation, illogical yet prompted by some higher logic, spreading meaning in several directions. The childlessness of Macbeth—with all its associations: sterility, futility, unnaturalness, lack of posterity—that is the main idea.

Like Florizel, Macbeth uses the figure of the killing of the seeds to express the idea of ultimate horror. Even if all Nature is in disorder, he asks the witches (act 4, scene 1), answer me—and the series of hyperboles in which he asks them culminates in:

> though the treasure
> Of nature's germens tumble all together
> Even till destruction sicken.
> (ll. 58–60)

The same image appears at the very climax of *King Lear*:

> And thou, all-shaking thunder,
> Smite flat the thick rotundity o' the world!
> Crack nature's molds, all germens spill at once
> That make ungrateful man!
> (3.2.6–9)

King Lear is about "unnaturalness between the child and the parent." The relation between Lear and Goneril is the precise opposite of that between Prospero and Miranda. And so when the old man casts about in his battered brain for the most terrible thing he can say, it is this:

> Hear, Nature, hear, dear goddess, hear!
> Suspend thy purpose if thou didst intend
> To make this creature fruitful.
> Into her womb convey sterility.
> Dry up in her the organs of increase,
> And from her derogate body never spring
> A babe to honor her!
> (1.4.297–303)

I dwell now on the primitive elements partly because scholars have indeed done justice to the nonprimitive elements and partly to show that "primitive" elements may be subtle and profound. Those who present Shakespeare as the practical man of the theatre who wanted to make money by providing a few evenings of soft emotion and broad fun will get as little comfort from the primitive part of *King Lear* as from its sophisticated, theological and Christian part. This, *en passant*: the main point is that *King Lear* is both primitive and sophisticated, and that the power in Shakespeare that most compels our admiration is the synthetic power, the ability to span two such worlds as these. Of this man, our supreme playwright, we may say: he encountered no gap which he could not bridge.

Modern scholars have performed a service when they have demonstrated how, in *King Lear*, Shakespeare miraculously managed to present the whole "Elizabethan world picture," the universe around, human society on earth, and individual man, center and model of the other two. It is a pity that after reading these modern accounts we sometimes have to wonder if Shakespeare also had a mind of his own. One may legitimately appeal back from purely scholarly interpretation to the judgment of the great humanistic critics, many of whom were not primarily scholars. It is the poet Dryden who reminds us that Shakespeare is not only to be commended for summing up the thought of his time: none was ever in livelier direct touch than he with life. "All the images of Nature," Dryden says, "were still present to him." And, just as he brought together the primitive and the sophisticated, he lived in the happy possession, not only of the world without, but of the world within. "He was the man who of all Modern, and perhaps Ancient Poets, had the largest and most comprehensive soul."

Having thrown out a hint or two as to what the drama was like in the beginning and what it became in the hands of its greatest practitioner, I turn to the modern stage. Necessarily, in this field, I shall be less concerned with attainments already completed than with problems reaching out into the future. But, first, what is to be inferred from the story I have been telling? Before asking what a new theatre can mean, should we not ask more searchingly what the old theatre means, what place it deserves in our lives? Shakespeare had such and such an intellect, such and such an imagination. To what end did he have them?

Some have said that the end of drama, and art in general, is pleasure, and others have said that it is instruction, and, though this is no place either to recapitulate or continue the argument, a remark or two about it may push the present inquiry one step further along. When, in her admirable book *Ancient Art and Ritual,* Jane Harrison chides those who see pleasure, not spiritual nourishment, as the end of art, is she not, like almost every contributor to this particular discussion, simply quibbling? Does she not find pleasure precisely in spiritual nourishment, just as we all do in nonspiritual nourishment? And, conversely, when Aristotle proposes pleasure as the end of art, does he not define pleasure so broadly as fully to appease those of Miss Harrison's persuasion, if they will read him sympathetically? One of the best commentators writes:

> Aristotle recognizes specific differences between pleasures. There is the harmless pleasure, which is afforded by a recreation or a pastime: but a pastime is not an end in itself, it is the rest that fits the busy man for

fresh exertion, and is of value as a means to further work; it has in it no element of that well-being or happiness which is the supreme end of life. . . . But art in its highest idea is one of the serious activities of the mind which constitute the final well-being of man. Its end is pleasure, but the pleasure peculiar to that state of rational enjoyment in which perfect repose is united with perfect energy.*

Such a form of pleasure is no less noble or moral than the objective proposed by those who take drama to be didactic—Shelley, for instance, who, in his preface to *The Cenci*, beautifully said:

The highest moral purpose aimed at in the highest species of the drama is the teaching the human heart, through its sympathies and antipathies, the knowledge of itself.

I propose to accept all three viewpoints—Jane Harrison's, Aristotle's, and Shelley's—and pass on to the problem of modern drama.

It could be that, in the eyes of the gods, there is no Problem of Modern Drama, no special and different task for the modern writer. Even so, we who are not gods can only see a perennial task in its urgent and present form. "Teaching the human heart the knowledge of itself," says Shelley. Assuredly he spoke for all time. Nevertheless, in the age following his death, the perennial task took a form which, it seems to me, can be roughly expressed in the words: teaching the human heart that it still exists. Or, better perhaps: teaching the human heart that it can exist again, that it can be brought back to life.

Ortega y Gasset says that man is the only creature who is made and not just born; for a man who simply exists is no man.

> What is a man
> If his chief good and market of his time
> Be but to sleep and feed?

Hamlet answers himself: "A beast, no more," and goes on to explain that this sleeping, feeding body of ours becomes human only when "godlike reason" inhabits it. Beasts are beasts, and gods are gods, but the human race is somewhere betwixt and between; that is the tragedy of our situation, and the comedy of it too. Now it may just be the way we feel about things, rather than an objective fact, but it does seem to us, does it not, that we live at a time when our humanity runs an unprecedented risk of total submersion in the beast? In such a time of death, the least flicker of life shines like a torch. In such a time of hate, the least murmur of love is music. In such a time of bestiality and unreason, the rediscovery of truly human impulse becomes the one thing necessary. And this is so far from being an original observation on my part that it is, on the contrary, the theme—one might almost

*S. H. Butcher, *Aristotle's Theory of Poetry and Fine Art*.

say, the obsession—of modern literature, including dramatic literature. There is a line of Schiller that sums it up in advance: "Dass der Mensch zum Menschen werde" ("That man may become man"). And this line is cited by Dmitri Karamazov in a crucial chapter that Dostoevsky calls "The Confession of a Passionate Heart in Verse." Or consider Browning's phrase, "and paint man man, whatever the issue." It is the second part of it that gives the modern application to the Shelleyan and perennial idea. "Whatever the issue!" There is a danger of man's being crowded out by "issues," a danger not just for people in general but particularly for the classes whose education should have made them champions of the human. We talk of "confusing the issue," but perhaps we should talk, rather, of issues that confuse us.

The aim, then, is the rediscovery of man, and one is tempted to say that the modern writer in the serious genres who ignores this aim is off the main track. Nor is it enough to be aware of the aim. The writer must be engaged in the process of search.

What is the difference between a novelist like Somerset Maugham and one like Joseph Conrad? In Aristotle's terms, Maugham offers us a pastime, Conrad the higher happiness which is the true end of human life. In more modern terms, Maugham is a proficient technician and entertainer, but Conrad is a searcher for the meaning that we too stand in need of, he is our companion and guide in the great quest.

The difference between Conrad and Eugene O'Neill is something else again. I believe that O'Neill wanted to achieve in the drama exactly what Conrad did achieve in the novel. If he didn't succeed, it could be simply that he had less talent, or it could be that, while he intended to search, he did not really do so. Reading *Mourning Becomes Electra*, we feel that here is an author who has said to himself: "What are tragedies like? They're about this, aren't they? They begin this way, proceed that way and end thus?" Reading *Lord Jim*, we join the author in a life-and-death struggle for meaning, for courage, dignity, identity, the humanly genuine, the human essence. And we forget how Conrad is doing it. Form is so perfectly handled that it disappears, and we confront the content in its nudity.

It is natural that, in approaching the topic of tragedy in modern times, we at once encounter Dostoevsky and Conrad.* There are no greater modern masters of tragedy than these, just as there are no greater modern masters of comedy than Jane Austen and Charles Dickens. Whatever justice there may be in saying that the drama has been dying, it would certainly be an error to imply that the energy that used to go

---

*Anyone who considers this statement either pat or vague should read, among other things, Vyacheslav Ivanov's book on Dostoevsky, *Freedom and the Tragic Life*, especially the chapter entitled "The Novel-Tragedy."

into drama has petered out. At worst, it has been deflected into another channel, that of fiction, leaving the theatre a cultural backwater.

It would not be reasonable to show surprise, let alone indignation, that many plays are not very good; many novels are not very good either. What is disturbing is the extent to which theatre people are simply out of touch—with just about everything. And a corollary of this proposition is that our theatre writers do not address themselves to the common task. Their plays are all rehash. Drama has become a ragbag for yesterday's notions and fads. More depressing than the mere lack of achievement is the lack of ambition, of dedication, of the sense of what the drama has been and should be.

One does not ask that every novelist be a Conrad. One does ask, though, that every novel that is to be read right through to the end bear witness to its author's adventurous spirit. He must battle with the materials even if he doesn't always win. He must search even if he doesn't always find. He *must*—if only for technical reasons. For it is the act of searching that brings writing alive. Just barely alive, perhaps. Great writing is *more* alive than that, alive in more ways than that. But the searching mind can create a minimum of life. And this is a minimum that most playwrights today neither meet, nor try to meet, nor have any idea they should try to meet. (Eugene O'Neill did not always meet it, but because he always tried to meet it, he is indeed a "distinguished" playwright; for this fact distinguishes him from nearly all his colleagues.)

Two mistakes are made. First, playwriting is regarded simply as a craft. Now, clearly, playwriting *is* a craft, just as fiction is a craft, *among other things.* It is another question whether it is advisable to isolate the craft from those other things, thus in effect replacing the playwright with the play-doctor, which is rather like replacing fathers and mothers with midwives. The notion has spread among writers, play-doctors, critics, producers, actors, public, that plays are "not written, but re-written"; that is, not written, but pieced together, not composed with one man's passion and intellect but assembled by the ingenuity of all who stop by at the hotel bedroom, preferably during the rehearsal period. In this way, dramaturgy is demoted from the fine to the useful arts; and is unique among the latter by not really being useful.

The second mistake is to write with the audience consciously in mind, instead of in the faith that there will be an audience for good work. Obviously when we say that a play is not a writer's exploration of reality but just a calculated arrangement of effects, there is no need to ask: effects upon whom? The *raison d'être* of these effects is to interest and please the audience. All writers, of course, *hope* to interest and please an audience; the exploratory writer decidedly hopes that his explorations will interest and please an audience. But for the nonexploratory writer, hope is not enough. He is not prepared to leave it, as it were, to chance. He puts his whole mind on audience, audience, audience—by God, he'll *make* them like it—and perhaps, by forgoing his claim to be an artist, becomes a remarkable craftsman. An artist cannot give *all* his attention to the audience; he needs to keep so much of it for his characters, his story, his subject. *

Now I am not prepared to argue with anyone who merely expresses an arbitrary preference for craft and pastime over art and exploration. The argument starts when someone, like Walter Kerr in his book *How Not to Write a Play,* seeks to confer a higher status on the lower phenomenon, raising craft above art, or so defining art that, to all intents and purposes, it *is* craft. Perhaps Mr. Kerr would say he hasn't done this; and it is probably as hard for me to sum up a book of his in terms acceptable to him as it has certainly proved for him to sum up a book of mine in terms acceptable to me. But I think it is true to say that he sees dramaturgy as a matter of adjusting the play to the audience; in no measure or fashion must the audience be asked to adjust itself to the play. * * They pay their money and they take their choice. *Vox populi, vox dei,* with *populus* defined as nonintellectuals, shopgirls preferred.

What about intellectual shopgirls? That they exist is news that apparently hasn't reached Mr. Kerr, though it is familiar enough to any book publisher; and, of course, they stay away from the plays that Mr. Kerr tries so hard to enjoy on their account. I believe Mr. Kerr's invitation to shopgirls will be turned down because the intellectual ones are busy with paperback books, while the nonintellectual ones are quite happy with their television sets; for, if we want a truly popular alternative to such highbrow pursuits as reading, we have it—in television. The theatre, as Mr. Kerr presents it, is something neither kind of shopgirl wants. * * * Nor is his sociology so up-to-date as he would wish it to be. For example, the notice in the window of the five-and-ten-cent store at the end of my street in Manhattan does not read: SHOPGIRL WANTED. It reads: SALESLADY WANTED. Call it elegance, call it snobbery, the cold fact remains that no candidate who appeals to The Shopgirl Vote, from this time out, is going to get it.

---

*In his book *The Inmost Leaf* Alfred Kazin speaks of "that morbid overconsciousness of the audience that afflicts even the most serious writers in this country." The problem is one, not for the theatre alone, but for our culture generally.

* *Contrast this with the attitude of a great playwright: "No matter how badly my *Carlos* fails as a stage-play, I must insist that our public could see it performed ten times more before it would comprehend and exhaust all the good in it which offsets its defects."—Friedrich Schiller.

* * *"By current measurements of audience size, the theatre hardly qualifies as a means of mass communication. But the films assuredly do, and increasingly since the successful marketing of the paper-backs, so does the book."—J. Donald Adams, *New York Times Book Review,* March 25, 1956.

Just as there is a word—patrioteering—for the kind of patriotism that is merely an appeal to the gallery or worse, there ought to be a word for that sort of "democratic" argument which is merely an appeal to mediocrity and the fear of distinction, for in America this is the appeal almost everyone makes when he runs out of real arguments: "democrateering," if I may coin a word and adjust a dictum, is the last refuge of a scoundrel. Mr. Kerr being no scoundrel, I shall dismiss his democrateering as simply unworthy of him, and turn to that part of his argument which calls for an answer. Discussing poetic drama, Mr. Kerr says: "Verse is of no value whatever unless, like every other part of the play, it mirrors the picture people have of themselves. . . . Writing verse is almost like taking the blood pressure of the age." If only Paddy Chayefsky would take up verse, one concludes, he would inevitably become Mr. Kerr's favorite playwright. For, even speaking prose, the actor who played Marty was awarded a golden urn with an inscription stating that he revealed "the meatcutters of America as friendly, humble, sincere, and accredited members of the human race." And this statement is guaranteed to give the picture the meatcutters have of themselves, as the urn was the gift of the Meatcutters' Union, Local 587, Santa Monica, California. It seems to me that Mr. Chayefsky is the playwright of the age of conformity, the age of "other-directed" yes-men, the age of democrateering salesmanship; and that Mr. Kerr is in some danger of becoming its critic.

"Every . . . part of the play . . . mirrors the picture people have of themselves." As the metaphor was presumably suggested by a famous passage in Hamlet, it may not be unfair to ask what that passage means. Hamlet spoke of the actor as holding up the mirror not to the picture people have of themselves but to nature, that is to people as they really are—a very different matter. In his use of this figure, Shakespeare was following an established tradition according to which the mirror was held up to human affairs to the end that men might be inspired by a good example or warned by a bad one. It was a normative mirror. Though art imitated life, it did not do so just for the record, but in order to improve life; far from saying: "This is how you see yourself, humble, sincere and accredited; keep it that way," it said: "You see what happened to this bad king, go thou and do differently."

The derivation of Mr. Kerr's view is not from the older medieval and Renaissance tradition at all, but from that much more recent historicism which encourages us to see in literature the background, and not the writer—the "Elizabethan world picture," and not the great William Shakespeare. One of the few authorities cited for Mr. Kerr's highly debatable remarks on Shakespeare is an able journalist, Marchette Chute. Admittedly, Miss Chute does not stand alone. She could easily appeal her case to a higher court, where such judges as Professor

Alfred Harbage of Harvard and Professor Allardyce Nicoll of Birmingham sit on the bench. For out of a few false analogies with our situation today, and a great deal of rancor against the idea of minority culture, these and other celebrated scholars have created the image of a Shakespeare who would have given one hand to Mr. Chayefsky and the other to the selection committee of the Book-of-the-Month Club.

Without wishing to deny that Shakespeare was popular, I decline to forget that, equally, he was "unpopular," aristocratic; his being both at the same time, his belonging to *both* the popular culture *and* the court culture, being another aspect of his universality, his comprehensiveness of soul, and another reason why we must consider him supremely great. Therefore, since we are citing authorities, I should like to appeal over the heads of the Shakespeareans of the past generation to the Shakespeareans of many earlier generations, as, for example, to Thomas Carlyle, who wrote, "Shakespeare is . . . the greatest intellect who, in our recorded world, has left record of himself in the way of Literature." And, of course, it is not a matter of Shakespeare but of theatre, drama, and literature generally. I should like to oppose to this idea of a poet who merely takes the blood pressure of the age the idea of a poet who raises the blood pressure of the age.

Not that this will surprise Mr. Kerr, who suspects that what I want to do with the theatre audience is to make it suffer, give it heart failure, and kill it off, except for that tiny circle of sophisticates, highbrows, aesthetes, longhairs, and eggheads, up there in the top left-hand corner of the second balcony, who are the fellow members of my mutual-admiration society . . . In his book, Mr. Kerr rebukes a playwright who said he wished to make his audience uncomfortable. Now, of course, if the choice is simply between comfort and discomfort, pleasure and pain, we're all going to be on Mr. Kerr's side, including, I am sure, the playwright who spoke of making his audience uncomfortable. Real life, however, mixes its pleasures and pains. Where is there more fun—in a comfortable play that gives auntie back her picture of auntie or an uncomfortable play which, while it may annoy auntie a bit, also intrigues her, tickles her, interests her, livens her up, and perhaps even shakes and moves her?*And in case anyone suspects that what I'm after is a little fun at auntie's expense, let me confess that sometimes I am auntie. Arthur Miller's plays pain me very much, but I would far rather see one of them than any play that, so to speak, merely reminds me of home, giving me back the pleasant picture I have of myself. Surely we

---

*On the fact that people say of a show that is the rage, "You *must* go, but for my own part it bored me to death," William Archer commented: "If the play is really a successful one, they misrepresent their sensations. . . . What they mean is, 'It interested me in spite of myself. I disliked it and it puzzled me; but it bored me much less than the trumpery pieces I like and understand.' "—*The Theatrical World of 1897.*

do *not* want back our own image of ourselves. That way lies a dull and even degenerate sort of art. We want someone else's image, and not necessarily of themselves, but perhaps of someone else again. (For example, William Shakespeare's image, not of himself, but of Richard III.) By all means, there has to be established an identification of the audience with the action and, often, with a protagonist; but this is effected, not by bringing the protagonist to the audience, but, contrariwise, by bringing the audience to the protagonist, lifting them out of themselves, placing them in the skin of a stranger.

> . . . the cardinal, the essentially dramatic conviction . . . that the worshipper can . . . become, can *be*, his god.

His god, says Jane Harrison; not himself, much less his flattering image of himself. The tragic hero, says Aristotle, is above life size; and comic characters are below life size. Absolutely no one, in the drama, is life size; no one is "the average shopgirl." Either our sense of reverence builds the hero up, or our sense of scorn cuts the shopgirl down. The theatre has a Brobdingnag and a Lilliput to offer, but absolutely nowhere for the common man to lay his head.

I am told that it is old-fashioned to speak of the "commercial" theatre, for everyone now knows that what Shakespeare and Shaw were after was money. Another false trail! No one denies that, so far from being against money, the artist is most often in the position of having to say to the business man, as Shaw did to Samuel Goldwyn: "You're only interested in art, I'm only interested in money." Human beings like money, and an artist is a human being. But he is also an artist, and while sometimes it may happen that the commercial theatre is mainly favorable to his art, it may sometimes happen that it is not— like the commercial anything else. Today, to choose a contrary example, commercial publishing in this country cannot, in my opinion, be said to be hostile to literature; on the contrary, any novel with merit in it has a strong chance of publication. In theatre, the situation happens to be very different. Not that there are great new plays lying idle in desk drawers; the trouble lies deeper than that. The plays don't get to be written at all, because those who might write them actually write novels. There are many answers to the question: what scares them off the theatre? One typical deterrent is the phenomenon of the Perfect Play.

The commercial play is the Swiss watch of dramaturgy. When properly manufactured, it is perfect, as only a piece of machinery can be perfect. And it is the prospect of such a perfection that current theatre criticism holds out to the young playwright, while enjoying itself noting the imperfections in plays by real writers. In this the newspaper critics live out their manifest destiny as spokesmen of the status quo—or rather, like the Devil in *Don Juan in Hell,* not of the status quo as it actually is, but as it aspires to be, not of Broadway as it actually is, but of the Platonic idea of Broadway, not of what people are, but of the picture they have of themselves. The Perfect Play being a good deal easier to put together (though not easy) than a significant imperfect play, one can indeed conceive of a Broadway on which every play is perfect. And since the standard by which perfection is judged is clear and objective (namely, show of hands), all plays in which imperfections are found could be promptly removed from the boards and from the record. I think I have stumbled here on a suggestion that should earn me a medal—or an aisle seat at a perfect play—in whatever mechanized utopia awaits us in the years to come.

Retreating to my customary persona, I realize that I am left with the unhappy task of championing imperfection. I idealize failure, says Mr. Kerr (to which it seems almost like nose-thumbing to retort: you worship success). Red herring upon red herring! It is not the price to be paid, but the jewel paid for, on which the case rests. But the price does have to be paid, the price of artistic success being, in general, a good deal of failure. To establish oneself as a VIP with a hit written at the age of twenty, and then to manufacture another hit every two years for life—this experience does not resemble that of any artist whose career is known to me. An artist begins as a fumbler, at best a brilliant fumbler, and, even after he has enjoyed some public success, he relapses continually into failures which no one should be so foolish as to idealize, since they represent to him nothing but bitterness and desolation of spirit. The lives of those two notorious career men, Shakespeare and Shaw, are not exceptions. Not even Shaw. The middlebrow critics of the 1890s were all against the young highbrow who wrote *Arms and the Man;* he had no success then, and he had very little success with the plays of his last twenty-five years. When today *The Lark* is spoken of as "second only to *Saint Joan,*" it is well to remember which show came second as a Broadway run. *

(If those who champion pastime tend to be against art, those of us who are for art must make it crystal clear that we are not against pastime. There have grown up particular pastimes, like Perfect Plays, which stand in the way of art, which in a sense are designed to replace art, but, no more than Aristotle when he formulated the distinction, need we in any way disapprove of pastime as such. On the contrary, we acquire in the theatre such respect for certain lighter works and forms that we are

*Namely, *Saint Joan,* with 218 performances (1923–24), as against *The Lark's* 229 (1955–56). Nor is it accurate to say that all runs were short in the twenties. During the 1923–24 season there were seventeen plays on Broadway that had run for more than 500 performances, the greatest classics among them being *The Bat* and *Abie's Irish Rose.*

ready to speak of the *art* in them, and so to pass beyond the dichotomy I have been using. The works of Labiche and Offenbach are pastimes. Are they therefore not art? The works of Dumas *fils* are not pastimes. Must we therefore rank them higher than Labiche and Offenbach? At this point, the terminology lets us down as, at some point, all critical terminology does. Before continuing to use the art-pastime dichotomy for what it is worth, I want, parenthetically, to concede this, and to insist that what I am trying to measure is the degree, not of earnestness, but of spiritual curiosity.)

I have been maintaining that the "serious" modern playwright is, or should be, engaged, along with other modern writers, in the search for the human essence. If it is possible to state in a word what moral quality the artist engaged in this quest needs above all others, I should say that it is audacity. Conversely, artists who are not searching, not reaching out for anything, but working comfortably within their established resources, and who are completely lacking in daring, who never "cock a snoot," "take a crack" at anything, "stick their necks out"— for them should be reserved the harshest adjective in the critical vocabulary: innocuous. In life there are worse things than innocuousness— forms of rampant evil which render innocuousness praiseworthy by comparison. But the devil doesn't write plays. And when Mussolini wrote them he didn't succeed in projecting anything of the force of his iniquity. Like many a better man, he only succeeded in writing innocuously. But that is the worst type of writing there is.

With the two conceptions of work—art and pastime, exploration and craft—go two conceptions of the worker. The master of pastime is the well-adjusted person, happily holding hands with the audience.* The artist, if not maladjusted, and I believe he is not, is not well adjusted either; perhaps we should follow Peter Viereck's suggestion and invent a third category, that of the *un*adjusted man, the healthy rebel. At any rate, it has been known, at least since Plato, that the artist is a dangerous character, and consequently that art is a subversive activity. I am not speaking of the philosophy, much less of the politics, of artists. Artists are disturbing, unsettling people, not by what they preach but by what they are, conservatives like Dante and Shakespeare being far more disturbing and unsettling than our little revolutionaries. The greater the artist, the greater the upset.

In the voice of every artist, however full-throated and mellow, there is an undertone of something very like insolence. The small boy who

* "The secret of your theatrical prosperity," Scribe was told in the speech that welcomed him into the Academy, "is to have happily seized upon the spirit of your century and to have made the kind of play which it takes to most readily and which closely corresponds to its nature." Allowing for differences in vocabulary, isn't this what a Broadway critic would say when conferring an award on a Broadway playwright?

said to Mme. de Pompadour: "*Why* can't you kiss me? The queen kisses me," was not the devastating Voltaire but the "mild" Mozart. "To kindle art to the whitest heat, there must always be some fanaticism behind it": Bernard Shaw was inspired to write this by seeing, not Ibsen's *Ghosts*, but the music-hall sketches and cabaret songs of Yvette Guilbert. The famous Tramp of Charlie Chaplin was gentle, and beloved by all the world, yet when I heard a candid spectator say of Charlie, "I can't stand the man," I realized how many others would say the same if they rigorously examined their responses; because, for all the charm and the high spirits, Chaplin is an alarming artist. Again, I am not referring to politics (though doubtless Chaplin took up Stalinism because he *thought* it was radical; there, history's joke was on Charlie). About any film of his, however slight, there is an air of menace; whereas most other comedians, for all that they make a lot more noise, are quite harmless.

Henri de Montherlant devoted an essay to the analogy of playwriting and bullfighting; and I have heard Martha Graham compare the dancer to the matador, and that, not in point of similarity of movement, but similarity of psychology: the dancer will attain to that razor-edge keenness when each move, each fall, each leap has that degree of urgency, that heightened sense of hazard.

"Live dangerously!" The artist follows Nietzsche's recommendation. Ortega y Gasset says there is some vulgarity in it because life is of its nature dangerous. True; but, as the fact is ignored and implicitly denied by modern culture as such, Nietzsche was fully justified in shouting it from the housetops. Even now, though editorials can be uselessly shrill about hydrogen bombs, though facts like the murder of six million Jews are common knowledge, that fundamental complacency of middle-class culture—the most imperturbable of all imperturbabilities—is still with us. The works of Nietzsche have not "dated." Nor has the artist's sense of danger: precisely from his "subversiveness" stems his utility to society.

And the theatre could make a special contribution. For though it has sometimes chosen to be the most unenterprising of the arts, the genius, and even the very technics, of the medium tend all the other way. Theatricality is, *by definition*, audacious. A comedian is, *by definition*, a zany. The impertinence, insolence, effrontery that I have speculatively attributed to the artist in general none would deny to the clown in particular. But have we begun to draw the logical inferences? We have been told often enough of all the gradual, thorough, and fine-spun things that the novel can do and that the stage fails to do, but have we explored the possibilities of theatre in the opposite direction—the realm of the sudden, the astonishing, the extravagant? The theatre is the place for the anarchist to throw his bomb.

Or perhaps for anyone *but* the anarchist to throw his bomb. For while theatre is the art of explosions, the trick is to have them go off at the right time in the right spot. Audacity has no place in the arts until it is brought under iron control. The rhythm of theatre derives from an alternation of explosion and silence; more precisely, there is preparation, explosion, and subsiding. The man of the theatre must not merely bring explosives in his bag; he must know exactly how to prepare the explosions and how to handle their subsidence. For the interplay between audacity and control produces the supreme artistic effects; the work of the masters of dramatic literature abounds in examples. And stage directing calls for the same combination of powers, though usually, even from the expert, we get either audacity without control, or control without audacity. The only man I know of who is endowed with both gifts to the greatest possible extent—and in both fields, playwriting and directing—is Bertolt Brecht. In that fact—and not in the theory and practice of propaganda—lies the secret of his unique importance in the theatre today.

But I am not coming forward with a messiah. No one man will provide the answer to our problem, and to part of it Brecht provides, in my opinion, the wrong answer. He is one of those writers who search less and less after what I have been calling the human essence, because they are more and more convinced that they have already found it. Even supposing that Brecht *has* found it, that fact would not augur well for him as an artist. The only artists today who remain artists after conversion to causes which claim a monopoly of the truth are those who are not wholly convinced. Graham Greene's work derives its vitality now from the fact that he is always fighting his own Catholicism. The minute he says to himself, "I am a Catholic writer," begins to ask the alleged truth of his beliefs to do duty for his personal grasp of truth, however tentative and unsure, he is through. I am not objecting here either to Communism or Catholicism but, rather, pointing out what kind of adherence to these causes, or any other that makes comparable claims for itself, is damaging to an artist. The audacity for which I have praised Brecht was not the product of such an adherence but, on the contrary, of that bourgeois freedom in which Brecht gradually came to disbelieve. As he was an artist by virtue of his subversive activities, and socially and overtly subversive activities at that, absolutely necessary to his art was a society which, first, he wished to subvert and which, second, would permit him to try and subvert it. Bourgeois capitalism met both conditions; Soviet communism neither. And so the *enfant terrible* of the Weimar Republic tried to convert himself into the yes-man of the Soviet bureaucracy and the DDR (Deutsche Demokratische Republik). Only in relation to the West could this political writer even try to remain audacious, and this is that easy audacity (common also among anticommunists) which is no audacity at all.* Meanwhile, those larger works which Brecht hopes will have some lasting value are most alive where some unresolved inner conflict forces its way in despite the author and the watching bureaucrats. Into both *Galileo* and *Mother Courage* have been smuggled elements which ar⌐ as subversive to Communism**as *The Threepenny Opera* is to capitalism. The Communist press has not been entirely happy about either play.

It is a mistake even to hope that an ideal will find its realization in a single man. It is a mistake to expect that the ideal situation will ever be realized at all. And it is above all a mistake to think that ages of great theatre come about through the critics' explaining how to write plays, or even how not to write them. The critic's influence is not directly on the creative act but on public opinion (the playwright being, however, a member of the public). What the critic influences is morale.

The theatre today is demoralized. It suffers from hysterical oscillation between cheap cynicism and idealistic euphoria. This could be because dramatic art nowadays attracts chiefly manic depressives, though to say so only provokes the query: how has this come to be so? Between flat despair and yeasty zeal, why is there nothing but a vacuum? The question puts the cart before the horse: it is precisely because of this vacuum, this void, this *néant,* that men can only admit defeat or simulate success, descend to cynicism or rise to feverish and showy enthusiasm. Which is to repeat that they are demoralized.

Now, if it isn't too late, what do we do about demoralization in any institution—the church, the army, the nation—but try to recall people to a sense of the past, the glorious origin of the institution, its great men, its highest moments? And this is what I have been doing in the course of this brief attempt to answer the question, What Is Theatre? (or rather, this lengthy attempt to ask that question). We of the theatre need the inspiration and the discipline of Shakespeare and Molière exactly as a musician needs the inspiration and discipline of Bach and Mozart. And we need a sense of where it all came from, this theatre of ours, and where it has been going, and where it seems to be going now. For the task that inexorably confronts us—the task of continuing—we need, also, to assign ourselves a master objective. I have

---

*My comments on Tennessee Williams and Arthur Miller in my books *What Is Theatre?* and *The Dramatic Event* are an attempt to describe the phenomenon of easy, or false, audacity in current American drama. This is not to deny that both these authors are capable of real audacity; their superiority to most of their colleagues derives to a large extent from such greater daring.

**At the date of writing, "Communism" meant "Stalinism." Second, some posthumous works of Brecht show him as less of a yes-man than is stated in this essay, written before Brecht's death. As for the insufficiency of my own formula, see "The Theatre of Commitment" above.

been suggesting that it is to search for our lost humanity. And, as weapons in this quest, I have been commending two that have been there from the beginning without losing any of their efficacity with the passage of time—the audacity of Dionysus and the controlling hand of Apollo.

(1955–56)

LETTER TO A WOULD-BE PLAYWRIGHT

In the fifties I had not only become a play reviewer (and ceased to be one), I had directed plays, and had even begun to interest myself in writing them. So when New Playwrights—a New York organization whose name is self-explanatory—invited me to talk to playwrights, I had a chance to get paid for talking to myself. When *Playboy* offered me the chance to reach their wider audience, I changed the talk to a letter, and when aspiring American playwrights wrote me in appreciation, I could feel I was no longer regarded as the enemy of Americanism in the theatre.

One does not write on theatre without receiving letters from playwrights. There is the playwright who tells me I have all the right ideas about drama and he has put all these ideas into a play—will I read it? There is the playwright who gets his attorney to write me demanding that every copy of my review of his play be removed forthwith from the market or he will sue me. Most ingratiating of all is the playwright who hasn't yet written a play and wants to know how to write one. I always feel that, if I really knew the answer, I would myself be the author of a list of plays at least as good as *Oedipus Rex*, *King Lear*, and *Phèdre*. But one such "playwright" recently raised questions I can at least begin to answer—as follows.

DEAR X:

So you have not yet written a play. One could wish some of our other dramatists had shown equal restraint. But then, you tell me, you have not yet reached twenty. The temptation to write a play may well be on the point of becoming irresistible. Once it does so, all anyone can do is try to keep you from writing a bad play. It will not be easy.

Many bad plays find favor in the great heart of the public, and most of them find favor in the heart, great or small, of their authors.

If you insist on writing a play, nothing can stop you from writing a bad one except the act of writing a good one. Can you learn to do this? Or, to give the question its classic form: can playwriting be taught? You tell me a friend of yours says it can't. But you tell *me* this because you assume that I believe it can. But do I? Well, yes and no, and more particularly—while I am feeling needled by your reading of my mind—No! There is a lot to be said for the unteachability of *any* subject. As I calm down, though, I shall agree with you in seeing no reason why playwriting should be regarded as *less* teachable than other subjects. Oh yes, it is less teachable than reading, writing, and 'rithmetic, but those are elementary subjects. Playwriting is an advanced subject, and at the advanced stage in any field a student has chiefly to work on his own. The point is that while the teacher, at this stage, may intervene less often, his intervention may still be valuable, even, in certain cases, essential. A coach of professional swimmers does not jump in the water and manipulate his men's limbs. A psychoanalyst does not interrupt his patient's every third word . . . In short, I would not exclude the possibility that a teacher might be useful to a playwright.

You tell me that even your friend who believes that playwriting *can* be taught adds that in practice it never is. Here my quarrel would only be with the word "never." I will grant you that most teaching of playwriting is ineffectual—if you will grant me that most teaching of everything else is ineffectual. Nature is said to be wasteful, but, if the art of education is anything to go by, art is even more wasteful. All these man-hours in classrooms—for nothing—possibly for that worse than nothing which is miseducation—the kind that has to be unlearned later, if indeed it still can be! And the pity of it, considering that the children being miseducated are not idiots! The energy of youth passes through our schools like so much unused water power. The years of opportunity between nine and nineteen are thrown away on mere sociability, and, of late, sociability has led through boredom to unsociability, otherwise known as crime. How can anyone believe in Education when the educators have provided nothing but awful examples of How Not to Do It?

But I hardly need tell you what a mess education is: you are, after all, educated. Or does your being educated *prevent* you from seeing the facts of education as of everything else? How *have* you spent the last ten years? On higher things, I should judge, for your letter bears witness to your neglect of lower things, notably grammar, syntax, diction, not to speak of style. You cannot write English. You propose to write plays; but you cannot write English; and presumably you see no great contradiction here. You will tell me that English could always be learned if absolutely necessary but that, first, plays aren't written in the language of Shakespeare, they are written in that of the gutter and, second, plays aren't properly said to be written at all, they are constructed, a Wright not being a Writer but an artificer, artisan, or fixer.

The *reason* you will tell me this is that you know I don't agree. You want to hear what I will say because you smell a rat: you yourself don't believe the stuff you are parroting. After all, you have not yet taken that course in playwriting, and so you are as yet incompletely indoctrinated with the antiliterary philosophy of its teachers. I will let you into the secret that underlies this philosophy—a secret deduction which perhaps those initiates don't even confess to themselves. It is this: because what is good as literature may be bad as theatre, it follows that bad writing is the first step to what is good in theatre. That is not undemocratic, you will admit: for such a first step can be taken by any citizen of whatever color, creed, or race. Some citizens are even willing to pay tuition for the privilege.

Why not learn the tricks of a trade that is nothing but tricks? Well, there *is* a reason why not, and it is that the path of foolishness isn't always simple. Bad taste has its pitfalls, just like good. For that matter, who has the courage of his puerility? The fool must perforce deny being a fool. It is even true, despite Machiavelli, that the knave must deny— even to himself—being a knave. Conscious knavery such as Machiavelli recommended is as much of a strain as virtue. For the price, one might just as well be good . . .

The teacher of play*wrighting* (despite Webster, it should be spelled that way) can start out cheerily enough with the declaration that the box office never lies, et cetera. The purpose of art is to please, et cetera. We aren't a lot of snobs, are we, et cetera. Just look what awful plays those highbrows write, et cetera. Shakespeare, on the other hand, is one of us, he took a course in playwriting from the horses outside the Globe Theatre, et cetera. Oh, those awful literati, those coteries, those cliques, I wrote a play myself once, and you know what was done to me by those awful literati, those coteries, those cliques, et cetera? In short, what we believe in is Democracy, and the people's choice is made known to Brooks Atkinson at 11:30 every evening by a process which may be mystic but which is no less Real. Et cetera.

When the tumult and shouting die, you realize, I hope, that, of all the gods, the public is a goddess and a bitch at that. *La donna è mobile.* If the public really ever had an opinion and stuck to it, one might at least be able to pay attention. But what is the public's verdict on *Abie's Irish Rose?* As of now, total indifference. As of thirty-five years ago, ecstatic approval. Now tell me—and don't use your head, use your public—is that a good play or isn't it? Don't bother to answer, just draw this moral: teachers who wish to teach the successful formulas are faced with the disturbing fact that the successful formulas change. It would even seem that a pattern sometimes fails precisely by becoming a formula, and has at that point to be replaced by another pattern, which in turn fails when it becomes a formula, and so on.

There is a bag of tricks in any profession, and young people will always learn the tricks, may often be the better for learning them, and may never be the worse for learning them—provided they accept them at no more than their actual value. I am attacking—yes, now you have brought out the aggressor in me—the notion that a play differs from a poem or a picture precisely in being all tricks. No one ever put that notion forward, you say. Perhaps not, I reply, but the teachers imply its truth and not once or twice, but all the time. Upon that sand they have built their theatres. Upon pure philistinism. Upon hostility to sensibility and imagination, not to mention thought.

This is the real reason why the books on How to Write a Play are so depressing. In many of them there's a lot of shrewd observation. What worked last time is offered to the student as what is likely to work next time and a thousand times thereafter. A list of the things that worked last time—this kind of exposition, this kind of curtain line, this kind of leading character, this kind of ending—is known as Dramatic Technique, is known as How to Write a Play.

In time the books on How to Write a Play became a joke. It was then that the total unteachability of playwriting began to be talked about. No one can help you, because playwriting proceeds upon no principles! With the silly simple rules of the how-to books, these counterrevolutionaries throw out critical understanding altogether, falling back upon an extreme relativism—so many plays, so many rules—and an extreme subjectivism—each playwright a law unto himself. This philosophy, whatever its truth, is likely to be just as cramping as the how-to books themselves, for it gives the playwright nothing to lean on but Inspiration, a creature far too whimsical and elusive to keep him from the bottle.

Those who hold this view make the same mistake as those who hold the opposite: they conceive of playwriting as a thing apart, an art somehow exempt from the normal obligations of art. I want to start at the other end. The playwright is, first, an artist and, second, he is a particular kind of artist—a writer. This would be an utterly uncalled-for formulation were it not more and more assumed that the playwright is neither a writer nor an artist but only a manipulator.

Not long ago a playwright was summoned to the hotel room of a producer. The producer had read the script, and was proceeding not only to talk about it but to rewrite it as he paced the carpet. He redid the first scene on his feet, reciting all the roles. "You aren't taking it down," he then said to the playwright. "No," said the playwright. "I'm taking it in. I go home. I let all this rest in my mind. What I can't absorb evaporates. What remains gets into the play later—if I like it and know how to work it in. The play needs time for the absorption of the new ideas, the new material. These things must happen organically, sir." That playwright spoke as an artist and a writer. That producer* spoke as a charlatan, not to say an egomaniac. The producer dropped the play on the grounds that the playwright didn't know his business. He meant, of course, that he didn't know his place. That place was the place of a stenographer—or shall we say an echo chamber for His Master's Voice? It isn't egomania I want to call your attention to, but the failure to cope with the psychology of the artist.

The artist has learned his craft but is never content to be a craftsman. The craft serves the art or, as Goethe put it, one only writes out of personal necessity. The endings of plays, for example, are not a gamble on the audience's response. They are a matter of what the playwright feels to be necessary. They cannot be open to discussion. Discussion with whom anyway? A work of art springs from its author's nature. No one can tell him what that is. Nor can he guarantee that any play he is working on will turn out well. That is where he differs from the craftsman. Craftsmanship can be perfected.

Consider what is happening when we take a work of art with a bad ending and stick on a good ending supplied to us by a craftsman or play-doctor. It can be true that we are perfecting the imperfect. I imagine a good craftsman could improve on the ending of Chekhov's *Ivanov.* However, from an artistic point of view, Chekhov's bad ending is necessary. The play could be fixed up externally with an ending that is neater and more logical, yet I don't think anyone could find an ending that would grow organically from the three preceding acts. If anyone could, he would be Chekhov's true collaborator—Beaumont to his Fletcher—and not a mere mechanic. It seems more likely that *Ivanov* is an impasse that can never become a thoroughfare. In *Ivanov* we have three superb acts from which there is no way out. When this sort of thing happens, an author writes another play. As for the public, it must settle for three great acts and accept one that is less than great.

If you have ever wondered why the newspaper critics often have more to say against the great writers than against the currently fashionable craftsmen, the example of *Ivanov* may make the reason clear. A craftsman can achieve a dead perfection. His work is the rearrangement of known elements—the solution of jigsaw puzzles. The artist's material is that greatest of mysteries, human nature. He feels his way in the dark. In philistines such things create anxiety and defensive

*Otto Preminger. The playwright: myself. The play: my adaptation of *Filumena Marturano* by Eduardo De Filippo.

resentment, but for anyone in the audience who has an inkling of what art is about, and an ounce of sympathy for it, there is more enjoyment in the imperfection of an *Ivanov* than in the bright, shallow perfections of the craftsmen.

Yet mustn't I get to know the theatre, you ask, greasepaint and gelatines, spots and teasers, flats and wings—that celebrated other world behind the footlights which is so notoriously "not literature"? I think you must. Or I *would* think you must if your own letter did not suggest that you already know that other world better than this one. You certainly know more of theatre practice than of literary practice. I think you should be urged to restore the balance.

"Shakespeare and Molière . . ." you begin to retort. I know. I have reason to know because I've been told so often: Shakespeare and Molière were actors. Molière was even a good actor. May *I* tell *you* something about them which I can guarantee you have not heard a thousand times before? They both managed somehow to see a lot of the world outside the theatre—of the two worlds outside the theatre, in fact, the direct experience they had of human living and the indirect experience of it that is acquired through reading. Molière learned a lot not only from clowns but from Jesuits.

We have no certain knowledge of what Shakespeare was doing in the crucial decade of young manhood, his twenties. There is an old tradition to the effect that he was a teacher, though not of playwriting. This tradition has been discounted only because people haven't wished to believe in a possibly erudite Shakespeare. Yet the plays themselves prove that he had studied and absorbed the whole culture of his day. He was steeped in the thought of his time as Thomas Mann, say, was steeped in Freud. Freud, you tell me, is known on Broadway too; he's even the only thinker who is. Ah yes, but to be steeped in Freud, as Mann was, is one thing, and to have dabbled a little in Freudianism is to have acquired the little knowledge that is worse than none.

Is there time, you ask, is there time to read more than a little? Life is real, life is earnest, and one ought to be seen a good deal at the Algonquin and the Plaza. The smoke-filled room cannot also be thought-filled,

> For at my back I always hear
> Time's wingèd chariot hurrying near . . .

And *Time* is as nothing compared to the *New York Times*. The young playwright will be glad of the help of more practical heads (arms, legs?) from the Theatre. They can rewrite him, right there in the hotel. In various hotels, changing with the stage scenery, New Haven, Boston, Philadelphia . . .

To this, the answer is that more time would be left if less time were wasted. Every timesaving device from the telephone to the airplane ends up as a timewasting device. The speeding-up of playwriting that takes place in hotels is a slowing-down of playwriting—in fact, a complete stoppage. Of course, it is true that playwrights must learn the art of the theatre, and above all its central art: that of acting. I would complain that most of them don't learn *enough* of it, partly because acting is a hard thing to learn about and very few people are especially sensitive to it, partly because the theatrical life generally consists in anything but the pursuit of essential theatre. It will be time to tell you to spend your days and nights with theatre people when theatre people spend their days or nights with the theatre art. At present, the injunction to be practical and get to know the working theatre is an injunction to squander the best years of your life in agents' offices, producers' offices, hotels, the right restaurants—or anywhere else in telephonic communication with these places.

We hear of the playwright's need of the theatre, but what of his need, equally real, to keep his distance? Henrik Ibsen "got to know the working theatre" as a young man, and that sufficed. To write plays, he went away from the theatre, nor did he return to see them through rehearsal. The most eminent of American playwrights, Eugene O'Neill, got his bellyful of theatre in childhood (maybe that's the best time), and considerably before middle age he felt the need to put a healthy distance between himself and the gentlemen who know all about it. Even Bernard Shaw, who was sociable, and who liked to direct his own plays, took up residence, as soon as he could, out of reach of bus and train. Every morning, as long as he could walk, he went down to his garden hut. To write. In solitude.

Does that sound rather grim? If you think it does, then we are making an interesting discovery: that you are not a writer. You may want "the theatre," but what you do not want is to write. Either it must be some other theatrical job you are cut out for, or it is not even theatre you want: it is prominence or parties or la vie de bohème.

A writer, *qua* writer, does not "need the theatre." He only needs a typewriter, a table, a chair and, surrounding these objects, four walls and a door that locks. Even a hotel room will do, if the lock is a strong one and the phone is out of order.

Lonely? But isn't loneliness the modern writer's favorite subject? Should he belie its importance? Then again, what about "the lonely crowd"? It is visible enough on Times Square, and in all public buildings adjacent thereto. Solitude, in fact, can be borne only by those who suffer least from loneliness—by those, that is, who feel that their solitude is amply peopled. Writers are such persons. Their philosophy is that of Pirandello: people exist for you insofar as they have been taken into your thoughts and feelings. These thoughts and feelings stay on after the "people" leave the room. Amazing to think how crowded was the solitude of a Tolstoy or a Dickens! At the opposite pole, we have people whose solitude is a terrifying emptiness; it even hurts them that Sardi's is closed on Sunday.

Think about this when next you hear that some so-called writer is a "real man of the theatre." He may just be gregarious. Solitary work makes demands and he cannot meet them. Doubtless you remember Shaw's quip: those who can, do; those who cannot, teach. It requires but slight adjustment to our theme: those who can, write; those who cannot, write plays.

And those who cannot write plays, write television plays. The writer who cannot write is an institution nowadays, and makes more money than the writer who can write. Otherwise, why would he devote so much time to nonwriting?

Do you want money? No, don't say anything. It really doesn't matter what a person *says* to that question. There are few persons who cannot be tempted by money. A poet is a person whose temptation to write poetry is so strong that it swamps the temptation to go after money. The poet has a simpler time of it than the dramatist: he makes a vow of poverty and leaves it at that. The dramatist never knows what will happen next. He may suddenly find himself as rich as the rich; but he cannot count on it. The situation is not easy on the nerves. Can *your* nerves stand it? And, if you did get rich, would you survive the experience as an artist? I am not assuming that you would wish to live like Aly Khan. I am thinking (among other things) of the following archetypal experience in twentieth-century America.

A man is born in the slums of Brooklyn or the Bronx. His writing is his response to that milieu. Broadway and Hollywood enable him to move to the East Sixties. It's only half an hour by cab from where the folks live, but, humanly speaking, it might as well be in outer space. Perhaps guilty conscience dictates a play saying how awful are the inhabitants of the East Sixties? But this play is not a good play. None of his plays are good plays any more. The theatre is now "hailing" a goodish play by a younger man—from Brooklyn or the Bronx—who is already in the taxi moving to the East Sixties.

I am (yes, you're right) only saying that, if you're going to be a writer, you will need a sense of identity. A firm one. Otherwise, "that undisturbed, innocent, somnambulatory process by which alone anything great can thrive is no longer possible." I am quoting a writer. He continues: "Our talents today lie exposed to public view. Daily criticisms, which appear in fifty different places, and the gossip that is provoked by them among the public, hamper the production of anything that is really sound. . . . He who does not keep aloof from all this and isolate himself by main force is lost." The author of *Egmont* and *Faust* is describing what would later be called the absorption of the intellectual by modern society. The creative process, he is saying, must not be disturbed, must not be deflowered. It must be a form of sleepwalking. Now Johann Wolfgang von Goethe was as worldly as any poet could afford to be. He spent much time on love affairs, and probably even more on affairs of state. But as for the world of the press agents and the press, he says: keep aloof or you will be lost.

Perhaps you are a stronger man than Goethe?

Let's assume you are strong enough to be a writer. That lonely room to which you are strong enough, and interested enough, to commit yourself must not be peopled exclusively with your personal memories. Nineteen years old as you are, you must not sit down and go to work without more ado on The Great American Play. Many have. And some of them have made a lot of money. What they have not made is The Great American Play.

In addition to memories, you need culture, all art being a crystallization of personal experience and secondhand experience. America is probably the only country in the world where a young person who wants to write a play (poem, novel) can imagine he is all set to go ahead on the basis of personal experience alone. (How many American short stories are but slightly more sophisticated renderings of the high-school theme, written in the autumn: Something That Happened to Me This Summer.) Everywhere else there is Culture. Which at its worst means: find out how it was done a hundred years ago and do it again, but at its best means: a sense of tradition.

A sense of tradition implies respect for the Masters. When the French actor Jean Vilar spoke in New York recently, many were surprised at his repeated allusions to "our fathers" and what they have left us. Where many Americans think they can "do it themselves" and deserve praise for trying to, your Frenchman unashamedly lives on inherited cultural wealth—without necessarily omitting to invest it properly and add the fruits of his own enterprise. Other Americans spend a good deal of emotional energy envying France. There is no need to; the Masters belong to all mankind. Among musicians, even in America, that fact is admitted. In the drama, as in all literature, there are language barriers. Yet have these stopped Balzac and Tolstoy from being an inspiration to novelists? Per contra, drama written in English—by Shakespeare—has inspired writers all over the world.

Why do the classics matter? They certainly do not perform all the functions that people have been pleased to assign to them. One could easily defend the thesis: The Classics Don't Work. They are nothing, or they are a fount of inspiration, especially to artists.

A few of the classics at a time, that is. For the artist is seldom a man of catholic tastes. Indeed it is doubtful if anyone really has the kind of taste which higher education supposes that he has: equally receptive to all kinds of greatness. If you are looking one way, you cannot be looking the other way; and a proper education would just help you to see, without claiming to give you eyes in the back of your head. To the artist, anyhow, the Masters are not a row of marble statues of equal size and indistinguishable features. Groupings and relationships change. Sometimes the artist must rebel against a particular Master, as the son against the father. There was Shaw's long campaign against Shakespeare. What one would deplore in a playwright would be indifference to Shakespeare, not hostility to him. In any case, Shaw was really attacking the public's attitude to Shakespeare rather than the man himself. Brecht later had to fight Goethe and Schiller. All that these things prove is that you can't have healthy religion without a certain amount of blasphemy.

The playwright's interest in the Masters is different from the scholar's interest. The scholar is concerned to place and appraise them. The artist is concerned only with what he can get out of them for his own practical purposes. His disrespect for information about them puts him at the opposite end of the scale from performers on a quiz program. But his need of the Masters is greater than anyone else's. They are his food. Goethe revealed to Eckermann that he could not let a year go by without reading some Molière.

It is hard, I think, for the aspiring American playwright to acquire such an attitude. I call your own letter to witness. "How," you rhetorically ask, "can one possibly imitate the classics today?" Who asked you to? Why so defensive? Stravinsky doesn't imitate earlier music. He makes legitimate use of it. And you might give a little thought to Bertolt Brecht's use of *The Beggar's Opera*—except that it is not so much the direct exploitation of classics that you need to know about at present as their subtle, indirect, pervasive, fructifying force.

It is not just a matter of the Masters. It is a matter of the relation between the playwright and the whole past of the art he serves. That relationship is always important and has in our time become even more so.

The last hundred years has seen the attempt to create a new kind of theatre that is the reverse of classic in any of the accepted senses of the term. The aim of the new, nonclassic theatre has been to present on the stage the illusion of ordinary life. The audience looks through a keyhole at the private life of its neighbors. A play is praised for the accuracy of its reporting and photography—"accuracy" here meaning the absence of exaggeration, interpretation, or even accent. Sometimes the severity of this formula has been relaxed, and a little democratic good will or Christian sentiment was admitted. I am speaking, as I trust you recognize, of the naturalistic play, still very much with us in the form of what Boris Aronson calls "the play about one's relations." At the time when I was reviewing Broadway plays and saw them all, I was surprised if I ever got to see anything on stage besides the middle-class

American home. An American designer only needs one set for his whole repertoire. It consists of an American house, shown inside and out, and possibly upstairs and down. Such is the richness and variety of naturalistic design. What is called in this country the Method in acting is largely devoted to creating on stage the illusion of ordinary behavior. And the word "ordinary" receives a push downward. According to this philosophy, a belch would always seem more real than a song. Such is the richness and variety of naturalistic acting.

But mark this paradox. Although naturalism is the dominant mode of modern drama, all the leading modern dramatists have tried to get away from it. They have one and all tried to get back to that classic theatre in which the figures are larger or smaller than life but never of average size. For the classic theatre does not present the illusion of ordinary life; it presents a vision of life both better and worse than the ordinary. Life is caught at its magnificent and its terrible moments, and so we are taken out of the banal moment in which we find ourselves, caught in a swifter rhythm, a heightened mode of existence. We do not go to the classic theatre in order to recognize the familiar—"just what my uncle George always says"—but to be astonished at revelations of the unsuspected. And though it is a long way from Uncle George's frame house to Macbeth's blasted heath, a classic drama could be set in Uncle George's frame house if the playwright were able to see through the familiar to the unfamiliar, beyond the cliché to the archetype.

There is no important modern dramatist who has not tried to do this, and it is surprising how many of them, in their search for the classic, have hit upon the classical in its historical sense—the Greek. What is attempted in *Mourning Becomes Electra* is not, it seems to me, entirely achieved, but the nature of the attempt is clear and right. It is an attempt to remove the clutter of naturalistic irrelevance and get down to a classic base. In order to arrive at a classic drama of American life, O'Neill used a classical Greek story. In that instance, I believe, the Greek cargo was too heavy for the ship, and the vessel sank, yet it sank nobly, with all on board singing an older and finer song than Nearer, My God, to Thee.

A more recent case is Arthur Miller's *A View from the Bridge*. The play was improved by the removal of explicitly Greek elements. Greece remains the inspiration of the play, or, rather, Greece is what helped Mr. Miller several steps along the road from naturalism to classic drama.

Even the so-called "masterpieces of naturalism" turn out, when looked at more closely, to be departures from naturalism. Take Strindberg's *The Father*, a play usually assigned an important part in the naturalistic movement. The fact is that Strindberg had been pondering the *Oresteia* of Aeschylus, and had come across the theory that it reflects the struggles leading to the creation of the patriarchal family. In *The*

Father he had in mind the breakup of the patriarchal family and the threatened return of matriarchy. He thought of *The Father* as his *Agamemnon.* Here is another play that is not only classic but classical.

Even the man who made the word naturalism heard all over the world—Émile Zola—did not champion the tame version of it that has been its main manifestation, nor did he let his own theories limit his creative writing. It was his pleasure to invoke science. Nonetheless, when he uses the idea of heredity, we are less close to any scientific genetics than we are to Moira, the Greek Fate. From Zola's hereditary criminal of *La bête humaine* it is only a step to hereditary disease as treated by Ibsen in his *Ghosts;* for although critics bred in the naturalistic tradition continue to speak of syphilis as the subject of this play, and some even add that the play is obsolete now that syphilis can be cured, the real subject is the curse on the house of Alving. It is not accidental that, in approaching a Sophoclean subject, Ibsen resorts to Sophoclean technique: the truth is forced out in a swift series of catastrophic discoveries.

In comedy there is a similar story to tell. Our only great modern master of comedy, Bernard Shaw, always described himself as an old-fashioned playwright, explaining that he went back over the heads of his contemporaries to Dickens, Fielding, Molière, the *commedia dell'arte* for his methods. Though he belonged to the same generation as Stanislavsky, and had in his friend and colleague Granville Barker a champion of naturalistic staging, he himself reserved his praises for what he called the classical actor. And he maintained that only classical actors could do his plays, because he had revived in them so many features of the classic theatre, and notably the tirade or long set speech which the actor has to articulate for us with the cool clarity of a musician performing a Bach suite.

By about 1920 the permanent crisis of the modern theatre reached a new stage. What Ibsen had done to the naturalistic theatre might be called boring from within. He had accepted its conventions and its stage. The generation of 1920 refused these concessions. The work of Cocteau, Brecht, Meyerhold meant the rejection of the established type of theatre altogether. A new start was proposed. From zero, one is sometimes told. Yet no movement ever goes back *that* far, because—as I was saying—no artist draws solely on his own experience: he always asks some support from tradition. And when one tradition lets him down, or he chooses to reject a tradition, he does not—whatever he may say—operate without tradition. He falls back on some other tradition. Even painters who have rejected all Western history end up, not as "original" in the sense which the man in the street gives to the word, but as neo-African and the like. Rejection of tradition usually implies nothing more than the rejection of recent traditions in favor of earlier ones. In the more interesting drama of the twenties we find that, while the naturalistic approach of the immediate past is taboo, every other avenue is open. Brecht explored the Spaniards of the Golden Age, the English Elizabethans, even the oriental theatre. It was again a search for the classic in dramatic art, and again the Greek note was the one most often struck. I've mentioned O'Neill. I'm thinking also of Cocteau's *Antigone* and *Orpheus*.

With all this goes a technical change that some people think the most important change of all. The dramatists are no longer writing for a box set hidden behind a proscenium arch. The proscenium arch may still be there, because the buildings can't be made over in a hurry, but it is ignored, canceled out, defied. The box set has been carted off stage forever. What the new generation clamors for is some sort of open stage, possibly Elizabethan, possibly also a Roman circus or a Greek arena. Whether such a physical change is the most important change or not, it is one that implies the others. The different shape and functioning of such a stage implies a fundamentally different technique of drama and, with that, a different view of art and life. Take one feature alone, the relation of the action to the eye of the spectator. In the nineteenth-century theatre, the spectator is asked to peep through a little door, like Alice, into an illuminated garden; in the twentieth-century theatre, the actors are brought out to him. In the one, the spectator is a voyeur; in the other, the actor is an exhibitionist. Here too, in the demands they make on the physique of the stage, the more alert modern playwrights have been searching for the classic theatre. The naturalistic theatre offered a peep through the keyhole into the room across the way. The classic theatre provides a parade ground for passions and thoughts and for the human beings above or below life size who experience them.

Since this is what has been going on, you would, from the artistic point of view, be wasting your time to write the kind of play that one generally sees on Broadway. If you have talent, you should join that pursuit of the classic theatre which is, paradoxically, the search for a truly modern theatre. A great future will be born, if at all, from the fruitful union of our present with such a past.

What do you want, actually? It's your wishes that carry the weight. Not what you tell your friends are your wishes. Not what you sometimes think are your wishes. Not what you habitually assume are your wishes. But what you finally find to be your wishes. Your real wishes.

Emerson warned us against wishing, really wishing, for things—because one is likely to get them. If your real wish is to become a prostitute, you will become one; in the theatre, it will be quite easy; and you will never live to regret it; even your old age will be provided for in articles you can write on What Made Me What I Am Today.

Your letter to me suggests, rather, that you wish to be a dramatist. If you do, you will have to try it and find out. Time will show if you really are one. Meanwhile, see yourself as a writer and, by consequence, an artist.

Even if you *are* a dramatist, you may not "succeed." That will hurt your feelings very much, especially when you see your nondramatist friend becoming The Successful Dramatist. An artist wants success. He does not, however, insist on it. His failure to insist on it, though a source of glee among those who exploit him, stems from strength in the artist himself: success is something he can do without, if with difficulty. His pride clamors for satisfaction even more than his vanity; he is a serious chap; he will buy lasting reputation even at the price of immediate fame.

As for you, young sir, if you find you are not a dramatist, and Broadway agrees with you, you will try something else willy-nilly; if there are agonies, they will not be agonies of choice. If you find you are not a dramatist, but Broadway finds you *are* one, the inducement will be considerable to change your mind and become convinced of what you know is not true—a common type of conviction nowadays, and one which is the tie that binds the two most famous streets in America: Broadway and Madison Avenue.

If you find you are a dramatist, and Broadway agrees, try to *stay* a dramatist; it will not be easy. If you find you are a dramatist, and Broadway doesn't agree, that will not be easy either; but you *will* stay a dramatist; you won't be able to help it.

Can playwriting be taught? You have just been the would-be playwright and I have been the would-be teacher. Have you learned anything? Not anything, certainly, that comes between the rise and fall of the curtain. We have stood all this time outside the theatre wondering whether to go in, and I have said: "Do you wish to enter? Then enter—tentatively. Do you have talent? When you know, decide whether to stay." Which is all very preliminary. But then, you aren't yet twenty. And I have met "students of playwriting." Their average age seems to me to be about ninety and probably is in fact over twenty-five. Few of them have explored their wishes (or notable lack of wishes), their talent (or truly remarkable lack of talent). So perhaps they missed that first lesson, which had for theme: TO WRIGHT OR NOT TO WRIGHT? You have just had it. Sincerely yours,

ERIC BENTLEY

(1960)

THEATRE AND THERAPY

No one decade is responsible for the idea of group therapy, but it was the sixties that made the most of group therapy—as of group everything else—and I originally set myself the task of looking into all the group therapies to see what secrets they might have to reveal to a theatre man. But, though I knocked at various doors, the only therapist who made me really welcome (as myself, that is, not as a prospective customer) was the late Dr. Jacob Levy Moreno. One eminent therapist threw me out as soon as I grew at all critical. Another seemed to me to be showing How Not to Do It. Others would not tolerate an outsider-observer in the sacred presence of The Group. Only Dr. Moreno made both his New York headquarters and his quarters in Beacon, New York, liberty hall for me: I could come and go as I liked, and I could either join in or remain at a distance observing—I did some of both. And so my piece on therapy represents exclusively what I learned from Moreno's psychodrama. Since this was the principal intellectual event in my life at the moment, I suggested to *Playboy,* when they asked me to review the current New York theatre season, that they commission a review of Moreno's psychodrama season instead. *Playboy,* though trying hard at the time to be serious, did not wish to be that serious: I was never asked to write for them again. I went ahead with the Moreno piece because it seemed a necessary extension of things I'd said in *The Life of the Drama.*

For better or for worse, the principal event of the 1968–69 theatre season was the visit to New York of the Living Theatre. Of their offering, they made a kind of take-it-or-leave-it proposition. I was one of those who "left it," but not in the sense that I left off thinking about it. What I propose to pursue here is the question: What has all the talk of the Living Theatre and kindred theatres really been about?

There is no one correct answer, but a central topic has certainly been "audience involvement." The Living Theatre was trying to change the character of the theatrical event. They wanted to move the audience onto the stage. They wanted to exercise a therapeutic influence. On the audience, of course; but also, as they proclaimed, on themselves: the audience was to help cure *them*. I asked myself when had I heard something of the sort before. The whole conception seemed to be one of group therapy, rather than theatre as previously conceived, but had not one celebrated group therapist already effected a merger of these two, and, in his system, was the actor not indeed the patient, and did not the audience assist in treating him?

The therapist was Jacob Levy Moreno; his name was in the Manhattan phone book, and I had no difficulty getting myself invited to attend the group-therapy sessions of the Moreno Institute on West 78th Street. Meanwhile I was seeing various shows around town that claimed to be doing something special with audience participation, and/or trying to give theatre a push toward therapy. I saw *The Concept, The Serpent, Dionysus in 69* . . . Even the current nudism proved relevant. Insofar as it was more than a pursuit of a quick buck, it was an affirmation of the body, the health of the body, and was related to "nude therapy," sensitivity training, encounter groups, et cetera. I visited some of these groups and also saw *Hair, The Sound of a Different Drum, We'd Rather Switch, Geese, Che!, Oh! Calcutta!* and so on. Of the theatres, I think the Play-house of the Ridiculous and the Ridiculous Theatrical Company were probably the most cathartic, being founded on the deepest rejection of The American Way, and inspired with the cockiest faith that they can get along without imitating that form of life. But gradually I found myself seeing shows less and Moreno's "psychodramas" more. If one wanted therapy in the theatre, why not go the whole hog? At the Moreno Institute, therapy was the acknowledged and sole aim in view, yet the sessions there were emotionally affecting and intellectually interesting to a much greater degree than the New York theatres. What more did I want?

For the moment, nothing. And I concluded that, rather than attempt any sort of survey of the new trend in theatre, I would simply try to explain what is at stake. Should drama be psychodrama? Is psychodramatic therapy the same as dramatic art? Are certain mergers called for? Or are certain separations—certain firm distinctions—in order? If we could attain to a degree of clarity on these matters, "current trends on and off Broadway" would be child's play.

Since it was psychodrama that prompted this approach and underpins the reasoning that follows, it will be as well to state in advance just what a psychodramatic session is. Perhaps a hundred people are placed on three sides of a platform. The platform itself has steps on all sides, is in this sense an "open stage." A patient, here called a protagonist, presents himself for a psychodramatic performance. A director-psychiatrist talks with him briefly, to find out what he sees as his problem, and what scenes from his life might be enacted. A scene being chosen, the roles of others taking part in it are played either by trained assistants or by anyone else present who might volunteer. What and how they are to play is briefly explained to them by the protagonist and director. If they then seem too far wide of the mark, the protagonist may reject them. But in each session, successful scenes do develop, "success" here being measured by the degree of spontaneity attained: if the protagonist does not "warm up" to his role, he cannot play it in its vital fullness.

Generalizations about the course of psychodramatic sessions are hazardous, since one session differs widely from another, but a typical line of development would be from relatively trivial scenes with friends in the recent past to serious and crucial scenes with parents in the more distant past. It will often happen that a protagonist will have an illumination, or at least a surprise, in one of these later scenes. He may suddenly realize that where he had seen only love there was also hate, or vice versa, in one of his main relationships. And here the stress should be on the word "realize," for it is likely to be a powerful emotional experience: a given insight is borne in upon a person in the midst of a very lively distress. The distress has opened the channels of communication. It may also have reached a kind of climax. The patient may, for the time being, feel cleaned out. The director now ends the playacting and asks the audience to share common experience with the protagonist. The point is not to elicit interpretations but to discover what chords were touched in the onlookers, what degree of therapy was in it all for them.

1

Dramatic art and psychodramatic therapy have a common source in the fact that life itself is dramatic. In other words, life is not a shapeless stuff which is given form only by a dramatist or clinician. Human life, like the rest of nature, has been shaped, indeed so markedly that this shaping has always been the leading argument for the existence of God. As the beauty of leaves or seashells is attributed to God the Creator, so the shape of events, large or small, is attributed to God the Dramatist: life, as Dante classically stated it, is a divine comedy. The idea that "all the world's a stage / And all the men and women merely players," is not a clever improvisation casually tossed off by Shakespeare's cynic Jaques, it was written on the wall of Shakespeare's theatre, the Globe, in a language older than English: *Totus mundus facit histrionem*. To speak of life, as many modern psychiatrists do, as role playing is only to make a new phrase, not to advance a new idea.

I shall return later to role playing and would only at this point call attention to the positive side of the pattern. The negative side is all too familiar: it is that people are often hypocritical—use a role to pretend to be better than they are and deceive other people. It is curious how the phrase "playacting" has come to be a slur: it implies insincerity. Yet the commonplaces I have cited imply that one has no alternative to playacting. The choice is only between one role and another. And this is precisely the positive side of the idea: that we do have a choice, that life does offer us alternatives, that one's will is free within whatever limits, and the end is not yet determined. Life is not merely going through the motions, it is an adventure: which is often all that people mean by calling it dramatic.

What else might they mean? In the vernacular, these days, "dramatic" means little more than thrilling, and if it also means "spectacular" the sense of an actual theatrical spectacle is probably not intended. Dramatists and psychodramatists give the term "dramatic" a much more elaborate interpretation. Just as they see more roles to role playing than Jaques' seven, they break down the "stage" which "all the world" is said to be into various departments. Given that there are roles to play, how are they played? A full answer to this question would be by way of a description of myriad different roles and relationships. A short answer, aiming at providing a basic scheme, might run somewhat as follows.

A role is properly and fully played by being brought into living contact with another role played by another actor. The "full" playing of the role implies that living contact is made, that if "I" am playing one role, "I" feel that the other role is a "Thou" and not an "It." (I am using terminology that most people will associate with Martin Buber, though J. L. Moreno has long thought along these lines too.) Buber's point has been that the modern person reacts to others as an It, and so forestalls communication. "I," too, become an It, if the other is an It. Neurosis walls us off from each other. That's modern life.

Now drama does not depict a utopia in which neurosis is absent, but, with an exception to be noted in a minute, it is utopian to the extent that it normally, not exceptionally, shows human beings in living contact with each other, shows couples who are "I" and "Thou" to each other. It may be living hatred that communicates, as in Strindberg's *Father*, or love, as in *Romeo and Juliet*, but that there *is* direct and lively communication is not only obvious, it is what interests us, it is what we want from theatre. Could it be said, then, that life is not dramatic in this respect, only theatre is? Perhaps. But the point is that this is a norm, not just for our theatregoing, but for our living. The "I" and "Thou" relationship is present enough in actual life for us to want to see more of it, and when we do see it in the theatre, our attitude need not be, "but that's because theatre is not life" but rather "this is what is trying to happen in life if only we would let it." For art need not be regarded as a more abundant life, but unreal. It can be regarded as an attempt by the life force (or what have you) to make our real life more abundant.

If life does afford real I/Thou relationships, and also, which is crucial, holds out the hope of ever more successful I/Thou relationships, drama can, for its part, portray the failure to achieve such relationships. But how could this possibly prove dramatic? Wouldn't the absence of live contact kill the stage action stone dead? It would—if nothing else is added. Drama characterized by a mere absence of emotion is dead. Suppose, however, the absence of emotion, of flow, is the very point? That, you say, is ridiculous. Then, I reply, the way to give it life is to give it ridiculous life. The dramatic form which regularly presents people who are out of contact with each other is the art of comedy, whose mode is ridicule. The role playing in *The Importance of Being Earnest* is all a game of pretending to have living I/Thou relationships—friend to friend, parent to child, man to woman—when such relationships are not in the cards. Again, when we say comedy presents types, not individuals, we might just as well say it presents individuals who cannot make contact with other individuals because of a crust of nonindividual class characteristics. This is not a *man*, Molière or Shaw is forcing us to say, it is a *doctor*.

The question whether tragedy or comedy is closer to life becomes rather a snarled one. Tragedy presents us in our emotional fullness; it has, therefore, more of life in it. Comedy presents our customary failure to live that way and, in presenting less of life, gives a more characteristic version of it. As for I/Thou relationships, if they are per se dramatic, then we may say that life aspires to the condition of drama.

Does the I/Thou relationship, granted that it includes role playing, amount to drama? If we would be inclined to say yes, that is because we have taken ourselves for granted. *We* are watching the "I" and the "Thou." We are their audience, and from their viewpoint a "They." Theatre is this completed circuit: an "I" and a "Thou" on stage and a "They" out front. Which is a very radical, if schematic, version of the rudiments of living: *I* relate to *you*, while *they* watch. I, Romeo, relate to you, Juliet, while the other Montagues and Capulets watch. This example, if extreme, serves to remind us how much those watchful eyes modify the I/Thou experience. We live out our lives in full view of other people. We do not live in a world of our own. We live in "their" world. How much tragedy, both of life and literature, lurks in that formula!

2

This, at any rate, is the image of life which psychodrama has appropriated: an "I," talking on stage to a "Thou," in front of a "They."

By that token, psychodrama may be said to resemble life or even to be a slice (many slices) of it. Visitors are surprised how close it comes to the real thing. And its watchword is spontaneity. Nonetheless, psychodrama has to depart from life in a number of ways, notably:

(1) The "I" is not presented in a sheer, naked, literal state but buttressed, clothed, supplemented by another person. When the protagonist, at a psychodramatic session, is found to be reluctant, silent, overdefensive, another person is asked to play his double and to come forward with exactly those responses which the protagonist is holding back. Thus to take a crude instance, in the matter of ambivalence, if the protagonist keeps saying, "I *love* my mother," and clamming up, the double will say, "I hate her guts." This is as different from life as can be, since help is being given precisely where it was, perhaps disastrously, lacking. (The double can of course guess wrong, but this fact will probably emerge from what the protagonist then says and does. In any case, there is nothing definitive in a possibly false suggestion. The situation remains open.)

(2) The "Thou" is rendered in more or less the form not of life but of drama, namely: impersonation. Any partner the protagonist's story requires is enacted either by a trained assistant or by a member of the audience at the session in question. Since this is a "stranger" to the protagonist, the difference, for him, from the real thing is very great indeed. Often it is necessary for the protagonist to reject outright what the player of such a role says. Sometimes he has to have him replaced. "My father just wouldn't react that way."

But—and this is what matters—some degree of I/Thou relationship is generally worked out before a session is over. Indeed what needs calling attention to is not the difficulty of reaching a degree of direct communication under the conditions of a psychodramatic session but the fact that life is outdone by psychodrama in this respect, somewhat as it is by dramatic art, though not by as much. It must be galling, for example, for a parent to learn how his child enters into rapport with a substitute parent far more readily than with the real one, but a moment's thought explains this: the "objection" is precisely to the real parent, and the "false" one is the real one minus the objection. Hence psychodrama is not "naturalistic," is not a duplication of actuality but, in the most relevant way, an improvement on it in exactly the same way as nonnaturalistic art is, for nonnaturalistic art is actuality not merely reproduced, but interpreted normatively, which means: to a certain extent transformed. Psychodrama and drama have in common a thrust toward human *liberation.*

To take up a single example. When a person fails to communicate with his nearest and dearest, he is apt to reach the extreme conclusion: "If I cannot reach them, I can reach no one." Actually, it is only they whom he cannot reach. The rest of the human race is more accessible. And psychodrama is not an argument to this effect but the living proof written in letters of emotion upon a person's whole nervous system: the kind of proof even philosophers don't easily reject when it's their own nervous system that is responding.

The form taken by scenes created in psychodramatic sessions stands, correspondingly, at a remove from actuality. The patient-protagonist is not encouraged to rack his brains for accuracy in reporting, as when someone tries to be very honest and self-disciplined in telling the police what occurred on a given occasion. What he does, after reminding himself as vividly as possible of the actual moment and location, is to let go and *throw* himself into the situation with a lack of reservation that at the time he hadn't actually achieved. Thus what is "brought back" from that actual happening is, in one sense, more than was there in the first place—more than was *known* to be there, more than actually emerged. Which is, of course, the reason for going to all the trouble. Mere rehash is a waste of energy for the rehasher, as well as being a great bore for those who have to listen. But I shall leave further comment on the psychology of recapitulation till later. The point here is that the "Thou" who is less, in that he may be a mere stranger, is also more, in that he is really a "Thou" where the nonstrangers were not.

(3) A third way in which psychodrama deviates from life is in making use of a director. There are few who feel, these days, that the drama of their lives is directed by God. That was hard to believe with any constancy at any time; today, if there is a God at all, He is an absentee landlord, a director on perpetual sick leave abandoning the actors to their own resources. Jacob Moreno, though, always wanted to play God, and the modern age obviously placed no special obstacles in his path. He modestly called himself—or any of his standbys— directors; but they preside over the psychodramatic sessions in fairly godlike fashion.

In psychodramatic sessions, the director intervenes in several ways. In the beginning, he elicits the information on the basis of which a first scene is set up. He then *interrupts* whenever it seems to him the drama is (a) repeating itself, (b) wandering off, or (c) petering out. Since anyone could easily be wrong on any of these three matters, it is clear that considerable shrewdness is called for, not to mention knowl- edge. Interruption is, in any event, a very dynamic factor in itself, as some playwrights (e.g., Brecht) have known. It gives a jolt, which can be salutary or disastrous according to the moment when it occurs.

Interruption is the director's chief negative act. But he does some- thing positive, too, and usually right after the interruption: he *suggests* an alternative path. Having stopped the patient-protagonist from pur- suing one course, he propels him into another. Again, the possibility of error is considerable, but again much can be expected from knowledge and know-how. And again, errors need not be final. On the contrary, given the patient's set of mind, they will probably be exposed rather soon. A dead end is a dead end, and is seen to be so by patient and/ or audience.

In one sense, then, the director is *not* called on to be God and always right, but only to be resourceful and always quick. The right moment to reach a stop or institute a change passes fast. The director must have instantaneous reactions that indicate immediate conclusions such as: "This is when a double is needed," "We must go straight to the scene just suggested in the dialogue," "Let's reverse roles here."

Reversal of roles, incidentally, is one of the chief devices of psychodrama, and perhaps one of the most efficacious. At a word from the director, the protagonist plays the "other fellow" in the scene. Thus "I" is forced to see and feel out the situation from the viewpoint of "Thou." Which is not only morally edifying but generally illuminating and specifically therapeutic. Our whole failure as human beings can be found in the failure to take in the reality of the other person. But merely knowing this doesn't help. Psychodrama can help by the *work* involved in "I"'s playing seriously at being "Thou."

In a sense, too, the director is not outside the psychodrama, but inside it. His is a voice that the patient sorely lacked the *first time around;* which was why seemingly fatal mistakes were made. *This time,* on stage, the voice speaks, like that of another double. *Next time,* if all goes well, the voice will be that of a double successfully internalized: it will be the patient's own voice. It is a "He" that becomes a "Thou" and that ends up as an "I."

Obviously the most important single instrument in psychodramatic therapy is the director, and this is not just saying that the director is the psychiatrist: it is saying that he has to possess the specific talents required by the situations that arise on the psychodramatic stage.

(4) If the "I" and "Thou" of life are modified in the psychodramatic theatre, so is the "They." The "They" of life is by definition general and amateur. The "They" of psychodrama is specialized and professional. At Dr. Moreno's public demonstrations the audience consists partly of those who see themselves as possible patients, partly of students of psychodrama. Any third element—such as the scoffers or the visitor who finds himself there by accident—is minor. So we are limited to people with a preestablished involvement, a curiosity that is really keen because it comes from need or greed.

It is perhaps seldom realized that in all theatrical situations there is a specific, understood relationship between actor and spectator, a kind of unwritten contract between the two. And it is probably just as seldom realized that the contract holds for only one type of theatre, while other types make other contracts. Thus what an expense-account executive at a Broadway show is buying from the actor is different from what, say, the Athenian people were buying from their festival players, which in turn was different from what Louis XIV had contracted for with Molière, and so on. A clear difference in aim, not to mention relationships outside the theatre, produces a clear difference in the actor/spectator relationship.

Such relationships, insofar as the facts are before us, can be examined in such terms as the degree of passivity (or its opposite) on the audience side. Lack of passivity can show itself in what I have just called need or greed: a felt need for what the spectacle intended to convey, an eagerness to know and in some sense possess it. At one extreme, audiences are both bored and bossy. "Entertain me," they say with a patronizing yawn. The actors are their slaves, their jesters, and will get whipped if they failed to be funny: what sharper whip than economic boycott? At the other end of the scale, the performer is looked up to: much is expected of him. The spectator is humble: it is he who hopes to profit by the exchange. The psychodramatic audience inclines to this other end of the scale, and its humility, combined as it is with neurotic involvement and intellectual curiosity, will show itself largely in the form of sympathy and human understanding.

It is not the audience's attitude in itself that is interesting but the way it functions in the reciprocal actor/spectator relationship. And it is necessary here to anticipate somewhat and say that one of the chief differences between drama and psychodrama is this: while drama is judged, fairly enough, by the effect the actor has on the audience, in psychodrama the highest priority goes to the effect the audience has on the actor. This effect, like that of the director's interventions, is by way of *propulsion*. The audience's sympathy oils the wheels; the audience's eager curiosity speeds things along. The whole occasion is a form of *public confession*. There is relief, and therefore pleasure, in such confession. The person who takes over-much pleasure in it is called exhibitionistic. But if a degree of exhibitionism is normal, so is a degree of shyness. The presence of an audience makes it harder to be frank. Psychodrama addresses itself to this shyness and asks that it be tackled, not avoided, as it largely is by psychoanalysis.

(5) A psychodramatic session differs from another two hours of living in that it is *literally* theatre while life is theatre only metaphorically speaking. I mean, to begin with, that there is a stage and that otherwise there is only an auditorium. This organization of space is so ruthlessly selective that most of the detail of actuality is omitted. To say the world is a stage is one thing. To represent the doings of this world *on* and *by* a stage is another. The physique of the psychodramatic theatre bears no resemblance to the world-in-general and not too close a resemblance

to the world-in-particular. A scene in a garden will be redone without the garden. A scene about a man as a child will be redone without a child—the physical presence of a child—on stage. Conversely, the physical characteristics of *theatre*—a floor of a certain type, steps, suggestive bits of furniture, the spectators' seats arranged in a certain pattern, the rows of faces above the seats—have a quality (reality, atmosphere) of their own which contributes to the character of psychodrama as a whole.

The sheer physical nature of a theatre does more to determine the nature of the whole theatrical event than has commonly been appreciated, except by recent writers on environmental theatre who have gone to the opposite extreme. Yet, if we turn now to the psychodramatic event as a whole, there is one feature more decisive than environment, and that is—it is so obvious, one could forget to notice—reenactment itself. Such and such was done in life: it will now be acted. Or, to return to the premise of role playing, such and such was enacted in life: it will now be reenacted. The first thing the director does is to ask the patient to *show* (instead of narrating) what once happened. Psychodrama is not life but recapitulation of life, living life over a second time, having your cake and eating it.

And this, which is indeed the key idea of psychiatry as we know it, can properly be the cue for a comparison of psychoanalysis with psychodrama. It was Freud who encouraged us to believe that, if anything at all could be done about our mental illnesses, it would be by going back to the time of their origin and reliving it. *The first time around,* we retreated at a certain point or stood still. The hope which therapy holds out is that, returning to this exact spot, we can *this time* make the needed advance from it. It is a repetition with a difference: an innovation, a nonrepetition.

All life is repetitious. There is the salutary and needed repetition by which good habits are formed. There is the baleful repetition by which bad habits are formed. There is the endless repetition of therapy sessions before the point is reached when any positive result is attained. Then, in the midst of repetition itself, the breakthrough. A paradox, if you will, and yet one which seems built into the process of living. Even lovemaking is all repetition—of words, of caresses, of body movement—until the breakthrough of orgasm. Scientists report similarly of the breakthrough into discovery; artistic performers of the breakthrough from the repetition of the rehearsal into performance.

As for bad habits, by innumerable repetitions an undesired action has become a habit. The habit is to be broken by yet another repetition, the repetition of perhaps the earliest performance, the original act, which is then *not* repeated, even once. It now leads when it should have led in the first place. In order to be freed from the old captivity one reenters it one last time.

Now psychoanalytic therapy is itself psychodramatic—up to a point. At one time, certainly, it specialized in the search for the early traumatic scene which was reenacted, with the patient playing his childhood self and the analyst, for example, the hated father. Freud's first great discovery in the therapeutic sessions themselves was that the analyst did become father, mother, et cetera, in other words, that the patient assigned him roles—the main roles in his personal drama. Such *transference* was the key to the whole patient/doctor transaction, and therapy came about through the pain the patient endured in reliving the old troubles. If the patient fought back, he could hope to work through neurotic darkness into light.

It is unfortunately impossible to make any survey of the results of Freudian therapy and compare them with the results of any other therapy. One can only assert the a priori likelihood that one person might get more help from one form of therapy, another person from another. One can also point to what for many patients would be an unnecessary limitation in Freudian procedure. Freud in his day had to be much concerned with what one might term the sanctity of the confessional. His patients would never have "got it out" had anyone but the doctor been listening. Even at that they needed further encouragement by the device of the couch. You lie down and avoid looking the doctor in the eye. So in a way you are alone and can get into a reverie and say things you couldn't say into anyone's face. Freud preserves his patients both from the "Thou" and the "They." The patients' efforts to convert the analyst into a "Thou" are stoutly resisted. They are seen only as interference with the intention of making the latter a receptacle for roles not truly his, a ghost. "Look," the analyst must always be imagined as saying, "you have attributed to *me* all these characteristics of your father, but that's *your* problem."

Whatever help may be provided by such constantly reenacted dramas of disenchantment, it may plausibly be maintained that there is often much to be gained by a contrary procedure: introducing the "Thou" by way of an actor and the "They" by way of an audience and letting the analyst emerge into daylight as a director. That the director can then be accused of pushing things too much is inevitable, but this risk may be worth taking, and there are self-corrective elements, as noted above. The "Thou" of the psychodramatic stage is neither the actual "Thou" nor a duplicate, but if he is a poor substitute in some ways, he is superior (as also noted) in others. The slow pain of free association, in conjunction with transference, produces certain realizations and has doubtless been curative on some occasions in some degree. But no patient is overly satisfied with the results, and that alone is justification for other methods than this Freudian one. And, as against transference, there is much to be said for engaging the other fellow, if not in his own person, at least in flesh-and-blood form. This encounter too inflicts a degree of salutary pain. And very painful indeed (as well as the opposite) is the presence of onlookers: something one has to face in life, something it may be needful to face in therapy. Many of us suffer specifically from fear of the others, and it may be doubted if psychoanalysis tackles this fear boldly enough. Many fear the flesh-and-blood actuality of the "Thou." It is often just this fear that makes a potential "Thou" into an actual "It." Here again, why not take the bull by the horns? There has been in the Freudian tradition itself a certain vestige of the Judeo-Christian hatred of the body. In this respect Karl Kraus may have hit the mark when he said, "Psychoanalysis is the disease of which it purports to be the cure." And after all, Dr. Moreno is not the only one to ask if Freud hadn't overweighted things on the mental side in reaction against the physiological emphasis of nineteeeth-century medicine. If today we talk in psychosomatic terms, by that token the somatic element is half of the whole. Is it not just as reasonable to get at the spirit through the body as vice versa? But these queries go beyond my topic, which is—to summarize this section—that, while there is drama as between couch and chair in the dimly lit office, there is an ampler drama when "I" meets "Thou" upon a stage in the presence of a director and an audience.

3

If psychodramatic therapy is at a remove from life, dramatic art is at two removes from it, for while the protagonist of psychodrama is "spontaneous" and presents himself, the protagonist in a play is held to a script on the basis of which he presents someone else.

If we see these two rearrangements of life—psychodrama and drama—as running in competition with each other, which one do we regard as the winner? It depends wholly on our own angle of vision. The psychodramatist inevitably looks with horror upon the written text. Dr. Moreno contemptuously terms it a "cultural conserve," and sees it exclusively as a hindrance to spontaneity, the highest value in his philosophy. From the viewpoint of therapy, I believe his point is well taken. Here there is nothing but advantage in improvisation. The protagonist is a patient, and only his life matters. I have remarked that even the audience in psychodrama exists for the sake of the protagonist, not vice versa, as in drama. The dialogue, a fortiori, is all his. Even the director is not an author but at best a sort of film editor. Nor are there any prescribed forms of dialogue or character, as with the *commedia dell'arte*, which the psychodramatic "actor" must follow. Improvisation in any art—*commedia dell'arte* or a jazz combo—is free only within narrow limits. By comparison, psychodrama offers its protagonist freedom indeed!

It is obviously possible that "confinement" within the rules of an art may become a neurotic problem for a given individual. Dr. Moreno reports that this was the case with John Barrymore. This actor was sick (literally) of playing Shakespeare: he wanted, he needed, to play Barrymore. (This is Moreno speaking. In fact Barrymore played Shakespeare seldom.) Of course, one thing one would need to know to make anything of this example would be whether psychodramatic therapy, if diligently pursued, would have cured Barrymore of alcoholism and of whatever else ailed him. That he wanted to play himself only proves him human: every infant wants the same. But I am prepared to grant that subjection to a written role may have compounded rather than solved this particular man's problems. No written role was ever intended to solve such problems anyway.

Spontaneity, as Dr. Moreno sees it, is a very useful, even an inspiring idea. I would define it as one of the forms of human freedom, a subjective form, in that it is a psychological, not a political, one. It is a matter of how one feels. A spontaneous man feels free. He feels disburdened of all the inhibitions and evasions and shynesses which normally hold him back from fully feeling what he could and would otherwise feel. If this is correct by way of definition, I would add that, like other forms of freedom, spontaneity operates within limits—within an iron ring of unfreedom, of unspontaneity. A completely free and spontaneous man would not only feel what he wants to feel but say what he wants to say—which would abolish politeness and saddle him with libel suits, to say the least. He would also do what he wants to—which would interfere grossly with the freedom of others. Life, then, has to set bounds to spontaneity. Indeed, some neurotic problems derive from such limits. Psychodrama moves the boundary posts out a little; but it doesn't throw them away.

What the psychodramatists have worked on, and worked for, is one particular kind of spontaneity which we may call solidification of the present moment. The neurotic's trouble is seen as the disintegration of the present: all is diffused into memories of the past and fantasies of the future. This entails great instability in the whole emotional system and, since joy is of the present, an incapacity for enjoyment: life is stale, flat, and unprofitable. To re-create the present tense, to create spontaneity, is to bring a person back to life, it is to enable him to experience life in its fullness. For, as Blake put it,

> He who catches the joy as it flies
> Lives in eternity's sunrise.

If all this makes it sound as if the purpose of psychodrama were to stimulate to momentary pleasure, I should go on to say, first, that this is no contemptible purpose but, second, that no one has claimed that a single achievement of that sort is a cure for any mental illness. Nor am I retracting the statement that psychodrama, like psychoanalysis, is painful: both therapies believe in possible progress through pain to pleasure. The difference between the two therapies, in regard to past and present, is that the Freudians keep constantly in mind the persistence of ancient hurts into the present and until recently have tried to refer the patient back just as constantly to the trauma of long ago, whereas the psychodramatist has always worked gradually back from the present. This labor, and not the discovery of trauma, is what "works through" the trouble: its pain, and not the vestigial pain of the trauma itself, is what the psychoanalyst assumes to be therapeutic. He begins "spontaneously" (i.e., as spontaneously as possible) in the present, works back to the obstacles, the rigidities, the nonspontaneities, only to help the patient back to the present, if he is lucky, with a true spontaneity.

Such a conception of spontaneity has in its favor that it is unpretentious. Its normal field of vision is a restricted one. Envisaged (initially at least) is not a whole life, a whole civilization, remade. In the clinical situation faced by the individual, doctor and patient can concentrate upon moment-to-moment experience. (If an invalid is still breathing, his breath will becloud a mirror.) Much psychiatry goes astray by overextending the field of vision: asking so many questions that there can be no coherent, compact answers. In psychodrama the question can usually be limited to: Is the patient's soul still breathing? Can this man warm up to an encounter with another man? Can he feel? Will his limbs go along with his feelings? Can he blush? Shout? Whisper? Kiss? Embrace? It is useful not to have to ask if a man is this or that type of neurotic, but instead: Is he in shape to survive as a human being among other human beings? Can he face the suffering? Can he experience the joy?

Limits are placed on spontaneity in life, in psychodrama, and in dramatic art. To the psychodramatic therapist the limits placed on spontaneity by art seem particularly threatening because, indeed, to impose a script and a role on someone would be to nip their psychodrama in the bud. This and the fact that psychodrama itself throws up scenes with considerable strength as dramatic *art* have encouraged Dr. Moreno to view the two activities as competitive and to feel that, in this competition, psychodrama wins. Actually, there is no competition. The problem, if it is a problem, is only that this therapy and this art overlap, and if chunks of a psychodramatic session are art, pure theatre could in some ways be therapeutic. More useful than taking sides, it seems to me, would be an attempt to sort things out a little.

To maintain flatly that theatre itself is or should be therapeutic will only lead us to the conclusion that it has less to offer than other therapies. If one had a serious mental illness, no amount of theatregoing in even the greatest of theatres could be expected to help very much.

Dr. Sophocles and Dr. Shakespeare would find themselves hopelessly unable to compete with Drs. Smith and Jones on Central Park West, neither of whom has ever laid claim to genius.

This is not to say that the notion of a *connection* between drama and therapy, between all the arts and therapy, is ill founded, only that it has been exaggerated, often by a kind of literal-mindedness. Take the most famous notion in the whole field: catharsis. There is a certain agreement, now, among scholars that the word should be taken as a medical term, that it signifies a purge, and not a moral purification as scholars used to think. Even so, there remains much to say, and chiefly that the word was pounced upon by psychiatrists of the 1890s and applied to a much lengthier and deeper process than any that a visit to a theatre could elicit. The word now described what happened in five years of psychoanalysis. Which, I would say, effectively takes it out of dramatic criticism altogether.

Was Aristotle wrong? Did he exaggerate? Did he mean something else? I doubt that a great pother is called for. After all, Aristotle said very little about catharsis, but the accepted modern interpretation of the word does apply to many works of art, provided we can forget psychiatry for a moment and remember art for quite a few moments. Is it the case that a psychiatric session provides a thoroughgoing catharsis, whereas a play provides an inadequate one? To be sure, patients have often been known to vomit after a session; the theatre could seldom achieve such a result even if it tried.

What is needed, perhaps, is not that we judge art as therapy but that we distinguish one kind of therapy from another. Society needs therapy on two different scales. In the case of individual breakdowns, something more drastic than art—any art—is needed: that's why we have psychiatrists. But these complete breakdowns do not exhaust the list of psychic ill that flesh is heir to. At present, it is true, the others are just let go, if not actually encouraged, because they serve this or that sinister interest. Mother Nature does what she can. Many mental illnesses arise, take their course, and are gone, like physical illnesses. As Freud noted, there are even happy therapeutic accidents. But by and large, mental illness is left to flourish, is *encouraged* to flourish, as physical illness was in the Middle Ages. Which means both that individual special therapy is needed by more and more people and that whole societies can be described as sick in something more than a metaphorical sense.

Now the arts are helpless in the face of such serious maladies. They can only help counteract such tendencies when other forces are doing so on a much larger scale than art itself: in other words when the situation is not as bad as all that. The Greeks viewed the arts as just a part of the good life, and the arts do need a good life to be part of, even if it's a good life that is beset by bad life. In such a context it makes sense to speak of a poet's "healing power" and even of the "corrective effect" of comedy. Poetry could not heal, and comedy could not correct, if things had gone more than just so far, *and not even then on their own*. But if there exists a real civilization, then, just as there are cures effected by nature, and others by lucky circumstances, so one could speak of the arts, too, as therapeutic, alongside other therapeutic agencies of a nonclinical sort. If it is a mistake to see art as standing alone, when it is in fact part of a common effort, a common culture, so it is a mistake to see art as therapy alone, when in fact, as we are all aware, it is other things as well.

What is the total function of art? That might seem too large a question to pose here, especially as there has never been any agreement on the answer. Yet there is no getting any further till the question *is* posed, and it is possible that the disagreements are not relevant. Suppose we just forge ahead.*

The function of art, say some, is to please. The function of art, say others, is to instruct. But what if being pleased is itself instructive? What if being instructed is itself a pleasure? The artistic impulse is the impulse to make something for fun. Why is it fun to make something?

The human creature has destructive urges. Little children wish to kill their parents. But destructive wishes trouble the conscience. We would like to atone for the sin of "thought crime." We would make restitution. We would repair the crockery we have broken, and restore it to its owner. The toy that a child willfully breaks but then guiltily repairs—or better still, replaces—and returns to its owner is perhaps the prototype of artwork. What arouses that "pity and terror" of which Aristotle spoke? Destruction and the resultant disorder. The tragic artwork is the poet's restoration of order and restitution for wrong. And his audience receives it as such. I offer these sentences only as thoughts that might help us understand the actual effect of tragedy, which is in part a healing effect, not indeed in the outright sense that tragedy would cure a case of epilepsy or schizophrenia, but in the sense that it springs from a need to feel that one can make good one's destructions. Without such feelings, I suggest, one would go mad. I am not saying nothing but tragedy, or nothing but art, can provide them. I *am* saying that art, that tragedy, can provide them.

If the therapeutic element is only part of a whole, what is the whole? I'd suggest that the best name for the whole is *education*, though you may prefer, at one pole, *child-rearing* or, at the other, *culture*. I mean

---

*Not, of course, alone. In the following paragraphs I am drawing upon Shaw's preface to *Misalliance* and two articles by the Scottish psychoanalyst W. R. D. Fairbairn, "Prolegomena to a Psychology of Art" and "The Ultimate Basis of Aesthetic Experience," which appeared in volumes 28 and 29, respectively, of the *British Journal of Psychology*.

that art is the pabulum of the people, and that they should be nourished by it from childhood on: this (along with other contributions) makes a culture, makes up the spiritual life of a civilized community. The function of art is to educate, but to say so is not to plump for a didactic type of art: rather, for the idea that art per se is didactic, whereas what is called didactic art tends to fail to be didactic, fails actually to teach because it is boring and therefore soporific. It is because art is *fun* that it can succeed in being didactic, for there is no true teaching except in eagerness, amusement, delight, inspiration.

On the one side, then, all the deadly hate and destructiveness; on the other, the desire to make restitution by creating something for fun. Such restitution is therapeutic, among other things, not to the extent that it alone can clear up the acute sicknesses of either individuals or societies, but on a smaller scale which is nevertheless not all that small and which, in any case, is without time limit. Once there is a good society, even a society good enough to earn the name of civilization not chronically sick, art will join with Mother Nature and with Happy Accident, as also with other branches of culture, to attend to the psychopathology of everyday life, neutralizing many minor toxins, killing many small germs. Which is but a modern and clinical way of restating the ancient belief that art is part of the good life.

Returning to the idea of spontaneity: if all spontaneity is a little unspontaneous too, as I believe, one can certainly find in art—and specifically in theatre—a kind of spontaneity. And indeed a true theatre person is one who craves this type of spontaneity. John Barrymore's problem, as I see it, was that he didn't want to be a theatre person, even though he had the talent for it: which is like being allergic to your own hormones.

Let me try to describe the spontaneity of an actor in a play. On the face of it he has surrendered it to the playwright: Barrymore mustn't be Barrymore, he must be Hamlet. But consider what really happens—from the first rehearsal on. At the first rehearsal, the actor hasn't yet built his characterization, so presumably what he brings along is himself and nothing but himself, and no script ever made an actor feel inhibited about this. As rehearsals progress a little, he comes into contact with his colleagues on stage. Maybe a little electricity is generated. He's attracted by the leading lady. He hates his male partner. Or vice versa. The electricity, in any case, is not between characters, it is between actors. Now the fondest hope of any professional actor (as of his director) is that the electricity generated in rehearsals will be preserved in the performance. That, to a large extent, is what rehearsals are for. Is such electricity a form of byplay, an additional stage effect like background noise? Just the opposite. Properly handled, it does not damage or distort the characterization itself, but is combined with it. Quite a trick! The characterization is to be what the author wanted: that, to be sure, is a principle of drama that there is no getting around. But the actor still meets the eye of another actor, not of a character, which is to say that both actors are still present: their own bodies and all that two human beings have that is not body. And they continue to use all of this, in live contact, as "I" and "Thou."

Should they fail to maintain the contact, could we say, "The actor having now withdrawn his own personality, what is left must be the character"? By no means: when the actors seem dead, as now they would, the characters would never be born. In other words, the life of the stage is a dual life, and through one of these two lives the principle of spontaneity enters, and is indeed essential: that the character may *seem* to have a spontaneous existence, the actor must *actually* have a spontaneous existence. The pulling-off of this "trick"—it is of course much more—is perhaps the main task to which the actor addresses himself. Other things are important. There has to be a characterization to animate. But unless the actor animates it, a characterization has no theatrical value whatever. Conversely, if an actor comes on stage as his spontaneous self, and throws characterization to the winds, we may possibly get something of *psycho*dramatic interest—but even this not really, because the other actors won't relate to it properly, nor will we ourselves relate to it properly: it isn't what we "paid our money for." Whether we know it or not, we have different criteria for dramatic art, different expectations. Barrymore was finally ruined precisely by playing himself instead of the stage character. Life is life. Therapy is therapy. Drama is drama. All afford some freedoms, some opportunities for spontaneity, but, in all, freedom and spontaneity are very strictly circumscribed, so that the acceptance of the circumscription is as necessary an attitude to human beings as love of freedom. Freedom, says Engels, is the recognition of necessity. Goethe says, "In der Beschränkung zeigt sich erst der Meister"—"only in his confronting his limits does a master show his mettle." This is another way of saying: we marvel that spontaneity exists at all; and we marvel how much spontaneity can be created by masters of living, of therapy, or of art.

(1969)

QUANTITY AND QUALITY

For Louis Kronenberger and Marshall Lee

My friend the critic Louis Kronenberger and his friend Marshall Lee asked critics of various arts what *quality* consisted of in the art of their choice, mine being drama. I hesitated over the proposal. Did it have a real point, or should one ask, who cares? And, if one attempted an answer, would it either be a list of high-quality dramas or an over-abstract account of what the word "quality" has meant or should mean? But when I found myself not wanting to comment on the word "quality," the word "quantity" came, or so I made bold to believe, to my rescue; and, after tossing both words in the air a couple of times, I concluded there was something I could say about the special intensities of theatre. For, if one is drawn to serious theatre, year after year, decade after decade, it is not because of the "entertainment value," much less the playwright's bright, or even deep, ideas about Wall Street or the Universe, it is by the *intensities* of theatrical experience. Kronenberger and Lee were giving me yet another chance to ask, what is theatre? and I might hope to present, if not different ideas from the limited stock in my head, at least a different emphasis. The same truth, but seen from another angle.

    It would be convenient if one could clearly and surely distinguish between quality in theatre and quality in the other arts. Certainly, most of us have our preferences as between one art and another. When D. H. Lawrence tells us that the novel is the one great book of life, he would seem to be implying that the novel is the greatest art. When Robert Frost says that everything written is as good as it is dramatic, he would seem to be saying that the drama is the greatest literary genre. How, though, can these claims be tested? Are they really anything more than heartfelt compliments, rhetorical expressions of enthusiasm, and applicable, with appropriate changes, to any art that takes one's fancy? It seems to me that preference of one art or genre to another might more sensibly be treated as a personal, temperamental, constitutional affair. Blind men, for example, seldom prefer painting, but one could not be surprised if a child who had shown a discriminating ear took easily to music—and perhaps ended up declaring music the highest, deepest, broadest—yes, the best—of the arts.

Furthermore, what blind men say about painting must be received with a certain amount of caution, for all their eloquence on the subject of music, and since no one is equally sensitive to all the arts and equally privy to their secrets, no one is really *in a position* to make those objective and definitive distinctions which alone could dispose of this matter. What one can learn at second hand—as, for example, by reading music history without having an ear for music—will not serve the purpose. The honest man, I fear, must admit that he can only take hold of those arts which take hold of him. Much of what he says about his favorite art may seem to others to apply just as much to their own favorites. This is natural, inevitable, and perhaps even valid. It is not clear that what people go to different arts for is always something different. Different arts, in some degree, perhaps a high degree, convey the same satisfactions, but to different people, people of different disposition.

Intensity, for example. But it is more than *an* example: it is *the* example. As surely as when they make love, when they expose themselves to an art human beings are seeking an intensification of their normal experience. That may be what they are mainly seeking; and it may be the principal and normal *raison d'être* for art. The quest may be seen in terms either of causes or results, antecedents or goals; and any such seeing yields an aesthetic. Nietzsche, for instance, stressed one result of such intensification: it invigorates, and thereby leads us to affirm existence, however irrationally. Which proposition implies a view of the causes and antecedents too. In advance of exposure to art, modern man tends to boredom, nausea, despair, nihilism. Nietzsche could see art as a cure, even, at times, as the sole cure and therefore our one hope of salvation.

And so the art which has the greatest intensity for you, though it will not have the greatest intensity for all and cannot claim to be, objectively, the intensest art, must for you represent a special opportunity and may well seem a special dispensation, a special revelation— God's way of getting through to you. As a theorist, you can grant that another art may be as intense to someone else, but as a man you will have great difficulty really believing this. I, for instance, like to think I have a fairly lively response to painting and architecture, and yet for the life of me I cannot conceive how a painting or a building could take hold so hard, could move so deeply, as *Oedipus* or *Lear.* I am even tempted to marshal arguments why drama in general is more intense than fine art.

It is more sensible, though, to drop the competitive mode and deal with the intensities of the theatre in their own right. Where to begin? To begin with *Oedipus* and *Lear* would be beginning at the end—that is, with the noblest and most intricate intensities, those with the largest human and spiritual meaning. Where is the beginning? The point, surely, where there is a performer's body on stage and a spectator's eye out front. Whence the intensification of the spectator's experience? From whatever the performer's body communicates. Goethe said of the theatre, "It is corporeal man who plays the leading role there—a handsome man, a beautiful woman." The art of the theatre starts in the simple sensuousness of direct physical attraction (as against the indirectness of painting and sculpture where we do not encounter the actual human body). The first reference the word "quality" would have in this context would be to the beautiful bodies of performers. The public's love of matinee idols, insofar as it is founded in the good looks of the stars, is basic and sound. The theatre, if it does nothing else, should exhibit fine male and female specimens, so that the spectacle may, at the very least, be a sort of human equivalent of a horse or dog show.

And of course the theatre can do *much* else. It can present the whole sensual lure of this world, and that through the world's darling allurement, the human body. So no wonder the theatre incurred the wrath of Saint Augustine and of all those for whom man's body, and the world's, represents mainly a threat. Saint Anthony, tempted, might just as well be depicted in an orchestra seat as in a garden, for what is theatrical spectacle but the literally shameless exhibition of all that which Saint Anthony is committed to fighting?

Yet only Saint Anthony's commitment can make pure sex appeal all that interesting and keep it so. For persons less committed, and less deprived, the mere exhibition of bare bodies palls sooner than they probably expect. In modern America there has to be tremendous ballyhoo about it, lest people lose interest altogether. Before American youth becomes preoccupied with breasts, millions of dollars are spent on establishing the prestige of breasts. Bare bodies also represent *the easy solution.* Their effect is overrated, and so is exploited to divert attention from poverty in other departments. And thus the physical appeal of other things than skin and the shape of mammary glands is forgotten about. Acrobatics is also purely physical; and yet need not have any sex appeal at all. What interests us in the acrobat's body is not how it looks but what it does: not bodily beauty but bodily prowess. Even the Folies-Bergères do not just "look": they find it necessary on stage to be going somewhere, doing something. Drama, as our teachers delight to mention, is action. And prowess is action, whereas handsomeness is not. The agile body is a truer archetype of theatre art than the beautiful one.

But, then again, beauty and prowess are not antagonists. On the contrary, they unite at the very threshold of theatre art to produce admiration. I wonder if we realize how crucial a product that is. We tend to think of admiration as but a stamp of approval added at the end but, psychologically, it is a prerequisite at the outset and throughout. One cannot pay attention with any pleasure unless admiration is aroused; and that one should pay attention *without* pleasure, in art, is never intended and would indicate a fatal breakdown. Once again the naivest, commonest responses are a reliable guide to the rudiments. When spectators whisper, "Isn't he marvelous?" as an actor goes to work, they are "with it," they are "into" theatre, "warmed up" to the theatre experience. Words like "competent" and "adequate," which in some fields would convey sufficient praise, are as damning in theatre as words like "dull" or "bad," because theatre is an engine which competence and adequacy will not drive. "Astonish me," Cocteau reports Diaghilev as saying to him. It was tantamount to saying, "Make me admire you inordinately"; and I am adding that this, functionally speaking, may not be saying much more than, "Hold my attention in the theatre." For, in the theatre, when there is nothing to marvel at, there is likely to be nothing, period. "Theatre of marvels" is a phrase to describe not only the special phenomenon of miraculous scenery and the like but any true theatre, any theatre that really "works." Every theatrical artist must be an acrobat in his own way, and the acrobat himself is the purest possible example of theatre, exhibiting, as he does, the most breathtaking feats that the human body is capable of. Nietzsche maintained that art embodies the will to power. If we apply the thought to acrobats, the operative word will be "embodies." Generally, the word "power" brings only politicians to mind, men in search of an abstraction, whom we can admire, if at all, only rather guiltily. The acrobat's power is concrete and corporeal. The wonder it arouses in us is lovely and innocent.

I once heard a man exclaiming upon the wonder of a trapeze artist's movements and being put down by his neighbor who said, "What's so wonderful? A bird would think nothing of it." Now one can wonder at the flight of birds too, but one would probably not wonder at a bird whose performance duplicated that of a trapeze artist. Why then do we wonder at the trapeze artist himself? That we do is the proof that movement is not found wonderful in itself but only as we hold a certain opinion about the mover's capacity for it.

> He floats through the air with the greatest of ease,
> The daring young man on the flying trapeze.

Ease. That is, nonease overcome. Our admiration for the daring young man has its root in the knowledge that, for a human body, such feats are not easy, as they are for birds. They require prowess, they require daring. And here we stumble upon a *difference* between acrobatics and regular theatre, namely, that the stage, unlike the circus ring, is not dangerous in the literal sense, only in the metaphorical. But the prowess circus artists and actors have in common. In order to understand our respect for it we should recognize that we do not make our minds a *tabula rasa* for artists to write upon but, on the contrary, bring to art all manner of attitudes and assumptions. In the present case, we bring our own estimates of what is difficult and of how difficult it is, and we respond to the acrobat's prowess insofar as we see it as a conquest of very considerable difficulties. In that sense, watching acrobats is an intellectual pursuit. More important, what the intellect addresses itself to is the will to power. It measures mastery. "All the world loves a winner." The Spanish proverb may bring to mind much that is dubious in ethics, but it embodies a truth of psychology that is not to be ignored by any student of the arts.

The stage is dangerous only in a metaphorical sense. "When you go out on stage," Sir John Gielgud once told a cast of actors whom he was directing, "think of it as a battlefield—because, by God, it is." In a metaphorical sense. And good theatrical work which comes across to us through our sense of difficulty overcome also comes across to us through our sense of danger survived, of risk successfully taken. Actors are heroes in the most primitive way: voyagers through perilous seas, climbers of crags, leapers of chasms, slayers of dragons. Those who are not are boring and, in effect, not actors.

What gives the actor his best chance of bringing to his audience that intensification of experience which is the aim of all art? It depends what is meant by "best." His simplest and most direct chance would be afforded by the simplest and most direct forms of dramatic art—such forms as melodrama and farce. Thrillers thrill. "Hilarious comedies" do induce hilarity. And indeed it is often assumed that nonthrillers thrill less, as also that less farcical comedies are less hilarious. It might even seem to stand to reason that the more *thought* you inject into a play the less *feeling* goes into it. But what would follow from this? That any successful melodrama or farce would be marked by greater emotional intensity than *Oedipus* or *Lear*, than *Volpone* or *The Misanthrope*. Which is not so: I need only appeal to the opinion of anyone who would claim to have experienced these works for an answer. Evidently the highest intensity is not reached by the most direct route.

Returning to our first postulate, which was that the theatre presents the beautiful body, the simplest and most direct procedure would be to take the actors' clothes off and send them out on stage; and since we live in a simplistic time, we find this procedure being adopted nowadays. What we do not find is any notably heightened intensity. Nor may we expect to find it even when—as is now being threatened—the actors make love on stage to the bitter or sweet orgasmic end. In doing this, the actors may indeed be experiencing intensity, but an actor's orgasm does not give me one. If I were brought to the point of orgasm by an enactment, it would presumably be through *non*orgasm on stage, through seductive cunning and device, erotic calculation and fantasy—in short, not through life but through art.

Sir Kenneth Clark has taught us that, in painting and sculpture, nudity is a kind of norm. But on stage it is not: it is a kind of exception. I affirm this, in the first instance, as a matter of history in all parts of the world of which I have any knowledge, but it could equally be affirmed as a matter of principle. Nothing seems more clearly written into the lawbook of dramatic art as it is known to us than that its first principle is concealment, its first implement (as well as symbol) the mask. True, this concealment can be regarded as a paradox. Just as one can *reculer pour mieux sauter,* so to conceal can be preparatory to revealing: dramatic plot might be cited as a leading example. But here again we are in the realm of metaphor. Nothing physical is uncovered at the end of a comedy, or, if it is, as for instance by the removal of a disguise, there are other clothes underneath. This last point is of importance to others than puritans and policemen. Pirandello called his plays "naked masks," not "naked faces," to express, among other things, his sense that the mask is itself an ultimate in the theatre. Nudity there, when it exists, will be a spiritual nudity; physically, the method of theatre is to cover, drape, and swathe. Hence the importance to naturalistic theatre of walls and ceilings, even of carpets, wallpaper, paint, light fixtures, everything that covers the nakedness of nature. But the great nonnaturalistic theatres go in for concealment every bit as much, and in some cases more. What is the baroque stage but this world decked out for carnival or upholstered to simulate a rather materialistic heaven? As for Shakespeare's stage, even if it was as bare of scenery as critics have liked to suppose (and it probably wasn't), it undoubtedly liked to flatter and distort the human form in all manner of rich raiment.

Seeing Edgar undressed, King Lear makes his famous speech about nakedness and himself starts to strip:

> Thou art the thing itself. Unaccommodated man is no more but such a poor, bare, forked animal as thou art. Off, off, you lendings, come, unbutton here!

He doesn't continue stripping, however, and the playwright twice tells us that Edgar's loins remain covered. Even if this latter point be regarded merely as a concession to a puritanic age, what is in question here is not what Sir Kenneth Clark calls nudity. The nudity of art, as Clark defines it, is an idealization of the human form, the human form transfigured by an idea of the *super*human. In other words, this idea itself becomes a kind of clothing. Quite different is your nakedness or mine, signalizing, as it does, the absence of an important part of our normal image, an impoverishment of our total ego, and it is this our nakedness—not Clark's nudity—which Shakespeare introduces into *Lear*, though even then not literally. Similarly, the taking off of clothes is shown in *Lear* not as an act of liberation but as an act of degradation, almost of mutilation. Lear may come to appreciate his common humanity in such a process, yet this is only to say he learns humility by being humiliated. Lear may speak of unclothed man as "the thing itself," as man in his essence, his animal essence, but there is no implication that the playwright agrees. The Shakespearean image of human dignity is an image of man as king, in other words, of man not only clothed but sumptuously arrayed, crown on head and scepter in hand. One might make the point that in this Shakespeare was a man of his time, but I am making the point that he was a man of the theatre—where *Homo sapiens* is not unaccommodated, poor, bare, and forked, but accommodated, rich, clothed, and raised above the animal by all the lendings and buttons that the dramatic poet can devise.

My larger point is that the theatre does not, cannot, go right at its intensities. If it could and did, showing copulation on stage would be a piece of theatre which no dramatic literature and no feats of what is normally called acting could possibly compete with. Even those modes, like melodrama and farce, which I have described as the *most* direct are still not *entirely* direct. They have their indirectness, and are dependent for their success on the operation of certain dualities. Farce depends upon a contrast between appearance and reality, lightness of heart and violence, gravity of manner and zaniness of substance. Melodrama is as close to a direct, unmediated image of life as the art of the drama ever comes. It may often be a pretty literal mirror image of our fantasy life. But since it offers itself as art, not as raw fantasy, it is permeated by a sense of irony. We recognize this at those points in a melodrama where we laugh at it without ceasing to enjoy it. In pure melodrama the smile is never quite absent. If we received these heroisms, these disasters, these secrecies, without a smile we would be taking them seriously, taking them as more than melodrama, attributing to them a greater and higher complexity. But even melodrama, which, since everything is relative, we can refer to as simple, is not as simple as all that.

At this stage in the argument we have to admit that intensity itself is not as simple a thing as is commonly assumed. The archetype of intensity, in common assumption, is sudden sharp sensation, such as a twinge of pain or a spasm of pleasure. Of late years, some advocates of drugs have offered to increase the intensity of such spasms for us as well as their frequency, and, logically enough, the suggestion has been made that the arts might prove unable to compete with the pleasures that drugs afford. I obviously cannot tackle here the whole topic of psychedelic experience, but it might be relevant to touch at least upon a claim for it that was put forward by its most widely known spokesman. In a lengthy exposition published by *Playboy*, Dr. Timothy Leary laid the stress on pleasure in the most directly physical sense: specifically, on many, many orgasms in place of the good old-fashioned single orgasm. It is not surprising that some of his colleagues immediately jumped on him. They wish to make a far more spiritual claim for psychedelic experience, and perhaps in the end, who knows? they will be able to make this stick. For the present, however, one may be justified in complaining that the talk of spiritual exploration is fairly vapid, like the talk of expanded consciousness, since one is given no clear account of *what* territory is explored or *what* the drug takers are aware of that they weren't aware of before. Even to say that drug experience improves one's experience of art itself—Beethoven sounds even greater when you're high—is to communicate very little if neither the previous experience of art nor the allegedly improved experience of it is adequately described. And at this stage, I find, most drug users fall back on the traditional copout of the mystics: their experience is by definition ineffable.

But while some things inaccessible to reason may be above reason, others may just be below it, and I would take my cue from Leary's confessions to *Playboy* for assuming that what he mainly looks to drugs for is *sensation*. The experience seems mostly subrational, and the experiencer's stance antirational. Art, including dramatic art, has to be considered, I'm afraid, in less animal and more human terms, much as one may resist the rhetoric that surrounds the word "human," and even though one may suspect that the human/animal dichotomy is unfair to animals. What I have in mind is not so much man's high claims for himself but rather what seems to be a fact of his makeup, namely, that with him, feeling does not exist separately, but is bound up with his thoughts. "Deep thinking," says Coleridge, "is attainable only by a man of deep feeling." And this is not all. There would seem to be some dynamic relation between a particular "deep thought" and the "deep feeling" of the man to whom the thought, as we say, "comes." Gabriel Marcel says, "Emotion is actually the discovery of the fact that 'this concerns me after all' "; which may not be a definition of all emotion but is certainly a very astute adumbration of the kind of feeling we find in dramatic art. Indeed we often find it twice over: in *Oedipus Rex* as in Ibsen's *Ghosts*, both characters on stage and spectators out front discover that "this concerns them after all," and are thereby deeply moved. Now to discover facts is the work of the intellect, and both

Sophocles and Ibsen ask the intellect to perform its most characteristic chore: puzzle solving. Spectator and leading character must carefully and logically piece together a case history. It is in this sense that one theorist of the drama calls plot its most intellectual element: the most intellectual in order that the play may be most emotional.

But the intellectuality inherent in plot is by no means the same thing as "the thought" in a play. Does the latter as well as the former contribute to the emotional impact? There is plenty of thinking in plays which contributes to nothing, least of all to thought itself, and thoughts thrown in for whatever interest they may have in themselves are so much dead weight dramatically. Hebbel, as cited above (p. 43), wittily said that characters in plays shouldn't have thoughts at all—thought should be something that emerges only from the play as a whole. The word "thought" is being used here in two quite different senses. In the first sense, a thought is an idea, often a general idea about life stated by an individual character with no special bearing on the plot and theme of the play. Oscar Wilde's characters get off such ideas all the time. The other kind of thought may have no general interest or reference. It is simply the intellectual part of the process of discovery and realization, either by a character or a spectator: "I see that that is so." Marcel is speaking exclusively of the latter kind of thought. First, one sees that that is so; then one recognizes that "it concerns me"; finally one is moved.

Possibly even this kind of thinking seems closer to crossword puzzles than to thought in the higher sense, but it need not be so. People who take *Oedipus Rex* as a crossword puzzle—and there have been some, even among classical scholars—regard the play as melodrama, which is to say that it has not brought them to any "this concerns me." Those who do derive this message from the play will unanimously claim that there is more to it than ingenious plotting. To say what this "more" is would be to offer a whole theory of the drama, or at least of tragedy. What is pertinent here is that when the thought is made a matter of personal concern it is deeply felt. Which is the obverse of the fact that we are narcissistic: we feel very little except when we take things personally.

The psychiatrist Victor Frankl has observed that while life and philosophy can normally be regarded as separate, as per the adage "First live and then philosophize," extreme situations can break down the separation and bring men to believe, "First philosophize and then die." Knowing that they must die, prisoners in the Nazi camps were desperate to find the meaning of death, of life: their extreme emotion drove them to an unwonted intellectuality . . . In tragedy we watch the inmates of this prison the world (as one of Shakespeare's tragic heroes calls it) in *their* desperate search for meaning, and, as has been known at least since Aristotle, we do more than watch. We enter in. We say, "This concerns me." It might seem a miracle that a single work can make all men feel that it concerns them personally. Certainly, the tragic writer has to be blessed with genius to practice successfully, and genius is a miracle. At the receiving end, however, neither miracles nor genius need be presupposed, but only the humanistic postulate of Montaigne: "Each man carries within himself the complete structure of the human condition."

Without breaking my promise not to claim that drama is a superior genre, I might point to a unique feature of it which for many of us has great appeal and which helps to explain the intensity of the genre. Although the playwright's characters are imaginary, like the novelist's, and cannot walk on stage (though Pirandello can imagine that they can), they are presented *to* human beings *by* human beings, and this is a degree of actuality and humanity unique in the annals of art. Its uniqueness is so striking and so attractive that I for one find it hard to believe that the theatrical scheme of things could ever be replaced by cinematography or any other mechanism. Its intensities are all its own, in that vibrations move from actor to spectator and back again, as they obviously cannot in the movies and television. In this respect, theatre is closer to group therapy than to "the media." J. L. Moreno's psychodramatic therapy is indeed based on theatre and can be regarded (though by me it is not) as the ultimate form of theatre.

What first strikes one about this scheme—human beings presenting other human beings to yet other human beings—is that it makes of theatre the most directly sensuous of the arts. That is why I mentioned physical beauty at the outset. But I hurried on to state that prowess was more important than looks; and perhaps by now my reasons for doing so are apparent. It would be hard to overestimate the importance of the actor's physical presence, but easy to overestimate the importance of his looks, because the dynamic of theatre is not beauty but interaction, as between human beings. A double interaction: first, between actor and actor; second, between actor and spectator. Thus the quintessential event in theatre is the human encounter. In one respect, this art is very simple. A child's impression, "All that happens is that a few people keep coming and going," is very proper, provided the child has also noticed that, before going, these people *meet*. Jean Racine remarked that his plays were quite easy to write once he had figured out the entrances and exits. This remark could be misunderstood only by someone who failed to realize what a Herculean labor the figuring out represents. Why, it is everything! For, as Nietzsche put it, "In every action of a human being the complete evolution of his psychic life is gone through again." The actions which playwrights show are encounters, and the great playwrights have known in their bones that each encounter is somehow crucial and comprehensive. That is the meaning of classical concentration in Racine and his Greek masters. But, equally, Shakespeare, whose methods were so different, evinces the fullest awareness of the possible bigness of the smallest encounter. The encounter of Cinna the Poet with the Roman mob is one of the shortest scenes in drama, and contains no character present in the rest of *Julius Caesar*, yet it both takes its place in the design of the play and remains indelibly stamped in the mind as a universal image.

"There seems to be no agent more effective than another person," writes Erving Goffman in his book *Encounters*, "for bringing the world alive for oneself." This is another of those principles of human life which are incorporated in the art of the theatre. Bringing things alive would, I think, be widely recognized today as the purpose of the arts in general, a purpose doubly worthy and urgent in a civilization like ours which is actually less a civilization than a massive assault on all forms of vitality, not to mention on life itself. Modern poets have stressed the need to give back to words their full emotional content. Dramatic poetry could be included in this proposition, and one might add that, the subject of drama being what is nowadays called "interpersonal relations," the art of the theatre, in which persons present persons to persons, is in a specially favorable position to set up live vibrations, to set the human engines revving again.

I would like to squeeze another idea out of Goffman's dictum: that one *needs* another person. A page or two back I was saying that one encounters oneself in the theatre. "This concerns me" means "this *is* me," and our identification with the tragic hero is perhaps the most celebrated fact in all theatrical psychology, finding its last squeaky echo in the newspaper reviewer's search for "human" characters whom he can "identify with." It is very well to begin with the hero as long as one proceeds to acknowledge the villain. But even a melodrama has a villain as well as a hero; tragedy, like serious modern drama, has many characters who may be neither heroes nor villains; and comedy can present a whole cast of characters whom one cannot identify oneself with, a world of "other" persons.

It is a recognized principle—Goethe, for one, states it—that one must find oneself, if at all, not by turning in on oneself but through human activity and relationship. This is something else that the dramatists intuitively know; it is implied already in Aristotle's insistence on character as doing rather than being. And so, in seeing a play, one can begin by feeling, "this concerns me, this is me"; one can go on to feeling, "this concerns others, this is the other fellow"; and one can end up feeling that the Me that "this" is has been redefined by the Non-Me, by the other fellow, or, more precisely, by interactions between the Me and the Non-Me—more precisely still, by interactions between aspects of the Me and aspects of the Non-Me. One realizes at this point why a playwright might need a big cast of characters. One realizes, too, that if he operated in abstract awareness of what he was doing (as most artists do not), he might well lay out the cast list in terms of various aspects of the Me and Non-Me, possibly with subdivisions according to which elements of the Me could be mixed with elements of the Other. Strindberg went some distance toward such a procedure in his dream plays, as did the German Expressionists who followed his lead.

I am assuming that Schopenhauer was right to believe that the stage offers the perfect mirror of life, but if it be asked, "How then is it to be distinguished from life itself?" one would have to admit that the image is misleading. On stage we see the "interpersonal conflicts" of real life in their full intensity; in life, however, we do not see them, or not in their full intensity. The effect of "full intensity" is, if you like, a trick, achieved above all by excluding from view all that is irrelevant to the conflict. Selectivity is the first principle of all art. But it is not a sufficient principle: another one enters in, more of an X-ray than a mirror, in that underlying realities, normally unseen if not necessarily invisible, are exhibited in art, not least in dramatic art. Now the words "underlying" and "exhibited" are both metaphors. The stage cannot literally exhibit either of the two sets of realities involved—the inner facts of individual lives or the general facts of social and historical life—but what it does make visible—and audible—will make these realities real. Art is life even more than life is.

The intensities of theatre are very many. Thousands of pages could easily be filled illustrating their variety. Let me provide one illustration which I consider unusually important. Its character will best come clear if I permit myself a comparison, but not an invidious one, with fiction. Whereas a great, long novel can give an unmatched impression of the ramifications of experience, its extent, and many of its undulations and slow developments, and so may be regarded as having an enormous horizontal range, a supremely great drama can claim to pack in as much of life, but one will more easily see it as a vertical structure, layer on layer or floor on floor. *War and Peace* presents human lives with an incomparable richness of personal detail; it also places them within a particular span of history, and seeks to relate them to history in general. *King Lear,* on the other hand, forgoes much that a long novel has to offer in detail and process; willingly accepts instead what critics, with gratuitous sneers, call "melodrama" and "mere intrigue"; but all the same contrives to present the life of man "whole" and on the grandest scale, a life cosmic, social, and individual—all the time, all three.

As a schoolboy, I was puzzled by the description of Sophocles as seeing life steadily and seeing it *whole:* I could mention many things about life which Sophocles does not mention, so how could his account be "whole"? Well, it is the outline of a whole, without most of the details. This would be part of the answer, but, finally, a more important part, I think, is that, for Sophocles, life possessed a *wholeness*, and that his work communicates a sense of it. Unity of action, for example, flows from this sense: drama can have beginning, middle, and end when dramatists feel that life has beginnings, middles, and ends. Today, when, on the contrary, the consensus is that "things fall apart, the center cannot hold," it is harder to write drama, easier to write the kind of prose fiction which doesn't require unity of action.

Unity of action makes for the highest intensity in drama, as Aristotle knew, but the phrase "unity of action" goes only a short way toward describing the unified and unifying vision of such a work as *Lear,* or even of smaller masterpieces like those of Ibsen. I have been saying that the playwrights portray the essential conflicts of human beings. It should be added that they do not situate the conflicts outside time and space. On the contrary, the playwright who can manage it projects the very archetypes of his epoch. The characteristic intensity of Ibsen arises from the feeling we so irresistibly receive of being at the very nerve center of his civilization. Critics of an "aesthetic" bent shake their heads over Ibsen's choice of the middle-class drawing room as his "favorite" locale, but favoritism is not involved; rather, an unerring instinct for the significant. And the setting is just one example. Everything about an Ibsen play helps to provide a theatrical image, not of individuals, or even families alone, but of a culture.

In our own time, what would be the status of *Waiting for Godot* if we did not believe it rendered a state of soul which is that of an epoch? No wonder that such a work arouses emotion, for in it I recognize not only *me* but *us.*

In setting up intensity as the criterion, one is attempting to speak in terms of quantity rather than quality. On the one hand, one asks how much emotion is generated in people, a purely quantitative query, and on the other one answers that the emotion is the greater the more the dramatist can pack into his play, a purely quantitative answer. It remains only to measure the quantities.

Only! Ay, there's the rub. One might believe in the eventual measurement of responses if indeed one simply wished to measure twinges and spasms, but if one believes that the total response of a human being is evoked by art, and that human beings—for worse as well as better— are what has been called spiritual as well as physical entities, then all prospect of measuring responses vanishes for the indefinite future. As for the amount of life that the playwright can pack into his play—life on the cosmic, social, or individual scale—this could definitely be measured so long as by *amount* is meant what a sociologist might mean and not what a dramatist has to mean. By the sociologist's standards more is recorded of human life in the *World Almanac* than in Dante's *Divine Comedy.* The almanac's account of things is a lot "truer," too. When one says Shakespeare packs *everything* into *Lear,* one is using not only hyperbole but also irony. One means that Shakespeare makes certain things so important that everything else shrinks into insignificance. Yes, he packs a lot in, but an even greater achievement was to reduce to nothingness, in our minds, the larger lot that he left out. In short, our apparently rather "objective" comment on *Lear* depends on a whole cluster of value judgments, and these judgments have been made not by the eye of an all-seeing deity, but by me—or you, dear reader—in the somewhat murky depths (and shallows) of our limited and muddled being. God can think, no doubt, of greater or less intensity in a play much as we think of it in an electric bulb—a matter of pure quantity. You and I can see His point in principle, but when we try to measure these differences in watts, we begin to flounder. The straw to clutch when, in such circumstances, we find ourselves drowning is the word "quality."

(1968)

INDEX

Index compiled by David W. Beams